Go Tell the Good News

by
Bob and Sandra Waldron

ISBN 1-58427-115-9

Guardian of Truth Foundation
P.O. Box 9670
Bowling Green, Kentucky 42102

Table of Contents

History of the Early Church

Bible history:

Creation
Flood
Scattering of the people
The Patriarchs
Exodus from Egypt
Wandering
Conquest of the land
Judges
United Kingdom
Divided Kingdom
Judah alone
Captivity of Judah
Return from captivity
Years of silence
Life of Christ

***Early Church**
***Letters to Christians**

Never lose your perspective in Bible study. The scheme of redemption is one complete story.

Go Tell The Good News is the eighth of nine books in a series on the Bible narrative, a series that begins with Genesis and finishes with Revelation. These books are designed as a guide to Bible study, a help to teachers and students alike. They are much more than Bible story books and much simpler to use than commentaries. Each book in the series can stand alone as a study of its particular period of Bible history, or it can be used in sequence with the others to form a detailed survey of the whole Bible story.

Go Tell The Good News is the story of the beginning of the church and of the spread of the gospel through the end of Paul's life. It encompasses the book of Acts and the epistles of Paul. The ninth book covers the rest of the epistles and the book of Revelation. Instead of giving a verse-by-verse exposition, we study the book of Acts as a narrative. When we get to the place where an epistle of the apostle Paul fit into the narrative of the history, we introduce it, outline it, and summarize the message of the letter.

This book covers the major portion of the last two parts of our outline of the Bible: the early church, and letters to the Christians. Never lose your perspective in your Bible study. The scheme of redemption is one complete story, the unfolding of the plan for man's salvation which God devised before time began (Eph. 3:11). Your study of the New Testament will be greatly enriched if you keep in mind where it fits in the overall picture of the Bible narrative.

If you are studying *Go Tell The Good News* in sequence with the other books in the series, allow at least two quarters for this study. We like the following sequence best in the survey of the whole Bible story: two full quarters on the life of Christ; plus one quarter combining the death, burial, resurrection, and exaltation of Christ, and the beginning of the church; two quarters on the book of Acts and Paul's epistles; and one final quarter on the last part of the first century. Even though this makes one quarter overlap with two books, it allows a little extra time for the New Testament study, and it shows the close connection between Jesus's sacrifice, His exaltation, and the beginning of the church which is His kingdom.

If you are studying this book with children, emphasize the history that is told in the book of Acts. The epistles were written to adults, to saints who needed to know how to live as subjects in the kingdom of Christ. As you come to the place where an epistle fits into the history, explain to the children that Paul wrote a letter to a congregation or individual, with a very brief explanation of the main message. Fit the explanation to the maturity of the children.

The Book of Acts

From the ascension of Jesus, to Paul the prisoner in Rome:
- **The story of how the great commission was carried out.**

Acts 1-12: Peter
Acts 13-28: Paul

Some of the acts of a few of the apostles.

4 B.C. - A.D. 29:
- **Gospel accounts**

A.D. 29 - A.D. 63:
- **Acts**

A.D. 64 - A.D. 96:
- **Roman persecution**

Go tell the good news:
- **Salvation is available!**

The King: Christ
His kingdom: The church
His subjects: Those who obey

The book of Acts tells the early history of the church which Jesus established. It begins with the ascension of Christ, and is the record of how the great commission began to be carried out. It is written from the standpoint of the activities of the apostles, particularly those of Peter and Paul. The book can be outlined in two broad divisions based on the work of these two men: Acts 1-12: Peter; Acts 13-28: Paul.

Be aware that the events told in the book of Acts are only a sampling of the work that was being done by all of the apostles and by other disciples, as they went about spreading the news about the Christ. This was certainly not the only work being done by the men of the day, nor were these the only events that took place in the lives of Peter and Paul. The gospel spread throughout the world during the first century, so there were many people working hard to spread the good news. The book of *Acts of the Apostles* might be more appropriately named, "Some of the Acts of a Few of the Apostles."

Span of the book:

The book of Acts does not take us through the entire first century. The gospel accounts cover nearly 35 years, Acts covers the next 30 years, and then the epistles and Revelation give us a glimpse into the last third of the century. Even though Acts covers only about thirty years, it is a very important thirty years, during which the church begins in Jerusalem and grows to cover the Roman world. The book begins with the ascension of Christ and ends with Paul in prison in Rome.

Importance of the book:

The book of Acts stands as a high point of the whole Bible story. The story of the death, burial, resurrection, ascension, and coronation of Christ is the climax of the history of all time — but it still would have done mankind no good if the story had not been told. Jesus came to pay the price for sin and to offer mankind the opportunity to accept His terms and to be forgiven for sins, but mankind had to learn those terms before the opportunity could be accepted. The gospel accounts end with the admonition to the apostles to go tell the good news to all the world — to every person.

Those who heard the good news and accepted the message were saved. But what about those who were saved? Did they just continue in their old way of life as if nothing had happened? No, those saved people became part of the kingdom of God, with Christ as their King ruling at the right hand of God; they became the loyal subjects of Christ. As each individual heard the message and accepted the terms of salvation, he was added by God into the body of saved individuals — thus becoming a part of the body of Christ, the church.

The church is the kingdom Jesus came to establish. The Jews wanted a military king on a throne in Jerusalem, but Jesus did not come to be that kind of king (John 6:15; 18:36). Instead, He came to earth to make it possible for men to have their sins forgiven and to become part of a spiritual kingdom, one in which its citizens would give their complete allegiance to Christ their King, with the hope of someday going to live in heaven itself with their King.

It is the process of being saved that puts one into the company of the saved:
- **Into the church.**
- **He is then a citizen of the kingdom of Christ.**

In keeping with the total commitment one makes when he becomes a citizen of the kingdom, the only way to become a part of the church is to be saved (Acts 2:47), to be born again (John 3:5). It is the process of being saved that puts one into the company *(the assembly)* of the saved ones. The church *(ekklesia, which means "assembly")* is the assembly of the saved ones from all the centuries, and from all nations under the sun, since Jesus established His church on the first Pentecost after His resurrection. There was no church before the day of Pentecost because Christ had to die, to be raised from the dead, and to be exalted to the right hand of God before the plan of salvation was available. There could be no "body of the saved" until men could be saved. There could be no subjects in Christ's kingdom until He was King over His kingdom. We are highly blessed to be privileged to be a part of that church, to be a part of that kingdom, to be a part of the saved ones.

Authorship:

It is agreed by virtually everyone that Luke wrote the book of Acts. There are four main reasons why:

Luke, the author of:
- **The gospel of Luke**
- **Acts**

- The preface in Acts addresses the book to Theophilus. No additional facts are known about Theophilus. Some think he was not an individual at all, but a lover of God in general, since the word Theophilus means "lover of God."

  The writer says that he wrote a "former treatise" to Theophilus telling about all that Jesus began to do and to teach. Sure enough, one of the gospel accounts is addressed to Theophilus — the book of Luke. Also, the preface of Acts overlaps with the end of the gospel of Luke in such a way as to make it evident that this was a design on the part of the writer of both books.
- The language of the book contains a number of medical terms which would be expected of a writer who was a physician, and Luke was "the beloved physician" (Col. 4:14).
- There are certain sections of Acts where the writer joins Paul's party and includes himself by using the term "we." These sections are called the "we-sections" of Acts. These sections are 16:11-18; 20:5-16; 21:1-18; and 27:1-28:16. We know from other passages that Luke was a companion of Paul during his imprisonment (Col. 4:14; 2 Tim. 4:11; Philemon 24), and he is the only companion who we know was a physician.

- The early church fathers *(early church historians)* who lived in the first century, and in the years immediately after that century, counted Luke as the author.

Time of writing:

During Paul's second missionary journey, when he and his companions arrived at Troas, they were joined by the writer of the book of Acts, Luke (Acts 16:6-10). It is certain that he did not start writing his account before this time (c. A.D. 51). Acts closes with the note that Paul remained in prison in Rome for two years (28:30). This latter date was A.D. 63. Obviously the book was completed after this date, but not long after, because it contains very few facts about Paul's imprisonment, and no further facts after Paul was released. We have therefore narrowed the period during which Luke could have written Acts to the time from A.D. 51 to A.D. 63. We can, however, narrow our estimate even more.

Time of writing the book of Acts: A.D. 60/61-64

Time of writing the book of Luke: A.D. 58-60

In his preface to the gospel of Luke, the writer emphasizes the careful research he did in compiling his facts about Jesus (Luke 1:1-4). That means that even though he was guided by the Holy Spirit, as were all the writers, he also talked to those who had been eye-witnesses of the events in Jesus' life and carefully compiled his information in a logical pattern. When is the most likely time for Luke to have been able to do such research? Judea and Galilee were the places for him to find the most witnesses of Jesus' life. The time that immediately comes to mind is the two years that Paul was a prisoner at Caesarea (Acts 24:27). On that last trip to Jerusalem when Paul was captured by the Jews and put in prison at Caesarea, Luke was with him (Acts 20:5-6). Luke was still with Paul when it was time for him to make the trip to Rome for his trial before Caesar (Acts 27:1). Those were the years A.D. 58-60. Almost certainly, therefore, this is the period when Luke wrote his gospel account.

Clearly, however, the gospel of Luke was written *before* the book of Acts (Acts 1:1). Most likely Luke began writing the book of Acts only a short time after writing his account of the gospel. Perhaps he started it before they left Caesarea, since the first part of the book tells the history of the church in Jerusalem, or perhaps it was written during the winter they were forced to spend on the island of Malta as he accompanied Paul to Rome, or shortly after they arrived in Rome (Acts 28:1-16). At the latest, it was written during the time Paul was a prisoner in Rome, being finished shortly after Paul's release, but before the outbreak of Nero's persecution of the church (July 19, A.D. 64). We can therefore say with assurance that Acts was written between A.D. 60-64.

Tell the story:

Tell the story:

- **Present it as history.**
- **Use synonyms to define words.**
- **Use geographical, historical, or archaeological facts to clarify a point,**
    - **Not to bury it.**

- **It is beyond the scope of this book to go into involved, technical arguments to refute false doctrines:**
    - **Though we do include information to clarify details.**

- **The narrative cycle of the Bible story has been neglected too often in the Bible classes of recent years.**

The teacher should not "argue" his way through the book of Acts, but rather present the story in a fascinating way. It is a book of history, telling the story of the spread of the gospel. Put words from the scripture into terms that your students can understand (*such as, using the word "language" for "tongue"*), and you will have answered many questions before they arise. As other questions come, answer them plainly from the scripture, using explanations and supporting evidence suited to the age of your students, and then move forward quickly into the next part of your narrative. Remember to use any geographical, historical, or archaeological fact to clarify a point, not to bury it!

Even though this book is history — and we stress the need to treat it as such — since it deals with the establishment of the Lord's church, many false doctrines are refuted in the book of Acts. Our study would not be complete if we ignored these important lessons. Therefore, there are many notes throughout the material to help you and your students understand what the Bible does and does not teach on various points of doctrine. Make your points clearly, but do not dwell on them to the loss of the overall story.

Though many points of doctrine are discussed in the material, we are fully aware there are many points that are not included here that are equally important. It is beyond the scope of this series of books to go into involved, technical arguments to refute false doctrine. That is a very important realm of Bible study, and a necessary one in our world that is so full of error, but that is not the purpose for this study. This study of Acts and of the epistles is part of a series of studies on the narrative cycle of the Bible. It is an effort to show how the history of the early church unfolds, why the epistles were written, and what their basic messages were. This book should serve as a foundation to enable students to be ready for the more complex studies of various subjects that arise in a more detailed study. It is this narrative cycle that has been so often neglected in Bible classes of recent years, so that is why we have tried to fill that gap in this series of books.

The necessity of a map study:

A map of the Mediterranean world is a *necessity* in the study.

It will be *absolutely necessary* to use a map in teaching this course. From Jesus' reference to Jerusalem, Judea, Samaria, and the farthest part of the earth at the very beginning of the book (Acts 1:8), all the way until Paul the prisoner walks into the city of Rome (Acts 28:16), a map will be essential to understand what was happening in the story. Use it constantly, even with the very youngest classes of children. A very simple map of Palestine, and a simple map of the Mediterranean world, with a bare minimum of names written in bold letters, will help the children begin to learn the basic facts about the lands in which Bible events took place.

The Great Commission (Matt. 28:16-20; Mark 16:14-20; Luke 24:44-53):

During the forty days between the resurrection and the ascension, Jesus gave His disciples a great commission — a great task that they were to perform throughout the rest of their lives. It was their task to go tell the whole world about Jesus: that the long-awaited Messiah had come, that He had done the work God intended, and that salvation was now available. We call that commission the "great commission," because of the greatness of its scope *(to the whole world),* and because of the greatness of its message *(that of salvation)*. The book of Acts tells how that commission began to be carried out. It tells the results that came with the preaching of the gospel: how people heard the story of the Christ and responded either in obedience to the terms of salvation, or in bitterness and in persecution of the messenger.

"And He said unto them, 'Go ye into all the world, and preach the gospel to every creature. He that believeth and is baptized shall be saved; but he that believeth not shall be damned'" (Mark 16:15-16)

Response of the hearers:

- **Believers responded in obedience to the terms of salvation.**
- **Unbelievers responded in bitterness and persecution of the messenger.**

Though we are not apostles and cannot tell the story of Christ as ones who heard and saw Him, the great commission is an on-going mission that will need to be carried out until the end of time. We can read and study the evidence recorded by the inspired writers of the New Testament, and we can tell that evidence to others. It is a task, a commission, we must be about as Christians.

See the table on the next page. Carefully observe the commandments given by Jesus in each of the accounts of the great commission. Then see the reasoning behind the combination of the commandments. As you go through the book of Acts, compare each conversion with the combination of commands shown here in this chart.

Matthew 28:19-20:	**Mark 16:15-16:**	**Luke 24:47:**	**Combination:**
Teach all nations	Preach to every creature	Preach in His name among all the nations	Preach/Teach
Baptizing them in the name of the Father, Son, and Holy Spirit	He that believeth	Repentance	He that believeth
Teaching them to observe all things commanded you	And is baptized	Remission of sins	Repentance
	Shall be saved/ He that believeth not shall be condemned.		And is baptized/ baptizing them
			Shall be saved/ Remission of sins
			Teach to observe all things commanded

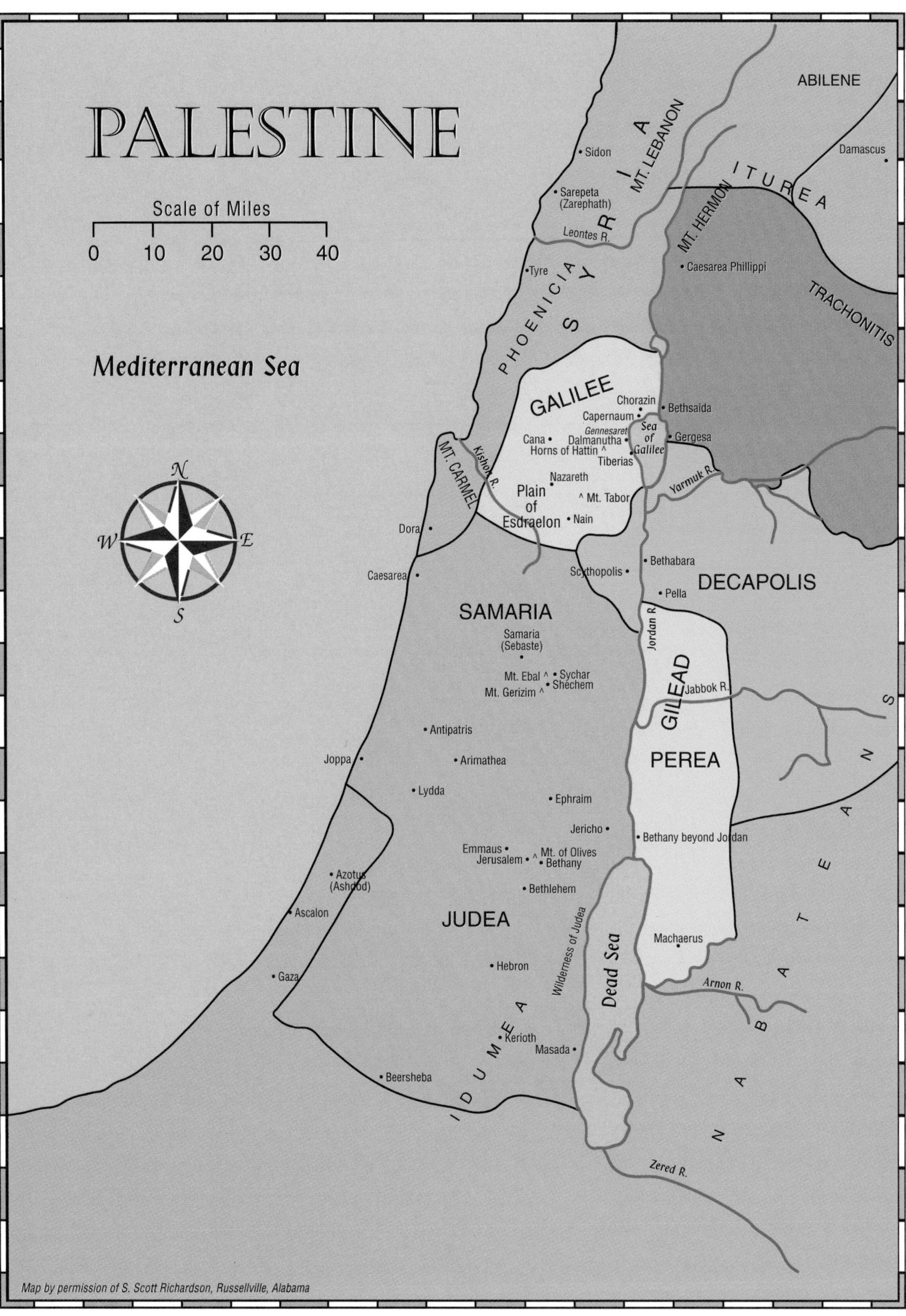
PALESTINE
Scale of Miles
0 10 20 30 40
Mediterranean Sea
ABILENE
Damascus
Sidon
Sarepeta (Zarephath)
Leontes R.
MT. LEBANON
SYRIA
ITUREA
MT. HERMON
Caesarea Phillippi
TRACHONITIS
Tyre
PHOENICIA
GALILEE
Chorazin
Capernaum
Bethsaida
Gennesaret
Sea of Galilee
Gergesa
Cana
Dalmanutha
Horns of Hattin
Tiberias
Kishon R.
MT. CARMEL
Nazareth
Yarmuk R.
Plain of Esdraelon
Mt. Tabor
Nain
Dora
Caesarea
Scythopolis
Bethabara
DECAPOLIS
Pella
SAMARIA
Samaria (Sebaste)
Jordan R.
Mt. Ebal
Sychar
Mt. Gerizim
Shechem
GILEAD
Jabbok R.
Antipatris
Joppa
Arimathea
PEREA
Lydda
Ephraim
Jericho
Bethany beyond Jordan
Emmaus
Jerusalem
Mt. of Olives
Bethany
Azotus (Ashdod)
Bethlehem
Ascalon
JUDEA
Wilderness of Judea
Dead Sea
Machaerus
Hebron
Gaza
Arnon R.
Kerioth
Masada
Beersheba
IDUMEA
NABATEANS
Zered R.
N
W
E
S
Map by permission of S. Scott Richardson, Russellville, Alabama

Section One

Primarily the Work of Peter

"And ye shall be my witnesses
in Jerusalem, in Judea, and in Samaria..."

Acts 1-12

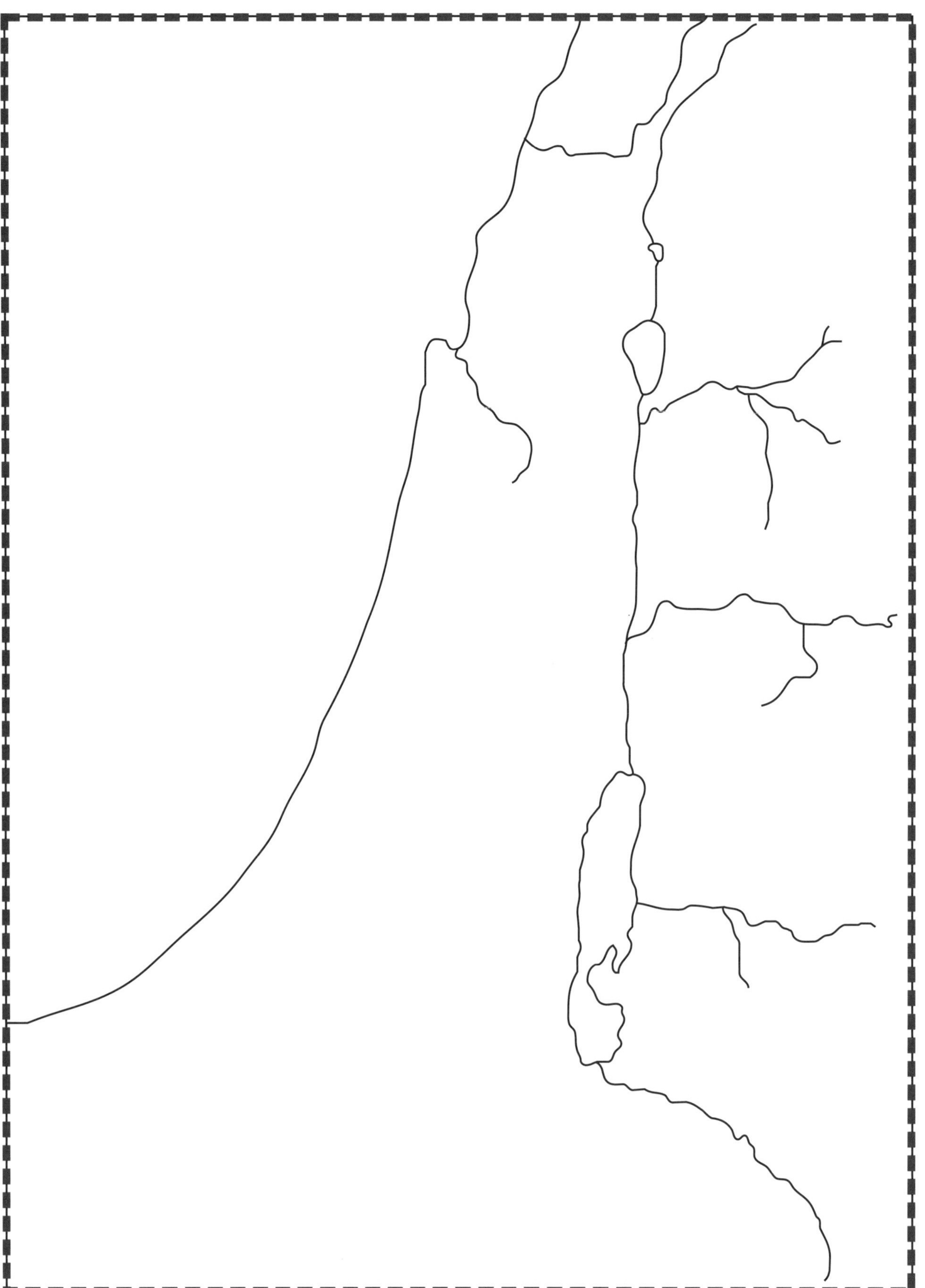

The Work Begins
(Acts 1-2)

All of the apostles are named in Acts 1:13. Between the ascension of Christ and the day of Pentecost *(no more than ten days)*, a new apostle is chosen to replace Judas Iscariot. His name is Matthias (1:15-26). The apostles are mentioned collectively several times through chapter 15. Peter is mentioned by name many times; John is mentioned four times in the story recorded in Acts 3-4. The death of James, the brother of John, is described in Acts 12:2. Otherwise, no other of the twelve is named in Acts. Peter and John continued to be associated for a long time with the church in Jerusalem (Gal. 2:9). The other apostles remained in Jerusalem through the first wave of persecution (see 8:1), but it seems evident that most of them left to go to other places before Paul's return to Jerusalem after his conversion (Acts 9:26-29; Gal.1:19), and certainly before Acts 15 (see Gal. 2:9). We point out these facts to avoid the thought that Peter was the chief apostle, or that he was the only one doing any work. But because his name is the main one used in the first part of Acts, we use his work as the basis for organizing the book in this manner.

In the first twelve chapters:
- **The gospel spread from the city of Jerusalem,**
- **To the whole eastern shore of the Mediterranean.**

The Gospel in Jerusalem
(Acts 1:1-8:3)

Prologue (Acts 1:1-5):

Luke wrote his first essay to Theophilus concerning all that Jesus did and taught until the day of His ascension *(the book of Luke)*. By the time of His ascension, Jesus had shown Himself alive by many indisputable proofs — proofs that could not be denied. He had appeared to His disciples during a period of forty days and had spoken to them of the kingdom of God. Finally, He commanded the apostles to remain in Jerusalem, and to wait for the promise of the Father which, as He said, "You heard from me, because John indeed baptized with water, but you will be baptized with the Holy Spirit not many days from now."

Jesus' work was effective:
- **His actions and His teachings matched:**
- **"...all that Jesus began both *to do* and *to teach*."**

Look back to the account of the Passover supper the disciples shared with the Lord on the night before He was arrested (John 13-16). During that supper, Jesus told His disciples that even though He was to be killed and would be leaving them, He would send a Comforter,

The Holy Spirit would:
- **Abide with them.**
- **Teach them all things they did not yet know.**
- **Bring to their remembrance the things Jesus had taught.**
- **Testify of Jesus.**
- **Guide them into all truth.**

the Holy Spirit, One who would abide with them. He said the Spirit would teach them all things they did not yet know, and would bring to their remembrance all things that Jesus had shown them and taught them. He said the Spirit would testify of Him (that is, bear witness to the truth of what Jesus had said), and that He would guide them into all truth (John 14:16-17, 26; 15:26; 16:7-15). At that supper, no time frame was given for the Spirit's coming except that it would be after the Lord died and returned to the Father. Now, here just before the ascension, Jesus is giving the same promise, and He is telling them the Spirit will come within a few days.

The ascension (Acts 1:6-11):

When the apostles met with Jesus for the last time, they asked Him, "Lord, are you going to restore the kingdom to Israel now?"

The kingdom Jesus came to establish:
- **A spiritual kingdom.**
- **Unlike all physical kingdoms.**
- **The disciples found it hard to understand the concepts concerning His kingdom,**
  - **But the Holy Spirit would help them understand all things.**

From their question, it sounds as if the apostles still did not understand the true nature of the kingdom Jesus had come to establish. We know that before His death they were confused about the nature of the kingdom, because they had on different occasions argued about who would be the greatest in that kingdom, thinking it would be like earthly kingdoms. Jesus did not speak of, or groan in despair at, the lack of understanding shown by His apostles. He knew the Holy Spirit would lead them to comprehend the things they did not yet understand.

It is possible that they understood something of the nature of the kingdom by now, and were wanting to know a time frame for the beginning of His spiritual kingdom. In either case, Jesus answered that the time was in God's hands and was no concern of theirs.

Ye shall be my witnesses:
- **In Jerusalem**
- **In Judea**
- **In Samaria**
- **To the uttermost part of the earth**

Jesus merely replied, "It is not your business when the Father chooses to do His will. According to His authority, He will determine the times when things will be done. But you will receive power when the Holy Spirit comes upon you, and you will be my witnesses in Jerusalem, and in all Judea, and in Samaria, and to the farthest corner of the earth."

Verse 8 can be used as another way to outline the book of Acts. We will observe the apostles and other faithful men taking the message about Christ: to Jerusalem, to Judea, to Samaria, and to the uttermost part of the earth.

When Jesus had said these things, He arose in the air, as the apostles watched, and disappeared into a cloud. As they continued staring upward in amazement, two men *(angels)* appeared by them and said, "Men of Galilee, why do you stand gazing into heaven? This same Jesus whom you just saw go into heaven will return in the same way."

Acts is a continuation of the story of the scheme of redemption.

Notice that this first section of Acts overlaps with the last few verses of Luke (Luke 24:44-53). This is no accident. Luke designed the books this way in order to show that Acts is a continuation of the story of the scheme of redemption. In our material on the life of Christ, we went to Revelation 4-5 and took a look behind that cloud that hid Jesus on this occasion to see the coronation of the Lamb that had been offered for the sins of the world.

Witnesses:

Jesus told His apostles that they were to be His "witnesses." They had seen His life, His miracles, the proofs of His deity. They had heard Him teach lessons that the multitudes were not ready to hear. They had seen the empty tomb, and they had seen Him alive again. They had touched Him, and had eaten with Him after His resurrection. They were eye-witnesses of the events in His life. Now it was their task to go tell that evidence to the world.

The apostles were eye witnesses:

- **Therefore they had a unique role to fill.**

This is the same commission that was recorded in the gospels, except that in the wording of this charge, Jesus was emphasizing the particular role that the apostles were to fill, in contrast to all others who would also be preaching and carrying the good news. It was this unique task of performing the work of witnesses that made them apostles. This is the work that Jesus had been preparing them for since He first selected them. If they had not been given a unique task to perform, then they would have been no different from other disciples. They would have been just twelve men out of many, many more disciples just like them. But these were men with a special task to perform —these were apostles, that is, they were "ones sent" on a mission. They were the eye-witnesses who could give testimony others would not be qualified to give.

We can be effective teachers:

- **But we cannot be witnesses.**

We can read and study the evidence the apostles and others recorded about Christ, and we can come to an understanding of who He was and what He did, but we cannot be witnesses. We do not live in the right generation to be witnesses. A witness is one who actually sees and hears an event. He knows first-hand what happened because he was there. In trials today, there may be witnesses to a person's character, ones who testify how this person has conducted his affairs in other situations and, therefore, can help predict whether he is capable of performing the crime he is accused of committing, but if there is an eye-witness to the crime, his testimony carries the greatest weight of all. In the same way, these apostles would give evidence of great weight. They were there when Jesus said and did these things. They were eye-witnesses.

No one:

- **Can be a "witness of Jehovah" today,**
- **Nor can anyone "witness" for the Lord.**
- **We live in the wrong generation to see Jesus on earth.**

Do not let someone confuse you today by claiming he is a witness of Jehovah, or that he is "witnessing" for the Lord. God does not work that way today. Throughout the biblical era, God was revealing His will and He sent angels, or appeared to men in dreams, or revealed His message in other ways. But in this era, God has revealed Himself to mankind through His Son (Heb. 1:1-2), and through His Son, the commission of giving eye-witness testimony was given to His apostles. If an angel did appear today, he would have to give exactly the message that is already revealed to us in the Bible, or he would be accursed (Gal. 1:8-9). Our work can be effective as we relate the evidence given in the Bible, but we are not witnesses.

The eleven apostles:
Peter
Andrew
James
John
Philip
Bartholomew
Thomas
Matthew
James
Thaddeus
Simon

The 120 consisted of:
- **The apostles**
- **Mary, Jesus' mother**
- **His brothers**
- **Faithful women**
- **Intimate disciples**

The disciples tarry in Jerusalem (Acts 1:12-14):

The apostles returned from the Mount of Olives to Jerusalem, just as Jesus had commanded, and went into an upper room where they waited for the promised coming of the Holy Spirit. Those present were: Peter, John, James, Andrew, Philip, Thomas, Bartholomew, Matthew, James the son of Alphaeus, Simon the Zealot, and Judas the brother of James *(the one called Thaddeus in other lists)*. They continued in prayer with faithful women, including Mary the mother of Jesus, with His brothers, and other faithful disciples.

Notice that Jesus' brothers are specifically mentioned in this group waiting for the coming of the kingdom. Yet, only a few months earlier, at the time of the Feast of Tabernacles in about October (our calendar), they still did not believe on Him (John 7:1-5). Now, by late May, His brothers are part of the inner circle of believers. Amazing events had occurred during those months, and obviously those events had convinced the brothers that Jesus was who He claimed to be, the divine Son of God. Paul lists James (almost certainly the Lord's brother) as one of the ones who saw Jesus after His resurrection (1 Cor. 15:7). Such an appearance to James would have been as convincing as the similar appearance to Paul.

Notice, also, that there is no sign of the deep grief and helplessness the disciples felt at the time of the crucifixion (Matt. 26:56; Mark 14:50; 15:40-41; Luke 22:62; 23:49), nor even the feelings of frustration they felt when they decided to go fishing (John 21:2-3). Their Lord has returned to heaven, but they now know their mission, and they are calmly waiting for the arrival of the Spirit as a signal that it is time to start their work.

Choosing of Matthias (Acts 1:15-26):

During the period of about ten days that they waited, Peter stood up in the midst of the brethren (there were about 120 of them) and said:

> Brethren, it was necessary for the scriptures to be fulfilled, which the Holy Spirit spoke through David concerning Judas who acted as guide to those who arrested Jesus. Judas was one of us and received his share in this ministry.

Then Luke interrupts his recording of Peter's speech to inform his readers that the money that had been paid to Judas was used to buy a field. Judas fell into the field after hanging himself (see Matt. 27:3-10). This story became known to all Jerusalem so that everyone called the field *Aceldama*, that is, the "field of blood."

Peter continued his speech, showing the scriptures which had to be fulfilled:

Requirements for the new apostle:
- **Been with us since John's baptism,**
- **A witness of the resurrection.**

> It is written in the Psalms: "Let his dwelling be made uninhabited, and let no man live in it," (Ps. 69:25), and, "His office let someone else take" (Ps. 109:8). Of the men who have accompanied us all the time Jesus was with us, beginning from the baptism of John until the day He was taken up from us: of these one must become a witness with us of His resurrection.

Two set forth:
- **Joseph Barsabbas**
- **Matthias**

One chosen: Matthias

Two men who met the standards Peter gave were chosen and put forward. One was Joseph Barsabbas who was surnamed *(given the name)* Justus, and the other was Matthias. Then the group prayed: "You, Lord, know the hearts of men. Show us which one of these two you have chosen to take Judas' place." They cast lots, and Matthias was chosen and was numbered with the eleven apostles.

Apostolic succession:

Jesus chose twelve apostles at first. When the first one died (Judas), another was chosen to replace him. Why it was so vital that the Lord's kingdom begin with twelve apostles is unknown. After the kingdom was begun, another apostle was chosen, Paul, fully equal to the twelve, yet not one of them (2 Cor. 11:5). But, when a second apostle died (James the brother of John, Acts 12:1-2), no successor was chosen, nor was there the slightest hint that there was any expectation of choosing a successor.

In the light of these facts:
- **Apostolic succession?**
- **Apostles today?**
- **Both totally without foundation in the Bible.**

It is important to note that Jesus gave no instructions for the perpetuation of the twelve apostles on earth. Not the slightest effort was made to replace them after the day of Pentecost. The subject is not even mentioned, and the early church never expected them to be replaced. They served a unique purpose in God's scheme of redemption, as special witnesses who had walked and talked with Jesus during His ministry and after His resurrection. They were specially guided by the Holy Spirit to reveal all truth and to confirm the message by special miraculous powers (Heb. 2:3-4). Since theirs was a unique position, there was no way it could be passed on to succeeding generations.

The Day of Pentecost
(Acts 2:1-47)

"And ye shall count unto you from the morrow after the sabbath, from the day ye brought the sheaf of the wave-offering, seven sabbaths shall there be complete: even unto the morrow after the seventh sabbath shall ye number fifty days; and ye shall offer a new meal-offering unto the Lord" (Lev. 23:15).

The Feast of Pentecost:

The first feast in the yearly cycle of feasts commanded in the law of Moses was the one-day Passover feast, immediately followed by the seven-day Feast of Unleavened Bread. This eight-day combination feast began on the fourteenth day of their first month *(called Abib and Nisan)* (Exod. 12:3, 6; Lev. 23:4-5). Passover was the time to commemorate the night the Israelites were freed from Egypt.

Leviticus 23:15 gives instructions about how to date the next feast after Passover. This feast, which was called the Feast of Weeks in the Old Testament (see Num. 28:26), was the time for the people to offer God the firstfruits of their crops. They were to begin numbering with the day after the sabbath, and count seven full weeks *(seven sabbaths)*, making the one-day feast fifty days after the Passover. In the New Testament, the Feast of Weeks is called Pentecost *(from the Greek word "pentekonta," "fifty)*.

Jesus partook of the Passover feast with His apostles on the night He was betrayed. He died the next day, and was raised on the first day of the week following that Passover feast on Thursday night. The day of Pentecost that is described in Acts 2 is the one that occurred fifty days after the bringing of the sheaf of the wave offering (Lev. 23:15-16) during the Passover Feast\Feast of Unleavened Bread that took place at the time of the crucifixion and resurrection.

The Holy Spirit:
- **Fell on the twelve apostles,**
- **Not on the 120 disciples.**

The Holy Spirit is one of the most misunderstood subjects in the New Testament:
- **We must be sure we and our students understand the passages as we come to them.**
- **Do not preach on the Holy Spirit in each class,**
- **But when you come to a passage on the subject:**
- **Make the point clearly,**
- **Then move on with your story.**

The apostles are filled with the Holy Spirit (Acts 2:1-4):

When the day of Pentecost had fully come, the apostles were all together in one place, when suddenly there came from heaven a sound like a tornado, and it filled the entire house where they were sitting. Tongues which parted like flames of fire appeared and sat upon each one of them, and the apostles were filled with the Holy Spirit. They began to speak in other languages, which they had never studied, as the Spirit gave them the ability to speak.

The Holy Spirit fell on the twelve apostles, not on the 120 disciples mentioned in 1:14-15. There are several reasons for this belief:
- *The Holy Spirit was promised only to the twelve (Acts 1:2-5, 8; John 14-16).*
- *The pronoun "they" in 2:1 refers back to the twelve apostles, including Matthias (1:26).*
- *The only ones who did miracles on the day of Pentecost, or at any time afterward until Acts 6:8, were the apostles (see 2:14, 43; 3:1-10; 4:33; 5:12). If the 120 received the Holy Spirit as the apostles did, why were they silent on the day of Pentecost and totally inactive in performing miracles both on that day and afterwards?*

- *The men who were speaking in tongues were all Galileans (2:7) and such would not have been true of the whole 120. Remember Nicodemus, Joseph of Arimathea, Cleopas and his wife Mary, Martha, Mary, and Lazarus, and a host of others.*
- *Peter stood up with the eleven (2:14), not with the 119.*

Impact of the miracle upon the people in Jerusalem (Acts 2:5-13):

Jews had come from all over the Bible lands to be at the feast of Pentecost. When the sound of the great wind was heard, the multitude rushed together and began to hear the apostles speak. As they listened, everyone was at a loss to explain how every man heard the apostles speaking in his own language. They said, "Look, aren't all these men Galileans? How then can we hear each man in our own native language?"

There were Jews present all the way from Parthia in the east, to Rome in the west, and they could all hear and understand the apostles telling of the mighty works of God in their own tongues. The audience was amazed and greatly puzzled.

But some mocked and said, "They are filled with new wine!" *(Or, as we would say, "They are drunk!")*

All the people present were either Jews or proselytes (that is, Gentiles who had accepted the law of Moses) (2:5, 10). No Gentiles were converted until Acts 10. This was a Jewish feast, and it was, therefore, Jews who had assembled to attend it.

A proselyte was a Gentile who had accepted the whole law of Moses with its rituals and sacrifices. The text will soon introduce us to "God-fearers" among the Gentiles. These were Gentiles who believed in the God of the Jews, but who did not follow the rituals and laws of Moses. Cornelius was a God-fearer, not a proselyte. A Gentile God-fearer, in contrast to a proselyte, would not have been allowed to participate in the Jewish feast of Pentecost.

Notice that the "tongues" were not ecstatic languages; they were not the language of angels. Instead, they were languages that could be understood by the people listening. The words "tongue" and "language" are used interchangeably in the passage (see 2:4, 6, 8, 11). Also, the statements of the people present show that these tongues were languages spoken by the people from the various nations.

The miracle of tongues was that the apostles were able to speak in languages they had not known before. The miracle did not take place in the ears of the listeners, but in the mouths of the apostles. Consider these arguments:

- *The text says the apostles spoke in other tongues (2:4, 11).*

Proselyte:

- **A Gentile who had accepted the whole law of Moses with its sacrifices and rituals.**

God-fearer:

- **A Gentile who believed in the God of the Jews, but did not follow the rituals of the law.**

Look at the places named in 2:9-11. Find all the places on the map at the end of this chapter. Notice that the map of the Mediterranean world that will be used for Paul's journeys is too small to show all the places mentioned.

1. **Parthia, Media, Elam, and Mesopotamia were all to the east of Palestine, across the Arabian desert. They were in, or near, the territories of old Assyria, Babylon, and Persia — near the Tigris and Euphrates rivers, and even beyond the Zagros mountains to the east of the rivers.**
2. **Cappadocia, Pontus, Asia, Phrygia, and Pamphylia were provinces on the northern shores of the Mediterranean in the peninsula called Asia Minor.**
3. **Egypt, Libya, and Cyrene were all in Africa.**
4. **Rome was in Italy; Cretans were from the island of Crete; and the Arabians were from the desert.**

- *If the miracle had taken place in the ears of the listeners, then everyone would have automatically understood the words he heard. None would have heard a "babble" of languages to lead them to the cynical charge that the apostles were "filled with new wine" (2:13).*
- *If the miracle were in the ears of the listeners, what need would there have been for an interpreter? Yet, as the history progresses, we learn that there were inspired interpreters who should be present if one were going to speak in an "unknown tongue" (see 1 Cor. 14:5, 13, 26-28).*

Peter's sermon (Acts 2:14-36):

The sermons of Acts are richer to us when we take time to see the exact points the Holy Spirit was making through the speaker each time.

Peter's sermon is the one recorded here in chapter 2, but notice that he stood up with the eleven (2:14). There were twelve sermons being preached on this occasion, with each of the apostles meeting with a group speaking a particular language or dialect. Those who could understand one apostle listened to him; those who could understand another apostle, listened to him. But of the twelve sermons, it is Peter's that is recorded for us. Also notice that we are given only the basic points that were made. Verse 40 says that "with many other words did he testify and exhort" the multitude.

As we proceed with an analysis of Peter's sermon, watch carefully for the exact points made. Each sermon in the book of Acts makes a particular point as its primary lesson. This one in chapter 2 is saying that all the events of that day of Pentecost and the preceding events of the death, burial, resurrection, and exaltation of Christ were part of the eternal plan of God. The Jews had rejected and killed Jesus, expecting that to be the end of Him, but God had planned for Him to suffer and then be raised from the dead. Indeed, He had predicted it all through His prophets. After the Jews' rejection of Jesus, God raised Him from the dead and highly exalted Him to His own right hand.

Peter, standing up with the eleven, spoke to the multitude and said:

Joel predicted:
- **The coming of the Holy Spirit,**
- **But he also predicted the hope of salvation.**

Peter is about to tell the people how to call upon the name of the Lord.

> Men of Judea, and all of you who are staying in Jerusalem, listen to me. These men are not drunk as you suppose. It is only nine o'clock in the morning, too early for men to get drunk. Rather, all of this is in fulfillment of Joel's prophecy in which he said:
>
>> God says "In the last age, I will pour out my Spirit upon all humanity. Your sons and your daughters will prophesy, and your young men will see visions, while your old men will dream dreams. Yes, and upon my servants and on my maidservants, in those days, I will pour forth my Spirit and they will prophesy.

Prophecies of the Bible, in Old and New Testaments, compact time.

"And I will show wonders in the heaven above and signs on the earth beneath: blood, and fire, and smoke. The sun shall be turned into darkness and the moon into blood, before the day of the Lord comes, that great, noteworthy day. And it shall be that whoever calls on the name of the Lord will be saved" (Joel 2:28-32a).

Through Joel, God said He would send His Spirit, not upon every individual human being, but upon representatives of all segments of society: men, women, young, old, slave, and free. The signs referred to are the signs of judgment which were typical of Old Testament prophecy (see Isa. 13:9-10; 24:23). These signs depict the judgment which would come upon Jerusalem and the Jewish nation in A.D. 70, because of their rejection of the Christ. Thus the fulfillment of this prophecy began on this day of Pentecost in A.D. 29 or 30, and continued the process of fulfillment for about forty years, until the destruction of Jerusalem in A.D. 70.

Prophecies of the Bible, in both the Old and New Testaments, compact time. This prophecy from Joel is an excellent example of that practice: from reading the passage, it would seem that everything described was to happen in one day. Yet, in the fulfillment of the prophecy, it is evident that it began at one point and continued over a period of years until its completion.

Look at Peter's exact points:

- **The happenings of today begin the fulfillment of the prophecy of Joel (2:14-21).**
- **Jesus of Nazareth demonstrated He was approved by God by the signs which He did — as you know (2:22).**
- **But according to the plan and foreknowledge of God:**
  - **You delivered Him to be killed; you crucified Him (2:23).**
  - **But God raised Him from the dead (2:24).**
  - **As had been foretold by David (2:25-31).**
    - **David spoke of One whose body would not be left in the realm of the dead, who would not decay (2:25-28).**
    - **Yet, David's body did decay; he was left in Hades, so he was not speaking of himself (2:29).**
    - **David knew God had promised to set a descendant of his upon the throne, One to reign forever (2**

Peter continued:

Men of Israel, listen to these words: Jesus of Nazareth was a man approved of God among you by the mighty works and wonders and signs which God did in Him in your midst, as you very well know. He was given into your hand by the plan and purpose of God. You took Him and, by the hand of lawless men, crucified and killed Him. But God raised Him from the dead, loosening the grip of death because it was not possible that He should be held by it. David predicted this concerning Him when he said:

I beheld the Lord always before my eyes, because He is at my right hand, that I should not be moved. Therefore, I was glad and praised God. Also my fleshly remains will dwell in hope because you, O God, will not leave my soul unto Hades *(the place of the dead)*, nor will you allow your Holy One to see physical decay. You made known to me the ways of life. You will make me full of gladness with your presence (Ps. 16:8-11).

Sam. 7:13, 16), so he predicted the resurrection of the Christ (2:30-31).

- **We are witnesses that God did indeed raise Jesus (2:32).**
- **God has exalted Jesus to His own right hand (2:33a),**
  - **As David also predicted (2:34-35).**
- **From there, Jesus has poured forth the Spirit as you see today (2:33b).**

- **Let everyone know that this Jesus, whom you crucified, has been made both Lord (Ruler) and Christ (the Anointed One) (2:36).**

"Then Peter said unto them, `Repent, and be baptized every one of you in the name of Jesus Christ for the remission of sins, and ye shall receive the gift of the Holy Ghost'" (Acts 2:38).

My brothers, I may speak to you freely of the patriarch David, that he died and was buried, and his tomb is with us to this very day. So David certainly was not talking about himself. David was a prophet. He knew that God had sworn with an oath to him that He would set one of his descendants upon his throne. Foreseeing the fulfillment of this prophecy, David spoke of the resurrection of the Christ, that He was not left in Hades, nor did His flesh decay. God raised up this Jesus, and we all are witnesses of this event.

The explanation of what you see and hear today is this: Jesus has been exalted to the right hand of God, and, having received that which the Father promised, He has poured forth the Holy Spirit upon us.

David has not ascended into heaven, but he himself said: "The Lord said to my Lord, 'Sit on my right hand, till I make your enemies the footstool of your feet'" (Ps. 110:1).

Let all the family of Israel know assuredly *(without any doubt; firmly believe)* that God has made this Jesus whom you crucified both Lord and Christ.

The people's response (Acts 2:37-47):

When the people heard this, their consciences hurt, and they asked Peter and the other apostles, "What should we do?"

Peter answered, "Repent and be baptized everyone of you in the name of Jesus Christ so that you can have the remission *(removal)* of your sins, and you will receive the gift of the Holy Spirit. The promise is to you, and to your children, and to all that are afar off, even as many as the Lord your God will call to Him."

Notice what these people were told to do to be saved. Before they asked their question, Peter had already told them to "let all the house of Israel know assuredly" (be convinced) that these things were true (v. 36). Now, in answer to their question about what they must do, he tells them to repent and be baptized. Do you see that Peter is telling them the commands Jesus gave in the great commission? You might start keeping a chart showing the commands given in the great commission and comparing them with what the people were told to do in each case of conversion.

Combination of the Great Commission:	Day of Pentecost:
Preach/teach	Peter and the eleven preached (2:14-40)
He that believeth	Let all the house of Israel know assuredly (be convinced) (2:36)
Repentance	Repent (2:38)
And is baptized/ baptizing them	Be baptized...in the name of Jesus Christ (2:38)
Shall be saved/ remission of sins	For remission of sins (2:38)
Teach to observe all things commanded	They continued steadfastly in the apostles' doctrine (2:42)

Peter said they would receive the "gift of the Holy Spirit." Did this mean that each believer automatically received a miraculous gift of the Spirit when he was baptized? There is no evidence of such in the chapters that follow. As we have already mentioned, no one besides the apostles did a miracle until after the Holy Spirit was specifically given to seven more men in chapter 6. Therefore, this gift that Peter refers to must be something else. What was it?

Many fine Bible students differ over what this gift is, but it seems most logical that it is the sanctifying, renovating influence of the Spirit — not in a miraculous way, but through His influence on our lives through the word. The result of this magnificent gift is our transformation (Rom. 12:2), our partaking of the divine nature (2 Pet. 1:4). It is through the Spirit and His work of revelation that God makes His light to shine upon us. It is through the Spirit's influence upon us that we are able to become all we can be in God's plan.

"...and you shall receive the gift of the Holy Spirit"
- **The renovating influence of the Spirit through His influence in our lives through the word.**
- **It is through this transformation that we may partake of the divine nature.**

The first great harvest of those who heard the Lord teach:
- **3,000 souls were saved,**
- **Were added to the apostles and to the body of the saved.**

The church, the body of the saved, had begun.

The new converts continued:
- **In the apostles' doctrine,**
- **In fellowship,**
- **In breaking of bread,**
- **In prayers.**

With many other words, Peter warned and encouraged the people saying, "Save yourselves from this perverse generation."

Those who gladly received his word were baptized, and there were added to them that day about three thousand souls. This response was the first great harvest of the work Jesus had done. The new converts continued steadfastly in the teaching of the apostles, in the sharing of spiritual interests and concerns, in the Lord's Supper, and in prayers. Every one was moved to fear God and reverence Him, and many miracles were done through the apostles. All those who believed continued to associate and to share their possessions. They sold their things to raise money and then distributed it to each one according to his need.

Every day, they continued to be together at the temple, and, eating their bread at home, they took their food with gladness and with great purpose of heart, praising God and making a favorable impression upon all the people. And the Lord added to their number day by day those that were being saved.

The church grew rapidly as the Lord added those who were being saved.

The church grew very rapidly during the first weeks and months after its establishment. The apostles were reaping the harvest from the work Jesus had done as He had taught up and down the land. Many of these Jews had seen Jesus perform miracles and had heard Him preach. They were, therefore, the first to be convinced that He was indeed the Messiah and that He fulfilled the prophesies of old even in His death.

Let there be no doubt that the Messianic kingdom promised in Daniel 2:44 was begun on this day of Pentecost. It was begun with power and grew mightily in spite of the opposition of the Jews and, later, of the Roman government. It was not buried under Judaism and given a "resurrection" in A.D. 70 as some teach. It was very much alive, growing and conquering during these years.

Notice that the believers were selling their possessions and sharing with those among them who were in need. This point will be mentioned again in the last of chapter 4 and in the first of chapter 5. We will discuss the matter in more detail at that point.

Here in this early period of the church, the new believers chose to be together as often as possible. The apostles taught daily in the temple and the disciples gathered to learn as much as possible about this new kingdom, the church. These daily gatherings and sermons also gave opportunity for many others to hear the message and to be convinced.

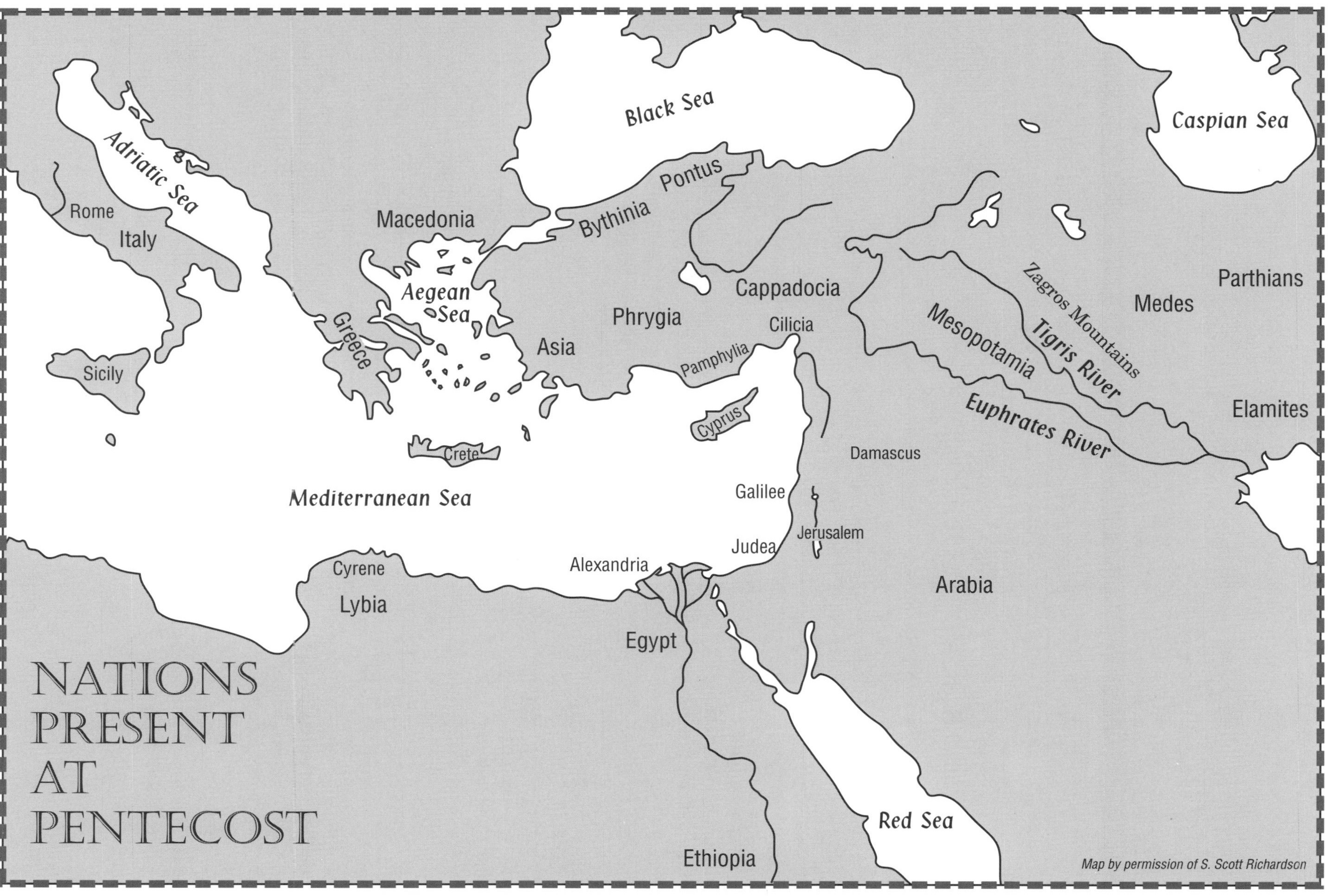
NATIONS PRESENT AT PENTECOST
Black Sea
Caspian Sea
Adriatic Sea
Rome
Italy
Sicily
Macedonia
Aegean Sea
Greece
Crete
Bythinia
Pontus
Asia
Phrygia
Cappadocia
Cilicia
Pamphylia
Cyprus
Mediterranean Sea
Zagros Mountains
Tigris River
Mesopotamia
Euphrates River
Medes
Parthians
Elamites
Damascus
Galilee
Jerusalem
Judea
Alexandria
Cyrene
Lybia
Egypt
Arabia
Red Sea
Ethiopia
Map by permission of S. Scott Richardson

Conflicts Begin
(Acts 3-7)

Peter and John heal a lame man (Acts 3:1-10):

One day Peter and John went into the temple at the hour of prayer *(3 o'clock in the afternoon; at the time for the offering of incense).* Their way led through the Beautiful Gate, which faced the east and opened into the women's court. By this gate a man who had been lame since birth was laid daily to beg alms from the passers-by. When he saw Peter and John about to go into the temple, he asked them for alms *(a gift of money).*

Peter, with John, looked at the man intently and said, "Look at us." The man paid close attention because he thought they were about to give him money. But Peter said, "I do not have any silver and gold, but what I do have, I give to you. In the name of Jesus Christ of Nazareth, get up and walk."

Can you imagine the joy of this man who had been crippled all his life, and now could walk?

Peter took the man by the hand, lifted him up, and immediately the man's feet and ankle-bones received strength. The man leaped into the air and began to walk and jump, praising God as he did so.

All the people saw him walking and praising God, and they recognized him as the beggar who had sat at the Beautiful Gate. They were filled with wonder and amazement at what had happened.

The money shared by the believers was for the needy among themselves.

Do you remember that the believers had been selling their possessions and sharing them as there was need (2:44-45)? We are told in 4:34-35 that the money was "laid at the apostles' feet" for distribution. That means Peter and John could have found money for a donation to this beggar, if that money were for all the poor of Jerusalem. But that money shared by the believers was for the needy among themselves. Peter and John might have even found some gift from their own personal resources — but what they had to give this man was of far greater value than any alms might have been. If we could have asked that man which he would prefer, alms or healing, which do you suppose he would have chosen?

A covered walkway, or colonnade, surrounded the temple courtyard on all four sides. Benches were found here and there. Solomon's Porch was the colonnade to the east, near the Beautiful Gate.

Peter preaches (Acts 3:11-26):

As the man who had been healed held onto Peter and John, the people ran together into Solomon's Porch to see what had happened. They were amazed and curious.

When Peter saw the people gather in astonishment, he said,

The primary lessons in this sermon are:

- **God has glorified His Servant Jesus (3:12-13a).**
- **You killed Him; you rejected Him (3:13b-14).**
- **But God raised Him from the dead,**
  - **We are witnesses of the fact (3:15).**
- **It was by faith in Jesus' name that this man was healed (3:16).**
- **You acted through ignorance (3:17).**
  - **But God was fulfilling all He had predicted through His prophets (3:18, 22-23, 24).**
- **You are the ones to inherit the fulfillment of all the promises God made,**
  - **You have been offered the first chance to share in the blessings (3:25-26).**
- **Take advantage of the blessings offered:**
  - **By turning from your ways so that your sins will be blotted out,**
  - **So that God can accomplish all He wants to accomplish through Jesus (3:19-21, 26).**

You men of Israel, why are you surprised at this man? And why do you stare at us as though we made him able to walk through our own power and holiness? The God of Abraham, of Isaac, and of Jacob, the God of our fathers, has glorified His Servant Jesus. You handed Him over to be killed, and you denied Him before Pilate, when he was determined to release Him. You denied the Holy and Righteous One and asked for a murderer to be released to you. You killed the Prince of Life whom God raised from the dead. Of this fact we are witnesses.

On the basis of faith in His name, His name has made this man strong — the man you see and know. It is Jesus' name and the faith that comes through Him that has made this man perfectly well before you all.

And now, brethren, I know that you acted in ignorance when you rejected and killed the Son of God, as did your rulers. But this is how God fulfilled what He had said through all the prophets, that is, that His Chosen One would suffer.

Therefore, repent, and turn from your way, so that your sins may be blotted out, so that times of refreshing may come from before the Lord, and so that He may send the Christ who has been appointed for you — Jesus. He must remain in heaven until the time comes for God to restore all things, as He promised long ago through His holy prophets. Moses said, "A prophet shall the Lord your God raise up unto you from among your brethren as He raised me up. You will need to obey everything He says. And it shall be that everyone who does not obey Him shall be completely destroyed from among the people" (Deut. 18:15, 18, 19).

Yes, and all the prophets from Samuel on have spoken of these days. You are the sons *(and, therefore, heirs)* of the prophets and of the agreement which God made with your fathers. He told Abraham, "In your seed shall all the families of the earth be blessed" (Gen. 12:3; 22:18). When God raised up His Servant, He sent Him first to you to bless you by turning each of you from your wicked ways.

Peter and John are taken into custody (Acts 4:1-22):

This is the first time the apostles come under persecution.

As Peter and John spoke to the people, the priests, the captain of the temple, and the Sadducees came to them. They were very disturbed because the apostles were teaching the people, and, in what they were saying about Jesus, they were proclaiming the resurrection from the dead. They seized Peter and John, and, because it was now evening, they put them in jail until the next morning.

The number of the disciples grew to 5,000.

Nevertheless, many of the multitude who heard the message that had been preached believed it. The number of men grew to be about five thousand.

It is the Sadducees who first object to the preaching of the apostles:
- **Because they did not believe in a resurrection.**

Since the healing of the lame man, and the sermon which followed, took place in Solomon's Porch at the temple, the priests and Sadducees were near by. The Sadducees had objected when Jesus spoke on the subject of the resurrection, so it is not surprising that they objected when they heard the apostles stating that Jesus had been raised from the dead. Neither is it surprising that it was the Sadducees who objected first to the apostles' preaching, even though they had not started their conflict with Jesus Himself as early as did the Pharisees. The Sadducees did not believe anyone would ever be raised from the dead, so they certainly did not believe that this man whom they had rejected had been raised.

In the conflicts which the disciples had with the Jews in the book of Acts, we will see them taken into custody for one reason, and then when they are tried before the council, that primary reason is ignored, and they are questioned as if they were seized for some entirely different reason. The explanation for this is that the Sadducees objected to the apostles teaching the resurrection, so they arrested them. But when the matter was brought before the council, the Sadducees knew better than to use the teaching of the resurrection as their charge, because the council was predominantly composed of Pharisees who believed in the resurrection of the dead (though they, too, objected to saying Jesus had been raised). We see this conflict in this story and in other places as well (see Acts 23:1-10).

All the persecutions told in the book of Acts:
- **Originate with the Jews,**
- **Or are a result of a local conflict.**

Pay careful attention to the source of the persecution as each occurrence arises. We think of the first century as a time when the Roman government persecuted the saints, and that is true of the last part of the century, but the Roman government did not know the church existed at this point.

This first opposition comes from the Jewish leaders: the priests, the captain of the temple, and the Sadducees. These, along with the Pharisees, were the ring-leaders in the opposition to Jesus, so now they object to the apostles' telling the multitudes that He was indeed the Messiah and wrongfully treated by the officials.

Trial before the Sanhedrin.

The next day, the rulers, elders, and scribes *(the Sanhedrin and possibly other leaders of the Jews)* gathered together. Annas and Caiaphas were both present, along with John and Alexander *(men unknown in the Bible story until this point)*, and others of the kinsmen of the high priest.

When Peter and John were brought before the assembly, the council asked, "By what power, or in what name, have you done this?"

Peter, guided by the Holy Spirit, responded:

> Rulers of the people and elders, if we are being tried today for an act of kindness done to a crippled man, and if you are asking how he was healed, then know this, all of you and

Note the points Peter made:

- **By the power of Jesus of Nazareth, this man stands before you in perfect health (4:9-10).**
- **You killed him (4:10).**
- **God raised Him from the dead (4:10).**
- **He is the stone you builders cast aside,**
  - **But He has been made the chief cornerstone of the building,**
  - **Just as the prophets predicted (4:11).**
- **There is salvation in no other (4:12).**

everyone else in Israel: It is by the name of Jesus Christ of Nazareth, whom you crucified, but whom God raised from the dead, that this man stands before you in perfect health. Jesus is the stone which you builders cast aside as worthless, and now He has been made the chief cornerstone of the building *(as the prophets foretold, Ps. 118:22).* In none other is there salvation, because there is no other name under heaven given among men by which we must be saved.

When the Jewish authorities saw the boldness of Peter and John, and realized that they were unschooled, ordinary men, they were astonished. They took note that these men had been with Jesus. Furthermore, the man who had been healed was standing with Peter and John, so the officials could not deny the miracle. Finally they commanded Peter and John to leave the council while they conferred.

They said, "What are we going to do to these men? A remarkable miracle has been done, and everyone in Jerusalem knows it. We cannot deny it. But to stop this thing from spreading any further among the people, we must warn them not to preach to anyone in this name again." Calling Peter and John back into their presence, they commanded them not to speak or teach at all in the name of Jesus.

"Whether it is right in the sight of God to listen to you more than to God, you judge. For we cannot but speak the things which we have seen and heard" (Acts 4:19b-20).

But Peter and John answered, "You may decide for yourselves whether it is right in God's sight for us to obey you — or God. As for us, we cannot keep from telling the things we have seen and heard."

When the Jews had threatened them more, they let them go. They saw no basis on which they could punish them, because the multitudes glorified God for what had been done. The man who had been healed was over forty years old and had been crippled since birth.

The officials saw the boldness of Peter and John.

The officials saw the boldness of Peter and John — although they were standing on trial in front of the very council that killed Jesus. It is only a few weeks since Peter was so afraid of this assembly he denied that he knew Jesus. The Sanhedrin is the same, with the same hatreds it had when it was trying Jesus, but many amazing events have taken place in those few weeks. Peter is a different man now. He understands how God's whole plan of redemption fits together, he understands why Jesus had to suffer and die before salvation could be available for mankind. He is no longer afraid of what the Sanhedrin may do to him.

Peter and John return to their own company (Acts 4:23-31):

"Their own company" is not identified. Since there were five thousand or more saints by this point, it does not seem likely that they returned to an assembly of all the saints. Also, at this time, only the apostles were doing the preaching and the working of miracles(4:29-

31, 33). Since this company to which Peter and John returned was composed of those who were directly involved with them in this work, likely "their own company" refers to the apostles.

Look at the exact points made in this prayer to Jehovah:
- **O Jehovah, Creator of all:**
  - **You predicted that the Gentiles, the kings, and the rulers would oppose your Anointed One (4:24-26).**
  - **And, indeed, it came to pass, just as predicted, in this very city (4:27-28).**
  - **Now, please be aware of their threatenings against us:**
    - **Help us have boldness to preach as we should (4:29),**
    - **While you continue to show miraculous signs in the name of your holy servant Jesus (4:30).**

When Peter and John returned to their own group, they told them all that the chief priests and elders had said to them. When the others heard the report, they lifted up their voices to God in total unity of mind, saying:

> O Lord, who made the heaven and the earth and the sea and everything in them: by the Holy Spirit you spoke through the mouth of our ancestor David, saying, "Why did the *Gentiles* rage, and the *peoples* imagine vain things? The *kings* of the earth set themselves in array, and the *rulers* were gathered together, against the Lord, and against His Anointed" (Ps. 2:1-2).
>
> And, indeed, Herod a *king* and Pontius Pilate a *ruler* met with the *Gentiles* and the *people* of Israel in this very city to conspire against your holy servant Jesus whom you anointed. They did what your power and will had decided beforehand should happen.
>
> Now, Lord, look upon their threatening, and help us, your servants, to have the ability to speak your words with all boldness, while you stretch forth your hand to heal and to perform miraculous signs and wonders through the name of your holy servant Jesus.

When they had thus prayed, the place where they were gathered was shaken. They were all filled with the Holy Spirit, and they spoke the word of God with boldness.

Every sermon so far has included these basic points:
- **Jesus showed He was approved of God.**
- **But you killed Him.**
- **God raised Him.**
- **We are witnesses of the resurrection.**
- **All of this was according to the plan of God.**
- **Take advantage of the salvation offered.**

The apostles did not pray for the persecution to stop. They realized persecution came with the task before them. Their Lord had been persecuted, and now it was their turn as they took the message to the world. Instead, they prayed for boldness to continue the work in spite of whatever came. The shaking of the building was God's way of assuring them that He heard their cry for help and was nearby.

These earliest subjects in the new kingdom of Christ had a feeling of love and generosity toward each other.

The disciples share their possessions (Acts 4:32-35):

The entire multitude of believers were of one heart and mind. Not one of them said that anything he possessed was his own; they shared everything they had. With great power, the apostles gave their witness of the resurrection of the Lord Jesus, and great grace was upon them all. No one among the believers had to do without. Those who owned lands or houses sold them, and brought the money they received from the sales and laid it at the apostles' feet. Then it was distributed as each one had need.

There was no commune where all the believers lived together and shared their property.

- **The situation described was a spontaneous sharing of necessities during a time of need.**

An unusual situation existed in Jerusalem at this time. A large number of Jews had come to the city to keep the feast of Pentecost. While they were there, many of them learned about Christ and His new kingdom, and became a part of it. These new believers chose to prolong their stay in Jerusalem and learn more from the apostles. Therefore, a need arose to provide the necessities for these so far from home. This was not a situation in which they all lived in some kind of commune, but rather it was the generous response from righteous people to meet a need that had arisen. After this early period, the disciples did not continue selling their possessions and sharing them as they did here. Therefore, we should learn from their example of generosity and be willing to share whenever a need arises, but we do not need to have a general sharing of all our possessions under normal circumstances.

The example of Joseph (Acts 4:36-37):

Barnabas:

- **Mr. Encouragement**

Joseph was a Levite from the island of Cyprus. Owning a field, he sold it and brought the money to the apostles for them to distribute as it was needed. The apostles named him Barnabas, which means "son of exhortation" *(or, as we would say, Mr. Encouragement).*

We will meet this man Barnabas again and again. It is the same man whom we meet here as Joseph, but he will wear the new name given him because of his actions.

There is a vivid contrast between the example of Barnabas and that of Ananias and Sapphira. It seems they wanted the kind of praise that was given to Barnabas, but they wanted to keep their money for themselves. Undoubtedly, the two stories are placed side by side to show this contrast.

Ananias and Sapphira (Acts 5:1-11):

A man named Ananias and his wife Sapphira also sold some property. With his wife's full knowledge, Ananias kept back part of the money and brought the rest of it to lay at the apostles' feet. He pretended that he had brought all of the money he had received from the sale of their property.

Peter said, "Ananias, how is it that Satan has filled your heart to lie to the Holy Spirit, and to keep back part of the price of the land? Before you sold it, was it not yours to do with as you wished? And, after you sold it, was not the money yours to do with as you wished? How could you decide to do such a thing? You have not lied to men, but unto God."

When Ananias heard these words, he collapsed and died. The younger men present prepared his body for burial, carried him out, and buried him.

Ananias and Sapphira wanted the praise without the sacrifice.

The disciples were not required to sell their possessions even during this time of need. Peter told Ananias that the property had been his, and it could have remained his. Then, after selling it, it was perfectly within his rights to bring part of the money to be used in the Lord's work and to keep the rest to do whatever he and Sapphira chose to do with it. The sin came when they decided to pretend they had brought it all. They were hoping to have the praise without the sacrifice.

Ananias lied to God by lying to men guided by the Holy Spirit.

Peter said Ananias lied to God, yet he had brought the money to the apostles. How could that be? Of course all sin is ultimately against God, but it was more than that on this occasion. The apostles were directly guided by the Holy Spirit as they spoke, so they were in a position to know whether this man was lying or telling the truth, and whether he deserved their praise or their rebuke.

About three hours later, Sapphira came into the assembly, but she did not know what had happened to Ananias. Peter asked her, "Tell me, did you sell your land for this amount?"

She said, "Yes, that is the price."

Peter answered, "How could you two agree together to test the Spirit of the Lord? Look, the feet of those who buried your husband are at the door, and they will carry you out also."

Immediately, Sapphira collapsed at his feet and died. The young men came in and, finding her dead, carried her out and buried her beside her husband. As a result of this event, great fear came upon the whole church, and upon everyone who heard what had happened.

Compare this event to the story of Nadab and Abihu:
- **God demanded obedience on the part of His priests.**
- **God demanded respect for the Holy Spirit on the part of the believers.**
  - **The multitude (as well as we ourselves) had to be impressed that the apostles were indeed inspired by the Holy Spirit so that their testimony would be believed.**

Sapphira came into the assembly three hours after her husband had died. This gives another glimpse into the activities of these early disciples. Though there were gatherings at the temple daily, and the apostles seemingly spent most of each day preaching to the crowds that gathered, the entire multitude of believers did not spend their entire days there.

Compare this event to the story of Nadab and Abihu who were struck dead for disobeying God's commandment in offering incense in the Old Testament (Lev. 10:1-2). God did not continue to strike people dead when they sinned under the old law, nor did He continue to strike people dead in the church. If He had done so, there would have been very few people left. But, in both cases, God was making specific points. Nadab and Abihu had just begun to fulfill their role as priests. They had just finished a special week of consecration to be priests, and were offering incense for one of their first times — and they ignored

God's laws for how it was to be done (Lev. 8-9; 16:12-13). God struck them dead to make the point that He demanded that His priests be careful to obey the details of His laws regarding sacrifices.

Now, in the case of Ananias and Sapphira, the church has just begun. The apostles have been given the Holy Spirit to guide them in their work —and these two people come expecting to be able to deceive the apostles just as they might deceive anyone else. God struck them dead to make, perhaps, more than one point. One was that He demanded that these new believers behave as obedient subjects of their King, the Christ. But, perhaps, the more specific point was that these apostles were no longer men with only their normal perception, but men with the power of Deity, the Holy Spirit, to help them. The multitude had to be impressed that the apostles were indeed inspired by the Holy Spirit so that their testimony would be believed.

The apostles continue their work of preaching and healing (Acts 5:12-16):

Multitudes were added to the disciples.

The apostles performed many miraculous signs and wonders among the people, and the disciples continued to meet regularly in Solomon's Porch at the temple. People from the general public did not dare associate themselves with the disciples, but they respected them very much. As the days passed, more and more people came to believe on the Lord and were added to the disciples, multitudes of both men and women.

Sick people were carried out into the streets and laid on beds and couches so that, as Peter passed by, at least his shadow might fall upon one here and there. Multitudes came from the cities around Jerusalem, bringing their sick and those who were afflicted with unclean spirits. All of them were healed.

It is still the apostles, and only the apostles, who were doing miracles.

Acts 5:12 is another verse which specifies that miracles were done by the apostles. In your study, associate this passage with 2:43; 3:1-10; and 4:33. There is plenty of evidence to show that the apostles preached and did miracles from the time they received the baptism of the Holy Spirit. There is no evidence that anyone else did any preaching or miracles until Acts 6:8. There is no evidence that the 120 disciples mentioned in Acts 1 received the baptism of the Holy Spirit; nor were the miraculous powers from the Spirit spontaneously obtained when one was baptized.

"And ye shall be my witnesses in Jerusalem, and in all Judea..." (Acts 1:8).

The influence of the message about the risen Christ is reaching out of the city of Jerusalem already. People from the outlying villages and cities of Judea are bringing their sick into the city to be healed, and they are hearing the message of the apostles. The plan for spreading the gospel is working exactly as Jesus described: the apostles are giving their testimony in Jerusalem, and now to the people of Judea (1:8).

The apostles are taken into custody (Acts 5:17-42):

More opposition arises:
- **From the Sadducees and priests,**
  - **Led by the high priest himself.**

Again, it was the Sadducees who moved against the apostles. They were very jealous of the success the apostles were having in making converts. Led by the high priest, they came and arrested the apostles and put them in the public jail.

That night, an angel of the Lord opened the prison doors and brought them out. He said, "Go, all of you, and stand in the temple courts and tell the people about this new life." Having heard this command, the apostles went into the temple about daybreak and began teaching.

Meanwhile, the high priest and his associates called the Sanhedrin together. When they sent to have the prisoners brought, the officers returned saying, "We found the prison completely secure with guards standing at the doors, but when we opened the doors, we found no one inside." When the captain of the temple and the chief priests heard this report, they were chagrined and wondered how the affair would turn out.

The officers bring the men without violence:
- **Because they fear the reaction of the people.**

Just then, someone came in and told them, "Hey! The men whom you put in the prison are standing in the temple teaching the people."

The captain went with the officers, and they brought the apostles back to the council, but they did so without violence because the officials feared the people. They were afraid the multitudes might stone them if they harmed the apostles whom they respected.

Earlier the Jews had said,
- **"Let His blood be on us..."**
- **But now they protest: "You intend to bring this man's blood upon us."**

When they got back with them, the officers set the apostles before the council. The high priest said, "We strictly charged you not to teach in this name any more, and yet you have filled Jerusalem with your teaching. You intend to bring this mans blood upon us."

Do you remember that when the Jews stood before Pilate and demanded that he crucify Jesus they said, "His blood be upon us and upon our children" (Matt. 27:25)? At that time they did not think there would be any further consequences. Now that it appeared there would be consequences, they wanted to avoid all blame for putting the Son of God to death. The only way these Jewish officials could have erased the blame for the terrible deed they had done would have been by humbly repenting and accepting God's plan for forgiveness. Instead, they continued their rejection and only increased their guilt by fighting against the apostles' message.

"We must obey God rather than men" (Acts 5:29).

Look at the exact points:
- **God raised the One you killed (5:30).**
- **God exalted Him to be Prince and Savior (5:31a),**
- **So that repentance and remission of sins could be given (5:31b).**
- **We are witnesses (5:32a),**
- **And, so is the Holy Spirit whom God has given (5:32b).**

Peter and the apostles answered, "We must obey God rather than men. The God of our fathers raised up Jesus, whom you executed, hanging Him on a tree. God has exalted Him at His right hand to be a Prince and a Savior, to bring Israel to repentance and to accomplish the remission of sins. And we are witnesses of these things, and so is the Holy Spirit, whom God has given to them that obey Him."

Instead of backing down, Peter repeated the very core of the message that the Sadducees hated so much. The message angered most of the Pharisees also because it placed the blame for the death of the Savior squarely upon their shoulders.

When they heard this, the Jews were so angry they wanted to kill the apostles. But a Pharisee named Gamaliel stood up in the council. He was a doctor of the law and was held in great honor. He commanded that the apostles be removed from the room, and then said to his companions:

Gamaliel said:

- **Let these men alone.**
- **If their message is from men, it will come to nothing.**
- **If it is from God, we do not want to be found fighting God.**

> Men of Israel, be careful what you do with these men. Remember a while back a man named Theudas arose proclaiming himself to be a leader. About four hundred men joined themselves to him. But then he was slain and his followers scattered, and it amounted to nothing. Afterward, Judas arose out of Galilee in the days of the enrollment for taxes and drew people after him. He also perished and all his followers scattered.
>
> My advice to you is to let these men alone, because if their cause is of men, it will be overthrown. But if it is of God, you will not be able to overthrow it. Instead you will find yourselves fighting against God.

The council agreed with Gamaliel's advice. Calling the apostles back, they beat them, commanded them not to speak in the name of Jesus, and let them go.

The apostles continue to teach and preach daily.

The apostles went out from the council rejoicing that they were counted worthy to suffer dishonor for the name of Jesus. And every day, in the temple and at home, they continued to teach and preach Jesus as the Christ.

The Grecian Jews murmur against the Hebrews (Acts 6:1-6):

Grecian Jews:

- **Those reared in the Greek world outside of Palestine.**

Hebrews:

- **Those holding rigidly to Jewish customs.**

As the number of disciples grew *(now well above 5,000)*, the task of distributing relief to the needy had grown to be very burdensome. Up until this point, the money was laid at the apostles feet (4:35, 37; 5:2), and they were responsible for seeing that it was distributed as needed. But by now, the work had outgrown their ability to handle the job alone.

Complaints arose from among the Grecian Jews that their widows were being neglected in the daily dispensing of relief. There is not the slightest hint that their complaints were untrue. The apostles dealt with it as a legitimate problem.

Grecian Jews were Jews reared in the Hellenistic (Greek) world outside of Palestine. Generally they were more comfortable reading their Old Testament in Greek (the LXX translation) than in Hebrew. Most of them were quite as pious and devoted as their relatives who lived in Judea, but, as might be expected, some of them had made accommodations in their customs to fit Greek society. These Jews made their visits to Jerusalem to attend feasts just as their Palestinian brethren did, although not as regularly, or as often, because of the greater distances and expense involved. During Paul's missionary journeys, they proved to be fully as fanatic against the story of Jesus as the Jews in Jerusalem. The term "Hebrew" is used in this passage to refer to those still holding rigidly to all Jewish customs.

By now the task of distributing to meet the needs of the people was so enormous, it is not surprising some were being overlooked. And, if some were going to be overlooked, it would most likely be those far from home, because they would not be as well known to the people living in Jerusalem.

This story illustrates the way to handle problems that arise in the church. It was handled:

- **Swiftly,**
- **By those in a position of leadership,**
- **Involving the whole multitude,**
- **Placing the solution in the hands of those most closely involved.**

The apostles called the multitude of disciples together and said, "It would not be right for us to forsake the word of God to serve tables. Therefore, choose from among yourselves, brethren, seven men with good reputations, full of the Spirit and of wisdom, whom we may appoint over this business. Then we will continue steadfastly in prayer and in the work of spreading the word."

This solution pleased the whole multitude, and they chose seven men meeting the qualifications which the apostles had set forth. They chose Stephen, who is described as a man full of faith and of the Holy Spirit, Philip, Prochorus, Nicanor, Timon, Parmenas, and Nicolas, who was a Gentile from the city of Antioch. He had been converted to Judaism before becoming a Christian *(a proselyte)*. They set these men before the apostles who, when they had prayed, laid their hands upon them.

The names of these seven men selected are all Greek names, but this does not prove that they were necessarily Grecian Jews. Several names among the twelve apostles are Greek names also (Andrew and Philip, for example). Yet mention of Nicolas, who was a proselyte, and the fact that all these names are Greek, indicate that the multitude may have chosen to put the work of relief into the hands of those from whom the complaints had come.

These men were all full of the Spirit, but they did no miracles until after apostolic hands had been laid upon them. That means the expression "full of the Spirit" refers to more than miraculous powers, including attitudes such as zeal and determination to serve God.

The number of disciples multiplied greatly,
- **Including a great number of the priests.**

Stephen performing miracles:
- **And he is not an apostle.**

This time the opposition:
- **Started with a local synagogue.**
  - **Not with the officials.**
- **This marks a major change in the origin of opposition.**

Stephen's speech was one of indictment rather than persuasion.
- **He would have been glad to convert,**
- **But he was talking to those who had already heard and had rejected the message.**

Stephen built to his climax:
- **Starting with Abraham, Stephen reminded the Jews of their history,**
- **The point he emphasized was that they had always rejected the leaders God had chosen for them: Joseph, Moses, the prophets, and then the Christ.**
- **By rejecting the leaders God had chosen, they rejected God Himself.**
- **In rejecting the Christ, they followed the pattern of rejection that had characterized the Jews for all their history.**

The word of God grows in Jerusalem (Acts 6:7):

As the word of God spread, the number of believers grew tremendously. Many even among the priests obeyed the gospel. No specific number is given this time.

Stephen's preaching brings him into conflict with the Jews (Acts 6:8-8:1a):

Stephen, one of the seven, was filled with grace and power. He worked great miracles among the people.

This is the first time someone besides the apostles performed miracles. Stephen is one of the seven men who have just been appointed for a special work and is one upon whom the apostles have "laid their hands" upon. The record tells us that the apostles prayed and laid their hands upon these men, but it does not tell us specifically why they did so beyond appointing them to the task for which they had been selected (6:6). Yet, here in verse 8, Stephen is able to perform miracles. Let us leave the question of how he received that power hanging for the moment. We will come back to the question and answer it from information we will learn in chapter 8.

Certain ones in a synagogue made up of Grecian Jews began to debate Stephen. They were, however, unable to resist the wisdom and the Spirit by which he spoke. These Jews included Libertines *(Freedmen, that is, those who had once been slaves but were now free)*, men from Cyrene in Africa, from Alexandria in Egypt, and from the provinces of Cilicia and Asia in Asia Minor. *(Find these places on your map on page 23. We will soon learn of a man named Saul from Tarsus of Cilicia. Acts 21:39; 23:34; 26:3.)* Since they could not answer Stephen's arguments, his enemies determined to destroy his influence another way. They paid men to lie, saying, "We heard Stephen speak blasphemous words against Moses and against God."

By these accusations, they stirred up the people, the elders, and the teachers of the law. They seized Stephen and brought him before the council. They set up false witnesses who said, "This man never stops criticizing this holy place and the law. We have heard him say this Jesus of Nazareth will destroy this place, and will change the customs which Moses delivered unto us."

All who were sitting in the Sanhedrin looked intently at Stephen, and they saw that his face looked like the face of an angel. The high priest asked him, "Are these things true?" And Stephen began his defense:

> Brethren and fathers, listen to me. The God of glory appeared to our father Abraham, while he was still in Mesopotamia before he lived in Haran, and said, "Get out of your land,

Stephen's speech:
Learn from your history:

- **God gave our family a great opportunity (7:2-8):**
    - **He called Abraham.**
    - **He promised this land to Abraham's descendants,**
        - **Though He predicted slavery and deliverance before time for their inheritance.**
    - **He gave the rite of circumcision as a sign of that covenant.**
    - **Isaac was born,**
    - **Then Jacob,**
    - **Then the 12 patriarchs.**
- **But the patriarchs rejected the brother God had selected to be their deliverer (7:9-16):**
    - **They sold Joseph.**
    - **Through God's hand, Joseph became ruler of Egypt.**
    - **Joseph saved his people from famine.**
- **Time approached for God to fulfill His promise to give the land (7:17-38):**
    - **People multiplied.**
    - **The king of Egypt oppressed our people,**
        - **Demanding the death of the babies.**
    - **Moses was born at this time.**
        - **Rescued as a baby,**

and away from your relatives, and come into a land that I will show you." So Abraham left the land of the Chaldeans and moved to Haran. From there, when his father had died, God sent him to this land where you now live. He gave Abraham no inheritance here — no, not even one square foot of land — but He promised that He would give the land to his descendants, even though at that time Abraham had no child.

God told him, "Your descendants will dwell for a time in a land that is not their own, and they will be made slaves and will be mistreated for four hundred years. But I will punish the nation whom they serve as slaves, and then I will bring them out of that land, and they will worship me in this place."

God gave Abraham the rite of circumcision as a sign of the covenant between them. After a time, Abraham became the father of Isaac and circumcised him on the eighth day. Isaac, in turn, fathered Jacob, and Jacob, the twelve patriarchs *(the sons of Jacob who became the fathers of the tribes).*

The patriarchs, moved with jealousy, sold their brother Joseph into Egypt. But God was with Joseph and delivered him from all his troubles. God gave him fame and wisdom before Pharaoh, king of Egypt, who made him governor over all Egypt.

Then a famine struck all Egypt and Canaan. It was a severe famine, and our fathers had no food. When Jacob heard that there was grain in Egypt, he sent our fathers on their first visit. On their second visit, Joseph told his brothers who he was, and even Pharaoh learned about Joseph's family.

Joseph sent for his father Jacob and for his whole family, a total of seventy-five people, and had them move to Egypt. There they remained, and Jacob and all our fathers died there. Their bodies were brought back and buried in Shechem in a tomb that Abraham had bought from the sons of Hamor.

As the time drew near for God to fulfill the promise which He had made to Abraham, the people grew and multiplied until another king came to power in Egypt, a king who did not recognize Joseph. This king dealt with our people in an under-handed manner and oppressed them by forcing them to throw out their newborn babies so that they would die.

It was at this time that Moses was born. He was a lovely baby in the sight of God. After being cared for three months in his father's house, he was cast out and was found by Pharaoh's daughter. She trained him as her own son, and he

- **But rejected by his own people at 40 years of age.**

was educated in all the wisdom of the Egyptians. He was mighty in his words and in his deeds.

When, however, Moses was about forty years old, he decided to help his relatives, the children *(descendants)* of Israel *(Jacob)*. Seeing one of them being mistreated, he defended him and killed the Egyptian oppressor. Moses thought that his own people would realize that God was using him to rescue them, but they did not accept this idea at all.

The next day, Moses found two Israelites who were fighting. He tried to reconcile them by saying, "Men, you are brothers! Why do you want to hurt each other?" But the one who was at fault pushed him away and said, "Who made you a ruler and a judge over us? Do you plan to kill me like you killed the Egyptian yesterday?" Moses fled, and he lived in the land of Midian, where he fathered two sons.

- **God sent the rejected Moses back to be the ruler and deliverer.**

After forty years, an angel appeared to him in the flames of a burning bush in the desert near Mount Sinai. When he saw the sight, Moses was amazed and went closer to have a better look. As he approached, the voice of God spoke to him saying, "I am the God of your ancestors, the God of Abraham, of Isaac, and of Jacob."

Moses was terrified and would not look. God continued talking to him: "Take off your shoes because the place where you are standing is holy ground. I have certainly seen the hardship of my people who are in Egypt. I have heard their groaning, and I have come down to deliver them. Now, I am sending you to Egypt."

- **Through Moses, God gave many blessings to Israel.**
- **This same Moses predicted a special prophet that God would send: the Christ.**

This very Moses, whom the people had refused by saying, "Who made you ruler and judge," God made both a ruler and a deliverer with the help of the Angel who appeared to him in the bush. This man led them by working all sorts of signs and wonders in Egypt, and at the Red Sea, and in the wilderness for forty years. This is the same Moses who told the Israelites, "God will send you a prophet like me from your own people" (Deut. 18:15). This is the same one who was in the congregation in the wilderness with the Angel who spoke to him on Mt. Sinai and received living words to pass on to us.

- **In rejecting God's leaders, they rejected God Himself, and turned to idols (7:39-50):**
  - **But our fathers refused to obey him, and made a golden calf to worship.**

But our ancestors would not obey him. They pushed him away and turned back to Egypt in their hearts. They told Aaron, "Make us gods to go before us. As for this Moses who led us out of Egypt — we do not know what has become of him!" So they made an idol in the shape of a calf and brought their sacrifices to it and rejoiced in the product of their own hands.

- **They preferred the shrine of Molech,**
  - **Though they had the shrine of God, the tabernacle, made according to His pattern.**

Therefore, God gave them up to serve the hosts of heaven, as it is written in the book of the prophets: "You did not offer me sacrifices for forty years in the wilderness, did you, O house of Israel? You took up the shrine of Molech and the star of the god Rephan, the figures which you made to worship. Therefore, I will carry you away beyond Babylon" (Amos 5:25-27).

Our ancestors had the tabernacle of the testimony with them in the wilderness. It had been made according to the directions God had given Moses. They brought it with them when, under Joshua, they entered the land and took it from the nations which God drove out before them. The tabernacle remained in the land until the days of David who found favor in God's sight and who asked to build a dwelling place for the God of Jacob. But it was Solomon who built Him a house.

- **But God showed you that even the tabernacle and temple were not His ultimate dwelling place:**
  - **God does not dwell in houses made by men.**
- **You stiff-necked people: You always resist the Holy Spirit (7:51-53):**
  - **Your fathers persecuted all the prophets:**
    - **The very ones who foretold the coming of the Righteous One.**
  - **And now, you have betrayed and murdered Him.**
  - **You received the law that was given through angels,**
    - **But you never obeyed it.**

However, the Most High does not dwell in houses made by men. As the prophet says, "Heaven is my throne, and the earth the footstool of my feet: what kind of house will you build me?" says the Lord, "Or what kind of place will you make for me to rest in? Did not my hand make all these things?" (Isa. 66:1-2).

You stiff-necked people, with uncircumcised heart and ears! You always reject the Holy Spirit. You are just like your fathers! Was there ever a prophet whom your fathers did not persecute? They even killed those who predicted the coming of the Righteous One. And now you have betrayed and murdered Him! You were the ones who received the law which was put into effect through angels — but you have not obeyed it!

Jesus was *standing* on the right hand of God as Stephen was stoned to death.

- **This is the only time the Bible speaks of Jesus standing, rather than sitting at God's right hand.**

When the Jews heard Stephen's charges, they were cut to the heart and gritted their teeth in rage at what he had said. But Stephen, being full of the Holy Spirit, looked up into heaven and saw the glory of God and Jesus standing on the right hand of God. He said, "Look, I see the heavens opened, and the Son of Man standing on the right hand of God."

At this, the Jews shrieked and stopped up their ears. Rushing forward, they seized Stephen and threw him out of the city where they stoned him to death. The witnesses laid their outer garments at the feet of a young man named Saul.

As they stoned Stephen, he called upon the Lord, saying, "Lord Jesus, receive my spirit." He kneeled down and cried with a loud voice, "Lord, lay not this sin to their charge." Then he fell asleep *(died)*.

Saul approved.

The young man Saul fully approved of what the mob had done to Stephen.

God did not spare Stephen's life:

- **He never promised that He would stop hardships that come from serving Him,**
- **But He has promised He will give us strength to bear whatever comes,**
  - **And that the reward for enduring will be worth whatever hardship is necessary.**

Stephen is the first person killed for his faith in Christ. Notice that God did not spare his life —yet Stephen was given a glorious glimpse of heaven and the throne of God with Jesus standing on His right hand. What strength this vision must have given Stephen in the midst of his agony.

There was nothing legal in this affair. The original charges were false ones, deliberately brought against Stephen to try to discredit him. Then, there was an official "trial" before the Sanhedrin, but instead of carefully listening to the defense and weighing the things said, the men in the Sanhedrin itself responded in rage. The stoning was not a lawful execution —but the actions of an angry mob.

The Church is Scattered
(Acts 8-12)

The Sanhedrin had feared the people, so had not mistreated the apostles (4:13-18; 5:26):
- **But now the opposition has originated with the common people, in a local synagogue.**
- **Watch as the persecution escalates.**

Look at the source of the persecution that arose against Stephen: the trouble started in a local synagogue. Stephen's defense was before the Sanhedrin, but he had been brought there by common men, not by the leaders themselves. This is a significant point because one of the reasons the Sanhedrin had not been harder on the apostles earlier was that they feared the people. Now opposition has arisen from the people themselves, so the leaders can vent their anger against the movement without fear of repercussions from the people. The many conversions that have occurred have removed sympathizers of the disciples from the Jews and has therefore created an undiluted opposition.

Severe persecution arose (Acts 8:1-4):

Faithful men buried Stephen and mourned his passing. The grief for him was only multiplied as others joined the ranks of the persecuted, because with the stoning of Stephen, it was as if the dam holding back the Jewish persecution of the church was broken. Immediately, a severe persecution broke out against the multitude of disciples in the city of Jerusalem.

Saul first held the coats for those who stoned Stephen.
- **Now he is a leading persecutor of the saints in Jerusalem.**

The young man Saul, who had held the garments for the men who stoned Stephen, became one of the leaders of the persecution. He devastated the church, making house to house searches to find believers. Those he found were cast into prison. As he himself later describes his actions, "I was convinced that I should do everything in my power to oppose the name of Jesus of Nazareth, and that is just what I did in Jerusalem. By the authority of the high priest, I put many saints in prison, and when they were put to death, I cast my vote against them. I went from synagogue to synagogue looking for those to punish. I tried to force those I found to blaspheme" (Acts 26:9-11).

The persecution encouraged the disciples to carry out the next step in Jesus' plan for the spread of the gospel (1:8):
- **Ye shall be my witnesses:**
  - **In Jerusalem,**
  - **In Judea,**
  - **In Samaria...**

It was a terrible time for the saints in Jerusalem, and all the new converts were scattered into Judea and Samaria. Soon, only the apostles were left behind in the city. The scattered disciples did not stop believing in Christ. Instead, they preached the message about Him everywhere they went, thus fulfilling the plan of God that the gospel be spread over all the earth.

The persecution was an effort to destroy the new church, but in reality, it had the opposite effect. It seems that the work of preaching had been confined to the city of Jerusalem up until this time. Now, due to the persecution, the disciples are scattered to the rest of Judea and into Samaria — and as they go, they preach to all they meet. Use the map of Palestine and see Judea and Samaria in relation to Jerusalem. They will soon be moving to places more distant, fulfilling the last major step in Jesus' plan: "to the uttermost part of the earth" (1:8).

Philip preaches in Samaria (Acts 8:4-24):

The inspired historian follows the scattered disciples as they spread the good news.

One of the scattered saints was Philip. He traveled north to Samaria and preached Jesus to the people there. When the multitudes heard Philip and saw the miracles which he did, they all paid close attention to what he said. Unclean spirits came out of many, screaming as they did so. Many who were paralyzed or lame were healed. There was great rejoicing in the city.

Philip was one of the seven men chosen in chapter 6.

After the apostles laid their hands on the seven men selected in chapter 6, they could do miracles (6:8; 8:6-7). These were the first ones besides the apostles who did miracles.

There was an apostle named Philip (1:13), but this Philip in Acts 8 was not an apostle, because the apostles were still in Jerusalem (8:1). This Philip is not called an apostle at all, nor could he do what the other apostles did, namely, give the Holy Spirit through the laying on of hands (8:14-18). Yet, he could do miracles. He was, therefore, another one of the seven men chosen in Acts 6. The story of Stephen, one of the seven, is told in chapters 6 and 7, and now we have two stories about a second one of the seven men told here in chapter 8.

Map Assignment:

- **Label the province of Samaria on your map.**
- **Label the city of Sebaste and the city of Sychar.**

The central portion of the land was called Samaria at this time, but the old city called by that name in the Old Testament had been rebuilt and renamed Sebaste in honor of Augustus Caesar (Sebaste is the Greek form of the name Augusta). From the wording here that Philip went to "the" city of Samaria, most assume he went to the chief city of Samaria which would be Sebaste. But, since some manuscripts just say "a city of Samaria," some think he may have gone to Sychar, near the site of old Shechem, where Jesus talked to the woman at the well and then to the people of the city (John 4). It could just as easily have been to another city in the area. It does not matter exactly which city it was. The important point is that the Samaritans heard the gospel and responded gladly. Philip was reaping the harvest of those who had heard Jesus teach, as well as reaching some who might never have seen Him personally.

Simon used trickery:

- **But he recognized that Philip was doing the real thing.**
- **Philip was performing *miracles* rather than using trickery.**

According to the great commission, the people of Samaria and Simon did the things necessary to be saved when they heard Philip preach.

There was a man named Simon in Samaria who, up until now, had used sorcery and had amazed the people of Samaria. He advertised himself to be some great one. He had managed to deceive everyone, small and great, so that they all said, "This man is that power of God which is called great — he is the Great One from God." They had paid attention to him for a long time because he continued to amaze them with his magical arts. But when the people of Samaria heard Philip preaching the good news concerning the kingdom of God and the name of Jesus Christ, they were baptized, both men and women. Even Simon believed the message and was baptized. He was so amazed at the miracles Philip could do, he followed him everywhere he went.

Great Commission:	**People of Samaria:**	**Simon the Sorcerer:**
Preach/teach	Heard Philip preach the good news of the kingdom of God and the name of Jesus Christ	Simon also heard the message Philip was preaching
He that believeth	They believed	He believed
Repentance		
And is baptized/ baptizing them	They were baptized, both men and women	He was baptized
Shall be saved/ remission of sins		
Teach to observe all things commanded	Peter and John preached in the Samaritan villages.	

Important details:
- **The Samaritans had been baptized,**
    - **But they had not received the Holy Spirit.**
- **The apostles in Jerusalem knew that Peter and John would be needed when they learned the Samaritans had been baptized.**

No mention is made of any miracles being done as a result of receiving the Spirit:
- **But miracles must have been done because Simon saw the results of the receiving of the Spirit.**

Luke, the inspired historian, writes what Simon saw:
- **He saw that *through the laying on of the apostles' hands, the Holy Spirit was given.***

Meanwhile, the apostles who were still in Jerusalem heard that the people of Samaria had received the word of God and they sent Peter and John to them. When they arrived, Peter and John prayed that the Samaritans might receive the Holy Spirit, because He had not fallen upon any of them. The only thing that had been done was that they had been baptized into the name of the Lord Jesus. Following prayer for the people to receive the Spirit, Peter and John laid their hands upon them and they received the Holy Spirit.

Important points regarding the Holy Spirit are learned here:
- *Receiving miraculous powers was not an automatic thing when one was baptized.*
- *The only connection between baptism into the name of the Lord Jesus and receiving the Holy Spirit in a miraculous way, was that it made the baptized ones fit subjects to receive the Spirit.*
- *Philip could do miracles, but he could not give the power of the Spirit to someone else.*
- *It was not left to the whims of even the apostles to give the Holy Spirit at random. They "prayed" that the Samaritans might receive Him.*

When Simon the sorcerer saw that the Holy Spirit was given through the laying on of the apostles' hands, he offered them money, saying, "Give me also this ability so that everyone on whom I lay my hands may receive the Holy Spirit."

Simon did not ask for the same gift that was being given freely to the believers:
- **He wanted the ability to *impart* the Spirit.**

Simon had believed and had been baptized, and had, therefore, been saved (Mark 16:15-16).
- **Now he sins.**
- **What was required when a saved person sinned?**
    - **Peter told him to *repent* and *pray*.**
    - **Simon asked Peter to pray on his behalf also.**

The Holy Spirit:
- **Apostles had to go to Samaria to give the Holy Spirit to others.**
- **Philip could not give the Spirit,**
    - **Nor did Simon have a right to that gift.**
- **That ability belonged to the apostles alone.**

Miraculous gifts of the Spirit came in only two ways:
- **Directly from heaven as in the case of the apostles and Cornelius.**
- **By the laying on of an apostle's hands.**

The Spirit was given in the first century in order to:
- **Deliver the message of God.**
- **Confirm the word of those who taught the message to others.**

Peter answered, "Your silver will perish along with you, because you have thought that you could buy the gift of God with money. You have no part at all in this matter, for your heart is not right with God. Repent, therefore, of this wickedness of yours and pray to the Lord that He may forgive you for having such a thought in your heart. I can see that you are in the very juice of bitterness and in the handcuffs of iniquity."

Simon answered, "Pray for me to the Lord that none of the things of which you have spoken will come upon me."

This is the passage where we learn how the Spirit was transferred from one person to another in the New Testament. Do you remember we left a question dangling back in chapter 6? At that time, the apostles laid their hands upon the seven men who had been chosen for a particular task. Not only did that proclaim they had been appointed for the task, Stephen, one of the seven men, was able to do miracles afterward (6:8). Now, in this story, another of those seven men (Philip) is performing miracles, but two apostles have to come from Jerusalem before any of the Samaritans can receive a like gift to do miracles. Notice that Simon did not ask for the gift to do miracles; he asked for the ability to pass the Holy Spirit on to others. He saw that was something the apostles were not giving freely. That right belonged to the apostles alone.

Throughout the New Testament, we find the Spirit either coming directly from God as in the case of the apostles in Acts 2 and upon Cornelius and his household in Acts 10, or from the laying on of the apostles' hands (Acts 6:6, 8; 8:14-24; 19:6; 2 Tim. 1:6). This is a very important point because if those who received the gift of the Spirit from the apostles could, in turn, pass it to others, then the gift could have been passed down through the generations to those of us today. But, if it could only be passed through the laying on of the apostles' hands, then it could not be passed after the last apostle died. The direct operation of the Spirit was given during the first century of the early church for the unique purpose of delivering the message of God and for confirming the word of those who taught it. That purpose was completed in that century, and there was no further need for the miraculous gifts of the Spirit.

Peter and John return to Jerusalem (Acts 8:25):

When Peter and John had preached the word of the Lord, they returned to Jerusalem. As they traveled through the countryside, they preached the gospel in many of the Samaritan villages.

The eunuch was deeply religious:
- **He had traveled at least six or seven hundred miles to worship in Jerusalem.**
- **As he rode home, he was reading from the prophet Isaiah.**

Map Assignment:
- **Find Ethiopia on the map on page 23 and see how far it was from Jerusalem.**
- **Look on the map of Palestine on page 8 and find the location of a road from Jerusalem to Gaza.**
- **Find Samaria and see where Philip had come from to join the eunuch.**
- **See God's providence. From the distances involved, Philip had to leave Samaria before the eunuch left Jerusalem for them to meet on the road to Gaza.**

This eunuch:
- **Was an Ethiopian,**
- **A Jewish proselyte,**
- **A "proselyte of the gate"**
    - **One who could be counted as a Jew in religion,**
    - **But who could not participate in the public worship because he was a eunuch.**

Philip preaches to an Ethiopian eunuch (Acts 8:26-40):

An angel of the Lord spoke to Philip and said: "Get up and go southward to the road that goes from Jerusalem to Gaza — the area that is deserted." Without question, Philip went south as he was told.

Meanwhile, there was an Ethiopian approaching the same spot that Philip was approaching. This man was a eunuch of great authority who served as treasurer to Queen Candace, queen of Ethiopia. He had made the trip to Jerusalem to worship and was returning to his own country. As he rode along sitting in his chariot, he was reading from the prophet Isaiah.

Ethiopia was a kingdom of primarily black people reaching from Aswan at the first cataract of the Nile, which marked the southern boundary of Egypt, southward to Khartoum where the Blue Nile and the White Nile join. The boundaries fluctuated through history, but Ethiopia was a powerful kingdom. It had two great royal cities during its history: Napata, just down-river from the fourth cataract of the Nile, and Meroe, located about midway between the fifth and sixth cataracts. (James Breasted, A History of Egypt, p. 561. Cf. fold-out map at the back of the book.)

The Ethiopians passed power through their queens. The queen mother transmitted the inheritance to her son, but she herself exercised the rule. Though the son was regarded as king and given divine honors, he was confined to the palace while his mother reigned. "Candace" was a title passed from one queen to the next.

Sometimes the word "eunuch" did not literally mean a man who had been emasculated, but a prince or officer of the court. The word had come to have that meaning because so many rulers of that day emasculated their officers to insure greater loyalty to the state. But this man was probably literally a eunuch since his official position is further described. If he were literally a eunuch, then he could be no more than a "proselyte of the gates" since his mutilation would prevent him from entering the inner temple courts (Deut. 23:1). Such proselytes were not circumcised and did not obey all ceremonial and dietary commandments of the law, but there were many of them in the world of the first century, and a great host of them proved receptive to the gospel.

This man was an Ethiopian, not a Jew, although obviously a proselyte, since he had come to worship at Jerusalem. He may well have been a black man. Certainly the word Ethiopia means having a dark or "burnt" face (Jer. 13:23); thus the Ethiopians were dark-skinned. Pictures on monuments, however, show that they were of mixed races: some Black, some Semitic, some Caucasian (Zondervan Pictorial Bible Dictionary, p. 262). There is evidence that there was a strong Jewish presence and influence in Ethiopia at this point in history.

Given the great power of the man and his probable wealth, there was likely a fairly strong bodyguard accompanying him, though no mention is made of anyone besides the eunuch.

The Spirit said to Philip, "Go on up to the chariot."

Philip ran to the chariot where he could hear the eunuch reading aloud from Isaiah. He asked, "Do you understand what you are reading?"

The eunuch replied, "How can I unless someone guides me?" Then he asked Philip to come up into the chariot to sit with him.

Isaiah describes the Messiah:
- **As a sacrifice who would willingly, humbly give Himself for us.**
- **He was deprived of any fair trial and was left with no descendants because His life was taken away.**

The passage the eunuch was reading was this:

> He was led as a sheep to the slaughter; and as a lamb before his shearers is dumb, so He opened not His mouth. In His humiliation His judgment was taken away; His generation who shall declare? For His life is taken from the earth (Isa. 53:7-8).

The eunuch's question, as he read the passage, was, "Who is the prophet talking about, himself or someone one else?"

Taking the scripture from Isaiah as his starting point, Philip preached Jesus to the eunuch.

What an opportunity! To take the One pitifully described in Isaiah 53:7-8 and show that, yes, His judgment was taken away, but He willingly gave Himself for our atonement (as Isaiah shows in that very chapter); and, yes, He had no descendants because His life was taken away, but that was not the end of it. He was raised from the dead, and ascended into heaven to sit at the right hand of God. And through the gospel, all men may be saved if they will believe and be baptized.

Look what the eunuch did when he heard the preaching about Jesus.
- **He believed it,**
- **And was baptized.**

Now the good news about Jesus will be carried all the way to Ethiopia.

Map Assignment:
- **Label Azotus and Caesarea on your map of Palestine.**

As Philip and the eunuch traveled along, they came to some water. The eunuch said, "Look! Here is water. Is there is any reason why I cannot be baptized?"

Philip answered, "If you believe with all your heart, you may."

And the eunuch said, "I believe that Jesus Christ is the Son of God."

Then the eunuch commanded the chariot to stop. He and Philip got out and went down into the water where Philip baptized him.

When they came back up out of the water, the Spirit caught Philip away, and the eunuch did not see him anymore. He continued on his way home rejoicing.

Philip, however, was found at Azotus. After passing through it, he preached the gospel in all the cities along the coast until he came to Caesarea.

Combination:	Ethiopian Eunuch:
Preach/teach	He heard Philip preach Jesus
He that believeth	He believed that Jesus is the Son of God
Repentance	
And is baptized/ baptizing them	He was baptized
Shall be saved/ remission of sins	He went on his way rejoicing
Teach to observe all things commanded	Nothing else is known about the eunuch

The conversion of Saul of Tarsus (Acts 9:1-19a; 22:1-16; 26:1-18; Gal. 1:13-17):

Saul of Tarsus became the one known best as the apostle Paul (see Acts 13:9).

Acts 9:1-19: Luke's record
Acts 22, 26: Paul's accounts
Galatians 1:13-24: Additional information about Paul's conversion, and the period immediately following.

We are including all the passages here in order to get the details together.

After giving this example of the preaching being done by the disciples who were scattered abroad, Luke brings us back to the main stream of the story to observe one of the most important events in the early history of the church: the conversion of Saul of Tarsus. The conversion of Saul had the immediate effect of stopping this first wave of severe persecution, and his conversion made his great work possible. It would be hard to over-estimate the impact of this man's work in the early church, and through his writings, in the church through all the generations since.

During the time Philip was working in Samaria and with the Ethiopian eunuch, the persecution was continuing to rage in Jerusalem with Saul leading in the effort. Believers were rooted out of synagogues, and Saul tried his best to cause them to blaspheme the name of Christ. He put many saints in prison, and when they were put to death, he cast his vote against them. He went from synagogue to synagogue to punish the saints, convinced that he should do all he could to oppose the name of Jesus of Nazareth. Still breathing threats and slaughter like some dragon, Saul sought and received authority from the High Priest and from the full Sanhedrin to go to Damascus and to other cities to search for disciples of Christ in the synagogues there and to bring them back to Jerusalem bound as prisoners.

Chronological Note:

Saul was probably converted no more than a year or two after the church began.

Though there are no specific facts upon which we can base a chronology of the first nine chapters of Acts, the evidence we do have implies that Saul was converted probably no more than a year or two after the church began on Pentecost. The main evidence to base this upon is that Jesus was crucified by the Jews at the time of the Passover feast. The opposition was at a fever pitch at that time. Less than two months later, on the day of Pentecost the gospel of a risen Christ was preached in the same city where Jesus was crucified, and the church began (Acts 2). The very next story in Acts is the healing of the lame man at the temple (3). As a result of that miracle and the sermon that followed, Peter and John were brought before the Sanhedrin and charged not to preach in the name of Jesus any more (4). The next chapter (5) tells of all the apostles being taken into custody, beaten, and strictly forbidden to preach in Jesus' name. In the following chapter (6), Stephen comes into conflict with the Grecian Jews, and, at the end of his speech in chapter seven, he is stoned and a great wave of persecution begins. The Jewish leaders would not have delayed long before trying to put a stop to the preaching of the gospel of Jesus of Nazareth. It is unlikely that even six months passed between Pentecost and the death of Stephen.

The persecution that began was against the whole church, and for a time raged just in Jerusalem and in the area immediately around the city. We are not told how long this period lasted, but the result of the persecution was to scatter the church quickly (8:4). Therefore, it was likely not long before Saul of Tarsus conceived of the idea of pursuing the fleeing Christians wherever they went, in an effort to destroy the churches which were beginning to spring up elsewhere. Regardless of the exact time involved, surely it is evident that Saul was converted early in the gospel era.

Label Damascus on your map of Palestine.

- **Those scattered were preaching the good tidings wherever they went.**
- **There were already saints as far north as Damascus.**
- **The Jewish officials are trying to destroy the church, but they are spreading it instead.**

Having received permission to persecute the saints, Saul and his companions set out for Damascus. As they approached the city about noon, suddenly a great light, brighter than the noonday sun, shined down upon them. Everyone in the group fell to the earth, and a voice spoke to Saul saying, "Saul, Saul, why are you persecuting me? It is hard for you to kick against the ox-goad."

Saul replied, "Who are you, Lord?"

The Lord answered, "I am Jesus of Nazareth whom you are persecuting." Saul later tells that even at this point, Jesus told him why He had appeared to him. He told Saul, "Now get up on your feet, because I have appeared to you in order to appoint you a servant and a witness both of your having seen me this time and of the times when I will appear to you in the future. I will deliver you from your own people and from the Gentiles to whom I am sending you. I am sending you to the Gentiles to open their eyes, and to turn them from darkness to light, and from the power of Satan unto God, so that they can have the remission of sins and an inheritance among those who are set apart by faith in me" (Acts 26:15-18).

Jesus appeared to Saul to:

- **Appoint him a servant and a witness of Christ.**
- **To send him to the Gentiles to open their eyes, so that they might have remission of their sins.**

Saul said, "What will you have me do, Lord?"

Jesus replied, "Go into Damascus and there you will be told what you must do."

The men who were with Saul were speechless, because they could hear a voice, but they could not see anyone speaking, nor understand what was said.

Acts 9:7 says the men "heard the voice" and Acts 22:9 says they "heard not the voice." There is no contradiction in the meaning, however. The Greeks used the word "hear" exactly as we do: to mean to hear the sound of something but not distinctly enough to understand what is said, and also to mean to hear with understanding. The Greeks, however, had a way of doing this that removed all doubt about which meaning was intended. Greek nouns have different endings to show whether they are used as subjects, objects, possessives, etc. The verb "to hear" in Greek sometimes takes the noun for "voice" in the genitive case for its object, and sometimes it takes the noun for "voice" in the accusative case for its object. When the noun is in the genitive case, as in Acts 9:7, "to hear" means to hear the sound. When the noun is in the accusative case, as in Acts 22:9, the verb means to hear with understanding.

The men with Saul heard the sound of the voice,

- **But they did not understand what was said.**

When Saul got up, he was blind from the bright light. He had to be led by the hand into Damascus. For three days, Saul would not eat or drink, and he continued to be blind.

Saul is not rejoicing as a saved man might at this point:

- **He is fasting and praying.**
- **He has discovered that Jesus is alive and in heaven,**
- **But he does not yet know what is required of him.**

There was a disciple named Ananias who lived in Damascus. He was a very religious, sincere man who was respected by all the Jews. The Lord spoke to him saying, "Ananias."

He replied, "Here I am, Lord."

The Lord said, "Get up and go to the street which is called Straight and ask at the house of Judas for a man from Tarsus named Saul. He is praying, and he has seen a man named Ananias coming in, and laying his hands on him so that he may receive his sight."

But Ananias answered, "Lord, I have heard a lot about this man, about how much evil he has done to your saints in Jerusalem. And he has come here with authority from the chief priests to bind all who call on your name."

But the Lord told him, "Go on your way because he is the vessel I have chosen to carry my name to the Gentiles and to kings, as well as to the children of Israel. I will show him how many things he must suffer for my name's sake."

The reason for Jesus appearing to Saul is repeated by Ananias:

- **"You will be a *witness* for Him unto all men of what you have seen and heard."**

Jesus did not save Saul on the road to Damascus.

- **Ananias told him to be baptized to *wash away his sins*.**

Ananias got up and went to the address Jesus had specified, and entered the house where Saul was. Laying his hands on Saul, he said, "Brother Saul, the Lord, even Jesus, who appeared to you on your way here, has sent me so that you may receive your sight and be filled with the Holy Spirit." Immediately there fell from his eyes as it were scales and Saul could see and he looked at Ananias.

Then Ananias said, "The God of our fathers has appointed you to know His will, and to see the Righteous One, and to hear a voice from His mouth, because you will be a witness for Him to all men of what you have seen and heard. And now, why delay any longer? Get up and be baptized and wash away your sins, calling on the name of the Lord."

Saul got up and was baptized. Then he ate food and was strengthened.

Combination of the Great Commission:	Saul of Tarsus:
Preach/teach	
He that believeth	He was convinced that Jesus was alive
Repentance	He fasted and prayed as signs of repentance
And is baptized/ baptizing them	He was baptized
Shall be saved/ remission of sins	And washed away his sins
Teach to observe all things commanded	He received the gospel as a direct revelation from God. He did not learn it from men (Gal. 1:11-12).

We will come back to the story of Saul of Tarsus as we begin Section Two.

By chapter 13 of the book of Acts, Luke changes the emphasis in his history from the early church in Jerusalem and its surrounding area to the spread of the gospel throughout the Mediterranean world. At that time, Luke tells the history by following the work of the apostle Paul as he traveled and preached. As we begin that major section of our book, we will come back to the story of Saul of Tarsus and tie together all the facts we are given about his life. At that time, we will examine the role the Holy Spirit played in his life, and we will observe as he carries out the charge the Lord has given him.

After Saul's baptism:

- **He preached in Damascus.**
- **He went to Arabia.**
- **Back to Damascus, where he continued preaching.**
- **He was let down through the wall to escape a plot by the Jews.**
- **He returned to Jerusalem, 3 years after leaving for Damascus.**
- **He was there only 15 days, before he was forced to flee again.**
- **The brethren sent him to Tarsus.**

Barnabas acted in his role as one who encourages.

The period immediately following Saul's baptism (Acts 9:19b-31; Gal. 1:13-24):

For a time, Saul remained in Damascus with the disciples. Immediately in the synagogues he began proclaiming that Jesus is the Son of God. Everyone who heard him was amazed and said, "Isn't this the man who in Jerusalem made havoc of those who call on this name? Had he not come here so that he might bring them bound before the chief priests?" But Saul continued to grow in strength and confounded the Jews living in Damascus, proving that Jesus is the Christ.

At some point, Saul went away into Arabia (Gal. 1:13-17). The Bible does not tell us how long he was there or his reason for going. Then he returned to Damascus and continued preaching. After many days had passed, the Jews plotted to kill him. Saul learned of their plot, and since the Jews were watching the gates of the city day and night so that they might kill him, the disciples took him by night and let him down in a basket through an opening in the wall of the city.

It had now been three years since Saul left Jerusalem (Gal. 1:18-24). When he returned, he tried to associate with the brethren, but they were afraid of him. They did not believe he was really a disciple. Barnabas, however, took him to the apostles and told them how Saul had seen the Lord on the way to Damascus and how Jesus had spoken to him. He told them how Saul had boldly preached in Damascus in the name of Jesus. Then Saul was freely accepted by the disciples and he associated with them, boldly preaching in the name of the Lord.

Saul particularly debated with the Grecian Jews, and they began planning to kill him. When the brethren learned of the plot, they escorted him to Caesarea, and sent him to his home town of Tarsus of Cilicia. He had been in Jerusalem only fifteen days before he was forced to flee for his life (Gal. 1:18; Acts 22:17-20).

With the conversion of Saul, the severe persecution against the church ended for the time.

With the conversion of Saul, the church throughout all Judea and Galilee and Samaria had peace. It was built up, and, walking in the fear of the Lord and by the comfort of the Holy Spirit, grew in number.

With the conversion of Saul, the main force behind the Jewish persecution of the church was removed. Therefore, the situation described in Acts 9:31 must have prevailed since shortly after Saul's conversion. Nevertheless, it is clear that the church in Jerusalem had been none too sure that Saul's conversion was genuine. Finding out that he had been truly converted must have been a relief to all the disciples in the region. Therefore, we find the passage describing the growth and peace of the church at this point.

According to Galatians 1:18-19, the "apostles" who were in Jerusalem at this time were Peter and James the Lord's brother, who is called an apostle in a secondary sense, not as one of the original twelve.

Now that the church had a time of peace, Peter left Jerusalem on a tour that took him among disciples:
- **In Lydda,**
- **In all the plain of Sharon,**
- **In Joppa,**
- **And finally to Caesarea.**

Follow his route on your map.

Peter preaches in Lydda and Sharon (Acts 9:32-35):

Peter left Jerusalem and traveled unhurriedly among the saints in the countryside of Judea. As he went throughout all the sections of southern Palestine, he came to the saints who lived in Lydda. There he found a man named Aeneas who had been paralyzed and bedfast for eight years.

Peter said to him, "Aeneas, Jesus Christ heals you. Get up and make your bed." Immediately Aeneas got up. Everyone who lived in Lydda and Sharon saw him and turned to the Lord.

People in the surrounding area learned of the healing of Aeneas, and turned to the Lord as a result.

Lydda is the Old Testament city of Lod mentioned in 1 Chronicles 8:12; Ezra 2:33; Nehemiah 7:37 and 11:35.

Peter raises Dorcas from the dead (Acts 9:36-43):

Only a few miles to the northwest of Lydda was the city of Joppa, situated on the coast. There a disciple lived by the name of Tabitha *(Aramaic language)*. In Greek, her name was Dorcas *(which means gazelle)*. She was rich in good works and in acts of mercy which she did for people.

In the passing of time, she became sick and died. When her friends had washed her, they laid her in an upper room. Since Lydda was close by, and the disciples had heard that Peter was there, they sent two men to ask him to come without delay. As soon as Peter got the message, he arose and went with the men.

When Peter arrived, they took him to the place where the body of Dorcas lay. Widows stood around weeping as they showed him the coats and other garments which Dorcas had made.

Again, many were converted as the report of the raising of Dorcas spread.

These stories at the close of chapter 9 prepare us for the conversion of Cornelius in chapter 10.

Peter put everyone out of the room and he knelt down and prayed. Then, turning to the body, he said, "Tabitha, get up."

Dorcas opened her eyes, and when she saw Peter, she sat up. Peter took her by the hand and helped her to her feet. Then he called the believers and widows and presented her to them alive.

The report of this miracle circulated throughout all Joppa and many believed on the Lord. After this, Peter stayed for many days in Joppa with a man named Simon who was a tanner of leather.

Peter preaches the first gospel sermon to Gentiles (Acts 10:1-48):

Caesarea:

- **A very large city (covering 3,000 acres),**
- **On the seacoast about thirty miles north of Joppa.**
- **All the Roman procurators of Judea after Pilate made it the seat of their government.**

A man named Cornelius lived in the city of Caesarea. He was a centurion of the Roman cohort known as the Italian cohort. Cornelius was a deeply religious man who feared God with all his house. He gave much help to the poor and he prayed continually to God.

Cornelius was a good man:

- **He feared God**
- **With all his house**
- **Generous to the poor**
- **Prayed regularly**

Though Cornelius knew of the God of the Jews and had come to worship Him regularly, he was not a Jew either by birth or by religion. He belongs in the category of people described as "fearing God" in the New Testament (Acts 10:2, 22; 13:16, 26). That is, he believed in Jehovah, but he did not attempt to become subject to the law of the Jews.

This is a significant point, because there had been many proselytes converted by this time. Remember that a proselyte was a Gentile by birth, but one who had been converted to the Jewish religion. There were proselytes present on the day of Pentecost when Peter and the other apostles preached the gospel for the first time (2:5, 10). Among the seven men who were chosen to help with the problem concerning the Grecian widows, there was Nicolas who was a proselyte from Antioch (6:5). The Ethiopian eunuch was a proselyte (8:26-40). But Cornelius was different. Almost certainly God selected him to be the first Gentile given the blessing of hearing the gospel because he already knew of Jehovah and would, therefore, be receptive to the message —but he <u>*was*</u> *a Gentile! As our story progresses, we will see why this presented a problem.*

Cornelius was a Gentile.

- **He worshiped the God of the Jews, and was, therefore, a "God-fearer,"**
- **But he was not a proselyte.**

A centurion was over 100 soldiers. This particular group of 100 men were part of an Italian cohort. A cohort was made up of 600 soldiers. There were ten cohorts in a legion. The Italian cohorts were composed of Roman volunteers, and were, therefore, considered the most loyal of the Roman soldiers. There were 32 such Italian cohorts stationed in the Roman empire.

About three o'clock in the afternoon, Cornelius was praying (Acts 10:30) when he saw an open vision *(that is, he was awake, not asleep and dreaming)*. In the vision, an angel of God came to him and said, "Cornelius."

Cornelius, staring at the angel and feeling very frightened, said, "What is it, Lord?"

God had noted Cornelius' good points and his prayers.

The angel said, "Your prayers and your good deeds are observed by God. Now send men to Joppa and bring back a man named Simon who is surnamed Peter. He is staying with Simon the tanner whose house is by the sea."

When the angel left, Cornelius called two of his household servants and a very religious soldier from those who were his closest aides. He told them everything that had happened and gave them their instructions. Then he sent them to Joppa.

Notice that a soldier and servants have been influenced by this good man Cornelius.

The messengers traveled the approximately thirty miles as rapidly as possible, to reach Joppa the next day. They approached the house of Simon the tanner about noon.

Meanwhile, Peter had gone onto the housetop to pray. He was very hungry, but while he was waiting for the meal which was being prepared, he had a vision.

The Jews usually ate two meals, the early one at about ten o'clock and the main meal which was eaten toward evening. This meal must have been a delayed breakfast, which helps explain why Peter was so hungry.

The trance into which Peter fell is from the Greek word "ekstasis" from which we get our word "ecstasy." It was a divinely induced condition in which one's external surroundings fade away from notice and one has a heightened awareness. In this state, Peter received his vision.

Peter saw the heaven *(sky)* open, and a great sheet was lowered by the four corners upon the earth. In the sheet were all kinds of four-footed animals, reptiles, and birds. A voice commanded, "Get up, Peter, kill one of these animals and eat it."

God teaches Peter a vivid lesson:

- **"What God has cleansed, do not call common or unclean."**

But Peter said, "No way, Lord, for I have never eaten anything common and unclean."

The voice replied, "What God has cleansed, do not call common or unclean."

This happened three times and then the sheet was taken up. *(It is hard to tell from the text whether the sheet was raised and lowered three times, or just the exchange in the conversation repeated three times.)*

While Peter was very puzzled about what he had seen and was wondering what it meant, the men sent by Cornelius arrived at the gate and asked if Simon who was called Peter were there. The Spirit told Peter, "Behold, three men have come looking for you. Get up and go down to them. Do not hesitate to go with them, because I have sent them."

Promptly, Peter went down to greet the men. He said, "I am the one you are looking for. Why have you come to find me?"

They said, "Cornelius, a centurion, a righteous man, one who fears God, and who has a good reputation among the Jews, was warned by a holy angel to send for you to come to his house, so he could hear what you have to say." Peter invited them in and provided them a place to stay.

Gentiles may be saved also:

- **Peter had preached: "The promise is to you and to your children and to *all that are afar off*..."**
- **Jesus had commanded: "Go ye into *all the world* and preach to *every creature*..."**
- **But Peter is just now understanding that means Gentiles also.**

On the day of Pentecost, Peter had preached saying, "The promise is to you and to your children and to all that are afar off, even as many as the Lord your God shall call unto Him" (2:39). Jesus Himself had commanded that the gospel be preached to all the nations (Matt. 28:18-20; Mark 16:15-16). So far, however, the gospel had been preached only to Jews and proselytes. Now comes this vision to encourage Peter to go to the home of Cornelius to preach the first gospel sermon to Gentiles. The problem was not that Peter did not want to obey God; instead, he had not grasped the implications of the words which had been revealed. We will continue to observe as those implications dawn upon Peter on this occasion and how he convinces his brethren that it was the will of God for the Gentiles to be given the right to salvation. Notice that he has already made one major step in his understanding because he has invited the messengers inside and has given them lodging —a Jew giving lodging to three Gentile men!

The stage is being set for a bitter controversy:

- **Must the Gentiles become Jews by religion, that is, be circumcised, before they can be Christians?**
- **It was not an easy question to settle in the first century.**

As Gentiles were converted, the stage was set for one of the bitterest controversies that plagued the church in the middle decades of the first century. Up until this point, the persecution against the church has come from unbelieving Jews. Soon, trouble will arise from within the church itself, as Jewish Christians begin insisting that before a Gentile could be saved, he must first be circumcised, that is, he must first become a Jew by religion. We will discuss this question over and over as we proceed through the rest of the history given in the book of Acts and also as we study the epistles. It was not an easy question to solve in that century.

So far persecution has come from unbelieving Jews.

- **Soon trouble will arise from Jewish Christians who demand that the Gentile converts be circumcised.**

Peter took six brethren with him to serve as witnesses.

The next day Peter left with the three men. He took six of the Jewish brethren from Joppa with him who will serve as witnesses to what was taking place (11:12). The day following, they arrived in Caesarea. Cornelius was waiting for them, and he had gathered his relatives and close friends to be there also.

When Peter entered the house, Cornelius fell down and worshiped him. But Peter lifted him up, saying, "Stand up. I am only a man."

As they continued to talk together, Peter went into the house and found many who were come together. He said to them: "You all know what an unlawful thing it is for a man who is a Jew to be in close contact with, or to be visiting with one from another nation. And yet, God has shown me that I should not call any man common or unclean. Therefore, I came promptly, making no objection. Now, may I ask why you sent for me?"

Cornelius said, "We are all here present in the sight of God, to hear all things that have been commanded thee of the Lord."

What an opportunity!

Most scholars estimate that Cornelius was converted about A.D. 38:

- **About eight years since the church was established on the day of Pentecost.**

Cornelius answered: "Four days ago, at this very hour, I was keeping the ninth hour of prayer in my house. Suddenly a man in bright clothing stood by me, and he said, 'Cornelius, your prayer is heard, and your deeds of mercy are noted in the sight of God. You are, therefore, to send to Joppa and call to you Simon, who is called Peter. He is staying at the house of Simon a tanner, by the seaside.' Immediately, therefore, I sent for you and you have done a fine thing to come. Now, therefore, we are all here present in the sight of God to hear everything the Lord has commanded you to say."

Cornelius is one of the very fine characters told about in the Bible. There are so many qualities in him worthy of being copied in our own lives. He was obviously looking forward to Peter's coming with excitement. He realized what an unusual opportunity this was and he wanted to share it with the people he loved.

What wonderful opportunities Peter has had since he left Jerusalem! What stirring experiences! How thrilling to stand here in this house before these people, knowing that they are ready to hear and to receive what he has to say about God's word.

Understand Peter's introduction:

- **God is no respecter of persons.**
- **To Israel, God sent the good news of peace through Jesus Christ: He is Lord *of all.***

Peter began to speak, giving as his introduction the lesson that he himself had come to understand within the last two days:

> Truly I am understanding that God is no respecter of persons. Rather, in every nation, he who fears Him and does righteous deeds is acceptable to Him. He sent the word unto the children of Israel, preaching the good news of peace through Jesus Christ: He is Lord of all.

Peter makes the same basic points that he had been making to the Jews:

- **Jesus of Nazareth:**
    - **You know of Him, because His work was done and told throughout Galilee and Judea.**
    - **God anointed Him with the Holy Spirit and power.**
    - **He went about doing good, because God was with Him.**
- **The Jews crucified Him.**
- **God raised Him from the dead.**
- **We apostles are witnesses of these things:**
    - **Unique witnesses, specially chosen by God to give testimony to all people,**
    - **That this is the One appointed by God to be judge of the living and the dead.**

The body of his sermon follows:

> All of you know about the events that began after John preached his baptism. These events began in Galilee and were told throughout all Judea. I refer to Jesus of Nazareth, how God anointed Him with the Holy Spirit and with power. He went about doing good, and healing all who were oppressed by the devil, for God was with Him.

- **The prophets of old had borne their witness of Him also,**
  - **Because this was all part of the plan of God.**
- **Through His name every one that believes on Him shall receive remission of sins.**

But notice this important difference in his message to these Gentiles:

- **Instead of saying, "*You* crucified Him," as he had been saying to Jewish audiences, Peter says, "*they* slew and hanged on a tree."**
- **Even though the Jews used the power and authority of the Roman officials to crucify Jesus, throughout the New Testament the blame for the deed is placed upon the Jews.**

And we are witnesses of all the things which He did, both in the Jews' country and in Jerusalem. The Jews put Him to death, hanging Him upon a tree. But God raised Him the third day and showed that He was alive, not to all the people, but to witnesses who were specially chosen by God, even us, who ate and drank with Him after He arose from the dead. And He charged us to preach to the people and to testify that this is the One appointed by God to be the Judge of the living and the dead. All the prophets bear witness to Him, that through His name every one that believes on Him shall receive the remission of sins.

See what Cornelius and his household did in order to be saved.

While Peter was speaking these words, the Holy Spirit fell on all those who heard him preach. The Jews who had come with Peter were amazed because the gift of the Holy Spirit was poured out upon the Gentiles also. They knew this was so because they heard the Gentiles speak with tongues and praise God.

Peter, seeing this also, said, "Can any man forbid water that these should not be baptized who have received the Holy Spirit just as we have?" In other words, in view of this sign from God, can any Jew deny that these Gentiles have the right to be saved? And Peter commanded them to be baptized in the name of Jesus Christ.

Afterward, Cornelius and all those with him begged Peter to stay with them for a time.

Peter was not asking permission to baptize these Gentiles, nor was he taking a vote among his Jewish brethren. Rather, he asked a rhetorical question: How could anyone refuse to let these people be baptized, since God obviously has accepted them?

Combination of the Great Commission:	**Cornelius and his household:**
Preach/teach	They were all present to hear everything the Lord had commanded Peter to say.
He that believeth	
Repentance	
And is baptized/ baptizing them	Peter commanded them to be baptized in the name of Jesus Christ.
Shall be saved/ remission of sins	The faithful brethren rejoiced that the Gentiles had been granted repentance unto life (11:18).
Teach to observe all things commanded	Peter stayed with them for a time.

Peter is called in question about his going to Gentiles.

The other apostles and the brethren that were in Judea heard that the Gentiles had also received the word of God. When Peter came back to Jerusalem, his Jewish brethren *(that is, those who had been circumcised)* objected to his actions, saying, "You went in unto men who were uncircumcised and ate with them."

Peter answered by carefully explaining exactly what had happened:

Peter must convince others:

- **The other apostles and the brethren in Judea had not seen the vision Peter had seen.**
- **Peter had to learn that God wanted Gentiles to be saved,**
    - **Now he must convince his brethren.**

> I was in the city of Joppa praying when, in a trance, I saw a vision. A vessel like a great sheet was let down to me from heaven by four corners. As I gazed, I saw four-footed beasts of the earth, wild beasts, reptiles, and birds of the heaven. I also heard a voice saying to me, "Rise, Peter: kill and eat."
>
> But I said, "No way, Lord, for nothing common or unclean has ever entered into my mouth."
>
> The voice spoke a second time saying, "What God has cleansed, do not call common or unclean." This was done three times and then everything was drawn back up to heaven.
>
> Just then, three men showed up at the house where I was staying. They had been sent to me from Caesarea. The Spirit told me to go with them, making no distinction. These six brethren also accompanied me, and we went into the man's house.
>
> He told us how he had seen an angel standing in his house who told him, "Send to Joppa, and bring back Simon whose surname is Peter. He will speak to you words whereby you will be saved, you and all your house."
>
> As I began to speak to them, the Holy Spirit fell on them, even as it did on us at the beginning. And I remembered what the Lord said, "John indeed baptized with water, but you will be baptized with the Holy Spirit." Now, if God gave them the same *(equal in quality or quantity)* gift as He gave us, when we believed on the Lord Jesus Christ, who was I, that I should oppose God?

The angel appearing to Cornelius did not save him:

- **The angel said Peter would tell him *words whereby he would be saved.***

Peter's conclusion after telling the full story:

- **If God gave them the same gift He gave us, who believed on the Lord, who was I, that I should oppose God?**

These faithful Jewish brethren agreed with Peter's conclusion.

When the Jewish brethren heard these things, they ceased their objections and glorified God saying, "Then to the Gentiles also God has granted repentance unto life."

This is the second recorded occasion of Holy Spirit baptism:

- **The 12 apostles (2:1-4).**
- **Cornelius and his household (10:44-46).**

There are two cases where it is clearly shown that the Holy Spirit came upon men directly from heaven, in baptismal form —Acts 2:1-4 when He fell upon the twelve apostles, and Acts 10:44-46 when He fell upon Cornelius and his household. A third time is implied in the case of Paul, but the details are not given (more about his case when we begin Section Two). There are several points to be observed:

- *Holy Spirit baptism is never connected with saving the person who received it.*

Specific reasons are given for Holy Spirit baptism in each case:
- **12 apostles:**
  - **To make them qualified witnesses,**
  - **To guide them into all truth.**
- **Cornelius:**
  - **To convince the Jews that God had granted repentance to the Gentiles.**

- *Those who received the Holy Spirit were doing nothing to try to get Him at the time.*
- *A special reason is given why the Holy Spirit fell on these occasions.*
  - *In the case of the apostles, it was to enable them to be qualified witnesses (Acts 1:8; 26:16);*
  - *In the case of Cornelius, it was to convince the Jews that God had granted repentance unto the Gentiles also (Acts 11:18).*

It is apparent that Cornelius received the baptism of the Holy Spirit, not just a measure of the Spirit, for these reasons:
- *It was administered the same way, straight from heaven.*
- *To find a comparable experience, Peter does not go the Samaritans who had received the Spirit through the laying on of apostolic hands (Acts 8:14-17), nor to the seven upon whom the apostles laid their hands (Acts 6:6). He went back to the beginning, the day of Pentecost. Thus Peter did not say, "Cornelius received the Holy Spirit just like everyone else has." He said the Spirit fell on him as it did on us "at the beginning."*
- *The experience reminded Peter of the Lord's promise, but that promise was of Holy Spirit baptism (11:16).*

Jesus' special commission to His twelve disciples made them apostles,
- **Not Holy Spirit baptism.**

Cornelius was not given the commission of being a special witness for Christ.
- **Therefore he was not made an apostle when he received the Holy Spirit.**

Did the Holy Spirit baptism make Cornelius and his household apostles? No, because it was not the baptism of the Holy Spirit which made Jesus' twelve disciples apostles. Their apostolic commission did that. In other words, Jesus had called them to be witnesses in a very special way. They had walked and talked with Him both during His public ministry and during the period after His resurrection. Therefore, they were given the special mission of carrying that message to the world. The Spirit's baptism merely enabled them to carry out their task. God's Spirit does what He sends it forth to do. In Cornelius' case, it was to convince the Jews that salvation was also being offered to the Gentiles.

Why did the Jews have trouble accepting the Gentiles?
- **The law of Moses specifically forbade their mingling with their neighbors.**
- **After the return from captivity, Ezra and Nehemiah bitterly opposed their intermarrying with their neighbors.**

Why was it so hard for the Jews to understand that the Gentiles were to be included in the blessing of salvation? That seems such an obvious point to us.

Anytime a race issue gets into a picture, there are conflicts that occur — but it was much more than a race issue in the first century. The law of Moses strictly forbade the Israelites' mingling with their neighbors (see Deut. 7:1-6; Exod. 34:10-17). There were at least two reasons for this command. First, God had chosen these particular people as His special possession, to have a people through whom He could show His care, and through whom He could bring His Son into the world and bring about the complete plan of salvation. Second, the neighbors of the Israelites were very wicked. God told them that if they became friendly with their neighbors, then their hearts would be turned away from Him and unto the idols. That is exactly what did happen.

- **Therefore the Jews had learned that God wanted them to keep themselves separate.**
    - **Even though they scattered all over the Mediterranean world, they carefully kept themselves separate from their Gentile neighbors.**

But now, the time of salvation for all mankind had arrived:

- **The prophets had predicted that the blessings of God would be for all.**
- **Jesus had commanded it in the great commission;**
- **Peter had preached it in the first gospel sermon.**
- **And now, God has demonstrated it by sending the Holy Spirit upon a family of Gentiles.**

Why so long to understand?

- **Long-standing beliefs do not change easily.**
- **Each city had to fight the battle.**
- **It took the rest of the first century for the question about the Gentiles to be understood and accepted.**

Throughout Old Testament history, the Israelites turned to the idolatrous practices of their neighbors over and over. Finally God carried them away into captivity for their sins. Even after He brought back a remnant, they started marrying their foreign neighbors and copying their ways. Ezra and Nehemiah each fought the practice bitterly, and even demanded that the foreign wives and children be put away (Ezra 9-10; Neh. 13:23-28).

By the end of the Old Testament, the devout Jews had learned that particular lesson. During the years of silence, Jews moved all over the then-known world, but they still determined to keep themselves as a separate people. The more devout they were, the harder they tried to keep themselves from others. This was pleasing to God at that time, because the old law was still in effect, and God was not finished with His plan for the salvation of all men. Jesus, therefore, came to a distinct people who should have been prepared to receive Him because of all the promises and prophecies they had in their scriptures.

But the time of salvation for all had come by chapter 10 in Acts. Those same Old Testament prophets who had predicted that the Messiah would come had also predicted that the blessings of God would be "for those who are afar off," as Isaiah said (Isa. 57:19). Peter could say those words on Pentecost, but he had to see a direct vision from heaven to understand what the words meant. The Jewish brethren who went with Peter from Joppa understood enough to be willing to go into a Gentile's home, but they were amazed that God would give them His Spirit. The brethren in Jerusalem objected when they heard that Peter had gone to a Gentile, but they were good men, so they accepted the explanation and glorified God when they learned the details of what had happened.

As we look back on the situation, we think the question should have been settled for all time from this point on. But long-standing beliefs do not change quickly. Even if it were understood in one town, the question would arise again as soon as Gentiles were converted in another town. It took the whole first century for this question to be finally understood and accepted.

The gospel spreads to Antioch (Acts 11:19-26):

Acts 11:19 takes us back to 8:4 where the church was scattered after the death of Stephen.

Those who were scattered abroad at the time persecution arose at the death of Stephen traveled as far as Phoenicia, Cyprus, and Antioch, but they preached only to Jews at first. After a time, some of the men, particularly men from Cyprus and Cyrene, began preaching to Gentiles also. The first place where they did so was in Antioch of Syria. The Lord blessed the work of these men, and a great number of people believed and turned to the Lord.

The report of this success came to the ears of the church back in Jerusalem, so the brethren there sent Barnabas to Antioch. When he arrived and saw the grace of God, he was very glad. He encouraged all

Mark these places on your first map of the Mediterranean world:
- **Phoenicia**
- **Cyprus**
- **Antioch of Syria**
- **Cyrene**

Do you see that our map of Palestine is no longer big enough to see where the gospel is spreading?

The Bible makes it clear that Peter was the first to preach the gospel to Gentiles (Acts 15:7).
- **Therefore the preaching referred to here occurred after Peter's sermon to Cornelius.**

The name Christian:
- **Began to be used for the first time here in this first congregation composed of both Jews and Gentiles.**
- **Means one who pertains to, or belongs to Christ.**
- **It was used with divine approval along with such words as disciple, saint, and other such terms.**

of the new disciples to remain true to the Lord with all their hearts. Barnabas was a good man, full of the Holy Spirit and of faith. Many people were added to the Lord.

After a time, Barnabas went to Tarsus in Cilicia to find Saul. Remember that Saul had been in Tarsus since he was sent there to escape the plot against his life in Jerusalem (9:29-30). When Barnabas found him, he brought him to Antioch to help in the work. For a whole year, they met with the church and taught many people. The disciples were called Christians first in Antioch.

There were many Antiochs in this part of the world. Two are mentioned in the New Testament: Antioch of Syria (11:19) and Antioch of Pisidia (13:14). For many years, Antioch in Syria was very prominent in the Bible story because the church there was strong and influential.

Some say that the name "Christian" was given to the disciples by their enemies. Others argue that it was given by God. We are not told how it originated. It was, however, accepted with divine approval (1 Pet. 4:16). It occurs three times in the New Testament: Acts 11:26; 26:28; and 1 Peter 4:16.

Many say the name "Christian" is the "new name" predicted by Isaiah in 62:2. To answer this question, we must go to the context of Isaiah 62. The words spoken in verse 2 are addressed to Zion or spiritual Jerusalem (v. 1). The glory of Zion would be in contrast to her misery of the former days. Her new name would be in contrast to her old name. What was her old name? "Forsaken," and her land was called "Desolate." But she would be called "Hephzibah" (My delight is in her) and her land "Beulah" (married) (v. 4). In this context, the new name is Hephzibah, not Christian. In other words, in the prophecy of Isaiah, God did not say that Zion would be called by a new name that was not revealed at that time; He went ahead and told what the new name would be. Also, the reference in Isaiah 62:2 is not to the individual members of Zion, but to Zion as a whole.

Reference is made in Isaiah 65:15 to "another" name which would be given to God's people. Chapter 65 is a contrast between the rebellious among God's people and the obedient. God tells the rebellious that they would leave their name for a curse, but that He would call His servants by another name. One might make an argument from this passage that Christian is the "other" name, but I do not believe that Isaiah was referring to the name Christian. Most students making the point that God predicted the name Christian refer to Isaiah 62:2 and the "new name," not to Isaiah 65:15 and "another name."

The church at Antioch sends relief to the brethren in Judea (Acts 11:27-30):

In those days while Barnabas and Saul worked at Antioch, prophets came from Jerusalem to Antioch. One of them named Agabus stood up and indicated with signs given to him by the Holy Spirit that there would be a great famine over all the world in the days of the emperor Claudius. So the disciples in Antioch, each man as he was able to do so, decided to send help to the brethren in Judea. This they did, sending their gift to the elders in Judea by the hands of Barnabas and Saul.

The saints in Judea:

- **Had borne the brunt of the persecution from the beginning,**
- **And would, therefore, be hardest hit by a time of famine.**
- **These disciples in Antioch are showing the same kind of generosity the first saints had shown after the church began on the day of Pentecost.**

The brethren in Antioch sent the help they gave to the elders (11:30). Which elders is unspecified except that the relief was for the brethren in Judea. Therefore, the elders would be the elders of the brethren in Judea. Jerusalem was not the focal point of this relief. There were many congregations in Judea by this time (Gal. 1:22), so the relief went to the elders of the various churches where the need existed. The gift was taken by Barnabas and Saul. There is no evidence that the church in Jerusalem acted in a supervisory capacity. At the end of the story, in Acts 12:25, when Barnabas and Saul finished their work of relief, they returned from Jerusalem, taking John Mark with them. But though they were in Jerusalem at the end of the time, that does not mean that Jerusalem was the only place they visited. Jerusalem was the largest city in the province of Judea, but it certainly was not the only one.

Barnabas and Saul take the gift to the elders where there was a need.

- **There is no indication that the church in Jerusalem acted in any sort of supervisory capacity in this matter.**

Chronological Note:

The mention of Claudius in Agabus' prophecy gives us a time reference. Claudius began his rule in A.D. 41 and ruled until A.D. 54. Much of his reign was plagued by famine, drought, and crop failures. It would help you to memorize the succession of Caesars who ruled in the days of the New Testament, because it is information about their reigns, and that of other officials, that gives us clues about the time and sequence of events in the early church.

The short reign of Caligula, the beginning of Claudius' reign, and the death of Herod Agrippa I all give us chronological anchor posts for this part of Acts, just before the missionary journeys of Paul begin.

Emperors in the days of the New Testament:

- **Augustus Caesar: 31 B.C. to A.D. 14**
- **Tiberius Caesar: A.D. 14-37**
- **Caligula: A.D. 37-41**
- **Claudius: A.D. 41-54**
- **Nero: A.D. 54-68**
- **Vespasian: A.D. 69-79**
- **Titus: A.D. 79-81**
- **Domitian: A.D. 81-96**
- **Nerva: A.D. 96-98**
- **Trajan: A.D. 98-117**

Herod Agrippa I was a prisoner in Rome until the death of Tiberius. He was then made tetrarch of Philip's tetrarchy in Palestine at the time Caligula became emperor. Then when Claudius became emperor in A.D. 41, he gave Herod rule over southern Syria and Palestine, which was virtually all the territory once ruled by Herod Agrippa's grandfather Herod the Great. The death of Herod Agrippa I is told in Acts 12:20-23. According to the historian Josephus, Herod's death occurred during the Passover feast in A.D. 44.

The prophecy of Agabus probably occurred first, followed by Herod's persecution of the church which is told in chapter 12, and then

The date at this point in Acts:

- **About A.D. 44,**
- **After the church was established in about A.D. 29/30.**

Herod's death. The predicted famine was probably already underway by that time. It seems that Saul and Barnabas took the relief from Antioch to Jerusalem about the time that Herod's persecution began. The last verse of chapter 11 tells of their taking the gift, then the story of Herod is told, followed by the last verse of chapter 12 which tells that Barnabas and Saul returned to Antioch.

Thus the date at this point in Acts is about A.D. 44. The missionary journeys will take place during the rest of the reign of Claudius and into the reign of Nero. The second missionary journey ended about the end of Claudius' rule (A.D. 54). We know this because Gallio, whom Paul encountered at Corinth during the second journey (Acts 18:12-17), was appointed proconsul for the year May 1, 52 to May 1, 53. The third missionary tour, and the rest of the book of Acts, took place during Nero's reign (54-68).

Herod's persecution of the church (Acts 12:1-19):

A new wave of persecution — from Herod Agrippa I:

- **He was a grandson of Herod the Great.**
- **The year is A.D. 44.**
- **It is Passover time, so it is early spring.**

This persecution is by a ruler, but it is still from the Jews:

- **Herod was acting out of zeal for the cause of the Pharisees.**
- **The Herod family had becomes Jews in religion,**
    - **Though their lives were a mockery of true service to Jehovah.**

James, the brother of John, is the first apostle to be put to death. What a sad day for the disciples!

The Herod in this story is Herod Agrippa I. He was the grandson of Herod the Great and the father of Herod Agrippa II whom we find in Acts 26. He was also the father of two daughters who play a part in the story: Bernice who accompanied Agrippa II in chapter 26, and Drusilla who was married to Felix the governor (24:24). The year was A.D. 44. The record in Acts shows that the time was Passover, about the first of April (12:3).

The Herodian family, who were Edomites by blood line, had accepted the Jewish religion during the years of Biblical silence when the Jews conquered the Edomites (Idumeans) and forced them to become Jews in religion. The Herodian family was so wicked they made a mockery of any service to God, but they still went through an outward form of obedience. This particular Herod had espoused the cause of the Pharisees, and Josephus speaks of his zeal for the Jewish religion. It was for these reasons that he persecuted the church.

About the time Agabus was making his prophecy in Antioch that there would be a famine over the land, Herod put forth his hand in Jerusalem and arrested some in the church, intending to persecute them. He executed the apostle James, the brother of John, with the sword. When he saw how much that pleased the Jews, he seized Peter also. Since this was happening during the days of unleavened bread, he placed Peter under guard, intending to bring him out for a public trial after the Passover was completed. While Peter was in prison, the church prayed earnestly to God in his behalf.

The Jews had learned how hard it was to keep Christians in prison, so Herod tried to be sure Peter was secure. There were four squads *(a quaternion)* of soldiers, a total of sixteen men, appointed to guard Peter. He was sleeping between two soldiers; he was bound with chains; and there were two soldiers standing at the door of the prison.

This story is charming:

- **It was still very early in the morning, before daybreak.**
- **These people had been praying through the night,**
  - **And possibly since Peter had been taken captive.**
- **What an example of effectual, fervent prayer!**

Rhoda *knew* Peter's voice:

- **She was a disciple,**
- **Well acquainted with Peter.**

The disciples are amazed:

- **They had been praying long and earnestly.**
- **They wanted Peter freed;**
  - **But James had been killed.**
  - **Other saints had died.**
  - **They did not know what to expect.**
- **Probably their prayers included the plea for God to give them strength to endure even if Peter were killed.**
- **Their joy at Peter's release was without bounds.**

Almost certainly, the James mentioned here is James the brother of the Lord whom we will meet again soon.

The persecution by Herod was only a minor set-back to the church. It continued to grow.

But an angel of the Lord came and stood by Peter in the night. A light began shining in the cell and the angel tapped Peter on the side and woke him, saying, "Quick, get up!" The chains fell from Peter's hands.

The angel said, "Put on your clothes and sandals." Peter did this, and then the angel said, "Wrap your robe around you and follow me."

Peter followed all the instructions, following the angel from the prison, but he did not know if it were really happening, or if he were seeing a vision. They passed the first and second guard and came to the iron gate which opened to the outside. The gate opened for them by itself and they went through it. When they had reached the first intersection, the angel disappeared.

When he was left alone, Peter realized this was no vision; he was free! He said to himself, "Now I know for sure that the Lord has sent His angel and has delivered me from the clutches of Herod and from the plans of the Jews."

As soon as he realized all this, he made his way to the house of Mary the mother of John Mark where many disciples were together praying. He went to the main gate and knocked. A maid named Rhoda came to the door and when she recognized Peter's voice, she did not even open the gate. She was so excited she ran back to tell the news to the crowd: "Peter is at the gate!"

Everyone said, "You are crazy."

But Rhoda kept insisting, "No, he really is there."

Then they said, "It is his angel *(spirit)*."

Meanwhile, Peter continued knocking. Finally they opened the door, and when they saw him, they were amazed.

Peter raised his hand to still the torrent of questions, and told them how the Lord had brought him out of prison. He said, "Tell these things to James, and to the brethren." Then he left and went to another place.

"Tell these things to James..." Yet James the brother of John has just been killed. This James is not identified at this point in the story. There was another James in the list of apostles, James the son of Alphaeus, but he never plays a prominent role in the Bible story. This is more likely James the brother of Jesus who soon comes into more prominence in the church at Jerusalem.

At daybreak, there was a great deal of consternation and confusion down at the prison because of the missing prisoner. Herod sent for Peter and found him gone. He grilled the guards about what had happened, and, finding no satisfactory answer, he commanded that the guards be put to death. But the effort at persecution seems to have fallen flat for him. Herod left Judea and went to Caesarea.

The death of Herod (Acts 12:20-24):

Herod had been quarreling with the people of Tyre and Sidon. The Bible does not tell us what had caused the contention, but Herod had cut off food shipments to Phoenicia. A delegation came to Caesarea from Tyre and Sidon, and they made Blastus, the king's chamberlain, their friend. Using the influence of Blastus, they asked for peace because they needed the supplies from Herod's country.

God struck Herod because he accepted the honor he was receiving as a god.

On a certain special day, Herod dressed himself in his royal apparel and sat on a special raised platform of honor and spoke to the people gathered to hear him, including the delegation from Tyre and Sidon. The people shouted, "The voice of a god and not of a man!"

Immediately, an angel of the Lord smote Herod because he took the glory being offered instead of giving the praise to God. Herod was eaten with worms until he died.

In contrast, the word of God grew and multiplied. Just as the early persecution from the unbelieving Jews only succeeded in spreading the gospel rather than stopping it, this persecution from Herod was only a temporary disturbance. The growth in the church continued.

Once again the Jewish historian Josephus furnishes us with some interesting details. This set day was the second in a great celebration of games after the Roman fashion to celebrate the triumph of Claudius on his return from Britain. It was on this day that Herod gave his answer to the ambassadors from Tyre and Sidon in the great theater where the games were being celebrated.

It was one of those occasions when Herod thought everything was going well. He enjoyed the full approval of Rome; he was at the height of his power. Everyone was filled with appreciation for the grandeur and magnificence of the occasion, and Herod's reply was favorable to Tyre and Sidon. Dressed in a robe made of silver threads, Herod positively gleamed in the morning sunlight, and he made a speech which suited the occasion. The audience, receiving the reply they wanted, and always willing to tickle the royal ear, cried out, "It is the voice of a god and not of a man!"

Since Herod was nominally a Jew, he knew enough about Jehovah to know the comment of his audience was blasphemous. But instead of suppressing such an idea, he allowed the cry to continue. He enjoyed allowing these idolaters to make a god of him. Therefore, God sent His angel to smite him because he did not give God the glory that was His alone.

Josephus says that Herod lived for five days. He does not say exactly what he died from, mentioning just pain and trouble in Herod's "belly." But Luke tells us exactly what it was. Masses of worms ate Herod's body as if he were already a corpse, and he died a most miserable death.

Barnabas and Saul return to Antioch (Acts 12:25):

Luke introduces John Mark:
- **He will accompany Saul and Barnabas on their first missionary journey;**
- **He is described as "sister's son to Barnabas."**
- **He wrote the book of Mark.**

Meanwhile, Barnabas and Saul were doing their work of distributing the relief sent from Antioch to the brethren of Judea. When they had finished the task, they returned from Jerusalem to Antioch. They took a young man with them. He was named John and surnamed Mark.

The dictionary defines surname in two almost opposite ways. The first meaning (and the modern one) is that of a family name, the last name. The second meaning is a name given. For example, King Richard was given the surname, "the Lion-hearted." This is the way the word is used in the Bible: Simon was surnamed (given the name) Peter (Rock); Joseph was surnamed Barnabas (son of consolation); and John was given the name Mark.

This young man John Mark is the one first mentioned by Luke in Acts 12:12. It was at his mother's home where the disciples had gathered to pray for Peter. We will read more of him during the first missionary journey; at the beginning second journey; and later toward the end of Paul's life (2 Tim. 4:11). Bible students agree that this is the one who wrote the book of Mark. In spite of a little shaky start, Mark proved to be a great disciple in the early church. In Colossians 4:10, there is a reference made to one named Mark who is described as a "cousin" to Barnabas, or as the King James Version puts it, "Marcus, sister's son to Barnabas." Almost certainly, this is the same Mark.

The end of Section One:

Luke changes the focus of his attention:
- **From Jerusalem to Asia Minor,**
- **From the work of Peter and others to the work of Paul and his companions.**

This completes the first major section of Acts. We have observed as the church began in the city of Jerusalem on the day of Pentecost, how persecution arose and scattered the saints, and thus spread the influence of the gospel to Judea, to Samaria, and on to other places in the eastern Mediterranean territory. Now the story continues with no break, but notice how the emphasis shifts from Peter and the events in the church in Jerusalem and in the surrounding area, to Saul and the church in Antioch of Syria and its surrounding area.

Notice that we will need a new map to see where Paul did most of his work. Through the rest of the New Testament our map of emphasis will be of the Mediterranean world with Jerusalem and Judea only one small section on the southeastern shores of the Sea.

Section Two

Primarily the Work of Paul

The Three Missionary Journeys
The Voyage to Rome
Paul's Epistles

"And ye shall be my witnesses...
unto the uttermost part of the earth."

Acts 13-28

Romans, 1 Corinthians, 2 Corinthians,
Galatians, Ephesians, Philippians, Colossians,
1 Thessalonians, 2 Thessalonians, 1 Timothy,
2 Timothy, Titus, Philemon

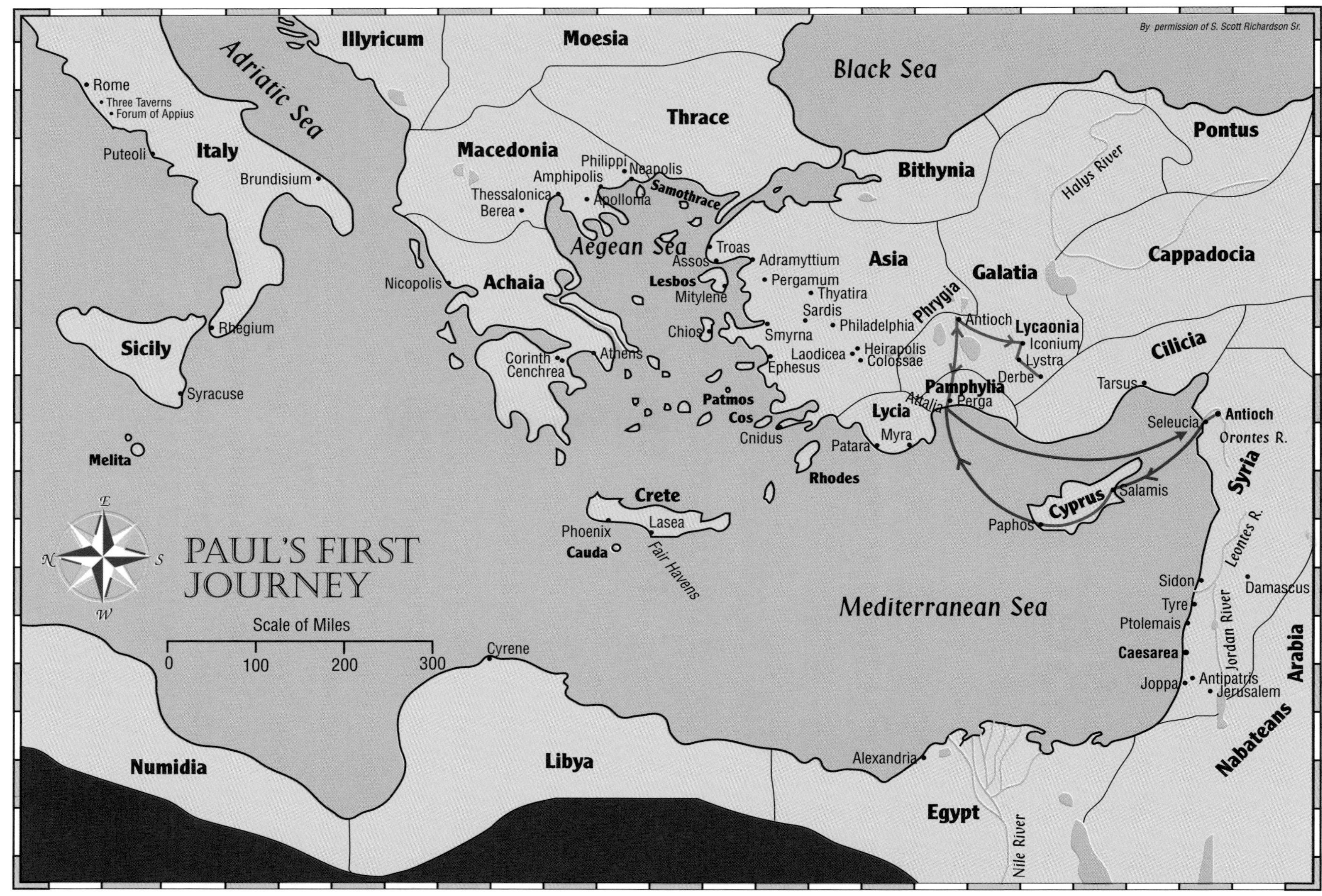
PAUL'S FIRST JOURNEY
By permission of S. Scott Richardson Sr.
Scale of Miles
0
100
200
300
E
N
S
W
Illyricum
Moesia
Black Sea
Adriatic Sea
Rome
Three Taverns
Forum of Appius
Puteoli
Italy
Brundisium
Thrace
Macedonia
Philippi
Neapolis
Amphipolis
Samothrace
Thessalonica
Apollonia
Berea
Bithynia
Pontus
Halys River
Aegean Sea
Troas
Assos
Adramyttium
Asia
Galatia
Cappadocia
Nicopolis
Achaia
Lesbos
Mitylene
Pergamum
Thyatira
Sardis
Phrygia
Antioch
Lycaonia
Iconium
Lystra
Derbe
Sicily
Rhegium
Chios
Smyrna
Philadelphia
Laodicea
Heirapolis
Colossae
Ephesus
Cilicia
Corinth
Cenchrea
Athens
Syracuse
Patmos
Cos
Cnidus
Pamphylia
Attalia
Perga
Tarsus
Lycia
Myra
Patara
Rhodes
Seleucia
Antioch
Orontes R.
Syria
Melita
Crete
Lasea
Phoenix
Cauda
Fair Havens
Salamis
Cyprus
Paphos
Leontes R.
Mediterranean Sea
Sidon
Damascus
Tyre
Ptolemais
Caesarea
Jordan River
Arabia
Joppa
Antipatris
Jerusalem
Nabateans
Cyrene
Numidia
Libya
Alexandria
Egypt
Nile River

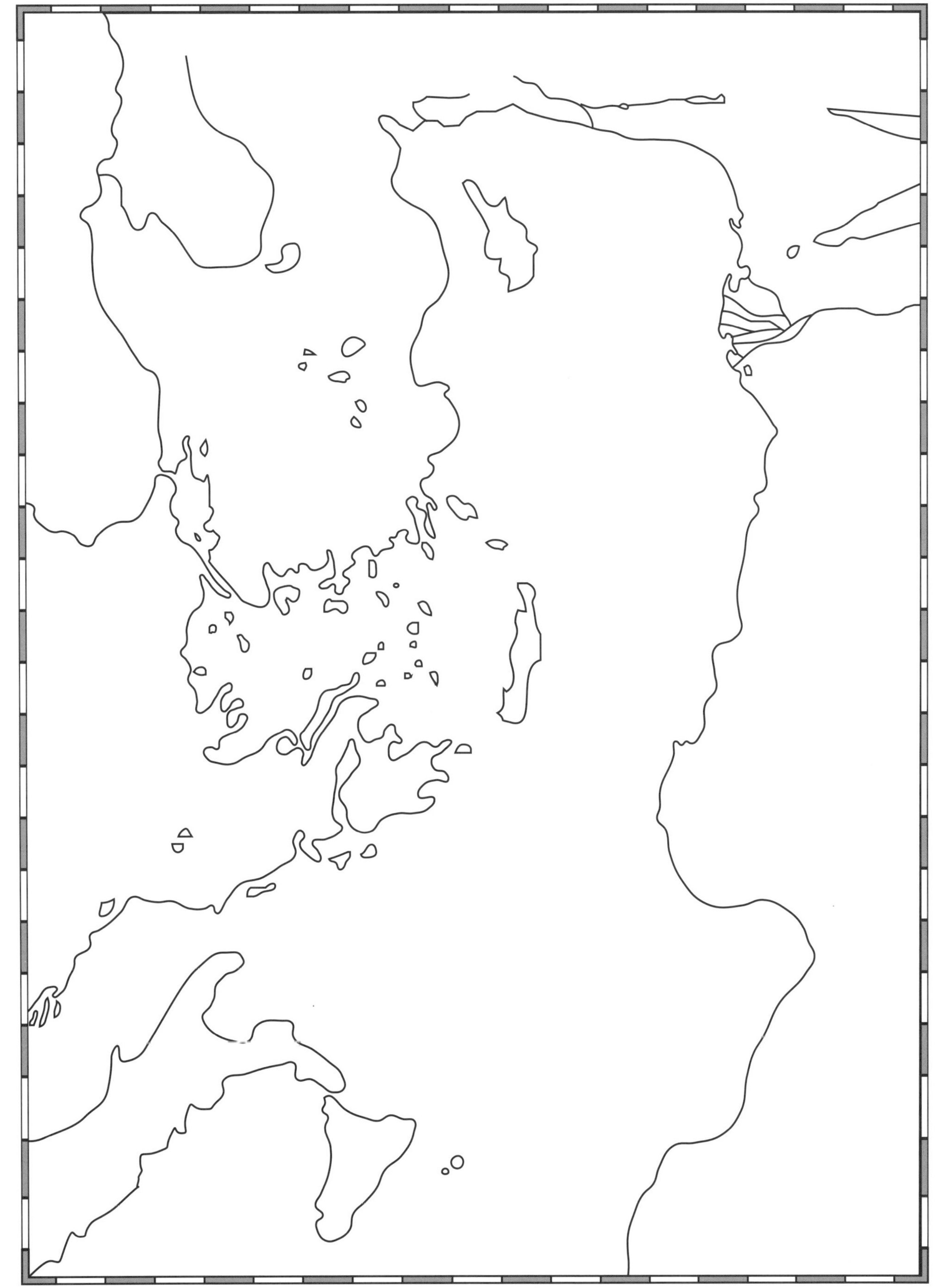

The First Missionary Journey

(Acts 13:1-14:28)

Saul of Tarsus

As we begin this major section of the book of Acts, let us review the information we are given about Saul's early life. We summarize and combine the information here so that we can have a clear picture of the man. Look at the passages included in the material to see how we learn each detail.

The contribution of Paul the apostle (as Luke will soon call Saul of Tarsus) to the success of the early church is of great importance. Though he had little to do with carrying the gospel "in Jerusalem, and in all Judea and Samaria," to him more than anyone else must go the credit for spreading the gospel to the "uttermost part of the earth." It was due to his influence, more than any other's, that the gospel was preached throughout Asia Minor, in Greece, in Macedonia, and all the way to Illyricum on the Adriatic Sea across from Italy (Rom. 15:19). Paul went on to preach the gospel in Rome, on the islands of Malta and Crete, in Nicopolis, and possibly as far away as Spain (Acts 28:1, 30, 31; Tit. 1:5; 3:12; Rom. 15:23-24). He also wrote thirteen (14, if the book of Hebrews is his) of the letters in our New Testament. There were many other people working at the same time, and in many other places, but since we have the account of his work, it is his work which has so affected the lives of all those that have lived in the generations since the New Testament days.

Saul (Paul):

- **Preached in Syria, Asia Minor, Macedonia, Greece, Rome.**
- **Wrote 13 (maybe 14) of the letters of the New Testament.**
- **Born in Tarsus of Cilicia**
- **Educated in Jerusalem**
- **Taught by Gamaliel**
- **A Pharisee**
- **A Roman citizen**
- **Led in the early persecution against saints in Jerusalem.**
- **Sought to go to other places to persecute.**
- **Converted in Damascus.**

Though born in Tarsus of Cilicia, Saul was educated in Jerusalem, instructed at the feet of Gamaliel who was one of the greatest of the Jewish teachers (Acts 22:3; 26:4). Saul was a Pharisee, the son of a Pharisee (23:6; 26:5). He was so zealous and energetic in his efforts to further the cause in which he believed, he advanced beyond many who were his own age (Gal. 1:13-14). In addition to his Jewish heritage, Saul was born a Roman citizen, which means his father was a citizen before him (Acts 21:39; 22:25-28). This proved to be a great asset to him.

Saul was not a leader in the persecution against Stephen when we first meet him, but he approved of the action that was taken (7:58; 8:1). Very soon afterward, however, he was clearly taking a leading role in the severe persecution which arose against the church (8:1, 3). After persecuting the disciples in and around Jerusalem, he asked for and received permission to go to Damascus to seek for saints there. He was planning to bring any he found to Jerusalem, bound as prisoners (9:1-2; 22:4-5; 26:9-12). He later called himself the chief of sinners as he remembered this period of his life. He said God showed him mercy because he did his deeds in ignorance and in unbelief (1 Tim. 1:12-16). He genuinely believed that Jesus was an imposter and should be opposed.

It was on that trip to Damascus that Jesus appeared to Saul and showed him that He was indeed alive and in heaven — therefore all He claimed to be. Saul was a changed man. He went into the city and fasted and prayed until Ananias came to tell him what was expected of him. As soon as he knew what to do, he arose and was baptized to wash away his sins (Acts 9:3-19; 22:6-16; 26:13-18).

- **Appointed to be a servant and a witness for the Lord**
  - **Specially appointed to take the gospel to the Gentiles.**

Even when the Lord first appeared to Saul, He told him that he would be a servant and a witness of what he had seen and heard. When the Lord asked Ananias to go to preach to Saul, He said, "This man is a chosen instrument to carry my name to the Gentiles, to kings, and before the people of Israel." It would be his task "to open the eyes of the Gentiles and turn them from darkness to light, and from the power of Satan to God, so that they may receive forgiveness of sins." Saul was warned that not only did he have a specially appointed task before him, he must suffer many things as a result of his work. Saul was obedient to the call and spent the rest of his life fulfilling the mission set before him (9:15-16; 22:14-15; 26:16-19). We have come to the point in the history for us to begin observing how he carried out the task before him.

The first three years after his baptism:

- **Preached in Damascus.**
- **Went to Arabia.**
- **Preached in Damascus again.**
- **Escaped a plot against his life by escaping over the wall in a basket.**

Immediately after he was baptized, Saul began to preach the gospel in the city of Damascus (9:19-22). Soon, however, he withdrew into Arabia (Gal. 1:13-17). The reason for his going there, and the length of time he stayed are not given. He returned to Damascus and continued preaching. But by now the Jewish officials who had once been his friends had become his enemies. "After many days," the Jews plotted to kill Saul. They watched the city gates day and night, so his brethren in Damascus helped him escape by lowering him in a basket through an opening in the wall (Acts 9:23-25). It had been three years since he had been converted (Gal. 1:18-24).

- **He returned to Jerusalem.**
- **Saints were afraid of him.**
- **Barnabas told his story.**
- **He preached in Jerusalem until there was a plot against his life — only fifteen days.**
- **Escaped to Tarsus.**

Saul returned to Jerusalem, but the brethren there were afraid of him. Barnabas learned his story and took him to the apostles *(Peter and James)* and convinced them that he had truly been converted (Acts 9:26-27). Saul was in Jerusalem only fifteen days on this occasion, and the only apostle with whom he had direct contact was Peter. He also met James the brother of the Lord (Gal. 1:18-19).

During those fifteen days in Jerusalem, Saul moved freely among the saints, and he preached boldly. Soon he was in conflict with certain Grecian Jews, and they began plotting to kill him. The brethren learned of the plot, and they took him to Caesarea and put him on a boat to Tarsus (Acts 9:28-30; cf. Acts 22:17-21).

- **Barnabas and Saul spent a year working in Antioch.**
- **Brethren in Antioch sent relief to poor brethren in Judea by the hand of Saul and Barnabas.**
- **When the task was finished, Saul and Barnabas returned to Antioch.**

He remained in Tarsus until Barnabas came from Antioch of Syria to ask him to go there to help in the work. He went and worked with Barnabas and others in Antioch for a whole year (11:25-26). During that year, almost certainly toward the end of the time, Agabus came and prophesied there would be a famine over the whole Mediterranean world. The brethren at Antioch decided to send relief to the poor saints in Judea, and they chose to send it by the hands of Barnabas and Saul (11:27-30). Therefore, Saul and Barnabas were in Judea about the time the apostle James was killed and Peter was imprisoned by Herod Agrippa (12:1-4).

When they finished their assigned task of distributing the gift to the elders of the churches in Judea, Barnabas and Saul returned to Antioch, taking the young man John Mark with them (12:25). That is where we find them as chapter 13 begins, and Luke's emphasis as a historian shifts to Saul and his work.

One of the interesting studies of Paul's life is to examine the influence of the gospel upon his temperament. His writings give a picture of a man of deep passions, a man of great resolution and will power. Saul was a man with a temper. He was, in short, one who could have become a fanatic in an unbalanced sense. Thus, while contending for Judaism, he says, "I strove to make them blaspheme; and being exceeding mad against them, I persecuted them even unto foreign cities" (Acts 26:11). In the gospel, however, Saul of Tarsus found that which he needed to stabilize his personality and character (2 Tim. 1:12).

Paul was an apostle as surely as the twelve were apostles:
- **Not a whit behind them.**

What Ananias did for Saul:
- **He laid his hands on Saul so that he might receive his sight.**
- **He told Saul how to wash away his sins so that he would be eligible to receive the Holy Spirit.**
  - **The Spirit would enable him to do the things God had appointed for him.**

Paul was an apostle as surely as Peter was an apostle, though he never walked and talked with Jesus during the years of His personal ministry. On more than one occasion in his writings, Paul makes the point emphatically that he had the same authority the other apostles had (Gal. 1-2; 2 Cor. 10-12). He did not receive his message from men; he received his knowledge of Christ and of the plan of God by revelation, that is, directly from God by means of the Holy Spirit (Gal. 1:11-12; 2 Cor. 12:1-7).

Some say that Ananias imparted the Holy Spirit to Saul because when the Lord sent him to Saul, Ananias said, "Brother Saul, the Lord has sent me that thou mayest receive thy sight, *and be filled with the Holy Spirit"* (Acts 9:17). Ananias' coming to Saul was necessary for both things to happen — for him to receive his sight and for him to be filled with the Spirit — but what Ananias did personally that these two things might take place was different. It is specifically said that Ananias was to lay his hands upon Saul "that he might receive his sight" (9:12). Nowhere is it stated that Ananias laid his hands on Saul that he might receive the Holy Spirit. After Saul's sight was restored, Ananias told him what the Lord wanted him to do with his life, and

Paul was a witness of the risen Christ and an apostle:

- **He received his knowledge of Christ and the plan of God by revelation.**
- **He had the full measure of the Holy Spirit that the other apostles had.**
- **He was "not a whit behind the other apostles."**
- **He did works that only apostles could do.**
- **Therefore, though the details are not given, Paul was baptized with the Holy Spirit.**

particularly what he was to do to be saved, in order to make him eligible to receive the Holy Spirit.

Nowhere do the scriptures describe exactly when or how Saul received the Spirit, but we do know that he received a miraculous measure of the Spirit, just as did the other apostles. Ananias stated that he came so that he might do so. Saul was an apostle "not one whit behind the other apostles" (2 Cor. 11:5; 12:11). He did works such as only the apostles who had been baptized with the Spirit could do (Acts 19:1-7). He was called by Christ to be an apostle and a witness, so the promise of the baptism of the Holy Spirit (Acts 1:8) applied to Saul as well as to the twelve. Since the baptism of the twelve apostles in the Spirit came directly from heaven without human hands, and since the baptism of Cornelius and his household came directly from heaven without human hands, and since Saul emphatically said he received his knowledge directly from God (Gal. 1:11-12; 2 Cor. 12:1-7), it is to be presumed that this is the way Saul received the Spirit as well. There can be no question that Paul had the full measure of the Holy Spirit that the other apostles had.

The first journey probably began in about A.D. 44/45.

The thirty years covered by the book of Acts are approximately half over by the time this first journey begins.

Chronological Note:

As we pointed out at the beginning of chapter 12, Herod Agrippa I died in A.D. 44. It seems that Barnabas and Saul returned from their trip to Judea about that same time, and then the very next story told is the beginning of the first preaching tour. We can, therefore, assume that this journey began in about A.D. 44 or 45. At the beginning of our study, we said the book of Acts covers about thirty years. Approximately fifteen of those years have passed by this point; the rest of Acts will cover about fifteen more years.

Map Assignment:

- **Memorize the places visited on this first journey.**
- **Know where the cities were located, and label them on your blank map.**
- **Know what happened at each place.**

Map Assignment:

Begin a chart in your classroom, or a special line on the map in your room to show this first journey. Help your pupils learn where Paul and his companions went, and what happened at each of the main places. Mark each place on your own blank map as you come to it in your study. Children as young as first or second grade can learn the information if it is made interesting, and if there is sufficient drill work to plant it in their minds. This first journey is the easiest of all to learn, so work on it in the younger classes even if you do not attempt to teach them the later journeys.

The Journey Begins

The call of Barnabas and Saul (Acts 13:1-3):

Five men worked as prophets and teachers at Antioch: Barnabas, Symeon who was called Niger *(a Greek form of the Latin word for black or dark-complexioned)*, Lucius who was from Cyrene, Manaen the foster-brother of Herod the tetrarch *(Herod Antipas)*, and Saul.

Manaen was reared with Herod Antipas as a child companion. Herod was born in 20 B.C., so Manaen was approximately 65 years old at this time. It was unusual to find men of his social status in the early church (see 1 Cor. 1:26-29). Herod Antipas ruled Galilee and Perea during the public ministry of Jesus. It was Antipas who beheaded John the Baptist and before whom Jesus appeared during His trial.

"Separate me Barnabas and Saul for the work whereunto I have called them."

The brethren fasted, prayed, and laid their hands on Barnabas and Saul as their way of expressing their concern and goodwill for them as they begin the task before them.

As these brethren engaged in the service of the Lord and in fasting, the Holy Spirit said, "Separate for me Barnabas and Saul to go to a work which I have chosen for them to do." Promptly, the Spirit's order was obeyed. When the brethren had fasted, prayed, and laid their hands on them, they sent the two men on their way.

Antioch of Syria was the third largest city in the Roman empire. It was built on the Orontes River and was about 20 miles from the Mediterranean. It was 16 miles from Antioch to Seleucia. Located about five miles north of the mouth of the Orontes, Seleucia served as the port for Antioch and was one of the most important harbors of the eastern Mediterranean in New Testament times.

Barnabas and Saul sail to Cyprus (Acts 13:4-12):

Antioch of Syria:
- **Their starting point**

Seleucia:
- **The seaport for Antioch**

Barnabas and Saul left Antioch, as guided by the Holy Spirit, and went down to Seleucia. From there they sailed 60 miles west to the island of Cyprus.

"Cyprus" means copper, so named because in ancient times the island was prized as a source of copper. The island is 140 miles long. It was ruled by the Romans from 58 B.C., and one of the governors was the famous Roman orator and writer Cicero. Its chief cities were Salamis and Paphos, on either end of the island. It became a very powerful center for Christianity in the early church. Barnabas was from this island (Acts 4:36). Some of the saints who were scattered after the early persecution in Jerusalem preached on the island of Cyprus (11:19).

John Mark is with Barnabas and Saul as their helper.

In Salamis, Barnabas and Saul preached the word of God in the Jewish synagogues. The young man John Mark whom they had brought with them from Jerusalem served as their helper. When they had gone

The Island of Cyprus:
- **Salamis: Preached in Jewish synagogues.**
- **Paphos:**
  - **Elymas the sorcerer;**
  - **Sergius Paulus was converted.**
  - **Saul began to be called Paul.**

through the whole island *(almost certainly preaching in various places along the way)*, they came to Paphos where they encountered a Jewish sorcerer who was a false prophet. His name was Bar-Jesus *(son of a man named Jesus)*.

A sorcerer (a magus) was not necessarily an evil man. The wise men who came to visit Jesus when He was a babe were magi. Such men were a combination of scientist/ magician, chemist/alchemist, astronomer/astrologer. There were those who sought knowledge and became very wise men; others sought power and control through the manipulation of rulers and of the wealthy whom they sought to influence through their knowledge.

"...being filled with the Holy Spirit..."
- **Paul was not acting out of a personal angry response to the interruptions by Elymas,**
- **He was acting with the approval and guidance of the Spirit.**

This sorcerer had managed to attach himself to Sergius Paulus, the proconsul of the island. Sergius Paulus was a man of intelligence and ability. When he heard about Barnabas and Saul, he sent for them to come to him for he wished to hear the word of God. But Elymas *(a free translation of the idea of a sorcerer, or a self-professed expert)* opposed Barnabas and Saul, seeking to turn the proconsul from the faith — probably by argument and ridicule.

Finally, Saul, who is also called Paul, being filled with the Holy Spirit, looked intently at Elymas and said, "O full of all deceit and having absolutely no scruples, you son of the devil, you enemy of all righteousness! Will you not stop perverting the right ways of God? Now, look, the hand of the Lord is upon you, and you will be blind, not able to see the sun for a while."

Immediately, a mist and a darkness fell upon Elymas and he went away trying to find someone to lead him by the hand. When Sergius Paulus saw what was done, he believed, because he was dumbfounded at the teaching of the Lord.

Just as Joseph was called Barnabas exclusively after the apostles gave him the name (4:36),
- **Now Saul is called Paul exclusively from this point on in the narrative.**
- **No information is given about why the change in the name.**

Paul is the prominent character from this time forward.

This is the first time Luke uses the name Paul instead of Saul in his narrative. Up until this point, the names of the men are given as "Barnabas and Saul," indicating Barnabas was the more prominent character. From this time on in the New Testament, Saul is called Paul exclusively, and his name is usually listed first when it is joined with the name of a partner.

Luke's reference to a proconsul on Cyprus was formerly challenged by critics on the ground that Cyprus was an imperial province governed by a procurator and not a proconsul. Such had been the case, but at this time Cyprus was a senatorial province and was, therefore, under a proconsul. In modern times, a Greek inscription was found on the north coast of Cyprus that was dated "in the proconsulship of Paulus," thus proving that Luke was correct in his terminology. No further information is known about Sergius Paulus. It is plausible to assume that when the text says he believed, it is saying that he became a Christian.

In Antioch of Pisidia

Paul is invited to speak (Acts 13:13-15):

Perga:
John Mark turned back

Paul and his companions sailed 170 miles north from Cyprus to the province of Pamphylia on the southern coast of Asia Minor. Since Attalia is not mentioned at this point, they probably sailed up the river Kestros and landed at Perga. There, John Mark turned back and returned to Jerusalem.

No information is given about why John Mark went back. Whatever the reason, Paul did not think it was a good one because when Barnabas wanted to take Mark along on the second journey, Paul refused because Mark "withdrew from them from Pamphylia, and went not with them to the work" (15:38). Some have suggested that he was overwhelmed at the work to be done, or that he was afraid of the arduous and dangerous journey up into the Pisidian highlands that Paul and Barnabas were about to undertake, but it is useless to speculate about his reasons since no details are given. Do not forget that this young man matured into a very valuable servant of the Lord.

Antioch of Pisidia:
- **They were invited to speak in the synagogue on the sabbath day.**
- **Paul was the speaker.**

Paul and Barnabas traveled on to Antioch in Pisidia, about 120 miles north of Perga. They went into the synagogue on the sabbath day and sat down. After the reading of the law and the prophets, the rulers of the synagogue sent to them, saying, "Brethren, if you have any word of exhortation for the people, please speak."

Portions from the law and from the prophets were read every sabbath day in Jewish synagogues everywhere.

The Pentateuch (Genesis through Deuteronomy) was divided into 54 sections, and selections from the prophets (including many books we do not normally think of as prophets, e.g. Judges, 2 Samuel) were likewise divided into 54 sections to be read in conjunction with the readings of the law. One section from the law and one section from the prophets was read each sabbath day. The sections of the law were called Parashas (or Parashioth) and the selections from the prophets were called Haphtarahs (or Haphtaroth). The Palestinian Jews and the eastern Jews (those of Syria and Babylon) used a Hebrew text which had been translated into the common Aramaic. The Jews in the other parts of the Roman empire, including these living in Asia Minor, used the Greek translation (the LXX) of the Old Testament.

It was after the reading of the law and the accompanying selections from the prophets that Paul and Barnabas were invited to speak. Knowing human nature, it is certain that the elders of the synagogue had met these men before the worship began, or had already sent the

Paul's speech consisted of three clearly marked sections:

- **Israel's history led them to the Christ (vv. 17-25).**
- **God fulfilled His promises to Israel by raising Jesus from the dead (vv. 26-37).**
- **In Jesus alone is forgiveness and justification (vv. 38-41).**

The speech:

- **Israel's history led them to the Christ (vv. 17-25):**
  - **God chose our fathers.**
  - **He led them out of Egypt and cared for them in the wilderness.**
  - **He gave them the land of Canaan.**
  - **He gave them judges until the days of Samuel.**
  - **When they asked for a king, He gave them Saul and then David.**
  - **From David's descendants God brought a Savior, Jesus — as John the forerunner predicted.**

- **God fulfilled His promises by raising Jesus from the dead (vv. 26-37):**
  - **To us this word of salvation is sent forth!**
  - **The rulers in Jerusalem did not recognize the Christ, though they had heard the prophets read regularly.**
    - **In their ignorance they fulfilled all that had been predicted about Him.**
  - **They killed Him.**
  - **But God raised Him from the dead, as the witnesses from Galilee testify.**
  - **The promise made to the fathers has been fulfilled in the resurrection of the Christ.**
  - **The prophecies agree: Psalms 2:7; Isaiah 55:3; Psalms 16:10.**
  - **The prophecies were not speaking of David; he died and decayed. But his descendant whom God raised did not decay.**

synagogue clerk to see who the visitors were. They would not have invited men to speak about whom they knew nothing.

Paul's speech (Acts 13:16-41):

Paul stood and motioned for silence and began to speak:

Men of Israel, and you who fear God, listen. The God of this people Israel chose our fathers and exalted the people when they were staying in the land of Egypt. With an outstretched arm He led them out of that country, and for forty years He cared for them and endured their conduct in the wilderness as a father with little sons. And when He had destroyed seven nations in the land of Canaan, He gave them the land as an inheritance for about 450 years. After giving them the land, He gave them judges until Samuel the prophet.

They asked for a king, so God gave them Saul the son of Kish of the tribe of Benjamin, for about forty years. When God had removed him, He raised up David to be their king, and said, "I have found David the son of Jesse a man after my own heart who will do my will."

Of this man's descendants, according to the promise, God has brought unto Israel a Savior, Jesus, after John had preached before His coming about the baptism of repentance to all the people of Israel. And as John was fulfilling his mission, he said, "What do you suppose I am? I am not the Christ, but, look, there comes One after me whose shoes I am not worthy to loose."

Brethren, sons of the genealogy of Abraham, and those of you who fear God, to us the word of this salvation is sent forth! For those who live in Jerusalem, and their rulers, did not recognize the Christ. They did not hear what the prophets, whose writings are read every sabbath, had foretold of Him. In their ignorance they fulfilled the promises concerning Him. Though they found no cause of death in Him, they asked Pilate to execute Him. And when they had fulfilled all the things written about Him, they took Him down from the tree and laid Him in a tomb. But God raised Him from the dead, and He was seen for many days by those who came with Him from Galilee to Jerusalem, men who now are His witnesses unto the people.

And we have come to tell you the good news about the promise made to the fathers: that God has fulfilled the same to our children in that He has raised up Jesus. To this agree the words of the second psalm: "You are my Son. This day have I proclaimed you as my Son." And concerning that He raised

- **In Jesus alone is forgiveness and justification (vv. 38-41):**
  - **Through this man Jesus remission of sins is preached to you.**
  - **All who believe on Him can be justified, in a way never possible under the law of Moses.**
  - **Beware of how you receive the message, lest the prophecy of Habbakuk apply to you.**

Him from the dead never to die again, He spoke these words: "I will give you the holy and sure blessings of David" (Isa. 55:3); because He says also in another psalm (Ps. 16:10): "You will not permit your Holy One to see corruption."

You see, David, after serving God's purpose in his own generation, passed to his rest and was buried with his ancestors and saw corruption. But the One God raised saw no corruption.

Therefore be assured, brethren, that through this man the remission of sins is proclaimed to you. Moreover, by Him every one who believes is justified from all things, from which you could not be justified by the law of Moses.

Be careful how you receive the message, lest you find the words of the prophets applying to you: "Look, you despisers, and wonder, and perish, because I am working a work in your day which you will not believe even if someone carefully spells it out for you" (Hab. 1:5).

The words of this warning closed Paul's speech. In the days of Habbakuk God had warned of the chastisement He would bring through the Chaldeans, but the people paid no attention. They despised, were incredulous, and perished. Paul was saying, do not let the words of this warning come to apply to you.

Similarities between this speech and those by others:

- **Paul tells of the death, burial, and resurrection of the Christ.**
- **He declares that it was all part of the plan of God for the redemption of mankind.**
- **He says the apostles were witnesses.**

Notice that there were God-fearers present (13:16, 26). These Gentiles were allowed to sit in the synagogues in a special place. They were found in most synagogues throughout the Roman world. They are the Gentiles referred to in 13:48. As Paul went from place to place, he usually found his most receptive audience from these God-fearers.

Differences between this speech and those by others:

- **Though these Jews were part of the chosen nation and were looking for the fulfillment of the prophecies, they were not directly involved in rejecting the Christ. The warning of how they responded to the message included the warning that they not be like their Judean brethren.**
- **Paul says the apostles *from Galilee* were witnesses of these things.**
  - **He was a witness of the living Savior, but he had not walked and talked with Jesus on the earth as had the twelve.**

Let us analyze Paul's speech in one more way. Notice that he spoke of the death, burial, and resurrection of the Christ just as the other speakers of Acts have. He also made it clear that all this happened in fulfillment of the promises and prophecies of God — therefore as part of God's plan for the redemption of mankind. He said the apostles were witnesses of these things.

But then there are some differences that need to be noted: Paul was speaking to Jews who were part of the chosen nation that had been so blessed through the years; therefore they understood the blessings and the promises that had been given and were looking forward to their fulfillment. But these Jews did not live in the land of Judea. They did not have a direct hand in rejecting and crucifying Jesus, therefore Paul says <u>they</u> killed Him, not <u>you</u>. The warning at the end of the speech not only warned lest they be like those in Habbakuk's day, but lest they be like their brethren in Judea who had rejected the Christ.

In both areas, the prophets were read every Sabbath day — but though the Jews of Jerusalem "heard" them read, they did not compre-

hend their meaning because they carried out exactly what had been predicted when the Christ appeared in their midst. The Jews of Antioch were not in a position to kill Jesus when Paul came into their midst, but they could just as certainly reject Him by rejecting Paul's message. Let us take the warnings seriously also.

Paul was a witness of the risen Savior:
- **But he never claimed to be the kind of witness who had walked and talked with Jesus upon the earth.**

Paul says that those who followed Jesus from Galilee (the twelve apostles) were witnesses to all the people of these things. Though Paul was an apostle as fully as the others, he does not claim to be the same kind of witness the others were. Jesus appeared to Paul on the road to Damascus, so Paul had proof He was alive in heaven, but Paul had not spent the years in day by day contact with Jesus that the others had.

It is very important to understand the message that each man gave as we study the sermons in the book of Acts. We cannot say we understand the passages until we understand exactly what points were made and why.

Jews and Gentile God-fearers were in the assembly (vv. 16, 26):
- **They asked Paul and Barnabas to speak again the next sabbath day.**
- **Devout Jews and proselytes followed them, and Paul and Barnabas taught them further.**
- **In order to continue in God's grace, they needed to believe and obey the message they had heard.**

Impact of Paul's speech (Acts 13:42-43):

As the people went out of the synagogue, there was great excitement among them. They begged that Paul and Barnabas speak further about these things the next sabbath day. In addition, when the assembly broke up, many of the Jews and the devout proselytes followed Paul and Barnabas, who talked with them and encouraged them to continue in the grace of God.

It is not to be thought that they, as Jews, without Christ, were in the grace of God. They were in the grace of God in that it was His grace which had provided salvation and had sent Paul and Barnabas to tell them about this salvation. The Jews had been God's chosen people until the coming of the new law, but now to continue in God's grace, they would need to believe the information about Jesus and then obey the message they had heard.

The next sabbath day:
- **Almost the whole city came to hear Paul and Barnabas.**
- **The Jews were jealous.**
- **Paul and Barnabas said they were turning to the Gentiles, since the Jews had rejected the message.**
- **The Gentiles rejoiced at the hope of salvation and the word of God spread through the area.**

The events of the following sabbath: belief and unbelief (Acts 13:44-52):

By the next sabbath, word had spread about what had happened, and almost the whole city came together to hear the word of God. But when the Jews saw the multitudes, they were filled with jealousy and began contradicting the things spoken by Paul, and they blasphemed.

Paul and Barnabas spoke out boldly to the unbelieving Jews, saying, "It was necessary that the word of God should first be spoken to you, but seeing that you thrust it away and judge yourselves unworthy of eternal life, we are turning to the Gentiles. For this is what the Lord commanded us when He said: 'I have set you for a light to the

Gentiles, that you may bring salvation to the farthest corner of the earth'" (Isa.49:6).

The part of the passage quoted by Paul and Barnabas is scarcely half of the verse. The first half of the verse says, "It is too light a matter that you [the Christ] should be my servant to raise up the tribes of Jacob, and to restore those who are preserved in Israel..." The verse addresses Christ, the Messiah, when it says "you." He was to be for the salvation not only of Jews, but also of Gentiles. What a blessing to all mankind!

When the Gentiles heard this statement they were glad, and as many as were disposed to accept eternal life believed. Consequently, the word of the Lord was spread throughout all the area.

Results:

- **The Jews stirred up the leaders of the city and had Paul and Barnabas expelled from the city.**
- **Paul and Barnabas brushed the dust of the city from their feet (see Matt. 10:11-15).**

The contrast of verse 46 where Paul and Barnabas rebuke the Jews, to verse 48 where the Gentiles rejoice and glorify God, is between the Jews who made a decision which put them out of the way that leads to life eternal, and the Gentiles of whom some were disposed to accept, to believe the words of the gospel. The context is not emphasizing something God did to them, but what they did to themselves in making themselves willing or unwilling to respond favorably to the message of salvation.

Source of the trouble:

- **Gentiles became involved in the trouble that arose at Antioch,**
  - **But it originated with unbelieving Jews.**
- **The Roman government has not yet discovered there is a new religion.**

The Jews, working through some devout women who were prominent in the city, and the leading men of the city, stirred up persecution against Paul and Barnabas. They expelled them from their borders. As they left, Paul and Barnabas brushed off the dust of their feet against them and moved on to Iconium, 80 miles to the southeast. Those who had been converted were filled with joy and with the Holy Spirit.

The devout women were proselytes. "Being of honorable estate" means they were married to the influential, leading men of the city. The Jews knew to whom the various women were married, and knew just how to use them to accomplish their goals.

Notice the trouble here in Antioch of Pisidia originated with the unbelieving Jews, although they influenced some of the leading Gentile men to take part in the trouble. As we continue through the journeys, look for the source of the trouble each time. Often there will be Gentiles involved, but it will either be over a local dispute between some individual Gentiles and Paul, or it will originate with Jews. The Roman government has not yet discovered there is a new religion.

Refresh your memory of the places Paul and Barnabas have visited so far:

- **Be sure you have each place labeled on your map,**
- **And that you know what happened at each place.**

Iconium, Lystra, and Derbe

Now on to Iconium:

- **Preached in synagogue for a "long time."**
- **A plot to stone them.**
- **They fled to Lycaonia.**

Paul and Barnabas in Iconium (Acts 14:1-7):

As usual, Paul and Barnabas went into the synagogue of the Jews when they reached Iconium. There they spoke in such a way that a great number of both Jews and Greeks believed. Once again, however, the Jews who were disobedient stirred up the Gentiles and poisoned their minds against the brethren. This bitterness did not immediately erupt in outright persecution, however the church needed special encouragement, so for a long time Paul and Barnabas stayed in Iconium preaching boldly what the Lord wished. The Lord added His witness to the gracious words which were spoken by granting various miracles to be done by Paul and Barnabas.

At Iconium:

- **The trouble originated with the unbelieving Jews,**
- **Who stirred up some of the Gentiles against Paul and Barnabas.**

Nevertheless, dissension grew. Part of the multitude sided with the Jews and part with the apostles. Finally a plot was made on the part of the Jews, the Gentiles, and their rulers to abuse the men and to stone them. Paul and Barnabas learned of the plan and fled to the neighboring province of Lycaonia, to the cities of Lystra and Derbe. There they continued to preach the gospel.

Gentiles were very much involved in this disturbance, but notice that it started from the Jews. Even the officials that got involved were local ones —not Roman officials from the hierarchy of the government.

Look on your map. They have gone to "Lycaonia" — which brings us to some more information about the circumstances in the land at that time.

The divisions of the lands of that day are quite confusing at times. When the Romans organized their conquered territories into administrative districts, they did not always respect old cultural and ethnic boundaries. Lycaonia, for example, was an old ethnic region, where the people were still in the habit of speaking their old language. But the Romans had divided Lycaonia into two parts. One part belonged to Rome — the part that contained Lystra and Derbe. Rome had made it a part of the district of Galatia and called it Galatica Lycaonia. The other part was not Roman, and was ruled over by King Antiochus and was, therefore, called Lycaonia Antiochiana. Paul and Barnabas did not go beyond the Roman part of Lycaonia.

Lycaonia and Galatia were two names for the same place.

The letter to the Galatians was written to the churches in Lystra, Derbe, Iconium, and Antioch of Pisidia.

This information explains why the area is called Lycaonia as the history tells of their going there, but later when Paul wrote a letter to the Christians of the area, the book was called Galatians. Both names applied to the same area.

Paul and Barnabas in Lystra (Acts 14:8-20):

Lystra was about eighteen miles southwest of Iconium. When they arrived, Paul and Barnabas found a man who was lame in his feet — a cripple who had never walked. This man heard Paul speaking, and Paul, looking intently at the man, and seeing that he had faith to be made well, said in a loud voice, "Stand all the way up on your feet." The man leaped up from the ground and walked.

Faith was never a requirement for a miracle to be accomplished in the New Testament.

- **But this crippled man was listening to Paul and he believed what he heard.**
- **Paul used the opportunity as a way of teaching the multitudes.**

Faith was not essential for a miracle to be done. The blind man of John 9 did not even know who Jesus was until He healed him. There were several dead people raised in the first century, and miracles were performed on inanimate objects such as turning the water to grape juice, stilling the storm at sea, and cursing the fig tree. Sometimes the person healed clearly had faith to be healed, such as the woman with the issue of blood. But faith on the part of the one healed was not a necessary condition for his healing, and not once was the lack of faith on the part of the one wanting to be healed used to excuse the failure of an attempt to work a miracle. The only time the apostles failed to perform a miracle, Jesus blamed their failure on their own lack of faith, not a lack on the part of the one to be healed (Matt. 17:19-21; see also Matt. 14:29-31).

This time Paul chose to do a miracle on one who did have faith. Where did that faith come from? "The same heard Paul speaking..." He got it from hearing the word of God (see Rom. 10:17).

Lystra:

- **A man was healed.**
- **The multitude was ready to worship Paul and Barnabas:**
  - **Calling them Mercury and Jupiter.**
- **Later, the same multitude at Lystra stones Paul nearly to death.**

When the multitudes saw what had been done, they became so excited they spoke in the language of Lycaonia and cried out, "The gods are come down to us in the appearance of men!!" They called Barnabas Jupiter *(Zeus in the Greek)* and Paul Mercury *(Hermes in the Greek)* because Paul was the chief speaker. *(Hermes was said to be the messenger of the gods.)*

The priests of Jupiter, whose temple was before the city, brought bulls with garlands of flowers about their necks to offer in sacrifice with the multitudes. As soon as Paul and Barnabas realized why a sacrifice was being prepared, they tore their clothes and ran into the crowd, shouting:

Paul's speech to these idolaters:

- **We are men like you.**
- **We have come to turn you from useless idols to serve the God who made heaven, earth, and everything in them.**
- **In times past, God let the Gentiles go their own way,**
  - **Though He gave witness of Himself.**

> Sirs, why are you doing these things? We are flesh and blood men just like you! We bring you the good news that you should turn from these useless idols to a living God, who made the heaven and the earth and the sea and everything in them. In generations past He allowed the Gentiles to go in their own ways. Yet, even then, He did not leave Himself without any witness among you in that He did good for you and gave you from heaven the rain and harvest seasons, thus filling your hearts with food and gladness.

Only with great difficulty did they succeed in stopping the multitude from offering sacrifices to them.

See the important point:

- **Contrast this sermon to the ones that have been made to believers in Jehovah.**
- **Compare it with the one to the idolaters of Athens Greece (Acts 17).**

Contrast this sermon to the idolaters of Lystra to the sermons that have been preached to Jews, proselytes, and God-fearers in the book of Acts. Notice that Paul did not call their attention to Jewish history or to the prophecies of the Old Testament. They would not have understood the significance. Instead he called upon them to listen to the information about the God who created the worlds —and to turn from their vain idols. Be impressed that the speakers and writers of the New Testament always made their lessons fit their audience. We must turn to Paul's lesson to the idolaters of Athens Greece in chapter 17 to find a comparable lesson. Let us learn to fit our lessons to our listeners. Begin teaching where the learner is ready to grasp what is being said.

A miracle:

- **Paul recovers and is able to go on to Derbe the next day.**

Then unbelieving Jews arrived who had followed Paul from Antioch of Pisidia and from Iconium. They persuaded the multitude, and they stoned Paul and dragged him out of the city, thinking he was dead. But as the disciples stood around him, Paul got up and went back into the city. The next day he went with Barnabas to Derbe, 30 miles to the southeast.

Paul's recovery was a miracle. From the wording of the text, it is evident that he was not completely dead when he was dragged from the city because the Bible says, they "drew him out of the city, supposing he had been dead." But, as the brethren watched, this nearly dead man got up and went into the city, and then went on his way to another city the very next day. A stoning that severe would have taken days or weeks to recover enough to be ready for a trip —especially on foot.

The return trip:

- **Lystra**
- **Iconium**
- **Antioch of Pisidia**
- **Perga**
- **Attalia**
- **Back to Antioch of Syria**

On their return trip:

- **They strengthened the brethren,**
- **They exhorted them to be faithful.**
- **They appointed elders in every church.**

Upon their arrival in Antioch:

- **They reported all the things God had done through them,**
- **And how He had opened the door of faith to the Gentiles.**

Paul and Barnabas return to Antioch in Syria (Acts 14:21-28):

When they had preached the gospel in Derbe, Paul and Barnabas returned through Lystra, Iconium, and Antioch, strengthening the disciples and encouraging them to remain true to the faith. They said, "We must go through many hardships to enter the kingdom of God" *(that is, the heavenly kingdom —see 2 Tim. 4:18).*

One of the very important things which Paul and Barnabas did on this return trip was to appoint elders in every church. When they had done this, and had prayed with fasting, they placed the disciples into the care of the Lord in whom they had believed.

Paul and Barnabas left the scene of their labors and went down from the Pisidian highlands to the province of Pamphylia. When they had preached in Perga, they went to Attalia and from there sailed back to Antioch of Syria.

When they arrived, they gathered the church together and told all the things that God had done with them and how He had opened a door of faith to the Gentiles. For a long time they stayed there at Antioch.

Appointment of elders:

- **The churches needed elders.**
- **Elders were appointed in every church.**
    - **Each church was independent and self-governing.**
- **Every major apostasy has involved misunderstanding and transgression of the role of elders and the independence of the churches.**

Many important points need to be made about the appointing of elders:

- *For these churches to be fully equipped, they needed elders.*
- *They needed qualified men.*
    - *That men could be qualified so quickly is easily explained by the fact that many of these converts were Jews. Being a truly good Jew would go a long way toward meeting the qualifications of elders recorded in 1 Timothy 3 and Titus 1.*
    - *The miraculous gifts of the Spirit would have greatly accelerated the growth and development of the disciples in the first century.*
- *It is important to observe that elders were appointed in every church, not in every district.*
    - *Each church had its own elders.*
    - *This passage is very important in establishing that each church is to be independent and self-governing.*
- *These concepts are easily taught, and we and our children need to be thoroughly grounded in the truth about the role of elders.*
    - *Every major apostasy of the church has involved the transgression of these principles.*
- *Other verses that need to be understood in conjunction with this one are: Titus 1:5; Acts 20:28; 1 Peter 5:1-2.*

Review this first journey:

- **Antioch of Syria**
- **Seleucia**
- **Island of Cyprus:**
    - **Salamis**
    - **Paphos**
- **Perga**
- **Antioch of Pisidia**
- **Iconium**
- **Lystra**
- **Derbe**

Their return:

- **Lystra**
- **Iconium**
- **Antioch of Pisidia**
- **Perga**
- **Attalia**
- **Antioch of Syria**

Chronological Note:

There is no way to know for sure exactly when the first missionary journey began, but fitting it with the account of Herod Agrippa's death, A.D. 44, seems to fit all the other data as well. The Jerusalem conference, which occurred between the first and second journeys, took place fourteen years after Paul returned to Jerusalem from Damascus, which was three years after his conversion (see Gal. 1:18-2:1). If we date the starting of the church in A.D. 29 or 30, and the conversion of Paul in 31 or 32, add three years between his conversion and his return to Jerusalem, plus the fourteen years before he returned for the meeting described in chapter 15, we arrive at the year 48 or 49 for the conference in Jerusalem. Therefore, it is fairly certain that this first journey occurred between A.D. 44 and 49.

How long did the first journey last? No one knows for certain. Some say barely over two years; others say three or four years. Consider these factors: After the death of Herod in A.D. 44, we do not know how long the disciples were at Antioch before the Lord called them to go forth on their special mission. Then, they went through the "whole island" of Cyprus (13:6) which would indicate a fairly thorough evangelizing of the island. There is no way to know how long it took them to pass through Perga, nor how long their stay was in Antioch of Pisidia, but they were there long enough for "the word of God to spread throughout the whole area" (13:49). They remained at Iconium a "long time" (14:3). There are no notes at all regarding how long they

About 20 years have passed since the church began.

- **This first journey probably took two or three years to complete, between A.D. 44 and 49.**
- **Only the highlights of these 20 years, and of this journey are told.**

were in Lystra and Derbe, nor how long they took exhorting the brethren as they passed back through all the cities. Then, upon their return, they remained at Antioch "no little time" (14:28). More than likely, therefore, two years is a short estimate for the length of this first journey, and five years is a long estimate. Dates given in this period, however, will vary from one scholar to another.

Remember, throughout the Bible story, only the highlights of the period of history are given. We have already covered about twenty years in the story of the early church, but think how few stories there are told about those years. The stories told are just examples of the work that was being done all around. Many, many other events were happening at this same time. There were many more things that happened even on this first journey. These are told so that we might know the type work being done. Paul's work was significant because of the writings he left behind, but he was not the only one working, just as Peter was not the only apostle working in Judea during the early chapters of Acts.

The Conference in Jerusalem

(Acts 15:1-35; Galatians 2)

Trouble Arises From Within

Many Gentiles have been converted.

- **Trouble arises from a new source.**
- **Instead of persecution from unbelievers,**
  - **This is a conflict in belief among the disciples themselves.**
  - **Some Jews who had accepted the gospel of Christ did not believe the Gentiles had a right to be saved,**
    - **Without their first becoming Jews,**
    - **That is, without being circumcised as a sign of their covenant relationship with God.**
- **Since this trouble was from within the church,**
  - **It proved to be the greatest hindrance yet to the progress of the gospel.**
- **It was the source of much conflict through the rest of the first century.**
- **It will be discussed over and over in Paul's epistles.**

It is now about A.D. 48 or 49.

By now innumerable Gentiles had become Christians. Men such as those mentioned in Acts 11:20 began preaching freely to Gentiles shortly after Cornelius was converted. And during their first preaching tour, Paul and Barnabas preached without restraint among the Gentiles. They "turned to the Gentiles" in Antioch of Pisidia when the Jews refused to accept their testimony (13:46).

When Peter converted Cornelius, he was called in question about his action by the brethren in Jerusalem. But as soon as they had been told the details of what had happened, it was the unanimous agreement among them that "unto the Gentiles also has been granted repentance unto life" (11:18). The men discussing the matter with Peter on that occasion were the apostles and other leading brethren in the church at Jerusalem (11:1). They were the ones in the best position to understand God's plan, but even they had to learn that the Gentiles were to be accepted on equal terms with the Jews.

Now trouble arises. There was strong opposition on the part of some of the Jewish Christians to baptizing the Gentiles without their first being circumcised. Notice, this trouble comes not from outside sources, but from within the church itself. These are Jews who have accepted the gospel of Christ. Their problem was that they thought the blessings from God could be given only to Jews, that they were God's only chosen people. Therefore, they were saying that the Gentiles must first become part of the covenant relationship with God (that is, through the sign of circumcision) before they had the right to be saved.

This issue was a very important one. It could have greatly hindered the progress of the gospel. It was the source of much conflict in the years that followed. Paul often deals with this question in his writings.

Galatians 2 adds a great deal to the study of Acts 15, so we will bring in points from Galatians at the appropriate places.

Chronological Note:

Except for the brief visit to Jerusalem from Antioch to carry relief to the poor (11:30; 12:25), it has been fourteen years since Paul was in Jerusalem, seventeen years since his conversion (see Gal. 1:18; 2:1). If the dates we have been giving are correct, and he was converted in A.D. 31 or 32, it would now be about A.D. 48 or 49. This date fits very well with all other facts known.

While Paul and Barnabas were still in Antioch after their first preaching journey, certain men came from Judea to Antioch and taught the brethren saying, "Unless you are circumcised as Moses commanded, you cannot be saved."

Men from Judea carried great weight with their message,
- **Because they are from Jerusalem where the gospel began to be preached.**
- **Paul and Barnabas knew these men were not teaching the truth,**
  - **But others at Antioch needed to be assured.**

Men from Judea would carry weight with any message they might bring, because Jerusalem, in the province of Judea, was where the gospel was first preached. For a long time after other disciples were scattered, the apostles remained in Jerusalem. Some were still there (Acts 15:4, 6, 22). So Jerusalem was still considered the source of very valuable information for the early Christians.

Paul and Barnabas had extensive debates with these men. After a time, it was determined that Paul, Barnabas, and certain others should go up to Jerusalem to the apostles and elders to discuss the matter with them. Paul did not feel the need to go to Jerusalem to learn anything, because the answer had already been given to him by the Holy Spirit. Nevertheless, the Spirit revealed that he should go with the men to Jerusalem (Gal. 2:2).

Look on your map:
- **See the overland route from Antioch to Jerusalem.**
- **Label Phoenicia and Samaria.**

On their way to Jerusalem, Paul and Barnabas visited the churches in Phoenicia and Samaria. At each place they told how the Gentiles had been converted. Their message brought great joy to all the brethren.

When they arrived:
- **Paul, Barnabas, and their companions were welcomed by the church, the apostles, and the elders.**
- **Paul met with James, Peter, and John.**
- **They were in full agreement.**

When they arrived in Jerusalem, they received a welcome from the church, the apostles, and the elders (Acts 15:4). Paul's first meeting was with James, Peter, and John in order that he might tell them what he had been preaching among the Gentiles (Gal. 2:2, 9). The result of this meeting was total agreement, which is exactly what we would expect of inspired men. Peter, James, and John fully understood that, as God had given Peter the responsibility to preach to the Jews, He had given Paul the responsibility to preach to the Gentiles. These three men extended to Paul and Barnabas the right hands of fellowship (Gal. 2:7-9). There was no jealousy or disagreement.

The James mentioned in this story was the Lord's brother (Gal. 1:19).
- **James, the brother of John, was already dead (Acts 12:1-2).**

Paul did not meet with these men because he doubted that the Spirit would give the same revelation to every inspired man, but rather because he wanted to see what each had done with that revelation. The story of how Peter behaved in Antioch (Gal. 2:11-14) just a short time after this conference shows that just knowing the truth does not always determine what one does.

Knowledge of right does not always assure correct behavior and teaching.

After his meeting with the three men, Paul and Barnabas told the whole congregation everything God had done through them. When all the brethren heard their story, certain ones of the sect of the Pharisees who believed rose up saying, "The Gentiles will have to be circumcised and they must be taught to obey the law of Moses."

Note that these are Pharisees who believe. We are so used to hearing the Pharisees object to the teaching of Jesus, it would be easy for us to think this was more opposition from unbelieving Jews. But these were men who had been Pharisees, but who had accepted the word of the gospel. Their problem was that they did not understand that the Gentiles were accepted on the same terms that they themselves were accepted before God. They had lived their lives being very careful to keep themselves separate from all customs of the Gentiles, so it was a hard lesson for them to accept.

This objection came from Pharisees who *believed.*

Paul did not give in to their demands for even one hour!

But Paul and those who stood with him did not give in to such demands for even one hour so that the truth of the gospel might flow without restriction (Gal. 2:4-5). Finally, during a meeting in which there had been much debate, Peter stood up and said:

Peter spoke, saying:
- **God chose me to be the first to preach to the Gentiles.**
- **God showed His approval by sending the Holy Spirit.**
- **God made no distinction between the Gentiles and the Jews, cleansing them by faith.**
- **He required nothing of Gentiles that He did not require of Jews.**
- **Why do you challenge God's will?**
- **Why demand they do what we and our ancestors could not do?**
- **We Jews will be saved by God's grace, just as the Gentiles.**

> Brethren, you know that some time ago God made choice among you that by my mouth the Gentiles should hear the gospel and believe. And God, who knows what is in everyone's heart, gave His witness to them, giving them the Holy Spirit just as He did unto us. He made no distinction between us and them, cleansing their hearts by faith. Now, why do you try God's patience by requiring the disciples to do what neither we nor our ancestors were able to do? Instead, we believe that we will be saved through the grace of God just as the Gentiles.

Peter's basic argument was that in the salvation of Cornelius by faith, God gave an example that showed all Gentiles were to be saved without being required to be circumcised, or to keep the law of Moses. Thus apostolic example is clearly established as a way in which God can make His will known, and in which He can require men to follow certain procedures.

After Peter's speech, everyone remained silent and listened to Barnabas and Paul recounting the signs and wonders God had worked among the Gentiles through them.

God demonstrated He approved of the message Paul and Barnabas were preaching among the Gentiles:
- **By allowing them to perform miracles among them.**

We are not told of any conclusion which Barnabas and Paul stated as they told of the miracles which God had done through them —and yet, were they not arguing a point? The point is that God blessed the work they were doing with signs and wonders. He would not have blessed them if He had not approved of their actions. But Paul and Barnabas had not required their Gentile converts to be circumcised or to keep the law of Moses. Therefore, it was a necessary conclusion that God had approved the Gentiles' being saved without circumcision and without the keeping of the law of Moses.

After Paul and Barnabas had finished their message, James responded:

James spoke, saying:

- **God showed His concern for the Gentiles by taking from them a people for Himself.**
- **This is what the prophets predicted:**
  - **For example, Amos.**
- **Do not make it difficult for the Gentiles who are turning to the Lord.**
- **Leave them alone, except to write to them, warning them to abstain from:**
  - **Contamination of idols,**
  - **Fornication,**
  - **Strangled animals,**
  - **Eating of blood.**
- **Moses' law is read and preached in the synagogues every sabbath.**

> Brethren, listen to me. Symeon *(another spelling for Simeon or Simon; the reference is to Peter)* has reminded us of how first God came to the aid of the Gentiles to take out of them a people for His name. And the words of the prophets are in agreement with this, as it is written: "After these things I will return and I will put up again the tent of David which is fallen, And I will set up the ruins of it so that *the remnant of men* may seek after the Lord, And *all the Gentiles* who are called after my name, saith the Lord, who makes these things known from of old" (Amos 9:11-12).
>
> Wherefore, as for my part, my judgment is that we not bother these who are turning to the Lord from among the Gentiles. Instead, we should write to them, telling them that they should abstain from the contamination of idols, from fornication, from animals which are strangled, and from blood. For Moses has been preached in every city for many, many years and is read in the synagogues on every sabbath.

Look at the things forbidden. All idolatry was forbidden, plus any contamination connected with idols. Fornication was included in the list because it was almost universally practiced in connection with idol worship.

Though some would relate the eating of things strangled to idolatry, it seems much clearer to relate it to the prohibition against eating blood since an animal strangled was not bled properly and would still have the blood in it.

"But flesh with the life thereof, which is the blood thereof, shall ye not eat" (Gen. 9:4).

"For the life of the flesh is in the blood... Therefore I said unto the children of Israel, No soul of you shall eat blood, neither shall any stranger that sojourns among you eat blood" (Lev. 17:11-12).

There have been questions about why the forbidding of eating blood is included in the list. Why this particular law from the law of Moses? Why not order them to be circumcised? The most logical answer is that the prohibition against eating blood was not peculiar to the law of Moses. The command was given to all mankind immediately after the flood (Gen. 9:3-4). The law was <u>repeated</u> in the law of Moses, but it did not <u>originate</u> with it (Lev. 17:10-16). Therefore, the prohibition against eating blood is found in all three dispensations of time. Look back to the passages in the Old Testament to see why the prohibition was given in each of the earlier dispensations. The same reason exists under the new law.

In mentioning the fact that the law of Moses was read each sabbath day all over the empire, it seems James was trying to reassure the Jews that the law would continue to be respected and remembered.

After James had spoken, the apostles, the elders, and indeed the whole church, decided to choose men to go with Paul and Barnabas to

Antioch to carry their conclusion to the brethren. They selected Judas Barsabbas and Silas, influential men among the brethren, and they wrote a letter for them to take to the Gentile brethren. The letter said:

The letter said:
- **Those men who came to you did not have authority from us.**
    - **They were leading you astray.**
- **We are sending Judas and Silas to confirm by mouth what we have written in our letter.**
- **The Holy Spirit places you under no burden except to refrain from:**
    - **Food sacrificed to idols,**
    - **Blood,**
    - **Meat from strangled animals,**
    - **Fornication.**

> The apostles and elders, as brethren, to the Gentile brethren who are in Antioch and Syria and Cilicia. Greetings.
>
> We have heard that some men who went out from us have bothered you with their words, leading you astray. We gave those men no such commandment. Therefore, it seemed good to us, having all come to the same conclusion, to choose men and to send them to you with our beloved Barnabas and Paul, men who have put their lives on the line for the name of our Lord Jesus Christ.
>
> We have, therefore, sent Judas and Silas who will tell you the same things by word of mouth. It seemed good to the Holy Spirit and to us to lay upon you no greater burden than these essential things: that you abstain from things sacrificed to idols, and from blood, and from things strangled, and from fornication, from which if you keep yourselves, you will do fine.
>
> We wish you the best.

Titus, the Gentile "test case," was *not* compelled to be circumcised.

One of the "certain others" who had gone with Paul and Barnabas from Antioch (Acts 15:2) was a man named Titus, who was a Greek disciple. He went on this occasion as a sort of test case. By the time the discussion was over, Titus was not compelled to be circumcised, as proof that Paul had been correct in his teaching (Gal. 2:1-3).

Paul and Barnabas and their companions return to Antioch (Acts 15:30-35):

The brethren in Antioch rejoiced when they heard the letter read from the brethren in Jerusalem.
- **It was a very encouraging message to the Gentile converts.**

When they had been dismissed, Paul, Barnabas, and their companions *(Titus, Judas, Silas, and others who are not named specifically but were included in the "certain ones" who had accompanied them to Jerusalem)* all went to Antioch. Having gathered the multitude of disciples together, they read the letter. Everyone rejoiced when they heard the letter because of its encouragement.

Judas returned to Jerusalem. Silas remained in Antioch.

Judas and Silas were also prophets, and they exhorted the brethren with many words and strengthened them. After spending some time with the disciples, Judas returned home, but Silas decided to remain in Antioch. Paul and Barnabas also remained in Antioch, preaching the word of the Lord along with many others.

"Please remember the poor..."
- **Do not forget this charge to Paul.**
- **It will play a part in the later history.**

As Paul tells the story of this meeting in Jerusalem, he adds one more fact which is not included by the historian Luke. When Peter, John, and James gave them the right hand of fellowship and encouraged them to take the gospel to the Gentiles as God intended, they asked Paul and Barnabas to be sure to remember the poor *(presumably among the Jews since they were the ones with whom these three men worked most)*. Paul said he continued to keep that goal before him from that time forward (Gal. 2:10.)

Why circumcision? Why choose that law to argue over?

- **Circumcision was given as a sign of the covenant between God and Abraham and his descendants.**
  - **If one were not circumcised, he was no longer an heir to the promises.**
- **But which promises were included in the sign of circumcision?**
  - **There were three primary promises made to Abraham:**
    - **Nation**
    - **Land**
    - **One to bless all nations (spiritual).**
- **But only the nation and land promises were tied to the rite of circumcision.**
- **The Jews thought the spiritual blessing was also tied to circumcision.**
  - **That is why they thought the Gentiles could not be heirs of salvation without the sign of the covenant.**

Why was there so much discussion in the first century over the question of circumcision? Why circumcision? Why not one of the other laws from the law of Moses?

In order to understand the thinking of the Jews, look back to Genesis 17 to the occasion when the law of circumcision was first given. At that time, God commanded Abraham to be circumcised as a sign of the covenant that had been made between them. Abraham was told that all the males in his household were to be circumcised — whether born in his family or bought as a slave. From that day forward, any male that was not circumcised was to be cut off and no longer counted as heir to the promises God had made to Abraham. It was, therefore, a serious matter if one refused to be circumcised.

But let us look at the promises that were part of the covenant for which circumcision was the sign. There had been three promises made to Abraham when God brought him to the land of Canaan: God promised that He would make a great <u>nation</u> of Abraham's descendants; He promised to give the <u>land</u> of Canaan to those descendants; and He promised to <u>bless all nations</u> through One who would come from Abraham's descendants (Gen. 12:1-7).

The Jews thought all three promises were tied to the sign of circumcision. But let us look closely at Genesis 17. God repeated His promise to make a great <u>nation</u> of Abraham's seed in the passage. He even enlarged the promise to say that Abraham would be the father of "many" nations. God also repeated the promise that He would give the <u>land</u> of Canaan to that nation. (See Gen. 17:4-8.) But God did <u>not</u> repeat the promise here that He would bless all nations through Abraham's seed (compare Gen. 12:3 to what is said in Gen. 17).

The Jews were correct in thinking that the sign of circumcision was a necessary part of being one of Abraham's chosen race, of being heir to the land of Canaan. But they were not correct in thinking that the right to share in the blessings that would come through Christ, the descendant of Abraham, hinged upon the rite of circumcision. They thought that Gentiles must be circumcised to show they were heir to the promises to Abraham before they could be part of God's chosen people. They did not understand the passages in the prophets that predicted a day when God's blessings would be available to all the nations (e.g. Amos 9:11-12; Hos. 1:10; Isa. 2:2-4).

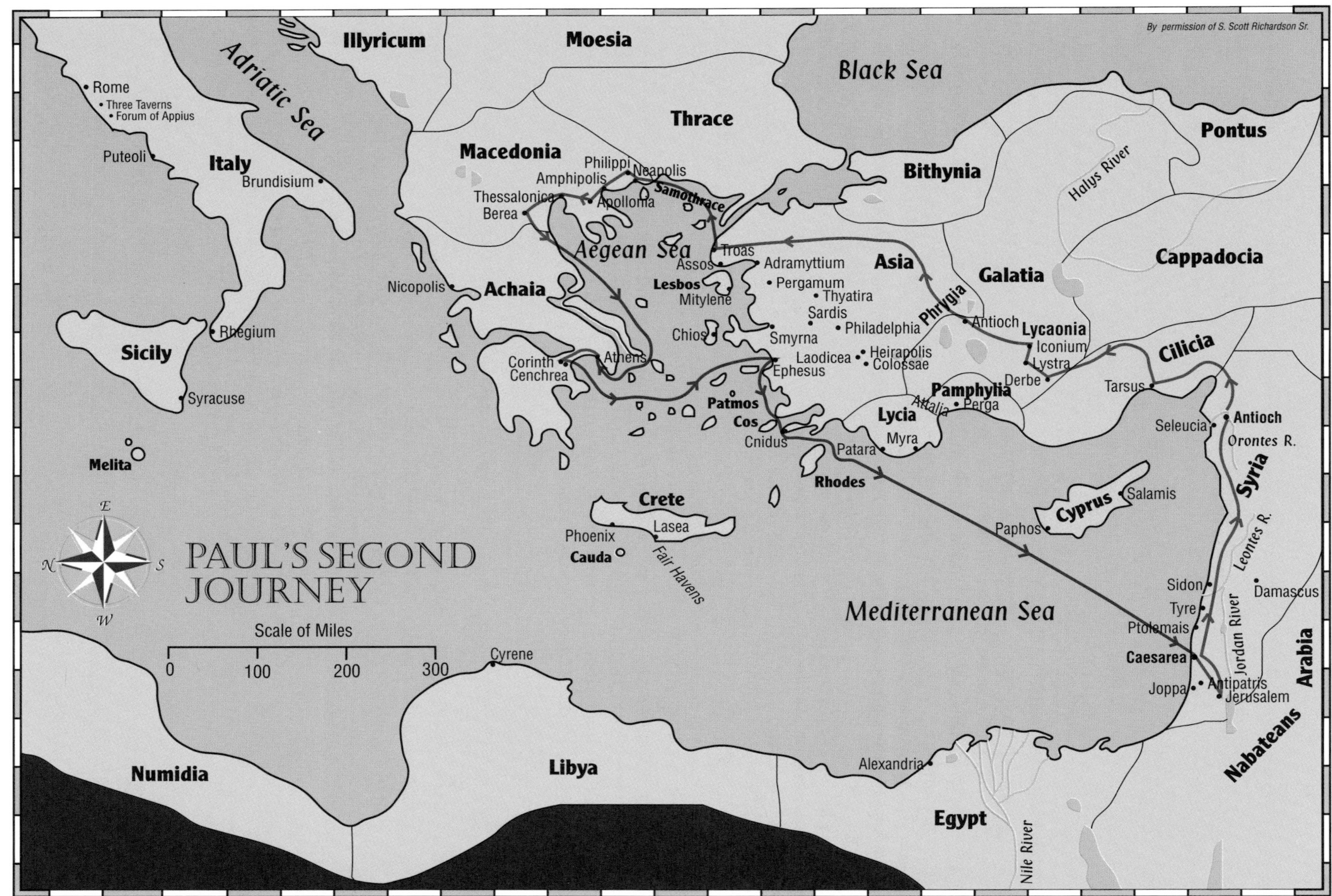

PAUL'S SECOND JOURNEY
Scale of Miles
0
100
200
300
N
S
E
W
By permission of S. Scott Richardson Sr.
Illyricum
Moesia
Black Sea
Adriatic Sea
Rome
Three Taverns
Forum of Appius
Thrace
Pontus
Puteoli
Italy
Brundisium
Macedonia
Philippi
Neapolis
Amphipolis
Thessalonica
Apollonia
Berea
Samothrace
Bithynia
Halys River
Aegean Sea
Troas
Assos
Adramyttium
Asia
Galatia
Cappadocia
Nicopolis
Achaia
Lesbos
Mitylene
Pergamum
Thyatira
Sardis
Philadelphia
Phrygia
Antioch
Lycaonia
Iconium
Lystra
Derbe
Sicily
Rhegium
Chios
Smyrna
Laodicea
Heirapolis
Colossae
Ephesus
Corinth
Cenchrea
Athens
Patmos
Cos
Cnidus
Syracuse
Pamphylia
Attalia
Perga
Lycia
Myra
Patara
Rhodes
Cilicia
Tarsus
Seleucia
Antioch
Orontes R.
Syria
Melita
Crete
Lasea
Phoenix
Cauda
Fair Havens
Cyprus
Salamis
Paphos
Leontes R.
Sidon
Damascus
Tyre
Ptolemais
Jordan River
Mediterranean Sea
Caesarea
Joppa
Antipatris
Jerusalem
Arabia
Nabateans
Cyrene
Numidia
Libya
Alexandria
Egypt
Nile River

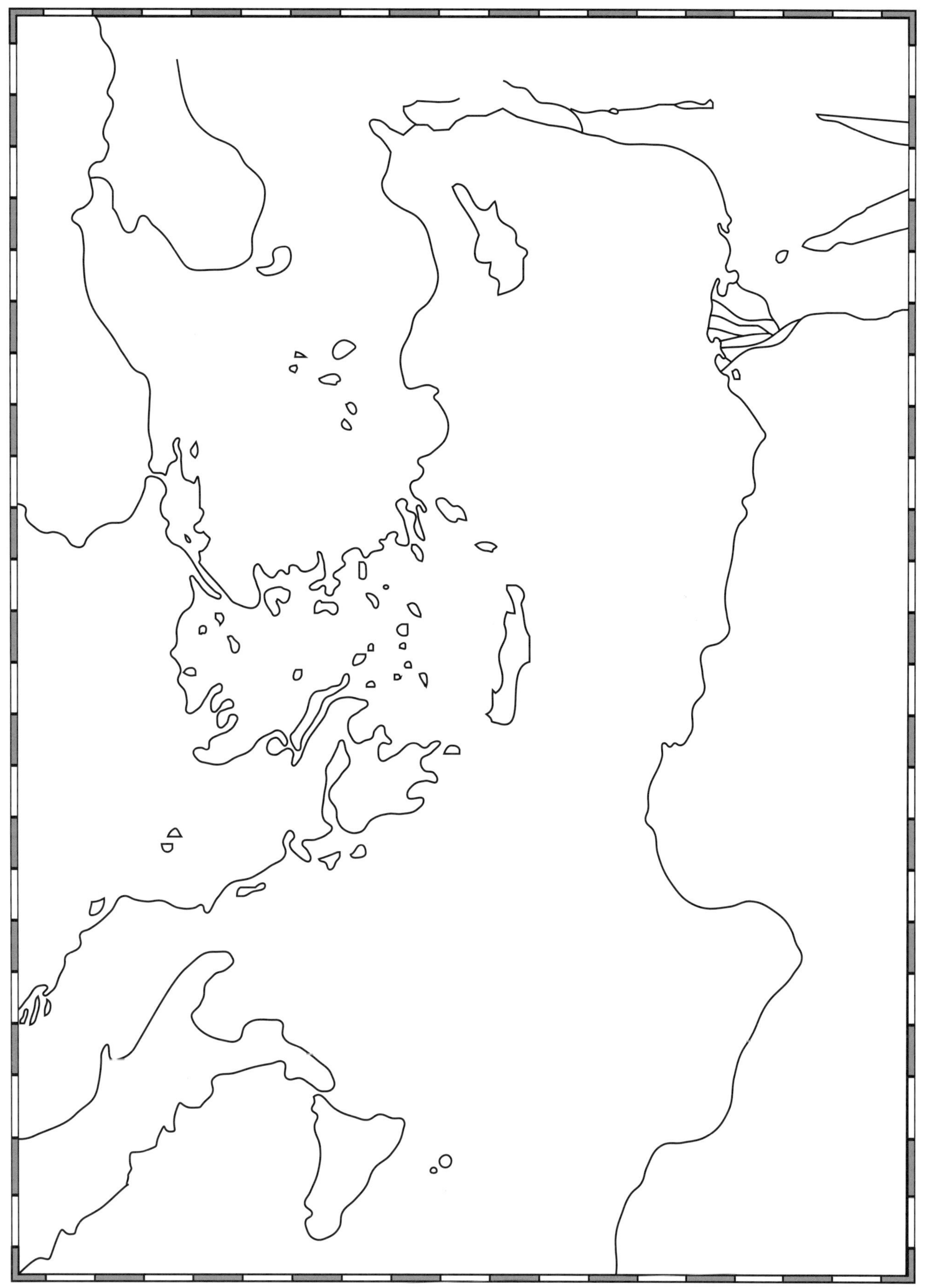

The Second Missionary Journey

(Acts 15:36-18:22; 1 & 2 Thessalonians)

A dispute arises between Paul and Barnabas (Acts 15:36-40):

The date: about A.D. 50/51.

After a time, Paul said to Barnabas, "Let us return to the places where we preached the gospel and see how the brethren are."

Godly men could disagree sharply, and still remain godly men.

Barnabas agreed, and he wanted to take John Mark with them again as their helper. But Paul did not think it wise to take one with them who had turned back at Pamphylia and did not go with them to the work. The disagreement was sharp. Each man thought he had good reasons for what he wanted done about John Mark, so neither man would change his mind. Yet, they were godly men, so they arrived at a workable solution to their problem.

Barnabas took John Mark and went to Cyprus.

They chose to separate and go different ways. Barnabas took John Mark with him and went to Cyprus *(the original home of Barnabas, 4:36)* to check on the churches there. The historian does not follow their journey. He goes back to the story of Paul's work.

Remember that Mark continued to grow in his service to God. In Paul's last letter, he asks Timothy to bring Mark with him "for he is profitable to me for the ministry" (2 Tim. 4:11).

Paul took Silas as his traveling companion and they went through Syria and Cilicia.

Paul chose Silas for his new traveling companion and they set out with the good wishes of the brethren in Antioch, who expressed the desire that the Lord would bless their labors. They traveled by land through Syria and Cilicia, strengthening the churches as they came to them.

Map Assignment:

- **Begin marking this second journey on your blank map.**
- **Label the route Paul and Silas probably followed through the mountains.**

The route Paul and Silas chose took them through the Syrian Gates, a famous pass in the Amanus Mountains. Likely Paul went through Tarsus as one of the places where he and Silas confirmed the church. Tarsus was Paul's home, and he spent time there before joining Barnabas in Antioch (9:30; 11:25). Though there is never a specific reference to a congregation in Tarsus of Cilicia, Gentile believers in Cilicia are addressed in the letter from Jerusalem (15:23), and now Paul and Silas strengthen "churches" in Syria and Cilicia.

After passing through the province of Cilicia, they traveled northwest and crossed the Taurus Mountains through a pass called the Cilician Gates. This brought them to the plain of Lycaonia, which they reached from the other direction on the first journey. Though the details of their route through the mountains are not given, the direction they took from Antioch, through Syria, Cilicia, and on to Derbe and

Lystra necessitated their passing through, or over, the mountain ranges. Certainly their logical route would be the one we have described.

Paul asks Timothy to accompany them (Acts 16:1-5):

Timothy is from Lystra:
- **Paul was stoned the first time he was in Lystra.**
- **Timothy would have known the story — if he had not seen it happen.**
- **Now Paul asks the young man to go with him as his assistant.**
- **It seems Timothy did not hesitate. His faith and courage are admirable.**

When Paul and Silas arrived at Lystra where Paul was stoned on the first journey, they found a disciple named Timothy. He was the son of a Jewess who had become a Christian, but his father was a Greek. Timothy enjoyed a good reputation, not only among the disciples at Lystra, but also in Iconium eighteen miles to the northeast.

Paul wanted Timothy to go on this journey with him. Obviously, Timothy was willing to go, but there was one problem: Timothy had never been circumcised. Paul took him and circumcised him because the Jews in the area knew his father was a Greek.

Timothy, though quite a young man at this point, became Paul's most trustworthy assistant. For the next sixteen or seventeen years, Timothy will be a companion and co-worker with Paul. As the aged apostle faced death, his last letter was to Timothy, urging him to come quickly, before winter (2 Tim. 4:9, 21a). The story of Timothy is a worthy one and his example commands our deepest admiration.

Why circumcise Timothy?
- **Paul opposed Titus' being circumcised,**
  - **Titus was a Greek with no Jewish background.**
- **But Paul insisted that Timothy be circumcised,**
  - **Timothy had been reared as a Jew,**
  - **But had never been circumcised because his father was a Greek.**

Why did Paul circumcise Timothy? Paul took Titus with him to Jerusalem for the meeting concerning circumcision and the keeping of the law. He opposed every effort to force Titus to be circumcised (Gal. 2:1, 3). Yet here Paul himself requires Timothy to be circumcised. Why the difference? The answer is that Titus was a Greek, not from a Jewish background, therefore the law of circumcision had never applied to him. Timothy had a Jewish mother, and he had been taught as a Jew (2 Tim. 3:15). He had been reared among Jews, and yet all the Jews knew he had never been circumcised because of his Greek father. It would greatly hamper their efforts among the Jews, if one of their group was of Jewish heritage, but had never been circumcised. Paul did not object to Jews living by the customs and traditions of Jews, but he <u>did</u> oppose binding those customs and traditions upon Gentiles and making them conditions of salvation.

The men delivered the decrees concerning circumcision from the apostles and elders in Jerusalem.

As the men traveled from city to city, they delivered the decrees from the apostles and elders at Jerusalem. So the churches were strengthened in their commitment to the Lord and increased in number every day.

The church continues to grow in number and in spiritual strength.

As word of the conference in Jerusalem is spread, the question of circumcision should have been settled forever, should it not? God's will had been definitely stated, and word is spreading about what that will was, but old beliefs are firmly ingrained. The question was not yet fully settled even in these congregations where the letter was delivered. It will arise again soon. Having a clear statement of God's will did not stop all arguments then, just as it does not always do so now.

Their journey so far:
- **Through Syria and Cilicia,**
- **To Derbe and Lystra,**
- **On through Phrygia and Galatia.**

They thought of preaching in the province of Asia, or perhaps north in Bithynia:
- **But the Holy Spirit urged them forward,**
    - **To the city of Troas.**

Paul sees a vision of a man from Macedonia asking for help (Acts 16:6-10):

Having been forbidden by the Holy Spirit to speak the word of the Lord in Asia, Paul and his companions traveled throughout Phrygia and Galatia, and on to the border of Mysia. From there they intended to go north into Bithynia, but the Spirit would not allow it. So, they passed just north of Mysia and came to the city of Troas.

The expressions "forbidden by the Holy Spirit," or "the Spirit suffered them not," seem a little strange at first. Did the Spirit not want the people of the provinces of Asia and Bithynia to hear the gospel? No, this was the way the Spirit chose to direct Paul's route. At this point, the Spirit had not yet revealed exactly where He wanted Paul to go, but as they approached an area and considered going there, the Spirit said, "No." Therefore, the men continued going forward until they had more specific information from the Spirit about exactly where they were needed most.

Their exact route during this early part of the journey is a little unclear. Some think Paul established several churches in northern Galatia on this trip and that the letter to the Galatians was written to those congregations. But, if so, those cities and churches are never mentioned by name in the New Testament. Most scholars discount that theory. The churches at Lystra, Derbe, and Iconium are the only ones from Galatia specifically mentioned, although Antioch of Pisidia was also a logical stopping place for Paul.

Consult your map regularly:
- **See the route Paul and his company followed as it is described.**

One other problem is that it says they traveled throughout Phrygia and Galatia as if they arrived in Phrygia first. Yet, they had traveled from the east and, according to the map, they reached Galatia first. This is another example of an old ethnic district, the borders of which were not respected when the Romans divided Asia Minor into administrative districts. A part of Phrygia was now in the province of Asia and a part of it in Galatia. After mentioning the cities of Derbe, Lystra, and Iconium in southern Galatia, Paul and his companions had to make a decision: should they go into the Roman province of Asia to preach? The Spirit said, "No." So, they kept to Phrygian Galatia (that part of the Roman province which overlapped the old district of Phrygia), and passed through Antioch of Pisidia and then across the northern part of Asia to the city of Troas.

Bithynia was a province to the north which extended to the shore of the Black Sea. Mysia was a section of the province of Asia between

The Spirit has now given them the direction to go:
- **God is sending them to preach to the people of Macedonia.**

Luke joins them at Troas. The group now includes:
- **Paul,**
- **Silas,**
- **Timothy,**
- **Luke.**

Paul did not establish the church in Troas.
- **There were saints in the city when he and his companions arrived.**

Continue to label your map.

Philippi was a Roman colony.

Adramyttium and Pergamum. Troas is a form of the name Troy and was located not far from the site of that ancient city.

During the night at Troas, Paul had a vision of a man from Macedonia earnestly begging him, "Come over into Macedonia and help us." When Paul reported his vision to the others, they all began making plans to go to Macedonia. It was now evident where God wanted them to go.

Luke joins the company at Troas because he, as the writer, begins to describe where "we" went rather than saying "they" did thus and so. This is the first "we section" of the book of Acts (16:10-17).

There was already a group of Christians in the city of Troas when Paul and his company arrived. Though there is no specific mention of a congregation at this time, Luke was there and was already one who could be a helpful companion in the work of preaching. As Paul has occasion to pass back through the city of Troas on other journeys, he worships with the saints there (20:5-11). This is further evidence that there were many others working for the Lord besides those mentioned in Luke's record.

The Aegean Sea lay between Paul's company and Macedonia. Crossing that sea would take them from the continent of Asia into Europe. Macedonia was a large province bordered on the north and east by Thrace and on the south by Achaia (Greece).

Lydia and her household are converted (Acts 16:11-15):

Setting sail from Troas, the company was able to travel straight to an island called Samothrace *(about halfway to Neapolis)* on one day, and the very next day they arrived at the seaport of Neapolis. From Neapolis they traveled along the Egnatian Way to Philippi.

The Egnatian Way was a road built by the Romans which led from Neapolis on the shore of the Aegean Sea, south through Thessalonica, and then west to the Adriatic Sea.

The city of Philippi was conquered in the fourth century B.C. by Philip of Macedon (the father of Alexander the Great) and was then named for him. In 42 B.C., the second Triumvirate of Rome (Octavian, Mark Anthony, and Lepidus) defeated Brutus and Cassius at Philippi. In commemoration, the city was made a Roman colony, which means it was regarded as a branch of Rome itself, with all the privileges that would entail.

After a few days in Philippi, Paul's company went out of the gate to a location by the river *(Gangites)* where it was said there was a place of prayer. When they arrived, they found some women gathered and they sat down with them and taught them.

Lydia:

- **A seller of purple, from Thyatira.**
- **Probably relatively wealthy, since she was in a business supplying only the rich.**
- **No husband is mentioned.**
    - **Lydia seems to be the one in business.**
- **Almost certainly, her household consisted of her servants and assistants.**
    - **She was meeting at the place of prayer with a group of *women*.**

One of the women, Lydia, who was a dealer in purple dye and cloth from Thyatira, was a worshiper of God. She listened to the preaching of Paul, and the Lord opened her heart to respond to the things spoken. When she and her household were baptized, she said, "If you judge that I am faithful to the Lord, come to my house and remain there," and she persuaded them to stay.

Since Paul went out to the riverside to find a group of people meeting for prayer, there must have been no Jewish synagogue in Philippi. It took ten Jewish men to organize a synagogue. That there were not that many Jewish men in Philippi may be because Claudius had already ordered the expulsion of Jews from Rome (A.D. 49). As a Roman colony, Philippi, learning of the emperor's actions, probably expelled the Jews from its borders. No Jew is mentioned in the story. Lydia was a proselyte of the gate, that is, a worshiper of God (16:14). The other women were likely proselytes as well. It is commendable that, though Lydia was far from home, she did not neglect the worship of God.

It seems there was no Jewish synagogue in Philippi.

- **It took ten Jewish men to have a synagogue in a city.**

Thyatira was the main city and a colony in the old territory known as Lydda (the kingdom of Lydda), now in the province of Asia. The main item of business in the whole area was purple dye and the cloth dyed with it. Thyatira was known as the source of the most superior dye of all. The dye was very expensive because only a drop of it could be secured from each shellfish. A cheaper product was made by crushing the fish. Only the rich could afford the clothes dyed with the purple (see Luke 16:19). The Romans trimmed their white togas with it and used it to color rugs and tapestries. Lydia was probably wealthy since she was in a business supplying only the very rich.

Look at what Lydia and her household did when they heard Paul preach.

There is much curiosity about Lydia, but almost no answers. We must be content with the facts given. Certainly it was a blessing for Paul, Silas, Timothy, and Luke to have a place where they could stay as they taught the word.

Combination of the Great Commission:	**Lydia and her household:**
Preach/ teach	Paul and his companions preached (16:13).
He that believeth	Lydia opened her heart, she believed (16:14).
Repentance	
And is baptized/ baptizing them	She and her household were baptized (16:15).
Shall be saved/ remission of sins	
Teach to observe all things commanded	Luke stayed behind with this group (16:40). Paul visited again (20:1-2, 6), and wrote them a letter.

Paul casts out a spirit of divination and is put in prison (Acts 16:16-24):

The unclean spirits always knew Jesus,
- **But neither Jesus nor the apostles wanted the testimony of the unclean spirits (see Mark 1:23-26).**

As the company of men traveled to the place of prayer, a certain girl met them who had a divining spirit. She made much money for her masters by telling fortunes. For many days she followed after Paul and his friends, crying out, "These men are servants of the Most High God; they tell you the way of salvation."

Finally, Paul could stand it no longer, so he turned and said to the spirit, "I charge you in the name of Jesus Christ to come out of her." At that very moment, it came out.

"Spirit of divination" means "the kind of spirit known as a Python." Opinions about this spirit are divided into the usual two categories:
- *Some say she did not really have a spirit at all, but rather a mental condition in which she thought she had a supernatural power to predict. This condition made her unusually sensitive to her surroundings so that she could pretend to tell the future.*
  - *Consistently, cases of spirit or demon possession are treated as real in the Bible.*
    - *Paul addressed the spirit himself, not a mental condition (16:18).*
    - *He "charged" the spirit, speaking in the second person, to come out of her. It, that is, the spirit, came out.*
    - *The only logical conclusion is that the spirit did exist.*
  - *In cases of demon possession:*
    - *The demon might give the victim strength which he would not normally have (see Mark 5:4); or cause seizures such as epilepsy might have caused (Mark 9:14-29); or other maladies (Mark 1:21-28).*
    - *The demon never gave special powers for his victim's benefit; instead, the demon used the powers to afflict the possessed.*
  - *The demons recognized Jesus in a way that the victim could not have done had he not been possessed (see Mark 5:7-12).*

Demon possession in the New Testament:
- **Was always treated as real, not some mental condition.**
- **God allowed Satan power to directly intervene, and to send his demons into people during the era when God was demonstrating His power through miracles.**
- **God's power was always superior when they came into direct conflict.**

- *Others say the girl had a spirit which possessed her and made her behave in a peculiar fashion, which enabled her masters to exploit her as a soothsayer.*
  - *Some would argue that this maiden could actually prophesy by the power of the spirit within her.*
    - *However, the text does not mention prophesying, but divination and soothsaying, both of which fall into the modern category of fortune-telling with a crystal ball or tarot cards.*
  - *If Satan could give the power to do miracles, then it would be pretty much a stand-off between his followers and God's.*

True prophecy:

- **The ability to predict the future with certainty:**
  - **Is a power belonging to Deity alone.**

This girl was demon-possessed,

- **And was being exploited to satisfy the greed of her masters.**

- *The miracles done by Jesus and by His apostles were designed to prove that they spoke for God, by God's power (John 20:30, 31; Mark 16:17-20).*
- *God treated the ability to foretell the future as a power peculiar to Deity.*
  - *Through Isaiah He challenged the false gods: "Let them bring forth, and declare unto us what shall happen: declare ye the former things, what they are, that we may consider them, and know the latter end of them; or show us things to come. Declare the things that are to come hereafter, that we may know that ye are gods" (Isa. 41:22-23).*
  - *According to this passage, if Satan could give men the power to foretell the future accurately, then he could give them the power to prove he is God.*

Source of this persecution:

- **It came from Gentiles,**
  - **But it started over a local dispute.**
- **The angry masters of the girl took Paul to the magistrates.**
  - **But notice they changed the charge.**
  - **Instead of admitting their selfish interest,**
    - **They pretended these men were in conflict with Roman laws.**
- **The Roman government had not set out to persecute them.**

Therefore, to summarize, this maiden definitely was possessed by a demon, one that made her able to give an impressive show of soothsaying, but not one that gave her one of the prerogatives of Deity. Her masters were exploiting her peculiarities for their own greed.

When the girl's masters saw that their hope of making money was gone, they seized Paul and Silas and dragged them into the marketplace before the rulers and the magistrates. There they charged, "These men, who are Jews, are stirring up our city exceedingly. They are proclaiming customs which are not legal for us to receive or to practice, since we are Romans."

A mob had gathered by this time, and a tumult arose against Paul and Silas. The magistrates were swept away by the frenzy and made no further investigation. Paul and Silas were stripped, and the magistrates commanded that they be beaten with rods. When they had been beaten severely, they were cast into prison, and the magistrates ordered the jailer to keep them securely. So the jailer took them into the innermost prison, the dungeon, and fastened their feet in stocks.

The jailer is converted (Acts 16:25-34):

Paul and Silas were praying and singing praises to God:

- **In the middle of the night, in a dungeon, and in stocks!**
- **No wonder the other prisoners were listening.**

In spite of their uncomfortable situation, about midnight, Paul and Silas were praying and singing songs of praise to God, and the prisoners were listening to them. Suddenly there was a severe earthquake which shook the very foundations of the prison. Immediately, all the doors sprang open and everyone's fetters came loose.

When the jailer was awakened from his sleep, he saw the prison doors open, and he supposed all the prisoners had escaped. Since the Roman officials would hold him accountable for the security of his prisoners, he drew his sword to kill himself, but Paul shouted, "Do not kill yourself, because we are all here."

"Sirs, what must I do to be saved?"

"Believe on the Lord Jesus Christ, and you shall be saved, you and your household."

Observe what the jailer and his household did in order to be saved.

Calling for lights to be brought, the jailer rushed in and, trembling with fear, fell down before Paul and Silas. He brought them out of the dungeon and asked, "Sirs, what must I do to be saved?"

Paul and Silas answered, "Believe on the Lord Jesus Christ, and you and your house will be saved." Then they taught the Lord's word to him and to all who were in his house. The jailer took them the same hour of the night and washed their stripes; then he and his family were baptized immediately. He brought them into his house and set food before them and rejoiced greatly with all his house.

Since none of the prisoners had escaped, the jailer was in no danger from the Romans. What did he wish to be saved from? Surely the salvation he craved was more than some kind of physical salvation. Obviously it was a salvation he felt he needed badly, because he fell before Paul and Silas trembling with fear. Paul answered him as if he questioned them about spiritual salvation. The subsequent actions of the jailer point in that direction as well.

Where did he learn about any such spiritual need? The text does not say, but there are many possibilities. He may have heard about the preaching that had been done for "many days" (16:18a). He may have been impressed by the demeanor of Paul and Silas in their suffering. He may have listened to their singing before he went to sleep and learned of salvation. We are not told.

Combination of the Great Commission:	**The Jailer and his household:**
Preach/ teach	Paul and Silas spoke the word of the Lord to him and to all the others in his house (16:32).
He that believeth	"Believe on the Lord Jesus Christ..." (16:31).
Repentance	He washed their wounds, and fed them before taking them back to the prison (16:33a, 34).
And is baptized/ baptizing them	Immediately he and his household were baptized (16:33b).
Shall be saved/ remission of sins	They were all filled with joy because they now believed in God (16:34).
Teach to observe all things commanded	Luke remained with this group (16:40); Paul visited again (20:1, 6); Paul wrote the book of Philippians to them.

Paul and Silas are released from prison (Acts 16:35-40):

When it was daylight, the magistrates sent officers to the prison with the word: "Let these men go."

Why the apparent change in plans on the part of the magistrates? The text does not say. Perhaps they thought the punishment was sufficient; or the magistrates may have realized they had over-reacted and decided to let the matter drop. These officers who were sent to release Paul and Silas were lictors. Each one carried a bundle of rods, from which protruded a mace or hammer. These were the symbols of Roman authority.

Paul's Roman citizenship was to his distinct advantage:

- **Though it had not spared him from receiving the beating that came as a result of mob action,**
  - **He was now treated with respect as he is released from prison.**
- **He will never again be in danger from these magistrates as he visits the city on future occasions.**

The jailer brought word to Paul: "The magistrates have sent to let you go. Come out now, and go in peace."

But Paul said, "We are Romans, and they have beaten us publicly, without a trial, and have thrown us into prison. Now they think they can just put us forth privately. No way! Let them come themselves and bring us out."

When the officers reported to the magistrates, they were frightened to learn that Paul and Silas were Romans. So they came and escorted them from the prison, begging them to leave the city.

Paul and Silas did leave the prison this time and went back to the house of Lydia. There they met with the brethren and encouraged them, and then left the city.

The magistrates were guilty of serious crimes. One of the advantages of Roman citizenship was that it protected one from the more vicious and cruel forms of punishment used by the Romans, such as beatings and crucifixion. Even when a Roman citizen was tried and found guilty of a crime, he might be exiled, or beheaded, but he could not be beaten or crucified. Paul was not about to let the Roman officials off this easily. His sense of justice and fair play forbade it. His actions were also in the interests of the believers who lived in Philippi. The church at Philippi was composed almost altogether of Gentiles, and many of them were probably Romans. The magistrates would be slow about condemning another one of the group without careful questioning of the charges.

Luke stays in Philippi as the others leave town.

- **Watch for him here later**.

Timothy is not mentioned in the events at Thessalonica.

Notice that Luke uses the expression "they" left the city (16:40). Luke stayed behind, and we will find him still at Philippi some years later. Therefore he was with the group only from the time he joined them in Troas (16:10) through their time in Philippi.

The congregation at Philippi was strong through the rest of the New Testament, no doubt, a testimony to Luke's influence there.

Paul preaches in Thessalonica (Acts 17:1-9):

So far as the record goes, they did not stop to preach in Amphipolis or Apollonia.

The small group of evangelists made their way to Amphipolis, 33 miles southwest of Philippi, and from there to Apollonia, 28 miles southwest of Amphipolis. They continued along the Egnatian way until they came to Thessalonica, 40 miles almost due west of Apollonia.

This Jesus whom I preach to you is the Christ:

- **He is the fulfillment of the plan of God.**

At Thessalonica Paul found a synagogue of the Jews and, as he usually did, he went there and for three sabbath days reasoned with them from the scriptures. He affirmed and offered proof that it was necessary in the plan of God for our salvation that the Christ should suffer and rise again from the dead. He affirmed, "This Jesus whom I preach unto you is the Christ, the Messiah."

This persecution began with Jews who did not believe Paul's preaching about the Christ:

- **But when they reached the local authorities, their charge was of treason:**
  - **"these men proclaim another king..."**
- **This time the charge did not hold.**
- **The officials allowed the brethren to go free,**
  - **But the charge was a serious one in the eyes of the Romans.**

Some of the Jews were persuaded, plus many of the God-fearing Greeks and prominent women. But the unbelieving Jews were provoked to jealousy and gathered vicious men from the rabble in the marketplace and formed a mob. They created a riot and assaulted the house of a man named Jason, trying to find Paul and Silas. When they could not find them, they dragged Jason and certain other brethren before the rulers of the city and said, "These fellows who have been turning the world upside down have come here also, and Jason has let them stay at his house. All of them behave contrary to Caesar's decrees because they say there is another king, a man named Jesus."

These accusations were very disturbing to the multitude and to the rulers. However, the rulers in this case *(unlike those at Philippi)* acted with restraint. They allowed Jason and the others to make bail and go their way.

Paul and Silas go to Berea (Acts 17:10-15):

The Jews of Berea heard the message gladly and searched the scriptures to see if the message were true.

The brethren at Thessalonica, fearing for Paul and Silas, sent them away by night. They traveled fifty miles southwest to Berea, where they promptly went into a synagogue of the Jews. They found these Jews more noble than those in Thessalonica in that they were willing to hear what Paul and Silas had to say, and then they searched the scriptures to see whether the things they had heard were true. Many of the Jews believed, as well as many of the prominent Greek men and women *(God-fearers)*.

Unbelieving Jews from Thessalonica went to Berea to try to stop the preaching:

- **Just as Jews from Antioch and Iconium caused Paul to be stoned at Lystra on the first journey (see Acts 14:19).**

Nevertheless, when the unbelieving Jews of Thessalonica heard that Paul was preaching God's word at Berea, they went there to stir up and to trouble the multitude. Immediately, therefore, the brethren sent Paul on his way to the sea, while Silas and Timothy stayed in Berea. Paul's escorts took him as far as Athens, where he told them to send Silas and Timothy to him as quickly as possible. His escort returned home and Paul was left alone in Athens.

Review this second journey so far.

There is considerable movement back and forth from Philippi to Corinth during this time, but Luke's references to such movements are incidental. We can be fairly confident about these movements by comparing passages in Acts, Philippians, and 1 Thessalonians.

- *Since Luke includes himself in the journey from Troas to Philippi (Acts 16:10-17), but does not include himself with the group leaving Philippi (16:40), it is assumed he remained there.*
- *Timothy may have remained in Philippi also for a short time.*
    - *There is no mention of Timothy in the passage telling of Paul and Silas among the Thessalonians (Acts 17:1-9).*
    - *Also, from Philippi someone brought an offering, or gift, for Paul "once and again" even while he was at Thessalonica (Phil. 4:15-16).*
        - *Who brought the offering, went back, and brought another?*
        - *The most likely candidate is Timothy.*
    - *From Thessalonica, Paul and Silas went on to Berea (Acts 17:10).*
        - *There is still no mention of Timothy.*
        - *At some point, however, Timothy joined them at Berea because when Paul was forced to leave the city, Silas and Timothy remained behind (17:14).*
        - *Paul sent instructions back from Athens that they should join him as quickly as possible.*
        - *There is no mention in Acts of their joining him in Athens, but there is evidence in the epistles that they joined him briefly, because he decided it would be better to be left alone in Athens than to be worried and uninformed about the condition of the brethren they had left behind in the little new congregations.*
            - *So Paul sent Timothy back to Thessalonica to check on the brethren there (1 Thess. 3:1-2).*
- *No specific facts are given about where Silas was while Timothy went back to Thessalonica.*
    - *But Paul was alone in Athens, so Silas was not with him.*
    - *Silas and Timothy joined Paul in Corinth when they "came down from Macedonia" (Acts 18:5).*
    - *Three churches having been recently established in Macedonia: Philippi, Thessalonica, and Berea.*
        - *Luke was at Philippi,*
        - *Timothy was at Thessalonica,*
        - *So the logical conclusion is to suppose that Silas went to Berea.*
        - *If that is true, then one of Paul's company was at each one of the new congregations established so far on this second journey.*
    - *When Timothy had completed his work at Thessalonica, he came through Berea where Silas probably joined him, and together they went to Corinth to join Paul.*

Actions of Paul's companions at this time:

- **Luke stayed in Philippi.**
- **Timothy:**
    - **No mention is made of Timothy's being in Thessalonica with the others (v. 10),**
        - **But he is with them in Berea by verse 14.**
    - **Timothy may have taken a gift (or gifts) from Philippi to Thessalonica,**
        - **Then joined Paul and Silas in Berea.**
- **Silas:**
    - **Was with Paul while he was in Thessalonica and Berea,**
    - **But he stayed behind when Paul was taken to Athens.**
- **Paul sent for Silas and Timothy:**
    - **Indications are that when they joined him, he sent them back to the new congregations:**
        - **Timothy to Thessalonica,**
        - **And probably Silas to Berea.**
- **Paul was alone in Athens.**
    - **Timothy and Silas join Paul again in Corinth.**

- *Their arrival in Corinth is described in Acts 18:5 and in 1 Thessalonians 3:6.*

Athens was the cultural center of the Greek way of life:

- **Which was based upon human wisdom.**

Important places in Athens:

- **The Acropolis:**
    - **An upper fortified part of a Greek city, on a natural or a man-made hill;**
    - **The city's civic and religious center.**
- **The Agora:**
    - **The public market place in ancient cities;**
    - **People gathered to buy and sell goods, to exchange news and information, to seek work for the day, or to do any number of other things one might do in a public gathering place.**
- **Mars Hill or Areopagus:**
    - **An out-cropping of rocks, 370 feet high, on the northwest side of the acropolis.**
    - **Named for the god Ares, or Mars.**
    - **The seat of the Greek Council in Athens.**
    - **Name for both the hill and the council.**
    - **The agora was just below it on the north side.**

Historical Note about Athens:

As Jerusalem had been the center of a way of life built around the revelation of God, Athens was the center of a way of life based upon philosophy and human wisdom. Athens' heyday was during the fifth century before Christ. Though Athens was still the philosophical and cultural center of the Roman world, Corinth had become the political capital of the province of Achaia (Greece).

Athens was about five miles northeast of the Saronic Gulf in the Aegean Sea. Its seaport was Piraeus. Connecting the two cities was a road about two miles long, which ran between two walls about two hundred yards apart. Greek writers tell of the many altars which were built along this road. Petronius, a Roman writer, wrote that in Athens it was easier to find a god than a man.

The city was scattered around the base of a hill five hundred feet high called the acropolis. Several temples, including the Parthenon, were built on this acropolis. The agora, or public marketplace, was north of the hill. Mars Hill, or the Areopagus, was on the western side.

Athens was filled with art, but most of it was connected with idolatry. Paul did not, therefore, admire the art. Instead his heart was stirred within him at the idolatry he saw on every side.

Two schools of philosophy in Athens are mentioned specifically: the Epicureans and the Stoics. The philosophy of the Epicurean originated with a man named Epicurus (340-272 B.C.). The Epicurean philosophy was humanistic: that is, that human beings are the greatest beings in existence. According to this philosophy, the world was formed by a chance combination of matter. While the Epicurean did not totally disbelieve in the gods, he believed them to be shadow beings who had no impact upon the world. At death, life and consciousness were over. Therefore, the highest aim for man was gratification of his every desire. Pleasure was the goal of life.

The founder of Stoicism was Zeno (336-260 B.C.). At the famous Painted Porch, or Stoa, he taught his followers; hence his philosophy came to be known as Stoicism. The Stoics possessed a higher moral code than that of the Epicurean. They condemned the worship of idols and the use of temples. Their god was the "Spirit of Reason" which gives order to the universe. The Stoics made strong efforts to be guided by neither pleasure nor pain, but by reason. They did not view pleasure as good, or pain as evil. Often the philosophy led its followers to commit suicide when reason saw no further value to life.

Two Greek philosophies:

- **Epicurean:**
  - **The highest aim for man was gratification of every desire.**
- **Stoic:**
  - **The Spirit of Reason gave order to the universe,**
  - **Therefore they tried to be guided only by reason rather than pleasure or pain.**

There was a synagogue of Jews in Athens:

- **Though it was such a center of Greek culture.**

In their minds, Paul was preaching about a demon:

- **Jesus, a "man-God."**

Paul spoke about the God which the Athenians admitted they worshiped in ignorance:

- **The true God:**
  - **Being the creator of all things,**
  - **He is completely independent of men,**
  - **He does not *need* anything men have.**
- **Instead, men are totally dependent upon God for their existence.**
- **God rules in the affairs of men.**
- **The conduct of God among men is calculated to draw men to seek Him,**
  - **Though He is not far away from each one.**

Paul reasons with Jews and with Gentile philosophers in Athens (Acts 17:16-21):

While waiting for Silas and Timothy, Paul's spirit was provoked. Instead of admiring the "art" of Athens, he was so full of indignation and spiritual outrage he could not forbear when he saw the city full of idols.

See Deuteronomy 7:26. The Israelites were told to abhor, to detest the gold, silver, or other precious materials they found in the idols of the wicked Canaanites. So Paul abhorred the trappings of idolatry in wicked Athens.

Paul reasoned with Jews and God-fearers in the synagogue, and in the marketplace with those who met there. As time went along, he began to have discussions with the Epicurean and the Stoic philosophers.

Some said, "What is this seed-picker *(this babbler)* talking about?" Others said, "He appears to be setting forth foreign demons." This was said because he preached Jesus and the resurrection.

Among Greeks a demon was not necessarily, or even primarily, an evil being, but one who was intermediate between god and men. A demon was not fully god, but neither was he fully human. From the standpoint of their imperfect understanding, they judged Jesus to be one of these demons.

Paul's audience grew in curiosity until they took him to the Areopagus (Mars' Hill) and said to him, "May we find out what this new teaching is that you are talking about? You have brought some strange ideas to our attention; we would therefore like to know what these things mean." For all the Athenians and their visitors had time for nothing except to tell or to hear some new thing.

Paul's speech on Mars Hill (Acts 17:22-31):

Paul stood up in the Areopagus and said:

> You men of Athens, I can tell that you are unusually religious, because as I passed along and observed your objects of worship, I found an altar with this inscription: "To the unknown God." What you therefore confess to worship in ignorance, I wish to tell you about.
>
> The God who made the world and everything in it, since He is ruler of heaven and earth, does not live in temples made with hands. Neither is He cared for as a patient, as if He needed anything, since He gives to everything life and breath and all things.

- **Since we are the offspring of God,**
    - **Do not conceive of God as an object of gold or silver or stone shaped by men's tools and art.**
- **God commands that all men everywhere should repent.**
    - **The reason: God will judge all men by the one He has chosen, Jesus Christ.**
    - **He demonstrated that Christ is His choice to be Judge by raising Him from the dead.**

From one man He made every nation of men to dwell on the face of the entire world, having determined the times of their existence and the extent of their territories. He did all this so that they should seek for Him, if indeed they might feel after Him and find Him. Indeed, He is not far from each one of us, for in Him we live, and move, and have our very existence, as certain of your own poets have said, "For we are also His offspring."

Since we are the offspring of God, we ought not to think that the Divine Being is something made of gold, or silver, or stone, carved and shaped by man's abilities and tools.

In times past, God allowed the ignorance of man to continue, but now He commands that all men everywhere should repent, because He has appointed a day in which He will judge the world in righteousness by the man He has chosen. Furthermore, He has certified this One as His choice by raising Him from the dead.

The results of Paul's speech (Acts 17:32-34):

When the philosophers heard Paul speak of the resurrection of the dead, some mocked, but others said, "We will hear you concerning this another time."

So Paul went out from among them. But certain ones were closely drawn to him and believed. Among those who believed were Dionysius, one of the council members, and a woman named Damaris, and some others.

The sermons in Acts were effective because they took into account the differences in the background of the audiences.

- **To Gentile audiences:**
    - **God is identified as the Creator of the universe.**
- **To Jewish audiences:**
    - **God is identified as the God of their fathers, the One who brought them out of Egypt.**

The results of Paul's work in Athens seem to have been meager. There is nothing said of multitudes of converts. Just a few seem to have been reached. We have no way of knowing what became of them. The New Testament never speaks of a church in Athens, but one of the early church fathers does. There is never again a specific mention of Paul's visiting the city, nor does the Bible mention a saint from there.

A survey of the different lessons taught in the book of Acts shows that, while the basic facts about God and the gospel are the same, each audience had its own peculiar background and circumstances. The sermons recorded in Acts were very effective because they took those differences into account. Compare the appeal to the Jewish prophets in speeches made to Jewish audiences (Acts 2, 3, 7, 13), and the lack of such references in speeches made before Gentiles (Acts 14:15-17; 17:22-31). Before Gentile audiences, God is identified as the Creator of heaven and earth, while before Jewish audiences, He is identified as the God who called "our father Abraham," or the God who "led our fathers out of Egypt."

Paul preaches in Corinth

Review this second journey so far.

Paul arrives in Corinth (Acts 18:1-4):

Still alone, Paul traveled forty miles west of Athens to Corinth, the capital of Achaia. There he met a Jewish man named Aquila with his wife Priscilla. Aquila, though a native of Pontus, had lived until recently in Italy. But the emperor Claudius had expelled the Jews from Rome, so Priscilla and Aquila had come to Corinth. Paul found it convenient to live with them for a time because they worked at the same trade as Paul — tent-making. Every sabbath Paul reasoned in the synagogues, seeking to persuade both Jews and Greeks *(God-fearers).*

Aquila and Priscilla:
- **Tent-makers with Paul**

Map Assignment:
Find and label:
- **Pontus**
- **Italy**
- **Corinth**

The emperor Claudius (A.D. 41-54) was a reasonable ruler who sought to respect the Jews' peculiar beliefs and practices; but when they continued to be involved in one dispute after another, Claudius showed that he could deal harshly. The trouble in Rome centered around one named Chrestus, according to the Roman historian Suetonius (who wrote in A.D. 120). Many have assumed that Chrestus was a variation of Christ ("Christos" in Greek), and this was, therefore, trouble and persecution against Christians. This theory does not fit, however. It would have Jews rioting in disputes with Christians in A.D. 49, and yet, twelve years later, when Paul arrives as a prisoner in Rome, he invites the Jews over for a discussion and finds them without rancor or ill-will. Instead they show a remarkable interest in hearing what Paul had to say: "We desire to hear of thee what thou thinkest: for as concerning this sect, it is known to us that everywhere it is spoken against" (Acts 28:22). It seems they had very little first hand information about "this sect" at that point.

Claudius is still emperor:
- **He is first mentioned as emperor in Acts 11:28.**
- **Ruled from A.D. 41-54.**
- **He expelled Jews from Rome in A.D. 49.**

It is uncertain whether Aquila and Priscilla were Christians before Paul met them. Usually Luke identifies people as disciples, if they are. We presume, therefore, that Aquila and Priscilla were not. Paul got acquainted with them at first because they shared the same occupation. They were, no doubt, soon converted to Christ, because they are certainly a strong influence for good very soon in the story.

The tents of that day were made of leather, or linen, or a cloth woven from goats' hair. Most of the tents, by far, were made of the goats' hair. The fabric was black and could shed the water of the hardest rains. Most authorities say that it was a lucrative trade. It was certainly an ideal trade for a traveler such as Paul.

Whether Paul converted Aquila and Priscilla, or found them already Christians, they soon become great assets in the Lord's work.

Historical Note about Corinth:

Though it was not famous for its philosophers, Corinth was well known for its industry and trade, and for its pursuit of immoral vices. A "Corinthian" came to mean a playboy without morals. "To Corinthianize" was a Greek expression which meant to spend one's

Corinth was well known for:
- **Its industry,**
- **Its trade,**
- **Its immoral vices.**

time with harlots. Other terms were also used which show how this city was identified with such ungodly activities.

Corinth was a Roman colony:
- **As Philippi was.**

Corinth was destroyed and sacked by the Roman general Mummius in 146 B.C. A century later, it was rebuilt by Julius Caesar and given the status of a colony. A temple to the goddess Venus, or Aphrodite, existed in the old city, with a thousand female slaves who served as priestesses to commit ritual fornication with those who came to worship the goddess of love and fertility. A new temple was built to Aphrodite in the new city, and, although we have no figures on the number of priestesses involved, it is certain that the same practice was carried on there.

Corinth commanded the trade routes of the Mediterranean.
- **Study your map:**
  - **See the location of Corinth, its isthmus, and its ports.**

Corinth commanded the trade routes of the Mediterranean. Ships from all countries docked at her harbors. Situated on an isthmus connecting the Peloponnesus with the mainland, Corinth was served by two harbors. Cenchrea, its eastern seaport, opened into the Saronic Gulf and into the Aegean Sea; while Lechaeum, its western seaport, opened into the Adriatic Sea. Through these ports the trade passed which made Corinth a wealthy city. Corinthian brass was highly prized and famous over the Roman world.

Paul converts many of the Corinthians (Acts 18:5-11):

Jesus is the Christ, the Messiah!

Your blood be upon your own heads!
- **I have no more responsibility on your behalf.**
- **I turn to the Gentiles.**

"Many of the Corinthians:"
- **Included idolaters, fornicators, homosexuals, thieves, and drunkards:**
  - **Who were not associated with the synagogue,**
  - **But were converted from their paganism.**
  - **(See 1 Corinthians 6:9-11).**

When Silas and Timothy came down from Macedonia, Paul was compelled by the message he proclaimed to testify that Jesus was the Christ. When the Jews refused to accept the evidence, and ranted and raved against the Lord's cause, Paul shook the lap of his robe and told them, "You are now guilty of your own blood. I am free of any fault in the matter. From now on I am going to the Gentiles."

He left the synagogue and moved his operations into the house of a man named Titus Justus, a God-fearer who became a Christian. His house was next door to the synagogue. Crispus, the ruler of the synagogue, also believed in the Lord with all his house. And many of the Corinthians, hearing the gospel, believed and were baptized.

Paul had been reasoning in the synagogue every sabbath, seeking to persuade both Jews and Greeks. When Silas and Timothy joined him, he began to do more than merely persuade. He asserted that Jesus was the Christ. Thus it became necessary for the Jews either to believe or to disbelieve — to accept or reject.

There are secular sources of information which indicate Titus Justus may have been from a very prominent family. He was a proselyte of the gate, meaning that he was not circumcised and did not accept the many ceremonial restrictions of the law, but he was a believer in God. It must have seemed a severe blow to the Jews to lose one of their most prominent proselytes and a ruler of the synagogue at one time.

We should not conclude that the Jewish synagogues had only one ruler. There is too much evidence to the contrary, both in the Bible and out of it, to believe that idea (Mark 5:22; Acts 13:15). Crispus was one of the rulers, or elders of the synagogue. There was an official called an archisynagogos who was a sort of presiding elder. Some say he may have exercised sole authority. Crispus could have been such an official.

Paul stayed in Corinth for a year and a half.

Notice what the Corinthians did when they heard Paul's message.

The Lord spoke to Paul one night in a vision and said, "Do not be afraid. Go ahead and speak freely. Do not remain silent, because I am with you, and no one will attack you to cause you harm, because I have many people in this city."

So Paul remained in Corinth for a year and a half, teaching the word of God among the people.

Combination of the Great Commission:	Titus Justus, Crispus, and many of the Corinthians:
Preach/ teach	Paul preached, testifying that Jesus is the Christ and many of the Corinthians heard him (18:5, 7, 8).
He that believeth	They believed (18:8)
Repentance	"Such were some of you..." (1 Cor. 6:9-11)
And is baptized/ baptizing them	They were baptized (18:8)
Shall be saved/ remission of sins	"Washed... sanctified... justified..." (1 Cor. 6:11)
Teach to observe all things commanded	Paul stayed a year and a half (18:11); he wrote two letters to them (1 & 2 Corinthians); and he spent the winter with them at the end of his third journey (Acts 20:1-2; 1 Cor. 16:6).

The Epistles Begin

Difference between the sermons and epistles:
- **Sermons given orally first.**
- **Epistles were written from the first.**

We have come to the time of the writing of the first epistle by Paul. The only difference between the epistles and the sermons we have studied in Acts is that originally the sermons were given orally and the epistles were written from the first. Luke, the historian, recorded a summary of the various sermons, and we have taken time to note the exact points made in each sermon. Now, in the epistles, Paul writes letters to specific congregations, or to individuals, and makes the points that are needed for that particular group. The epistles are letters, intended to be treated as whole thoughts, not dissected under a microscope. We understand their message best when we look at them as a whole —as a sermon expressing particular thoughts.

These letters can be analyzed for their exact points just as surely as the sermons recorded in the book of Acts can be analyzed. Do not bog down in the details in each verse. A detailed study is beyond the scope of this particular study of the New Testament.

Summary of 1 Thessalonians

First Thessalonians:
- **The first recorded epistle written by Paul.**
- **Written from Corinth when Timothy joined Paul after being at Thessalonica.**
- **Date: A.D. 51 or 52.**

It was at this time, when Timothy and Silas came from Macedonia to join Paul at Corinth, that the apostle wrote his first letter to the Thessalonians. It was a letter to newly converted Christians, from the man who was responsible for their learning the truth. Think what you would have wanted to say to these Christians if you had been Paul; and also think of the joy you would have felt to receive a letter from Paul if you had been a saint at Thessalonica.

As you study the book, be alert to the times Paul mentions their persecutions. This particular little new congregation was facing an unusual degree of persecution from those in their own city. Paul is worried about their ability to remain faithful. Remember that when the Jews stirred up a mob in Thessalonica and they came before the rulers, they made the charge that these people were "proclaiming another king —Jesus" (Acts 17:6-8). Such a charge sounded like treason. Therefore, the rulers would be quick to listen to any charge against these saints.

Let us see exactly what Paul wrote to these brethren.

The letter says:
- **We thank God that you turned from idols to God (1:2-10):**
  - **You were converted in spite of great affliction.**
  - **Now you serve as examples to others.**

Paul, Silas, and Timothy to the church at Thessalonica:

- We thank God that you turned from idols to God (1:2-10):

  We thank God for you continually, bearing in mind your work of faith, your labor of love, and your steadfastness of hope in our Lord Jesus Christ. Beloved of God, we know of His choice of you, because our gospel did not come to you in vain. It came in power, and in the Holy Spirit, and with full conviction. You became imitators of us and of the Lord, in that you were converted amidst much tribulation and in much joy. And now you serve as examples to all the believers in Macedonia and Achaia. We do not need to tell others how you received us, because they tell us how you turned from idols to serve the living and true God, and to wait for His Son from heaven.

The point of imitation Paul is emphasizing here is that the Thessalonians had faced affliction in their conversion, just as Paul had, as saints who had been converted elsewhere, and as the Lord Himself had faced affliction. They were, therefore, imitators of others who had chosen to serve God in spite of severe opposition. It is a way of telling them they are not alone in their suffering.

- **Our coming to you was not in vain (2:1-16):**
    - **You know how we conducted ourselves in your midst.**
    - **You responded by accepting the gospel as God's word, not our own.**
    - **You became imitators of the churches of Judea.**

- Our coming to you was not in vain *(that is, we did not fail)* (2:1-16):

Though we were mistreated at Philippi, we came to you with boldness, to speak the gospel to you in spite of much opposition. Our preaching to you was never of error, or impurity, or deceit. We did not seek to please men, but God; we did not use flattering words, nor did we preach out of greed. We did not seek glory from you or from anyone else, though we could have been a burden to you as apostles of Christ. Instead we were gentle with you as a nursing mother with her child. You know how we worked night and day to keep from being a burden to you. We behaved devoutly, uprightly, and blamelessly among you. As a father exhorts his own children, we encouraged you to walk in a manner worthy of the God who calls you. You responded by receiving our message, not as man's word, but as God's word, which it truly is.

You have also become imitators of the churches of Judea, because, as they have had to suffer at the hands of their own countrymen, so have you. The Jews killed Jesus, and the prophets, and drove us out. They are filling up the full measure of their sins, and God's wrath will come upon them.

It would have been easy for Paul and his companions to have been intimidated by their experience at Philippi to the point that they were afraid to preach, but they did not let their experiences stop them. He wants the Thessalonians to have the same determination.

- **I was worried lest persecution make you give up (2:17-3:10):**
    - **I was so worried I sent Timothy.**
    - **He has returned with a good report,**
        - **So I am comforted.**

- I was worried lest persecution make you give up (2:17-3:10):

I, Paul, wanted to come to you, but Satan has stopped us (*likely through the continuing persecutions that drove Paul on to the next city and did not permit him to go back*). Do you know what is our hope, our joy, our crown of rejoicing? It is you. You are our glory and our joy. When I could stand it no longer, I thought it best that I be left alone in Athens, and I sent Timothy to you to strengthen and encourage you.

We hope no man will be disturbed by these afflictions. When we were with you, we told you that we would suffer affliction. But I was afraid the tempter might have tempted you and our labor might have been for nothing.

But now Timothy has returned from you, and he tells us good news about your faith and love. So we are comforted, for we really live if you stand firm in the Lord. Therefore we pray night and day that we may see your face and may complete what is lacking in your faith.

- **May the Lord establish you (3:11-13).**

- May the Lord establish you (3:11-13):

May the Lord direct our way to you. May the Lord make you to increase and to abound in love for one another, and may He establish your hearts blameless in holiness before our God and Father at the time when the Lord Jesus Christ comes again with all His saints.

- **Walk so as to please God (4:1-12):**
    - **Conversion means a special kind of life.**
    - **Live quietly and take care of your own affairs.**

- Walk so as to please God (4:1-12):

  You received instructions from us about how to walk and to please God. Now we exhort you to abound more and more. God's will is for you to live special lives: Abstain from sexual immorality; do not take advantage of or cheat your brother in any way, because the Lord is the avenger of all wrongs. God did not call us to live immorally, but to be holy.

  You already show your love for your brethren, but do it more and more. Work to live a quiet life, to take care of your own affairs, to work with your own hands, so that you may walk properly before those who are outside of Christ, and that you may lack nothing.

- **Those who have died in Christ are safe (4:13-18):**
    - **They will return with Jesus.**
    - **The dead in Christ shall be raised first.**

- Be assured of the welfare of those who have died in Christ (4:13-18):

  If we believe that Jesus died and rose again, then we can be assured that God will bring with Him those that are asleep. Those of us who are alive when Jesus returns will not precede those who have died in Christ.

  When that day comes, the Lord will descend from heaven, with a shout, with the voice of the archangel, and with the trump of God. And those in Christ will be raised first, then we that are alive at the time of His coming will join them in the clouds to be with the Lord forever.

- **The time for His coming is unknown (5:1-11):**
    - **Be warned and ready.**

- The time for His coming is unknown; be warned and ready (5:1-11):

  You already know that the day of the Lord will come as a thief in the night. While others are saying, "Peace and safety," destruction will come upon them. But you do not live in the darkness, so the day will not slip up on you like a thief. Therefore, let us not sleep as others do. Neither let us get drunk. Those who sleep, sleep at night, and those who drink get drunk at night. Since we are of the day, let us be awake and sober, and let us put on the breastplate of faith and love, and, for a helmet, the hope of salvation. For God has not appointed us to wrath, but to obtain salvation. Therefore, whether we are awake or asleep when He returns, we will live together with Him.

- **Instructions for the church, and closing remarks (5:12-28).**

- Various instructions to the church and closing remarks (5:12-28):

  Appreciate those who labor among you; esteem them highly for their work's sake.

Warn the unruly; comfort the fainthearted; support the weak; be patient with all men.

Do not repay evil for evil. Seek what is good for each other and for all men.

Rejoice always. Pray without ceasing. Be thankful.

Do not quench the Spirit. Do not despise prophecies.

Examine all things. Hold fast to that which is good. Abstain from every form of evil.

May God set you apart completely, and may your whole spirit, soul, and body be preserved blameless at the time our Lord Jesus Christ comes again.

Brethren, pray for us.

Greet the brethren with a holy kiss.

I command that this letter be read to all the holy brethren.

The grace of our Lord Jesus Christ be with you.

A Thumb-Nail Sketch of 1 Thessalonians:

A summary concept:

- **Idolaters became worshipers of God:**
  - **In spite of persecution.**

The primary theme of 1 Thessalonians is an expression of joy for their conversion from idols to the true God. Paul thanks God for how thoroughly the Thessalonians were converted, in spite of the opposition they had endured. He and his co-workers encouraged the Thessalonians to accept the gospel by the example of their own conduct. He reminds the Thessalonians of their conversion and exhorts them to walk as children of God.

They were worried about what would happen to the dead saints at the time of the Lord's coming. Paul assured them that these saints would not be left behind, but would be raised from the dead and taken with the living saints to meet the Lord in the air. He closed the letter with various instructions to the church.

Summary of 2 Thessalonians

Second Thessalonians:

- **A follow-up letter to clarify some points of misunderstanding on the part of the saints at Thessalonica.**

Date: still A.D. 51 or 52.

Timothy reports some matters that still need to be clarified.

Very little time passed between the writing of 1 Thessalonians and 2 Thessalonians. Second Thessalonians was a follow-up letter in order to clarify some things the saints did not understand. It was written in the early part of the year and a half Paul spent in Corinth (18:11). We, therefore, place the summary of 2 Thessalonians next, and date it A.D. 51 or 52, no more than a few weeks, or months, after 1 Thessalonians. Remember, Paul is still on the second missionary journey.

It seems that Timothy took the first letter, and returned to Corinth to report to Paul. He told how the first letter had been received favorably, but he also told him there were some misunderstandings in the minds of the brethren at Thessalonica. There are indications in the book that false teachers had presented a letter to the Thessalonians, claiming that it was from Paul, but it was a fake (see 2:2; 3:17). Paul responded by writing a second letter to correct those misunderstandings.

The letter says:

The letter says:
- **Greetings**
- **Be comforted in your afflictions; God will avenge (1:3-12):**
  - **We give thanks for your steadfastness.**
  - **God knows your trials:**
    - **He will see that justice is done.**
  - **We pray you will grow in every way.**

Paul, Silas, and Timothy to the church at Thessalonica:

- Be comforted in your afflictions; God knows and He will avenge (1:3-12):

  We must give thanks for you because you continue to grow in your faith and love so that we boast to others of your faith and steadfastness in the face of your persecutions. By your enduring such things you show yourselves worthy of the kingdom of God.

  Remember that God is righteous and He will see that justice is done. Those who persecute you will themselves be punished in flaming fire and will be separated from the presence of God eternally while you are given rest.

  We will continue to pray that you will live as you should and will grow in every way so that you may glorify Christ, and He may glorify you.

- **Do not to be disturbed by false teaching regarding the Lord's second coming (2:1-12):**
  - **The Lord will not return right away.**
  - **An apostasy will come first.**
  - **Those who do not want the truth will be given the opportunity to believe a lie.**

- Do not be disturbed by false teaching concerning the Lord's coming (2:1-12):

  We want to reassure you about the coming of Christ so that you will not be disturbed by what some may preach or write. The coming of the Lord is *not* going to be right away, regardless of what anyone says. First there will be an apostasy in which the man given to sin, a man destined for destruction, will oppose God and everything that pertains to God. He will set himself up as God. Then he himself will be destroyed by the word of the Lord Jesus. This man will seek to persuade men by showing all sorts of false miracles. All those who do not want the truth will be given this opportunity to believe a lie and be condemned because they preferred sin to righteousness.

The man of sin who is described in chapter 2 has been explained in many ways. Two of the most common explanations are the papacy, or the cult of emperor worship. Good arguments are made by the best of students for both of these ideas. Another explanation is that the expression "man of sin" means "a man given over to sin." Thus Paul would not be referring to a particular, specific person, but to a kind of man who would appear after a while. If this is the explanation, then this prophecy would take its place alongside 1 Timothy 4:1-5. There is no way to be sure. Seemingly, in the context of that day, the Thessalonians knew who the "man of sin" was.

- **May God encourage and strengthen you (2:13-17):**

- But we give thanks for you; may God encourage and strengthen you (2:13-17):

- **We are thankful that God chose you.**
- **Stand firm.**

We always thank God for you because He chose you and called you through the work of the Spirit and your own belief in the truth, so that you could share in the glory of our Lord. So then, brethren, stand firm and hold tightly to what you have learned. May our Lord Jesus Christ and God our Father encourage your hearts and strengthen you in every good deed.

- **Please pray for us (3:1-5):**
  - **That our word will be received freely.**
  - **That we may be delivered from wicked men.**

- Please pray for us (3:1-5):

  Brethren, we ask that you pray for us that the word we preach will be received freely even as it was in you, and that we may be delivered from wicked, unscrupulous men.

- **Deal with those who walk disorderly (3:6-15):**
  - **Refuse to associate with them.**

- Deal with those who walk disorderly (3:6-15):

  Now we command you to refuse to associate with anyone who is out of step with the things we have preached to you and who will not obey our instructions which we have written. We have heard that some are such busy bodies that they do not have time for their own affairs. Let each person do his own work, minding his own business.

- **Benediction and close (3:16-18).**

- Benediction and close (3:16-18):

  May the Lord always give you peace.

  I have signed this letter in my own handwriting, which is the sign of genuineness in every epistle I write.

A Thumb-Nail Sketch of 2 Thessalonians:

One of Paul's primary points in this letter was that the Lord was not coming back right away, so continue the normal activities of life, particularly in earning a living. The thoughts can be expressed in four main points:

A summary concept:

- **<u>The Lord is not coming back immediately, so do your normal work</u>.**

- *Paul expresses his concern for their afflictions and places those afflictions in a divine perspective.*
- *He tells them not to be upset, or to think that the Lord will come back right away. An apostasy will come first.*
- *Then he gives a warning against those who walk disorderly by not taking care of their own affairs and by interfering with everyone else's. Thus they did not earn their own bread, but had to eat that of others.*
- *If anyone failed to obey these apostolic instructions, he was to be rejected.*

The Jews bring Paul before Gallio (Acts 18:12-17):

Again, persecution came from unbelieving Jews.

When Gallio was proconsul of Achaia, the unbelieving Jews made a united attack and brought Paul before the judgment seat to make accusation against him. They said, "This man persuades men to worship God contrary to the law."

Gallio behaved as a state official should in such affairs:

- **He refused to act as judge in religious matters.**

As Paul was about to open his mouth to respond, Gallio told the Jews, "If this were a matter of injury or some heinous crime, O you Jews, then the only reasonable thing I could do would be to put up with you. But if these things be questions concerning terms, and names, and your own law, deal with them yourselves. I am determined not to be a judge in such matters." And he drove them from the judgment seat.

Then they all laid hold on Sosthenes, the ruler of the synagogue, and beat him before the judgment seat, and Gallio paid them no mind.

There are perhaps two questions which need a little attention:

- *Is the Sosthenes mentioned here the one in 1 Corinthians 1:1?*

  The Sosthenes in 1 Corinthians joins with Paul in the salutation to the saints in Corinth. Possibly that means Sosthenes was a saint from Corinth, but with Paul in Ephesus at the time of the writing of the book. If so, he would be as deeply concerned about the work in Corinth as Paul was. The text gives us almost no information about the identity of Sosthenes either in this passage or in 1 Corinthians. He is called the ruler of the synagogue in this passage, but he could well have been converted after this occasion. But there is not enough information to know whether they were the same. It is useless to speculate.

- *Who beat Sosthenes in Acts 18?*

  Some say the Jews beat their own ruler because he bungled the job of accusing Paul before the proconsul. The KJV says the Greeks beat him, which would imply that some of the Greek bystanders beat him, and Gallio just ignored this "lynch justice." This explanation, however, does not fit well with the character of Gallio. Roman authorities had a severe dislike of any kind of mob action. It would have been contrary to Roman policy for a proconsul to sit idly while a mob beat someone.

  There is no way to know for sure, but the most reasonable explanation seems to be that the Jews were shocked at how suddenly their plan was thwarted by this proconsul. They had to be driven out (likely while loudly protesting), and in the process their leader, Sosthenes, was beaten by the Roman lictors who served the proconsul.

Gallio was proconsul of Corinth for one year:

- **Almost certainly A.D. 52 on our calendar.**

Scholars date New Testament events by events mentioned in the Bible text that can be verified from history:

- **Paul was in Corinth after the Jews were expelled from Rome in A.D. 49 (Acts 18:2).**
- **Gallio was proconsul while he was there (A.D. 52) (Acts 18:12).**

Historical and Chronological Note:

Achaia was a province which shifted back and forth from imperial control to senatorial control. Therefore it would be under a procurator at one time and then under a proconsul at another time. Luke is the only writer who calls Gallio a proconsul. Once again, however, Luke has been proven correct by an inscription found in 1909 at a quarry near Delphi. The inscription is from Claudius (A.D. 41-54) to the citizens of Delphi and he mentions Gallio as his friend "and proconsul of Achaia." It also contains a date in the reign of Claudius which is the year A.D. 52 on our calendar. Some authorities differ a year or so, but probably the most accurate estimate is 52.

Gallio was an older brother of Seneca, the Roman philosopher and writer. He was born in Cordova, Spain. Of him Seneca wrote: "No mortal is so pleasant to any one person as he is to everyone."

Notice from the dates that the reign of Claudius did not last much longer (his reign ended in A.D. 54). After Nero took over as emperor, Gallio and his brothers did not do as well. Some say they were forced to commit suicide by Nero, although there is some uncertainty among ancient writers as to the exact manner of death.

Cenchrea:
- **The eastern seaport for Corinth.**

Priscilla and Aquila:
- **Go with Paul as far as Ephesus.**

No mention is made of Silas or Timothy,
- **Though it was unusual for Paul to travel alone.**

Paul promised to return to Ephesus.
- **Do not forget the promise.**

Someone made a vow:
- **Either Paul or Aquila.**
- **From the wording, it could be either one.**

The vow may have been a Nazirite vow, as described in the law of Moses,
- **Or it may have been a vow of later origin.**

Paul goes to Ephesus (Acts 18:18-21):

After remaining in Corinth many more days, Paul said his goodbys to the brethren and sailed for Syria, taking with him Priscilla and Aquila. He had shorn his head in Cenchrea because he had a vow.

They landed at Ephesus and Paul left Priscilla and Aquila there. While he was there, he entered the synagogue and reasoned with the Jews. When they asked him to stay longer however, he refused, saying that he was on his way to keep a feast at Jerusalem (KJV, 18:21), but that he would return to them if it were God's will. After this he set sail from Ephesus to continue his journey toward Jerusalem.

Who made a vow as they were leaving Corinth (18:18)? Authorities are divided on the subject. Grammatically, the Greek indicates it was Aquila rather than Paul. It does not matter greatly. If this were a Nazirite vow, the hair was due to be burned on the altar at the temple; and since Paul, and not Aquila, was on his way to Jerusalem where the temple was located, then it is logical to think it was Paul who had made the vow.

The only kind of vow specified in the law of Moses that involved shearing the hair was the Nazirite vow, and that was either if the vow were interrupted by defilement (Num. 6:9-12), or at the end of the vow (Num. 6:13-20). According to the law, a Nazirite vow was taken to show a special dedication to God for a certain purpose or period of time. Such vows usually lasted only a few weeks or months.

The vow taken here seems to have been taken at the time of the shearing of the head and does not really fit the details surrounding a Nazirite vow. There is another vow involving the shearing or shaving of the head mentioned by Josephus in connection with Bernice, the sister of Herod Agrippa II (Wars of the Jews, Book II, Chapter 15, Section 1). The vow mentioned by Josephus was not commanded in the law, but was a purely voluntary vow one could take. As Josephus says, "For it is usual with those that had been either afflicted with a distemper, or with any other distresses, to make vows; and for thirty days before they are to offer their sacrifices, to abstain from wine, and to shave the hair of their head." Thus, in this vow mentioned by Josephus,

Regardless of which man it was, or which vow it was:
- **Paul did not object to Jewish Christians continuing to follow the customs of the Jews.**
- **But he did oppose their trying to make those same customs and laws binding upon the Gentiles.**

the hair was shaven at the beginning of the vow and perhaps kept cut during the period of the vow. It is not certain that the thirty days was a necessary part of this vow.

Whichever the vow, it illustrates a principle consistent with Paul's teaching. He thoroughly supported Jews acting as Jews (1 Cor. 9:20). Therefore, it was not wrong for either Paul or Aquila (both Jews who had become Christians) to take a vow. It was only when the commands of the Old Law were regarded as binding upon the Gentile converts that Paul objected.

One interesting note is that among Jews in the Roman world it was considered that a Nazirite could cut his hair as needed to keep it from getting too long, if all the hair thus cut were taken and added to the hair cut off at the conclusion of the vow and then burned on the altar at the temple.

Paul goes to Caesarea, Jerusalem, and then on to Antioch (Acts 18:22):

Paul landed at Caesarea,
- **Went to Jerusalem and saluted the church,**
- **Then on to Antioch in Syria.**

Find these places:
- **Ephesus**
- **Caesarea**
- **Jerusalem**
- **Antioch**

When he had landed at Caesarea, Paul went up to Jerusalem and saluted the church there, and then made his way back to Antioch where this second journey had begun. The cycle was complete, and this second journey was over.

Notice that Jerusalem is not specifically mentioned. Why then do we say that Paul went there?
- *He had told the Jews in Ephesus that he was on his way to Jerusalem to keep a feast (KJV, 18:21), so it is logical to think he went where he was headed.*
- *If his goal were Antioch, why did he detour to visit the church in Caesarea? So far as we know, Paul had no direct connection with the church in Caesarea before this time and we never find him placing emphasis on the church there in his life's work. He did, however, have close ties to the church in Jerusalem.*
- *Always in the scriptures the expression "going up" is used of a trip to Jerusalem. When he had landed at Caesarea, he "went up" and saluted the church. In other words, his going up was not in reference to Caesarea, but to what he did after landing at Caesarea. After saluting the church, he went down to Antioch. Jerusalem was located in the hill country, so to go to it, one went up, and to leave the city, one went down.*

Review this second journey:
- **Know where each place was,**
- **And what happened there.**

Review of the second journey:

The route:
- **Antioch**
- **Syria and Cilicia**
- **Derbe and Lystra**
- **Phrygia and Galatia**

- Paul and Silas traveled by land through Syria and Cilicia, strengthening the churches and delivering the letter from the apostles and elders in Jerusalem;
- On to Derbe, and Lystra where Timothy joined them.
- They continued on through Phrygia, and Galatia.

- **Troas**
  - But as they considered preaching in Asia, or north in Bithynia, the Spirit urged them forward to the town of Troas, where they were joined by Luke.
  - In Troas, they saw the vision of the man from Macedonia asking for their help.
- **Philippi**
  - They immediately sailed across the northern part of the Aegean Sea, and made their way to the city of Philippi.
    - Lydia and the jailer were converted, with their households.
  - They left Philippi at the request of the magistrates after Paul and Silas were arrested.
    - Luke stayed behind, and possibly Timothy did also.
- **Thessalonica**
  - Paul and Silas went on to Thessalonica where they preached until trouble arose. The brethren helped them escape by night.
- **Berea**
  - Paul and Silas preached in Berea until trouble arose, and the brethren escorted Paul to Athens. Silas and Timothy remained in Berea.
- **Athens**
  - Paul was alone in Athens. He spoke to philosophers on Mars Hill.
- **Corinth**
  - Still alone, Paul went to Corinth where he worked with Aquila and Priscilla as tent-makers.
    - He wrote a letter to the church at Thessalonica when Timothy and Silas joined him.
    - Soon he wrote a second letter to the Thessalonians because of mis-understandings they had.
    - Paul stayed a year and a half in Corinth, and many Corinthians heard the word, believed it, and were baptized.
- **Ephesus**
  - Paul and his company headed toward Syria.
    - Aquila and Priscilla went with them as far as Ephesus.
    - Paul promised to return to Ephesus as soon as possible, after he made the trip to Jerusalem to keep a feast.
- **Caesarea**
- **Jerusalem**
- **Antioch**
  - He sailed to Caesarea, went up to Jerusalem, and then returned to Antioch in Syria.

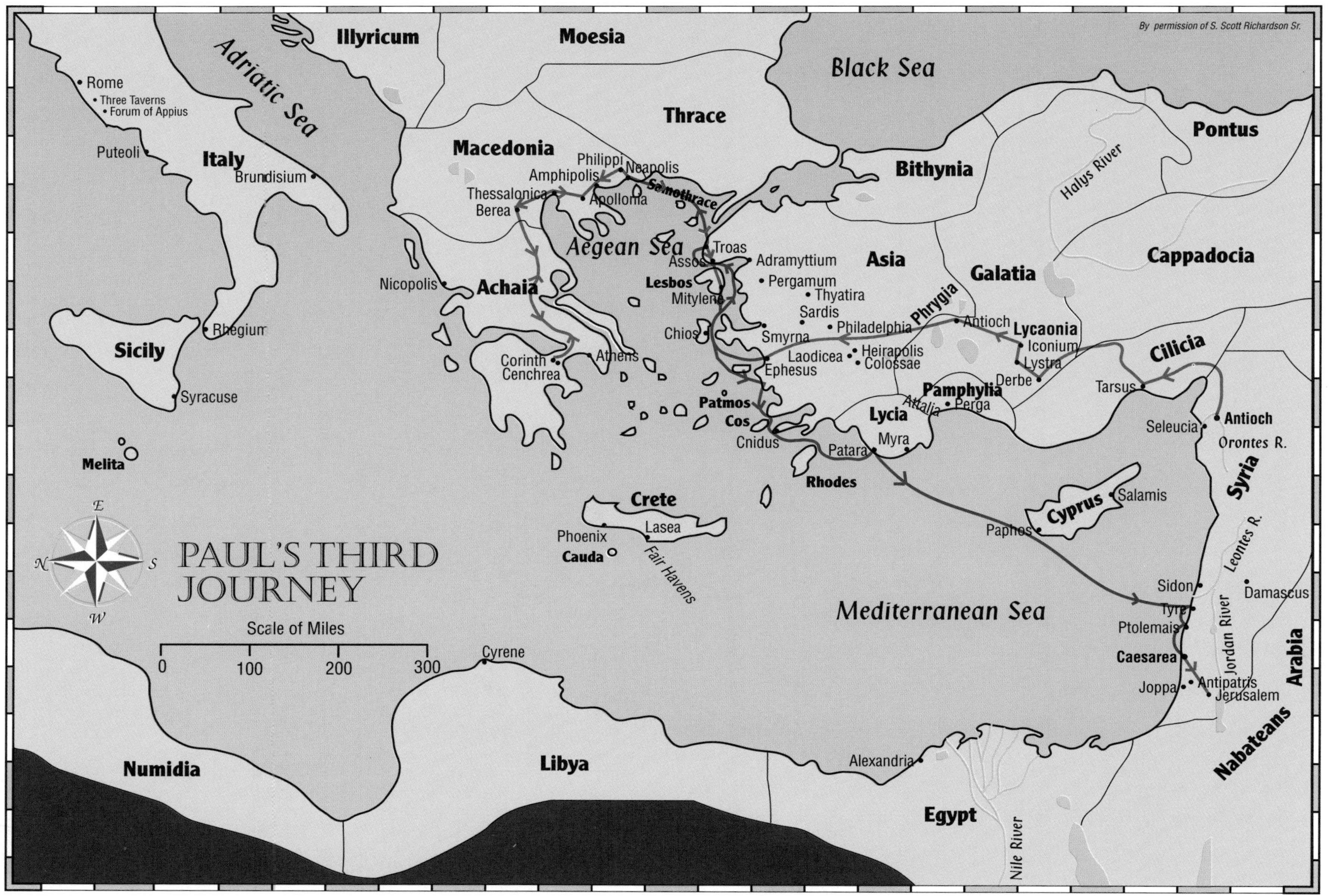

PAUL'S THIRD JOURNEY
By permission of S. Scott Richardson Sr.
Scale of Miles
0
100
200
300
E
S
W
N
Illyricum
Moesia
Black Sea
Adriatic Sea
Rome
Three Taverns
Forum of Appius
Puteoli
Italy
Brundisium
Thrace
Macedonia
Philippi
Neapolis
Amphipolis
Apollonia
Samothrace
Thessalonica
Berea
Aegean Sea
Bithynia
Pontus
Halys River
Cappadocia
Troas
Assos
Adramyttium
Asia
Galatia
Nicopolis
Achaia
Lesbos
Mitylene
Pergamum
Thyatira
Sardis
Phrygia
Antioch
Lycaonia
Iconium
Lystra
Derbe
Sicily
Rhegium
Chios
Smyrna
Philadelphia
Laodicea
Heirapolis
Colossae
Ephesus
Corinth
Cenchrea
Athens
Syracuse
Patmos
Cos
Cnidus
Pamphylia
Attalia
Perga
Lycia
Myra
Patara
Rhodes
Cilicia
Tarsus
Seleucia
Antioch
Orontes R.
Syria
Melita
Crete
Lasea
Phoenix
Cauda
Fair Havens
Cyprus
Salamis
Paphos
Leontes R.
Sidon
Damascus
Tyre
Ptolemais
Caesarea
Jordan River
Arabia
Joppa
Antipatris
Jerusalem
Mediterranean Sea
Cyrene
Alexandria
Nabateans
Numidia
Libya
Egypt
Nile River

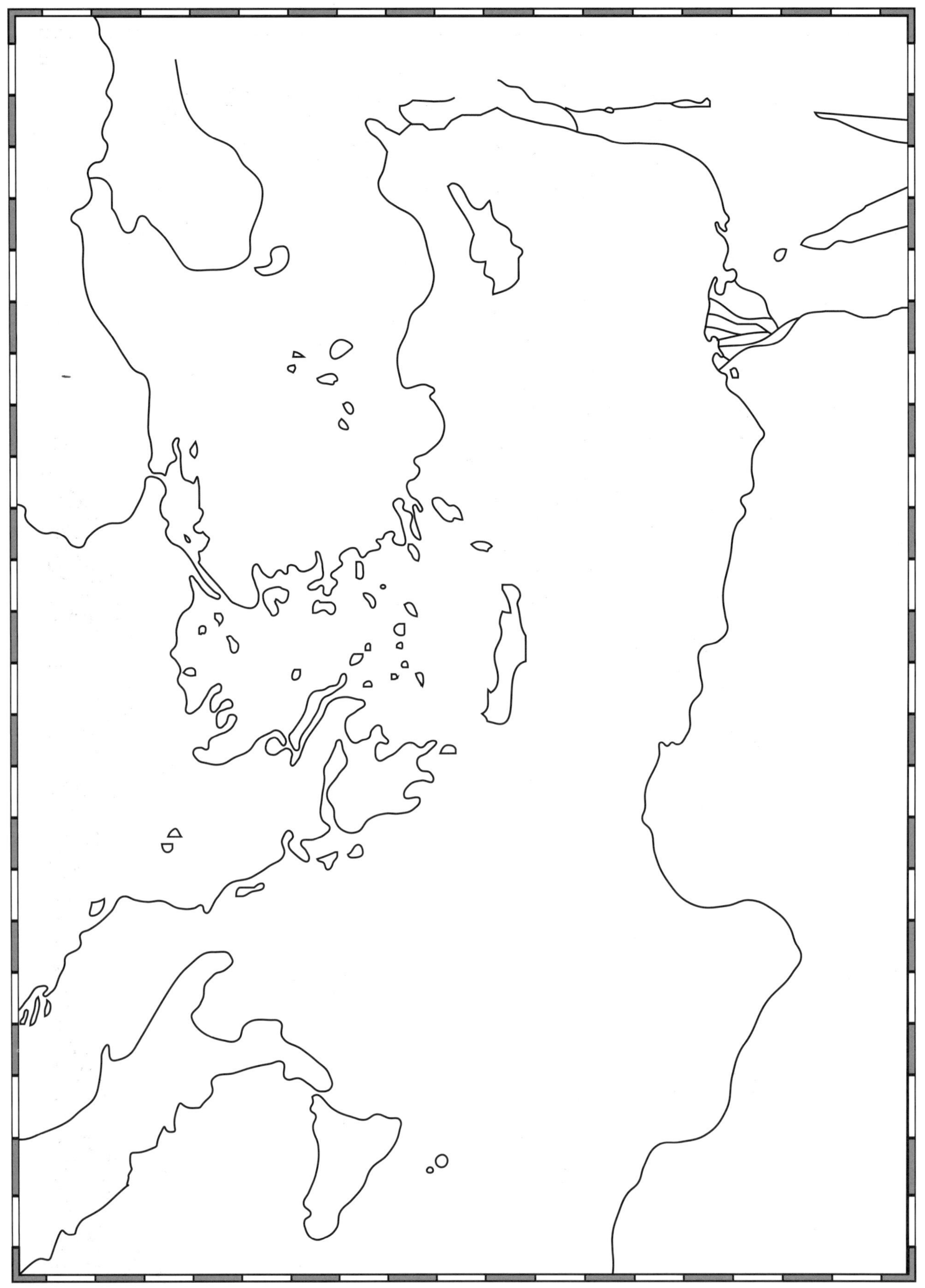

Paul's Third Missionary Journey

(Acts 18:23-21:17; Galatians, 1 & 2 Corinthians, Romans)

Late A.D. 53 or early A.D. 54.

Claudius died in A.D. 54:
- **Nero became emperor.**

Books written on 3rd journey:
- **Galatians**
- **1 Corinthians**
- **2 Corinthians**
- **Romans**

The journey will end in Jerusalem as Paul and others take a gift to the poor saints.

No mention is made of companions as Paul starts this third journey, but he rarely traveled alone.

Label this journey on your blank map on page 120:
- **Know the route,**
- **Know what happened at each place.**
- **Label Antioch of Syria, Galatia, and Phrygia.**
- **Label the cities of Derbe, Lystra, Iconium, Antioch of Pisidia.**

Apollos:
- **A Jews from Alexandria;**
- **An eloquent man;**
- **But he knew about Jesus only through the baptism of John.**

Chronology Note:

Let's take a moment to get our bearings. Acts 18:11 says that Paul "settled" in Corinth and preached the gospel for a year and a half. Then the text tells of the uprising that resulted in his being brought before Gallio, and he stayed in Corinth "many days" after that (18:18). We showed from historical evidence that Paul's encounter with Gallio was in about A.D. 52. From the wording of the text, it is difficult to know whether the uprising was within the year and a half already mentioned, or if it came at the end of that time and Paul stayed some while longer. From other dating information, the trouble was likely early in that year and a half, and the "many days" were the rest of the time mentioned. After he left Corinth, more time passed while he made his trip to Jerusalem and then to Antioch. By now it is probably the spring of A.D. 54. This is the year Claudius died, and Nero began his rule. The rest of Paul's life will be during Nero's reign. He will, in fact, be executed by Nero, as will Peter and many other Christians.

On this third journey, Paul will write Galatians (the most probable time of its writing), 1 and 2 Corinthians, and Romans. In the spring of A.D. 58, near the end of this journey, Paul, and a group of messengers from various congregations which were made up predominantly of Gentiles, will make their way to Jerusalem, taking an offering for the poor saints in that city. We are marking the end of the third journey with Paul's arrival in Jerusalem (21:17).

Paul travels through Galatia and Phrygia (Acts 18:23):

After spending some time in Antioch of Syria, Paul departed and retraced the route of the second journey through Galatia and Phrygia. He went to the churches, one after another, which had been established earlier *(Derbe, Lystra, Iconium, and Antioch)*. He further taught the brethren and strengthened them.

Apollos comes to Ephesus (Acts 18:24-28):

While Paul was on his way through the provinces of Galatia and Phrygia, a Jew named Apollos, from Alexandria in Egypt, came to Ephesus. He was trained in reasoning, in speech, and in debate, and he was mighty in the scriptures. He had been taught about the Lord, and, being the kind of man who wanted to share his faith, he discussed and taught accurately the things he had learned. But there was a problem: he knew about Jesus only in connection with John's baptism.

Aquila and Priscilla:
- **Had traveled with Paul from Corinth to Ephesus at the end of the 2nd journey (18:18).**
- **They remained in Ephesus when Paul went on his way.**
- **They taught Apollos the information he lacked.**

Apollos defended what the Jews attacked:
- **Jesus was the Christ.**

Label your map:
- **Achaia,**
  - **Corinth as its capital.**
- **Ephesus.**
- **See how their locations compare.**

Ephesus:
- **The foremost commercial city of Asia Minor;**
- **The administrative center for the Roman province of Asia;**
- **The "Temple Keeper" of the goddess Diana.**

Paul keeps his promise:
- **"I will return again unto you if God will" (18:21).**

Apollos began to speak boldly in the synagogue at Ephesus where Priscilla and Aquila heard him. They took him aside and taught him the additional facts which he needed to make his knowledge complete.

After a time, when Apollos decided to go to Achaia *(Corinth was the capital of Achaia)*, the brethren at Ephesus encouraged him and wrote a letter of introduction to the disciples in Achaia. When he arrived there, he greatly helped those who had believed because he powerfully refuted the Jews' arguments before everyone, showing from the scriptures that Jesus was the Christ.

There is much that we do not know about Apollos. Apparently he had been taught by one of John's disciples, a disciple who knew that John had pointed his own disciples to the Lamb of God who takes away the sins of the world (John 1:29) — but Apollos had not learned of Jesus' sacrificial death, of His resurrection, of His ascension, of His rule in heaven, or of the establishment of the church as His body. Was he baptized again? There is every reason to believe he was. John's baptism was for the remission of sins, but it was not in the name of Christ, nor into His kingdom. John's baptism was a preparatory baptism.

Historical Note about Ephesus:

Ephesus was the foremost commercial city in Asia Minor. Its harbor at the mouth of the Cayster River had to be continually dredged of silt. The former harbor of Ephesus is now seven miles inland, because they ceased to dredge the silt away as the years passed.

Though the city was the administrative center for the Roman province of Asia, its chief claim to fame was that it was the "Temple Keeper" of the goddess Diana (Acts 19:35). An earlier temple had burned in 356 B.C., according to tradition, on the very night Alexander the Great was born. The temple of Paul's day was ranked among the seven wonders of the world. It was 425 feet long, 220 feet wide; it had 127 columns which supported the roof, each 60 feet high; and it was made of the purest marble.

We know there was already a church in Ephesus when Paul returned here at the beginning of his third journey because the "brethren" at Ephesus had already sent Apollos on to Achaia with a letter of introduction from them (18:27). The church was probably the result of Paul's earlier brief stay (18:18-21) and of the work of Priscilla and Aquila. Now Paul is returning, just as he had promised he would.

Paul baptizes twelve men into Christ (Acts 19:1-7):

While Apollos was working in Corinth *(Achaia)*, Paul arrived in Ephesus. He found some disciples whom he asked, "Did you receive the Holy Spirit when you believed?"

They answered, "No, we did not hear anything about whether the Holy Spirit was given."

"Into what then were you baptized?" *(or, "In connection with what then were you baptized?")* Paul asked.

Paul baptizes 12 men who knew only the baptism of John.

"Into John's baptism," they replied. *(Their answer showed their misunderstanding — because one could be baptized at John's instructions, but no one was baptized "into" John's baptism. Their knowledge was so scant, Paul's question really did not make sense to them, so their answer made no sense either.)*

Paul said, "John baptized with the baptism of repentance. His message to the people was that they should believe on the One who was to follow him, that is Jesus."

When the men heard Paul's explanation, they were baptized in the name of the Lord Jesus. Paul laid his hands upon them, and the Holy Spirit came upon them, and they spoke with tongues and prophesied. In all, there were about twelve men.

John's baptism:

- **For the remission of sins,**
- **But it was not in the name of Jesus *(by the authority of Jesus)*,**
- **It did not require faith in Jesus as the Messiah.**
- **It was for the Jews.**
- **It was an act to show repentance.**

John's baptism today?

- **No one today was alive at the time John's baptism was preached.**
- **Therefore no one today could be baptized scripturally with John's baptism.**
- **It is a legitimate subject to study,**
    - **But do not let it divert you from the main study of the third journey of Paul.**

John's baptism was in order to have the remission of sins (Mark 1:4; Luke 3:3), as was the baptism begun on the day of Pentecost (Acts 2:38). Nevertheless, John's baptism was fundamentally different from baptism "in Jesus' name." John's baptism was directed to Jews and proselytes only, a baptism motivated by penitence. It was authorized by God, but it is never said to be "in Jesus' name." When Jesus' disciples baptized in the early days of His ministry, they baptized in the same way and for the same purpose that John had been baptizing — not in the name of Jesus (John 4:1-2). Faith in Him as the Christ was not required, because Jesus' work had not yet begun when John began his work, and it had barely started when Jesus' disciples baptized some in the same manner. The baptism of the Great Commission, however, was by Jesus' authority, it was in His name, it required faith in Him, and it placed men into a covenant relationship with Him.

It has been argued that John's disciples were not baptized again on, or after, Pentecost because the apostles were not baptized on Pentecost. In the first place, merely that no specific mention is made of the apostles' being baptized is no proof they were not. But even if the apostles were not baptized on Pentecost, there is a more appropriate explanation than that they had already been baptized by John:

- *When God created the world, He created things fully developed so they could function right away.*
- *Likewise, when Jesus established the church, the apostles were His specially chosen nucleus for His kingdom.*
- *What they did to be in the church can no more be compared with what all others must do than the special creation God performed at the beginning of time can be compared with the generation by natural law of all plants and animals since creation.*

When Paul explained the problem to these men, he did not say, "The baptism of John was only good until Pentecost. Since you men were baptized after that, your baptism is not acceptable." But who knows when these men were baptized? We assume that Apollos baptized them because he had just been there with an incomplete understanding of God's plan, but there is no way to prove that assumption. And, if John's baptism were the same as baptism in the name of Jesus, it should have been just as acceptable after Pentecost as before.

Baptism in the name of Jesus requires:
- **Faith in Him as the Divine Son of God,**
- **Understanding of His completed mission,**
- **Belief that He is the source of salvation.**

No, the problem with John's baptism was that it was for a limited time and purpose. It was to prepare God's people for the arrival of the Messiah. When Jesus commanded His baptism, He required that men believe in Him as the Divine Son of God, the Messiah. They were to understand His completed mission, and to believe that He was the source of their salvation.

The Holy Spirit did not automatically come upon those who were baptized in Jesus' name,
- **But their lack of knowledge about the Spirit alerted Paul that something was wrong with the understanding these men had about Christ and the subject of baptism.**

What connection was there between the Holy Spirit and baptism in the name of Jesus? Did the Holy Spirit automatically come in miraculous measure upon those who were baptized in Jesus' name? Paul's question: "Did ye receive the Holy Spirit when ye believed?" moves some to argue that the miraculous measure of the Spirit came automatically upon correct baptism in Jesus' name. But there is another explanation that fits all the passages better.

- *Evidence is conclusive that the miraculous powers of the Spirit did not automatically come at baptism. This is the second case in the book of Acts where it specifically says people were baptized in the name of Jesus and did not receive the Spirit immediately.*
    - *The people of Samaria were baptized in the name of the Lord Jesus without the Holy Spirit's falling upon any of them (8:15-16). It is specifically stated that Peter and John (apostles) <u>laid their hands upon them and gave them the Holy Spirit</u> (8:17-18).*
    - *In the present example, Paul baptized these men into the name of the Lord Jesus, but the Spirit did not come upon them immediately. "When Paul <u>had laid his hands upon them</u>, the Holy Spirit came on them" (19:6).*

Paul laid his hands upon the twelve men and they received the Holy Spirit.

- *When these men expressed ignorance about the Holy Spirit, it made Paul suspect that there was something amiss with their understanding about the whole story of Christ and with their baptism.*
- *The most logical explanation as to why Paul asked them if they had received the Holy Spirit when they believed was because he knew they could only have received it if they had been baptized at a time when an apostle was present.*
    - *It seems he was planning to impart the Spirit to them if they did not have it.*

- *Then their admitted ignorance about the Spirit alerted him to the problem with their baptism, and he dealt with that problem first.*

Paul preaches for three months in the synagogue in Ephesus (Acts 19:8-9):

Unbelieving Jews are the source of trouble for Paul and the brethren in the synagogue.

For three months Paul preached boldly in the synagogue at Ephesus, seeking to persuade concerning the kingdom of God. By then some of the Jews became hardened and disobedient. They began to say evil things about the way of Christ before the multitude. Therefore Paul left the synagogue, taking the disciples with him, and they went into the school of a man named Tyrannus (*the tyrant)*.

Summary of the book of Galatians

As you study Galatians:
- **Do not lose sight of the history of Acts.**
- **Paul is at Ephesus on the third missionary journey.**

The churches of Galatia:
- **Antioch of Pisidia,**
- **Iconium,**
- **Lystra,**
- **Derbe,**
- **And possibly others that had started through their influence.**

Paul and Silas delivered the decrees concerning circumcision and the old law to the churches at the beginning of the second journey.

Judaizing teachers:
- **Jews who had been converted to Christ,**
- **But who demanded that the Gentiles must become Jews (by being circumcised) before they could be accepted as brethren.**
- **These false teachers were a source of bitter opposition to Paul and others.**

The churches of Galatia were established during Paul's first missionary journey and included Antioch of Pisidia, Iconium, Lystra, Derbe, and possibly other congregations that had started from their influence (Acts 13-14). Paul passed back through the area at the beginning of both his second and third journeys (15:41-16:1-6; 18:23). The areas called Lycaonia, Pisidia, and part of Phrygia were included in the Roman province called Galatia. Though some of the Galatian Christians were Jews, many of them were Gentiles.

Remember that it was between the first and second missionary journeys that trouble arose at Antioch of Syria over the question of circumcision, and Paul and Barnabas went to Jerusalem to discuss the question with the brethren there (Acts 15:1-2). The Spirit guided the apostles to conclude that the Gentiles were <u>not</u> required to be circumcised, nor to keep the old law in any way. Decrees were written stating that conclusion, and Paul and Silas delivered these decrees to the churches they visited as they started the second journey, including the churches of Galatia (Acts 15:1-41-16:4). The problem of circumcision for the Gentiles was a complex problem to the Jews, so it took most of the first century to settle all the related questions. This letter was written after that trip to Jerusalem because Paul describes the trip in chapter two of the book..

Paul wrote the letter to refute destructive teaching that was being done in Galatia by Judaizing teachers. They were teaching that the Gentile converts must be circumcised before they could have the right to be Christians (Gal. 5:2-3; 6:12-13). Closely connected to that subject, but enlarging the topic to its full extent, Paul then deals with the question of the old law itself. Is anyone (Jew or Gentile) still subject to the Law of Moses? Or, has it been taken out of the way?

The false teachers were seeking to destroy Paul's influence by saying he was not really an apostle like the twelve before him (such as

If Paul's message were not directly from God:
- **How could the Galatians be sure his message was accurate?**

The book of Galatians is the Holy Spirit's statement on the relation of the Christian to the Old Law.

Paul begins the epistle with a warning instead of an expression of thanksgiving.

The book of Galatians:
- **Written between A.D. 52 and 54,**
- **But to pinpoint the date more definitely is impossible.**

The three most likely occasions were:
- **From Corinth at the close of Paul's second journey,**
- **From Antioch of Syria shortly before he set out on his third journey,**
- **From Ephesus, early in his stay there.**

Paul does not mention the gift to the saints of Judea:
- **Though the Galatians participated in the gift.**

The letter says:

Peter and John). It was absolutely necessary for Paul to convince his readers — of that generation and of all generations since — that his message could be trusted, because it came directly from God. After Paul vigorously defends his apostleship, he spends the rest of the book proving that the spiritual blessings the Galatians enjoyed were through Christ and the gospel, not through circumcision and the law. Since Paul was writing with the inspiration of the Holy Spirit, the letter is not just Paul's statement on the relation of Christians to the old law, it is the Holy Spirit's written statement on the subject.

Paul does not deal with the false teachers themselves in this book, but rather with the people who have accepted their teaching. He is saying, "How could you accept their message?" He does not begin this epistle with an expression of thanksgiving for the brethren of Galatia, as he does in so many of his other books (e.g. 1 Thess. 1:2; 2 Thess. 1:3; 1 Cor. 1:4). Even though he deals with problems and false doctrines in other books, he is especially concerned about these Galatians because they are already accepting the false doctrine they are being taught. Therefore, he begins with a warning, rather than thanksgiving.

No one knows exactly when the letter was written. Since Paul marvels that they had turned so quickly from the decrees they had been given, it is possible that he wrote the letter from Corinth while he was still on the second journey, but it seems more logical to place it here early in the time he was at Ephesus on the third journey. As he began this third journey, he passed back through the area, strengthening and encouraging the brethren. It may be that he observed trouble and misunderstanding on the subject of the old law as he passed through the area and is now writing to clarify the subject in the minds of all who read his letter. By determining that the letter was written from Corinth at the end of one journey or from Ephesus at the beginning of the next journey, we have narrowed the range of time for its date to one or two years. After Paul left Corinth at the end of his second journey, he made a quick trip to Judea, then on to Antioch where he spent "some time," passed back through the areas of Galatia and Phrygia, and then to Ephesus.

We are dealing with the epistle to the Galatians under the assumption it was written from Ephesus, probably early in Paul's stay there. It was written before Paul made the decision to collect a gift from the predominantly Gentile churches to take to the saints in Judea, because he does not mention the gift in this letter although brethren from Galatia participated in that gift (see 1 Cor. 16:1; Acts 20:4). We have chosen to discuss the letter at the point that Paul leaves the synagogue of the Jews and goes to the school of Tyrannus, between verses nine and ten of Acts 19, although we are not trying to pinpoint the time of its writing that precisely.

The letter says:

- **My message came straight from God (1:1-2:21):**
  - **God made me an apostle (1:1-5).**
  - **How could you accept another gospel?**
    - **There is no "other" gospel (1:6-10).**

- My message is true, because it came straight from God (1:1-2:21):

Paul, an apostle, not sent by men, nor made an apostle by men, but through Jesus Christ, and through God the Father who raised Him from the dead, to the churches of Galatia. May God's grace and peace be upon you.

I am amazed at how quickly you are abandoning Him who called you in the grace of Christ for another gospel, though it is not really a different gospel, but there are some who would trouble you by perverting the gospel. But though we, or an angel from heaven, preach a gospel contrary to what we have preached to you, let him be accursed. I repeat: if any man preaches any gospel besides the one you accepted, let him be accursed. *(There is a progression stated in verses 6-9: the gospel was preached to the Galatians, and they received it; how could they now reject it?)*

- **I know what I am talking about (1:11-24):**
  - **God revealed His message to me.**
  - **I was not taught it by men.**
  - **There was not time for me to learn it while I was in Jerusalem.**

The gospel which I preach did not come from man, but by revelation from God. There was never an opportunity for me to be taught the gospel which I preach. You know that I persecuted the church and tried to destroy it. I was advancing more rapidly than many of my own age because of my zeal for the traditions of my fathers. But when the One who had set me apart from my mother's womb called me and revealed His Son to me so that I might preach Him to the Gentiles, I did not consult other people, nor did I go to Jerusalem to those who were apostles before me in order to be taught. Instead I went away into Arabia and returned to Damascus.

It was three years before I went to Jerusalem and met Cephas *(Peter)* and James the Lord's brother. I was there only fifteen days before I went away to the regions of Syria and Cilicia. I was not even known by face to the brethren of Judea. They only knew that the one who had once persecuted the church was now preaching, and they glorified God.

- **The other apostles acknowledged my gospel (2:1-10).**
  - **Titus was not circumcised.**
  - **They added nothing to what I taught.**
  - **God sent Peter to the Jews, and sent me to the Gentiles.**

When I returned to Jerusalem after fourteen more years, my message was vindicated by the result of our meeting there. I made that trip by revelation *(that is, at the instruction of the Holy Spirit)*, and when I arrived I privately told those in positions of authority what I preach to the Gentiles. I had taken Titus with me, and not even he was compelled to be circumcised. This question of circumcision of the Gentiles came in by way of false brethren who were spying out our liberty in Christ Jesus, in order to bring us into bondage. We did not yield to them for even one hour.

Those in positions of authority did not add anything to what I taught. James, Peter, and John extended the right hand of fellowship to me and to Barnabas. They recognized that I had been given the task of preaching to the Gentiles, just as Peter had been given the task of preaching to the Jews. The only thing they asked was that we remember the poor, which I am eager to do.

- **When the need arose, I reproved Peter for acting contrary to what we both taught (2:11-21).**
- ***Paul reminded Peter:***
  - **No man can be justified by the law.**
  - **If righteousness came through the law, Christ died for nothing.**

Afterwards, when the need arose I did not hesitate to rebuke Peter for his actions: He came to Antioch, and at first he ate with Gentiles, but when certain brethren came from James, he withdrew himself. Even Barnabas and the rest of the Jews were led away by his actions. Therefore, I told Cephas: "If you being a Jew. live as a Gentile, then how is it that you compel the Gentiles to live as Jews? You as a Jew realize that no one can be justified by the Law *(law of Moses)*, but by faith in Christ Jesus — because no man can be justified by the Law. I died to the Law so that I might live to God; I have been crucified with Christ; it is no longer I that live, but Christ lives in me. The life I live now is by faith in the Son of God, who loved me and died for me. If righteousness came through the Law, then Christ died for nothing."

The connecting link between the first and second main points is this concept that Paul reminded Peter: if the Law of Moses had provided ultimate forgiveness when a law was broken, then there was no need for Christ to die.

- **Spiritual freedom is in Christ, not through the law of Moses (3:1-4:31):**
  - **Justification comes by *faith in Christ*, not by the law (3:1-14):**

- Spiritual freedom is in Christ, not through the law of Moses (3:1-4:31):

  You foolish Galatians, did the spiritual blessings you have received come through the law, or through the gospel of Christ? Having begun your growth by the Spirit, are you planning to be made perfect by going from the Spirit to the flesh? Did God work miracles among you by the works of the law or by the response of faith?

  - **Abraham was justified by faith.**
  - **All who *believe* are children of Abraham (3:6-9).**

  Abraham *believed* God and it was counted unto him for righteousness. Just as Abraham was justified by faith, so all men, Jew or Gentile, will be justified by faith. This good news was announced to Abraham long ago when God said, "In you all the nations will be blessed." Not all those who have been circumcised are children of Abraham: his children are those who follow in his footsteps of faith.

It is the justification made possible by faith instead of by perfect works that makes it possible for men to be blessed. That is what God meant when He promised Abraham that <u>all nations</u> would be blessed through him (Gen. 12:3). Through faith in Christ, I can become a child of faithful Abraham, and receive the promised blessing..

- **Those under the law were under a curse (3:10-12):**

Those under the works of the law are under a curse, because the law says: "Cursed is everyone who does not obey *everything* written in the law." It is clear that men have never been justified by the law because God said, "The righteous will live by faith." The law is not a matter of *trusting in* the commandments, but of *doing* them. *(It took perfect obedience in order to be justified by the law itself.)*

- **Jesus became a curse to make forgiveness possible (3:13-14).**

So Christ redeemed us from the curse of the law that we were under by coming under a curse Himself. For the law also says, "Cursed is everyone who hangs on a tree." He thus died so that the Gentiles might have the same blessing as Abraham so that we all might receive the promise of the Spirit through faith.

- **Adding the law did not void the promise God had made (3:15-4:7):**

Even among men, when an agreement has been made and confirmed, no one else can come along later and void it or add to it. Likewise, when God made a covenant *(a contract)* with Abraham, the law which came 430 years later could not do away with the promise. If the inheritance were by law, it could not be a matter of promise.

- **The law was added because of transgression until the seed came (3:19).**

Then what purpose did the law serve? It was added because of the transgressions of men until the seed of promise should come. This law was ordained through angels by the hand of a mediator *(Moses)*. The same God who dealt personally with Abraham to give him the promise dealt with a whole nation through Moses, but it was the same God in both cases. Obviously then, the law *(of God)* is not contrary to the promise *(of God)*. If a law had been given that was able to give life, then righteousness could have been based on the law. But all men were locked up under sin, until the promise by faith in Jesus Christ might be given to those who believe.

- **The law of God was not contrary to the promise of God (3:19-24):**
  - **But it could not give life.**
  - **All men were locked in sin.**

- **A form of bondage (3:23-29):**
  - **The law was the guardian to bring the heirs of the promise to Christ.**
  - **Now all are children of God...**
  - **A child under servants...**
    - **Jews were held in bondage...**
- **Christ freed men from the bondage of the law,**
  - **Gave them the privileges of sons (4:1-7).**
- **You Gentiles were released from another bondage, idolatry:**

But before *(the system of salvation by)* faith came, we were kept in custody, until the faith should be revealed. The law was our guardian to lead us to Christ so that we could be justified by faith. But now that Christ has come, we are no longer under a guardian. You are all children of God by faith in Christ, because as many as have been baptized into Christ have put on Christ. There is no distinction between us now, we are all one person in Christ, we belong to Him, we are Abraham's children, and therefore heirs according to the promise.

A child, though he may be in prospect master of all, is no better than a slave while he is under various guardians. So we Jews were held in bondage by the elementary things of the world. But in the fullness of the time God sent forth His Son born of a woman, born under the law, so He could redeem those who were under the law, so that we could be adopted as His sons and receive all the privileges of sons. This means we may call upon God as our father *("Abba" signified the intimacy that would be associated with "Daddy" in English)*. We are no longer slaves, but rather sons; and if sons, then heirs through God *(through what He has done)*.

You Gentiles were under a different kind of bondage: idolatry. When you did not know God, you were in bondage to those which

- **Are you willing to go under the bondage of the law (4:8-11)?**

by nature are no gods. Now that you have come to know God, or rather to be known by God, are you willing to exchange one bondage for another, that of the law? You observe days and months and years. I am concerned about you, that perhaps I have labored for nothing.

- **Why have your feelings for me changed (4:12-20)?**
  - **Have I become your enemy?**

I beg you to feel about me the way I feel about you. It was because of a bodily illness that I preached among you the first time. You could have despised me, but instead you received me as you would have Christ. Where is that joy you had in connection with me? Am I become your enemy because I tell you the truth? Those who are trying to win you over are not seeking your welfare. My little children, I am in anguish worrying about you until I can be satisfied that Christ is formed in you.

- **Allegory *(Illustration)*: Hagar and Sarah (4:21-31):**
  - **Sons of the bond-woman were slaves.**
  - **Sons of the free woman are free.**
  - **Which do you want? Freedom or slavery?**

Those of you who want to be under the law, please listen to what the law says. Compare Hagar the bondmaid of Abraham and her son Ishmael, with Sarah the wife of Abraham and their son Isaac. The situation between these two women and their sons corresponds to the situation today between Jews and Christians. Hagar was a slave, and her son was born of purely natural processes, whereas Sarah was free, and her son was born according to the promise of God. Hagar and Ishmael correspond to physical Jerusalem and to the Jews. Sarah and Isaac correspond to Jerusalem above and to Christians. But in the same way that he who was born according to the flesh persecuted him that was born according to the Spirit, so it is now (Gen. 21:8-21). Also remember that, as Hagar's son did not inherit, so the Jews will not inherit the blessings of God through the law.

- **You were set free; do not go back under bondage (5:1-6:18):**
  - **One who accepts circumcision is obligated to keep the whole law (5:2-12):**
    - **Falling under the curse again.**
    - **You were running a good race. What happened?**
    - **If I agree with them, why are they still persecuting me?**

- You were set free by Christ; please do not become entangled in bondage again (5:1-6:18):

If you accept circumcision you will lose all the spiritual advantages you have in Christ, because I tell you that the one who submits to the law cannot get by with keeping just one commandment. He must keep them all. You are cut off from Christ when you seek to be justified by the law; you are fallen from grace. We through the Spirit wait for the hope of righteousness by faith. Because in Christ Jesus neither circumcision nor uncircumcision amounts to anything, but faith working by love.

You were running a good race. Who cut in on you and kept you from obeying the truth? This persuasion did not come from Him who called you. A little leaven leavens the whole lump of dough. I have confidence in you, that you will adopt no other view, but the one who troubles you will bear his judgment, whoever he is. If I still preach circumcision, why am I still persecuted? Then the stumbling block of the cross has been removed! I wish that those who are disturbing you would even go beyond circumcision and castrate themselves.

Apparently there were some Judaizers who were willing to try any argument. If they could not discredit Paul's teaching, then they would try to argue that he actually supported their doctrine. After all, he had Timothy circumcised (Acts 16:3). So Paul says that if he is really agreeing with the Judaizers, then why are they still vilifying him and persecuting him? With their preaching of circumcision, the Judaizers are competing with Paul to take the Galatians away from his influence. But if they have no more to offer than Paul — in other words, if he, too, still preaches circumcision — how will they be able to outdo him? Paul argues that if they argue for circumcision, why not be castrated? This point would have had particular significance among the Galatians, because they had the castrated priests of Cybele, a Phrygian goddess. What an advance toward holiness this would be! This would really leave Paul behind, who, according to them, was still just preaching circumcision. Then the Galatians would really have something to admire!

- **Do not use your freedom as license to indulge the flesh (5:13-15).**

You have been set free, but do not use your freedom and forgiveness as license to sin. Through love serve one another. The whole law is fulfilled in this one statement: you shall love your neighbor as yourself. If you bite and devour one another, be careful lest you consume each other.

- **Walk by the Spirit and you will not fulfill the desires of the flesh (5:16-26).**

If you will let yourselves be guided by the Spirit, you will not be fulfilling the desires of the flesh. The flesh lusts against the spirit, and the spirit against the flesh. These are in opposition to one another. But if you are led by the Spirit, you are not under the law.

  - **Those who do the deeds of the flesh will not inherit the kingdom of God.**

The deeds of the flesh are evident. They are immorality, impurity, sensuality, idolatry, sorcery, enmities, strife, jealousy, outbursts of anger, disputes, dissensions, factions, envying, drunkenness, carousing, and other such things. I warn you that those who practice such things will not inherit the kingdom of God.

  - **Those who belong to Christ have crucified the flesh.**

In contrast, the fruit of the Spirit is love, joy, peace, longsuffering, kindness, goodness, faithfulness, meekness, and self control. Against such things there is no law. Those who belong to Christ have crucified the flesh with its passions and lusts.

  - **If you live by the Spirit: walk by the Spirit.**

If we live by the Spirit, let us also walk by the Spirit. Do not be filled with pride, provoking one another and envying one another.

- **Responsibilities to one another (6:1-10).**
  - **Restore the fallen.**

Brethren, when one among you falls into sin, those who are faithful should help him recover — and watch yourselves lest you also be tempted. Help to bear one another's burdens and you will

- **Bear burdens...**
- **Examine one's self...**
- **Share...**
- **You will reap what you sow:**
  - **If to the flesh: corruption.**
  - **If to the spirit: eternal life.**

fulfill the law of Christ. If anyone thinks he is something when he is nothing, he deceives himself. But let each one examine his own work, and then he will have reason for boasting in himself alone and not in regard to others. For each one shall carry his own load.

Let the one who is taught in the word share with him who teaches. Remember that God will not be out-smarted, nor can His laws be by-passed. What you sow is what you will reap. If you sow to the interests of your body's desires, you will reap corruption; but if you sow to the interests of your spirit, you will reap eternal life. Let us not be weary in well doing because we shall reap at the proper time if we faint not. So as we have the opportunity, let us do good to all men, especially to them that are of the household of faith.

- **The false teachers do not keep the law (6:11-16):**
  - **They want to avoid persecution,**
  - **They want to boast they have another on their side.**
- **May I boast only in the cross...**
- **My body is branded with the marks of Christ (6:17).**
- **Benediction (6:18).**

These false teachers do not keep the law themselves. The only reasons why they are trying to force you to be circumcised is so that they may avoid being persecuted for preaching Christ, and that they may boast they have another on their side.

May I never boast except in the cross of our Lord Jesus Christ, through which the world has been crucified to me, and I to the world It is not circumcision that matters, nor uncircumcision, but whether one is a new creature. May mercy and peace be upon as many as walk by this rule and upon the Israel of God

Do not let any man trouble me, nor question the genuineness of my apostleship, because I bear branded on my body the marks of Jesus.

May the grace of our Lord Jesus Christ be with your spirit, brethren. Amen.

A summary concept:
- **<u>Spiritual freedom is in Christ, not through the Law of Moses</u>.**

Thumbnail sketch of Galatians:

The primary points of Galatians are easily set forth. There are six chapters, and they can be divided into three sections of two chapters each:

- *The first section is a defense of Paul's apostleship.*
- *The second section affirms that spiritual freedom is in Christ through the gospel, not through the law.*
- *The third section shows that this freedom should not be regarded as permission to give free reign to the desires of the flesh.*

James:
- **The Lord's brother.**
- **Not an apostle.**
- **Wrote the book of James.**

The James mentioned in the book of Galatians is the Lord's brother, not one of the apostles (Gal.1:19; see Mark 6:2-3; Acts 15:13). He is the one who wrote the book of James.

Paul was asked to remember the poor, which he was eager to do (Gal. 2:10).

Remember that the men in Jerusalem at the conference concerning circumcision asked that Paul remember the poor (Gal. 2:10). This point will play a major role in the story soon.

Paul preaches in Ephesus so that all that are in Asia hear the word (Acts 19:10-20):

Look on your map:

- **See the province of Asia with Ephesus as one of the cities.**
- **Probably the churches at Colossae, Laodicea, Thyatira, and in other Asian cities were established at this time (Rev. 1:11).**

For two years Paul preached in Ephesus, with the result that everyone in the province of Asia had opportunity to hear the word of God, both Jews and Greeks. During this time God worked unusual miracles by the hands of Paul. For example, handkerchiefs and aprons were carried from Paul's body to the sick, and they were healed, and evil spirits were expelled.

There were some vagabond Jews in Ephesus, itinerants, who wandered about acting as exorcists *(pretenders who "drove out" demons by magic charms)*. These men overheard Paul casting out demons and they heard him use the name of Jesus. Such men were always on the lookout for a new and powerful charm which they could use. Therefore they undertook to use this name of Jesus with some who were possessed, saying, "I adjure you by Jesus whom Paul preaches."

Seven sons of Sceva:

- **Vagabond Jews, exorcists.**
- **They thought Paul was using some kind of very effective charm to perform the miracles which he did.**
- **They "borrowed" the charm.**

One group who tried such a plan was composed of seven sons of a man named Sceva, a Jew who was an influential priest. The evil spirit whom they were trying to exorcize answered them: "Jesus I recognize, and Paul I know about, but who are you?" The possessed man leaped upon the brothers and beat them and overpowered them so that they fled from the house wounded and naked. This episode became known to all the Jews and Greeks in Ephesus, and everyone was moved to fear the name of the Lord. His name was greatly enhanced in respect and honor.

The word for <u>both</u> in this passage is used sometimes to refer to more than two (see Acts 23:8). The passage indicates that the possessed man was chasing and beating all seven exorcists.

The tense of the verb "burn:"

- **Instead of piling up these books of magic and burning them at once, a fire was started, and people came and added their books to the fire.**
- **This burning was not imposed upon the people by any outside authority;**
  - **It arose from their own rejection of the magical arts.**

Another result of Paul's preaching was that many of those who believed came confessing that they had been doing wrong, and telling what they had done. Many who used magical arts brought their books *(scrolls)* together and burned them in the sight of all. When they counted the value of the books, the figure came to fifty thousand pieces of silver.

Since the confessing of wrong-doing from the believers is mentioned directly in connection with those who used magical arts, it seems that some of these Gentile converts had been trying to hold to their old superstitions and charms without realizing they were in conflict with God's power and law. There would be no way to prove that these were the only sins that were confessed, however, because an increased awareness of the greatness of God enhances one's desire to be right in His sight in all areas of life.

Paul's plans at this time:

- **To stay in Ephesus until late spring,**
- **Pass through Macedonia and Greece *(Achaia)*,**
- **Go to Jerusalem,**
- **Then to Rome to preach.**
- **Label these places on your map:**
    - **Visualize the route Paul is planning to follow in the months ahead.**
- **Soon his plans change due to circumstances that arise.**

Paul plans to collect a gift from the Gentile congregations to take to the poor Jewish saints in Jerusalem:

- **Timothy and Erastus have gone into Macedonia;**
- **Timothy is to continue on to Corinth.**
- **Someone unnamed has gone to Galatia.**

Paul decides to go to Jerusalem; he sends Timothy and Erastus ahead to Macedonia (Acts 19:21-22):

After these things, Paul decided that he would go to Jerusalem, passing first through Macedonia and Greece. His plan was, as he said, "After I have gone there, I must also visit Rome." He decided to send two of his assistants, Timothy and Erastus, on ahead of him into Macedonia while he himself remained in Asia a little longer. According to First Corinthians 16:8, he intended to stay in Ephesus until Pentecost, which would be mid spring (*about the middle of our month of May*).

We learn from the letters of 1 and 2 Corinthians and Romans that this trip to Jerusalem was for the purpose of taking a gift from the predominately Gentile congregations that Paul had established to the poor saints (mostly Jews) in Jerusalem (see Rom. 15:25-26; 1 Cor. 16:1-3; see also Acts 24:17). We will be studying more about this gift as we proceed with the history. As early as the Jerusalem conference, James, Cephas (Peter), and John asked Paul to remember the poor, and Paul says he was very energetic in doing so (Gal. 2:10). This journey will demonstrate how energetic he was in the matter. He will risk his life in order to take the gift.

Timothy and Erastus leave the work in Ephesus to go into Macedonia, checking on the welfare of the congregations and probably telling more about this planned gift. Paul expected Timothy to make his way south to Corinth after a time in Macedonia (1 Cor. 16:10). Someone has also been sent to the churches of Galatia to tell them about the proposed gift, although no name is given (see 1 Cor. 16:1). The gift to the saints is not mentioned in the book of Galatians, so it was written before this plan was made.

Summary of First Corinthians

1 Corinthians:

- **Written from Ephesus,**
- **Very early spring of the year A.D. 57.**

We come now to the writing of two of the major epistles of Paul: 1 and 2 Corinthians. They were written within a few months of each other. First Corinthians was written at Ephesus (1 Cor. 16:8-9). It is the mention of the "great door of opportunity" which was open (16:9) that leads us to conclude that the letter was written shortly after the burning of the magical books described in Acts 19:13-20.

Trouble in Corinth may have hastened Paul's decision to send Timothy ahead of him (Acts 19:21-22), because in 4:17 he says, "For this cause I have sent unto you Timothy..." It is evident from reading the book, however, that Paul hoped most of the problems would be solved before Timothy arrived. According to 16:10, Paul realized Timothy might not arrive in Corinth before he himself did, perhaps because of difficulties Timothy might face along the way . Aquila and

Priscilla were still in Ephesus when First Corinthians was written (1 Cor. 16:19). Paul planned to leave Ephesus soon, to travel through Macedonia to Corinth, and to spend the winter with the Corinthians (16:5-7). This was a change in plans from what he had earlier told them, and he will explain that change of plans in 2 Corinthians 1:15-17, 23.

Aquila and Priscilla were still in Ephesus.

Paul hopes to visit Corinth soon:
- **Perhaps to spend the following winter there.**

First Corinthians closes, mentioning a great door of opportunity open to Paul in spite of many adversaries (16:9), possibly the renouncing of magic on the part of so many in Ephesus. Second Corinthians begins by telling of Paul's great affliction in Ephesus, so severe he "despaired even of life" (1:8-9), probably the riot and its aftermath that was caused by Demetrius and the silversmiths. Obviously, therefore, in a short time, Paul's circumstances changed drastically at Ephesus. These facts also point to the interval between Acts 19:22 and 23 as the time when 1 Corinthians was written.

At Ephesus:
- **There is a "great door of opportunity open" (1 Cor. 16:9),**
- **But conditions are about to change drastically.**

Fitting the facts mentioned in Paul's letters with facts told in Acts helps us to determine what was happening during this time. Visitors from Corinth had come to Ephesus to see Paul. They brought a letter with some questions for Paul to answer, but they also told him that the saints at Corinth were acting like squabbling babes instead of mature Christians. When Paul wrote them a letter to answer their questions, he first scolded them for their actions (see 1 Cor. 1:11; 7:1; 16:6-8, 15, 17-18).

Visitors from Corinth:
- **Brought a letter with questions for Paul to answer;**
- **They also brought word of trouble among the saints at Corinth.**
- **Paul deals with some of the problems first.**
- **Most of the problems were "people problems," not false doctrines.**
  - **Paul shows them a "better way."**

Most of the problems at Corinth were internal; most were "people problems"—revolving around attitudes and relationships between the brethren themselves. Some of the questions involved false ideas also, but even these false ideas could have been solved more easily if the people had the correct attitudes. Therefore, the whole book can be said to revolve around the point Paul makes in chapter 13. He says, "Let me show you a better way ..." (12:31b), and then he describes genuine love and all its characteristics. If brethren truly love God, truly love His word, and truly love each other, then internal problems can be solved. That is one of the greatest lessons to be learned from the book.

Let's refresh our memory about the church at Corinth. Paul went there on his second journey, and that is where he first met Aquila and Priscilla. (Acts 18:1-2). Paul's work was very successful, in spite of the fact that the city was known for its wicked inhabitants. Some of the ones converted had themselves participated in the wickedness before their conversion. After listing some of the sins of immorality in 1 Corinthians 6:9-10, Paul says "and such were some of you" (v. 11). Perhaps it is not surprising, therefore, that there was still some spiritual immaturity in their midst.

The church at Corinth:
- **Established on Paul's second journey.**
- **People were converted from the wicked population of the city.**

There are some other interesting details that we learn from the epistles that are not included in the book of Acts. Paul wrote a letter to the Corinthians that the Holy Spirit did not see fit to preserve for us. In it, he told them they should not associate with immoral brethren (1 Cor. 5:11). There was also a brief visit to Corinth sometime after his

- **An earlier letter had been sent to them.**

- **Paul had visited Corinth during this time he was at Ephesus.**

- **They already knew about the proposed gift for the saints of Judea.**

long stay there and before the time of the writing of the letter we call First Corinthians, because in 2 Corinthians 12:14, as Paul is telling them his plans to come to them shortly, he says this will be his third time to visit them. The book of Acts records only one time with them so far. The Corinthians already knew about the proposed gift for the saints in Judea, because they were the first congregation to begin collecting their bounty. By the time Paul writes 2 Corinthians, they had already spent a year collecting their portion (2 Cor. 8:10).

Study the book:

- **But do not lose sight of your history.**

Take time to make a brief study of this long important letter, but do not lose sight of the history. Remember that at the time of the writing of this epistle Paul is still on his third journey and that he is still at Ephesus.

Since it is a long book, look at this brief outline first in order to get an overall picture in mind.

Summary Outline of 1 Corinthians:

- You have everything you need to keep you strong and blameless (1:1-9):
  - For which I am thankful.
- But there is trouble among you (1:10-6:20):
  - There is division over preachers.
  - There is gross immorality in your midst.
  - You are going to law with brethren.
- Now about your questions (7:1-11:1):
  - Marriage
  - Eating meat sacrificed to idols
- Back to more problems (11:2-15:58):
  - Disorders in your worship
  - Improper use of spiritual gifts
  - Some are teaching there is no resurrection.
- Now concerning the collection for the saints... (16:1-14).
- Closing remarks... (16:15-24).

:

The letter says:

- **Introduction (1:1-9):**
  - **We give thanks...**
  - **You have everything you need.**

The letter says:

Paul and Sosthenes to the church of God at Corinth:

We give thanks for the way God has enriched you in all speech and knowledge, just as the testimony about Christ was confirmed among you. Therefore you do not lack in any gift as you wait for the revelation of our Lord Jesus Christ. You have everything you need to keep you strong and blameless against the coming of the Lord.

- **But there is trouble among you (1:10-6:20):**
- **Divisions over preachers (1:10-4:21):**

- **But there is trouble among you (1:10-6:20):**
- Division over preachers (1:10-17):

My brothers and sisters, I have been told by the household of Chloe that there are divisions among you. This is what I mean: you are fussing about which preacher you like best. Some of you are

- **Personal preferences about preachers (1:10-17).**
- **I was sent to preach...**

saying, "I like Peter best," or, "I like Apollos," or, "I like Paul," or, "I like Christ." Is Christ divided? Was Paul crucified for you? Were you baptized in the name of Paul?

I am glad I baptized none of you except Crispus and Gaius so that no one could say that I baptized in my own name. I also baptized the household of Stephanas. I don't know if I baptized anyone else. Who did the baptizing is not the point. God did not send me to do the baptizing but to preach the gospel, not with wisdom of words, lest the cross of Christ should not count.

This thread of division, coupled with the threads of worldly wisdom and pride, continue through chapter 4.

- **Worldly wisdom versus God's wisdom (1:18-2:16):**
  - **Message of the cross (1:18-2:5):**
    - **Foolishness...**
    - **Power of God...**
  - **Not many wise called.**
    - **Glory in the Lord.**
  - **My message:**
    - **Jesus Christ and Him crucified!**
  - **We speak true wisdom (2:6-16):**
    - **God planned...**
    - **Unknown...**
    - **Spirit searched God's mind,**
      - **The hidden wisdom...**
      - **Revealed it to us!**

- Worldly wisdom versus God's wisdom(1:18-2:16):

You have been given the message of the cross — foolishness to men, but the power of God to those who are saved. God chose to avoid making an appeal to the world's wisdom. It pleased Him to save those who believed through the foolishness of the message preached. Jews seek for a sign, and Greeks seek for wisdom, but we preach Christ crucified: to the Jews an obstacle, and to Greeks foolishness, but to those who are called, Christ, the power of God and the wisdom of God.

Consider yourselves as an example: Not many of the wise of this world, or of the mighty, or of the nobility, have been called. God chose you to shame the wise. God wanted it to be so that, as it is written, "He who glories, let him glory in the Lord."

When I came to you, brethren, I did not come planning to impress you with oratory or worldly wisdom. Therefore my message was one thing: Jesus Christ and Him crucified. I did not want your faith to be in the wisdom of men, but in the power of God.

The truth is that we do speak wisdom, but it is not a wisdom that originates with this world. It is a wisdom that God planned before the worlds, which none of the rulers of this world have known. Had they known it they would not have crucified the Lord of Glory. But, as it is written, "No man has seen, or heard, or even thought of the things God prepared for those who love Him."

The Spirit of God searched the depths of God's mind, to find His secret wisdom — the wisdom that had been hidden through all the centuries before us — and has now revealed it to us! A worldly man does not understand the things of the Spirit, because they are foolishness unto him, but the one who is spiritual judges all things.

- ***God's Spirit has revealed the whole mystery — the one that was hidden in the depths of God's mind.***

Did you notice the thought Paul expressed about God's wisdom in concealing His plan? If Satan had known how God planned to save mankind from Satan's clutches, he would not have killed the Christ! But God's whole plan was built around the sacrifice the Christ would offer for the sins of mankind — so He made His plans, gave enough predictions to let mankind realize the full significance when it all came to pass — and then He kept it a mystery until it was time for it to be accomplished. But now it is revealed! The whole story is complete! What wisdom! What a blessing!

- **The message — not the messenger (3:1-4:13):**
  - **You think like babes.**
  - **We are nothing but servants, delivering a treasure that came from God (3:1-15).**
    - **Farmers...**
    - **Builders...**
  - **Do not admire worldly wisdom (3:16-23):**
    - **Mere foolishness,**
    - **You belong to God.**
  - **We are servants with a responsibility(4:1-5):**
    - **God will judge how we discharge that duty.**
  - **Do not be puffed up... (4:6-13)**
    - **All you have is a gift.**
    - **You are boasting...**
    - **We are nothing...**

- It is the message that is important, not the messenger (3:1-4:13).

You are acting like babies, so I have to keep talking to you as if you were babies. You are still thinking the way this world thinks. When there is envy, fussing, and divisions among you, aren't you behaving like people of this world? When you line up after Paul or Apollos, are you not acting like men of this world?

Who are we? Servants! You are God's field; we are just workers, planting and watering, but God gives the yield. I, as a wise master builder laid a foundation, because I preached Christ among you, and no other foundation can be laid than Christ. But let those who come later be careful how they build on that foundation. Each man builds of different materials: some gold, some silver, some precious stones, others of wood, or hay, or straw. In the day of trial everyone's work is shown to be what it really is. The day of trial is as a fire. The fire burns some things and purifies others. If a man's work is burned up, he suffers loss, though he himself will be saved.

Let no one therefore become enamored with the wisdom of this world. God considers the wisdom of the world to be foolish. Let no one therefore boast in men, because God has placed all things at your disposal to make you what you are, and you are Christ's and Christ is God's.

So think of us as servants of Christ who have been given a responsibility. Faithfulness is required in servants, but I am not concerned with the judgment of a human court as to my faithfulness. Even I am not the one to judge myself. That I know of no failure of mine does not justify me; the one who is my judge is God. Do not therefore anticipate the judging that God will do when the Lord comes.

Now I have made application of these point to myself and Apollos so that by our example you might learn not to think of men above what is written, so that none of you will be puffed up against the other. The one who has made you different is the one who has given you what you have, but if you have been given these things, then why brag as if it is something you devised?

You have it made! You have everything! You already rule like kings! I wish you did, because then we could reign with you, but I think that God has put us, the apostles, on display as men condemned to death. We are something for the world to stare at; we hunger and thirst; we are poorly clothed; we are beaten and homeless; we labor with our hands. When we are reviled, we bless, and when we are persecuted, we endure. We have been made as filthy wash water.

- **I hope to come soon — in love, not with a whip (4:14-21).**

I am writing to you as a warning, not to shame you. You have many instructors, but not many fathers. I am your father in the gospel. Imitate me. For this reason I have sent Timothy to remind you of my ways. Some are puffed up as if I were not coming at all. But I will come shortly, if the Lord wills, and I will not be "talking big," like some do, but I will know the power of God. Which do you prefer, that I come to you with a whip, or in love and gentleness?

- **Gross immorality (5:1-13):**
  - **You are proud of your leniency!**
  - **Turn him over to Satan, so that he can be saved.**
  - **You will ruin the whole dough...**
  - **I wrote you about this before.**
  - **Do not associate with a guilty brother:**
    - **Put him away.**

- There is gross immorality in your midst (5:1-13):

It is commonly reported that you are letting a man who has committed fornication with his father's wife *(likely a stepmother)* remain in the church, and you are even proud of your leniency! Even though I am not present with you, I know what needs to be done. In the name of the Lord Jesus Christ, gather yourselves together, along with my spirit, and turn such a one over to Satan for the destruction of the flesh, so that his spirit can be saved in the day of the Lord Jesus Christ. Your pride is not good. Don't you know that a little leaven will leaven the whole mass of dough? Get rid of the old leaven so that you can be a new, fresh mass of dough. I wrote to you about not keeping company with the immoral. I did not mean the immoral of the world — you would have to go out of the world to do that — but I meant that if one who is considered a brother be guilty of such behavior, have no association with him. Those who are outsiders God will judge. Put away the wicked man from your midst.

- **Going to law against brethren (6:1-11):**
  - **Is there no wise man among you?**
  - **Better to be wronged than to cause trouble.**
  - **The wicked will not inherit the kingdom of God.**
  - **You have been justified,**
    - **Live accordingly.**

- Brethren are going to law against brethren (6:1-11):

I have also heard that some of you are getting lawyers and suing your fellow Christians — and that before unbelievers. Do you not know that the saints will judge the world? If this is true, do you mean to tell me that you cannot judge even the smallest things among yourselves? When you have disagreements among yourselves about things of this life, why do you go to those who are least esteemed by the church to judge your dispute? Is there no wise man among you who can arbitrate between you? This is not right. You are defeated already because, instead of taking offense if necessary, you cheat and wrong your own brethren! Don't you realize the wicked will not inherit the kingdom of God? Do not be misled. Neither fornicators, nor idolaters, nor adulterers, nor homosexuals, nor sodomites, nor thieves, nor greedy, nor drunkards, nor revilers, nor extortioners will inherit the kingdom of God You used to be wicked like these, but now you are washed, sanctified, and justified. Behave yourselves accordingly.

- **Honor God with your body (6:12-20):**
    - **Do not be a slave to your appetites.**
    - **Your body belongs to the Lord:**
        - **Do not join it to a harlot!**
    - **Your body is the temple of the Holy Spirit.**
        - **You were bought.**

- Honor God with your body, rather than defiling it (6:12-20):

All things may be lawful for me, but not all things are helpful. All things may be lawful, but I will not be made a slave by any of them. Food was made for the stomach, and the stomach for food, but the body was not made for fornication, but for the Lord. Do you not realize that your bodies are members of Christ? Shall I take the members of Christ and join them to a harlot? Or did you not know that he who is joined to a harlot is one body with her? "For the two," said He, "are become one flesh." But he who is joined to the Lord is one spirit with Him. Flee fornication. Every other sin that a man does, he does outside the body, but one who commits fornication sins against his own body. Don't you know that your bodies are the temple of the Holy Spirit? Do not, therefore, allow your bodies to be defiled by fornication. You were bought with a price. Honor God in your bodies.

- **Answers to your questions (7:1-11:1):**
- **Concerning marriage (7:1-40):**
    - **God's basic plan for marriage (7:1-7):**
        - **Each person has his own mate.**
        - **Each mate fulfills his responsibilities.**

- **Now about the things you wrote (7:1-11:1):**
- Your question concerning marriage (7:1-40):
- God's basic law for marriage (7:1-7):

It is good for a man not to touch a woman (*sexually*). Nevertheless, to help you avoid fornication, let each man have his own wife, and each woman have her own husband. Let each husband and wife meet the responsibilities to satisfy the other's sexual urges. Do not deprive one another of sexual satisfaction, unless it be by mutual consent, for a time, so that you may devote yourself to prayer and fasting, and then come together again. Otherwise Satan might tempt you because of your lack of self control.

- **Advice to unmarried and widows (7:8-9):**
    - **Good to remain unmarried,**
    - **But better to marry than to burn with desire.**

- Advice to unmarried and widows (7:8-9):

I wish that everyone were as I *(unmarried)* in this regard, but each man has his own particular gift or ability. But I say to the unmarried and widows that it would be good if they remained as I. But if they cannot control themselves, then let them marry. It is better to marry than to burn with desire.

The comments of Paul in this chapter that "It is good for a man not to touch a woman" (7:1), his encouragement for the single and the widows to remain unmarried (7:8), and his encouragement to fathers to keep their daughters single (7:38) are all in view of a peculiar circumstance: the present distress that was upon them (7:26). In other passages Paul encourages marriage (1 Tim. 2:15; 5:14). Paul is not denying what God said in the beginning: "It is not good for the man to be alone" (Gen. 2:18) —but it was a time of trouble and persecution, and therefore less difficult if one were alone.

- **The Lord's charge to the married (7:10-16):**
  - **Remain married.**
  - **If a separation comes:**
    - **Remain unmarried,**
    - **Or be reconciled.**

- God's charge to the married (7:10-16):

Now to the married, I give charge — really it is the Lord who has said this, not I — a wife is not to separate herself *(original means divorce)* from her husband. If she should do this, then let her remain unmarried or be reconciled to her husband. The same law applies to the husband.

Paul is not for one instant saying that one may divorce freely as long as he does not marry again. No, he just reaffirmed what the Lord said in Matthew 5:32 and 19:9 on this subject. If the woman divorces for some cause other than fornication, she has sinned. However, if she gets married, she does even worse: she commits fornication (Matt. 19:9). Therefore her immediate options are to remain unmarried or be reconciled to her husband.

- **If a saint has an unbelieving partner:**
  - **Do not put the unbeliever away,**
  - **But if the unbeliever leaves,**
    - **The saint is not a slave.**

But to the rest I say — the Lord did not speak specifically concerning this situation — if a man has an unbelieving wife, and she is willing to remain married, let him not leave her. The same is true with the woman that has an unbelieving husband. The unbeliever is sanctified (*in regard to the marriage)* by the partner who is a Christian. However, if the unbelieving partner departs, let him depart. The brother or sister involved is not a slave to have to agree to any terms to preserve the marriage.

- ***Service to the Lord is of more importance than preserving a marriage.***

It is commonly argued that verse 15 is the "Pauline exception" for scriptural divorce in addition to the exception of fornication stated by the Lord (Matt. 19:9). However, it is clear that, even though Jesus did not deal specifically with the matter of a believer having an unbelieving mate, His statements underlie what Paul says about the matter. As in any marriage, they are not to divorce. If the unbeliever is not satisfied, and is determined to leave, the Christian partner is not at fault. And, as a slave, a Christian would have no choice about going with a master, no matter what the master required, but a Christian is not a slave. If a husband demanded that his wife give up her association with the saints to preserve her marriage, she does not have to do that. If an unbelieving partner divorces his wife, then the situation fits the general circumstances set forth by the Lord in Matthew 5:32 and 19:9. Neither partner would have the right to marry again. The unbeliever might not respect the Lord's teachings on this point, but the believer must do so. The law does not change — but Paul is saying that if the choice comes to serving the Lord or preserving the marriage, let the unbelieving partner go. Service to the Lord always comes first.

There was a special situation in the first century. The gospel went out all over the Roman world, and there would have been many cases where one partner in a marriage was converted — and the other not. That is the situation under consideration in 1 Corinthians 7. The New Testament never encourages a Christian to marry a non-Christian, though it never specifically forbids it. But any Christian who marries one who is an unbeliever should be aware that the problems that may arise are enormous. Let the saint beware!

- **One can serve God, whether (7:17-24):**
  - **Jew or Gentile,**
  - **Slave or free,**
  - **Married or single.**

- One can serve God in whatever state he finds himself (7:17-24):

  In the situation one was when he was called, let him remain. If one were called, being a Jew, he does not have to become a Gentile. If a Gentile were called, he does not have to become a Jew. It is not circumcision or uncircumcision that matters, but the keeping of the commandments of God. Were you called as a slave? Do not let that bother you. Even if you become free, count it merely as an advantage you can use. If you were free, realize you are now Christ's slave. Let each man remain in the circumstances in which he was called.

It is obvious from this very epistle that when Paul says to remain as one is, he is talking about social situations, not immoral, sinful ones. Those practicing the sins of 6:9-11 obviously had to cease sinning when they were justified. Therefore such verses as 7:20, 24 cannot be used to say that one may remain in an unscriptural marriage. If a marriage relationship is sinful in God's sight, it must be renounced as surely as a sinful homosexual relationship (Matt. 14:4) — or the lifestyle of the thief.

- **Times of distress are upon you (7:8, 25-39):**
  - **Do not change your marriage status.**
  - **Better if unmarried:**
    - **To be free from cares;**
  - **But you do not sin if you marry.**
  - **A father does not sin if he allows his daughter to marry.**

- Times of distress are upon you (7:8, 25-38):

  Now concerning what to do about letting your virgin daughters marry, I have no command of the Lord, but I give my judgment as one who has been regarded by the Lord as trustworthy. Because of the hard times that are upon us, I think it is better not to change one's marriage status. If you are married, remain married. If you are free of a wife, do not seek a wife, but if you marry you have not sinned.

  The sober truth is that many changes are going to be brought upon people so that those that have wives will be as those who have none, and those that weep as they that weep not, and those that rejoice as they that rejoice not. I am concerned that you be free from cares. One who is unmarried does not have a wife and family to be worried about. The widow and the woman who has never married can concentrate on the things of the Lord, but the woman who is married must also be concerned with her husband. I am saying these things to help you, not to put an obstacle in your path.

  If a father thinks that he is mistreating his daughter in not letting her marry, if she is getting past marriageable age, if he chooses to let her marry, he will not be sinning. But the father who can avoid the necessity of letting his daughter marry shall do well. So the one who gives his virgin daughter in marriage shall do well; and the one who succeeds in keeping her unmarried will do better.

- **The married is bound so long as the partner lives.**

A woman is bound *(tied)* by law to her husband as long as he lives. If he is dead, she can marry anyone she wants in the Lord. But she will be happier if she remains as she is in my judgment.

It must be continually borne in mind that these instructions on the inadvisability of getting married are not the normal ones. In 1 Timothy 5:14, the younger widows are strongly encouraged to marry. These instructions were given in view of a "distress" that was upon the saints, or was about to be upon them. Saints were already experiencing sporadic local conflicts because of their faith, and it was only a few short years before the Roman government itself began its terrible persecution of Christians. Paul's advice was timely.

- **Eating meat sacrificed to idols; "spiritual rights" (8:1-11:1):**
  - **You have knowledge:**
    - **No idol is a god;**
    - **Sacrificed meat is not contaminated (8:1-6).**

- Eating meat sacrificed to idols; the question of "spiritual rights" (8:1-11:1):
- "Knowledge" versus love for your brother (8:1-13):

Concerning the eating of things sacrificed to idols: We have knowledge, but knowledge can puff one up *(make one swell)*, whereas love seeks to do what is good for another. It is true that no idol is anything, and that there is no God but one. But not everyone has that knowledge. One used to idolatry might eat the meat as sacrificed to an idol *(still considering it as a sacrifice to the false god)*. But mere food is not what commends us to God, whether we eat it or not.

- **But what about the weak brother?**
  - **Will your "right" to eat the meat cause him to partake in idolatrous worship? (8:7-13).**
  - **You sin if your "rights" cause him to perish.**

But beware lest this liberty of yours becomes a stumbling block to someone else. If a weak brother sees you, who has knowledge, eating in an idol's temple, your example will make him think it is all right to eat meat in worship of idols. You could argue that you have the *right* to eat as you please, but would you be willing to pursue your right even if it caused a weak brother to stumble? If you sin against your brother because of your "knowledge," and cause him to perish — the one for whom Christ died — you have sinned. Therefore, if eating meat will cause my brother to stumble, then I will never eat meat again.

- **Paul says, "I have 'rights' too" (9:1-27):**
  - **But I have not used them,**
  - **Lest I hinder my work for the Lord.**

- Paul had "rights" that he had not used (9:1-27):

I have rights too. Am I not an apostle? Even if others do not consider me an apostle, you should: you are the stamp of my apostleship in the Lord. Have we no right to eat and to drink? Don't Barnabas and I have the right to marry, or to be supported while preaching the gospel? What soldier ever supported himself? Am I drawing illustrations only from men, or does not the law say the same? It is written in the law of Moses, "Thou shalt not muzzle the ox when he treads the grain." This statement is written, not primarily for the ox's sake, but for our sake, that we might understand this principle. Still, I have not used these rights, to make me more effective in my work. Do not the priests live from the altar upon which they minister? Just so, the Lord ordained that they that preach the gospel should live from the gospel.

- **I have lived in whatever style necessary in order to convert souls.**

Instead of seeking my rights, I have become all things to all men. Among Jews I lived as one under the law; among Gentiles I lived as one without the law, not being without law as far as God is concerned, but being under law to Christ. Other things must come before our "rights" sometimes.

- **Remember your goal...**

I do everything for the gospel's sake. Do you not understand that everyone runs in the race, but only one wins the prize? Even so, run so that you may attain. Every athlete exercises great self control and discipline, and they do it to win a corruptible crown,

- **I discipline myself for the gospel's sake.**

but we an incorruptible one. In the same way, I run with discipline *(self-restraint)*. I do not fight as one swinging at the air, but I beat my body black and blue to keep myself from being rejected after I have preached to save others.

- **Beware lest ye fall (10:1-13):**
  - **Your fathers fell.**

- Do not be over-confident of your ability to resist temptation (10:1-13):

I remind you that you can be over-confident of your ability to withstand temptation. Our forefathers had many spiritual advantages; yet we know God was not well-pleased with them, because

- **They became idolaters...**

they fell in the wilderness. These things were written about them to be our examples, so that we should not lust after evil things as they did (Num. 11:4). Neither be idolaters as some of them were

- **Their example is our warning.**

(Exod. 32:1-8). Neither let us commit fornication as they did, and 23,000 fell in one day (Num. 25). Neither let us test the Lord's patience, as some of them did, and perished by the serpents (Num.

- **Beware lest you fall...**
  - **You could become idolaters again.**
- **There is always a way of escape.**

21:6). Neither complain, as some them did, and perished by the destroyer (Num. 16:41-50). These things happened to them by way of warning. So let the one who thinks he is standing be careful lest he fall. There is no temptation to which you will be subjected that is not common to all men. Someone has been tempted as you are and has resisted. God will not allow you to tempted above what you are able to bear, but He will provide a way of escape for every temptation.

Stop and think for a moment. Many of these Corinthians had been very wicked men of the Gentile world before conversion (6:11) —and their conversion had taken place within the last five years. Yet Paul expected them to know the stories of Jewish history well enough for him to use the events to teach the lessons they needed now! Sometimes we excuse ourselves for not knowing the Old Testament when we may have been Christians for many decades. Would the writer of Hebrews scold us by saying "...for though by this time you ought to be teachers, you have need again for someone to teach you to elementary principles of the oracles of God" (Heb. 5:11-14)?

- **Do not join the worship at the idol temples (10:14-22):**
  - **Flee idolatry!**
  - **The idol is nothing...**
  - **But one has fellowship with the false worship when he joins in the sacrifices.**
  - **The recipient of that false worship is the Devil.**
  - **You cannot be joined to the Lord and to the Devil at the same time.**

- Do not participate in the worship at the idol temples (10:14-22):

Therefore, flee idolatry! Do not be overconfident in dealing with idols. Is there not a reality behind our worship? When we drink the cup of blessing, does it not represent the reality of Christ's blood? And when we eat the bread do we not share in communion of the body of Christ? All of us, being many are one bread, one body, because we are all partakers of the one loaf, and are made one by it. When physical Israel ate the sacrifices, did they not have fellowship with the altar?

What am I saying, that an idol is real? No. You are telling yourselves, "This idol is not really a god, so I can go to the false god's temple and be there when sacrifices are offered to it, and I can eat the sacrifice. It will not matter because he is not a god anyway." But it does matter! Even though the false god is not a god at all, you should have nothing to do with worshiping it. The one who receives the worship you give to that false god is the Devil! You know you cannot drink the cup of the Lord and the cup of demons. You cannot partake of the table of the Lord and the table of demons. Do you want to provoke the Lord to jealousy? So, do not go to the idol temples.

- ***Who receives false worship offered today?***

Who receives the worship offered in false religious services of our day? There is usually no idol sitting in the building, but is not the principle the same? We tend to be frightened by a newspaper report of "Satanic worship," but totally unalarmed by all the false religions around us. Why? A frightening thought!

- **Lawful versus expedient (10:23-11:1):**
  - **Eat meat from the market...**
  - **If you are offered meat with no comment, then eat.**
  - **But if it served as sacrificed meat, decline it.**
  - **Follow my example in this matter.**

- "Lawful" versus "expedient" (10:23-11:1):

Everything that is lawful may not always be expedient *(wise, appropriate, helpful)*. Let every man seek to do good for his neighbor. Whatever is sold in the street meat markets, eat. You need not question the source of the meat for conscience's sake, because you have bought it merely as meat to eat, and the earth is the Lord's and everything in it.

If an unbeliever asks you to eat at his home, and you desire to do so, eat whatever is set before you without asking questions. But if some man informs you that the meat has been offered in sacrifice, then do not eat it, not for your conscience, but for his. Whether you eat or drink, do everything to glory God. Do not cause anyone to stumble in his behavior by your actions. I seek to please men in all things, not seeking my own profit, but what is good for others. Be imitators *(follow my example)* of me, even as I am of Christ.

- **Back to more problems among you (11:2-15:58):**
- **Disorders in the worship (11:2-34):**
- **Forgotten roles (11:2-16):**
  - **God ordained our roles...**
  - **Show by your dress in worship that you remember your role.**

- **Back to more problems among you (11:2-15:58):**
- Disorders in the worship (11:2-34):
- Failure to show proper submission, based upon God's order (11:2-16):

I want you to remember that God is over *(head over)* Christ, Christ is head over every man, and man is head over the woman. Every man who prays or prophesies with his head covered dishonors his head *(Christ)*. Therefore let not the man cover his head because he is the image and glory of God. But let every woman who prays or prophesies do so with her head covered. The man is not from the woman, but the woman from the man. Also man was not created for the woman, but the woman for the man. Judge for yourselves: is it proper for a woman to pray to God uncovered? Doesn't nature *(long established custom)* itself teach you that if a man has long hair, it is a shame to him? But if a woman has long hair, it is a glory to her because her hair is given to her for a covering. But if any man intends to be contentious about the matter, we have no such custom, neither the churches of God.

- **Partake of the Lord's Supper with proper reverence (11:17-34):**
  - **You have made the Supper a mere meal...**
  - **The Lord ordained the Supper...**
  - **Showing disrespect brings judgment upon one...**

- Failure to partake of the Lord's Supper with proper reverence (11:17-34):

I regret to hear that when you assemble, it is not for the better, but for the worse. It is reported that there are factions among you. When you come together, it is not to eat the Lord's Supper. Each one eats before the other, and one is hungry, and another is drunken. The Lord's Supper is not a common meal, and should not be eaten as one. Don't you have houses in which to eat your common meals?

I received from the Lord that which I told you, that the night in which He was betrayed, He took bread, and when He had given thanks, He broke it and gave it to His disciples saying, "Take this and eat, because this is my body which is broken for you." In the same way, He took the cup after supper and said, "This cup is the new covenant in my blood. Do this, as often as you drink it, in memory of me." Whoever therefore eats the bread or drinks the cup of the Lord in an unworthy manner shall be guilty of the body and blood of the Lord. If you do not eat the Lord's Supper properly, you will bring judgment upon yourselves.

- **Improper use of spiritual gifts (12:1-14:40):**
  - **There is jealousy among you (12:1-31).**

- Improper use of spiritual gifts (12:1-14:40):
- There is jealousy among you (12:1-31):

Before you were converted you worshiped idols that could not even speak and you were led in whatever direction you might be. But the Spirit of Christ teaches all men the same things and the same attitude toward Jesus.

- **All spiritual gifts come from the same Spirit,**
- **The same Lord is served,**
- **The same God gives abilities.**

There are many kinds of gifts given by the Holy Spirit. There is a variety of services, but the same Lord is served, and there is a diversity of abilities but the same God who enables all. Some have the ability to teach wisdom, others can teach knowledge, some have the power to do miracles; some can prophesy. Some speak in languages they never studied, and some can interpret such tongues. But it is the same Spirit that makes these abilities work among you just as He wishes.

- **Many members, but we are all part of one body...**
- **We must function as a healthy body...**

The church has many different people in it. By one Spirit we were all baptized into one body. The body is not one member but many, and everyone does not do the same thing. It is like your body: do your ears do the same things as your eyes? Are you glad you have feet *and* hands? You need all the parts of your body. In the same way, you need all the people in the church. God has set us in the body in the same way it is with our physical bodies. Some of our members are not as presentable as others, but to them we give more honor. All the members of our bodies care equally about the other members, no matter how small or insignificant. Therefore, if one member suffers, the other members suffer with it, or if one member rejoices, the other members are happy with it.

- **No competition.**

So God has set functions and abilities of all different kinds in the church. They are not in competition with each other. Desire earnestly the greater and more helpful gifts— but let me show you a better way to deal with these things.

- **A better way — Love (13:1-13):**
  - **If I do the greatest of acts, but do not have love, it is worthless.**
  - **True love seeks the other's welfare...**
  - **Love never fails...**

- I show you a more excellent way (13:1-13):

  Love one another. Even if I speak with the tongues of men and of angels, if I have not love as my motive, I am just making noises. If I am able to do stupendous miracles, and though I give my body to be burned, without love it is all worthless. Love suffers long, and is kind. If you love one another, you are glad to see something good happen to your friend. You will not envy him. Neither will you brag when you have something he does not have. Love does not keep a list of grievances. Love goes on and on, but the speaking of prophecies will stop; tongues will cease; the giving of knowledge will cease. Now we know in part, and we prophesy in part, but when that which is perfect is come, then that which is partial will be done away. When a man is still a child, his speaking and his understanding are immature, and things are characteristic of him that will not be later. When he grows up, he puts away the things of his childhood, the things connected with his immaturity. Now faith, hope, and love remain, but the greatest of these is love.

- **The proper way to use spiritual gifts (14:1-40):**

- The proper way to use the gifts you have (14:1-40):

  You should have the greatest desire for the spiritual gift that will be most beneficial to the church. The one who speaks in a tongue edifies himself, but if no one understands what he is saying,

- **Desire the gifts most helpful to the church,**
  - **Not the most impressive.**

it is of no value to the church. The gift of greatest value is prophecy *(inspired teaching)* because this is how men learn God's will. Unless the inner man participates in the worship, the worship is vain. It is as when one gives thanks: if one does not understand what is being said, how can he say, "Amen" at the giving of thanks? I thank God that I speak with tongues more than you all. Nevertheless, I would rather speak five words with my understanding, so that I could instruct others, than ten thousand words in a tongue.

- **Do not be like children with a toy...**

Brethren, do not be like children in your maturity, but in malice, be like children. In the law it is written, "By men of strange tongues will I speak to this people, and even then they will not hear me." Therefore, tongues are a sign, not to them that believe, but to the unbelieving. But prophesying is for them that believe. If therefore the whole church be gathered together, and everyone is speaking with tongues, and some men, untaught and unbelieving, come in and hear you, they will think you are insane. But if everyone teaches, and a man comes in, untaught and unbelieving, then he will learn, he will be convicted, and he will fall down on his face and worship God.

- **Seek to build up, to teach by your gift...**
  - **Take turns, be orderly...**
  - **God is not the source of confusion.**

So what shall we say? Whatever anyone has to say or to teach, let it be done so as to build up and help. If any man speaks in a tongue, let there be only two, or at the most three who do so, and let them take turns, with someone interpreting what is said. If there is no interpreter, then let not the one who would speak in tongues address the assembly. Let those who prophesy also take turns. The spirits of the prophets are under the control of the prophets, so each can wait his turn. God is not the source of confusion.

- **Let the women be quiet *(not taking a public role)* in the assembly.**

As in all the churches, let the women refrain from addressing the assembly, for it is not permitted to them to speak, but let them be in subjection even as the law says. And if they would like to ask about what has been said, let them ask their husbands at home, for it is shameful for a woman to address the church.

- **If one will not accept these instructions, do not accept him.**

If any man thinks himself to be a prophet, or spiritually minded, let him acknowledge that the things I have written to you are the commandment of the Lord. If a man refuses to acknowledge this, then do not acknowledge him.

Therefore, my brethren, desire sincerely to prophesy, and do not forbid to speak with tongues, but let everything be done with decorum and in order.

- **Some are teaching there is no resurrection (15:1-58):**
  - **Jesus died, was buried, and was raised from the dead (15:1-11).**

- Some are teaching there is no resurrection (15:1-58):

Brethren, let me remind you of the gospel which I received and which I delivered to you: Jesus died for our sins as the scriptures foretold, He was buried, and He was raised on the third day, as the scriptures said He would be. Many witnesses saw Him after He

- **If this is true, how can some say there is no resurrection (15:12-19)?**
  - **All would be useless...**
- **But Christ *has* been raised (15:20-28),**
  - **He will reign until death is conquered.**
- **If the dead are not raised, why risk our lives (15:29-34)?**

arose, including me. So we all have believed, and so we have preached.

Since we have preached that Christ was raised from the dead, how is it that some among you are teaching that there is no resurrection of the dead? If that is true, Christ is not risen, and if that is true, then our preaching is useless, and you are still in sin.

But Christ has been raised, the very first of all the dead to be raised permanently. He must reign until the very end, when the last enemy shall be conquered, which is death. Then He will turn the kingdom over to God who will be over all.

If the dead are not raised, then why be baptized with a view to them? Why hazard our lives for the gospel? If the dead are not raised, we might as well eat and drink, for tomorrow we die. Do not be deceived: associating with the wrong companions will corrupt your morals. Be serious and do not sin, for some have no knowledge of God. I say this to move you to shame.

- **Do not let your questions about the resurrection disturb you (15:29-49).**
- **Some will not die, but all will be part of the resurrection (15:50-58).**
  - **Victory over death!**
  - **Stand firm.**

- Do not let your questions about the resurrection destroy your faith (15:29-49).

Don't let your questions about the resurrection keep you from believing that it will happen. For example, what kind of bodies will we have? Well, there are different kinds of flesh now, and different kinds of glory, so it is not surprising that we will have a different kind of body in the resurrection. Now we have a physical body; in the resurrection we will have a glorified body.

Not everyone will die. Those who are still alive when the Lord returns will be changed in a split second. Those who are dead will be raised incorruptible. Then will come to pass the saying which has been written: "O death, where is thy sting? O grave, where is thy victory?" But let us thank God who gives us the victory through our Lord Jesus Christ. Therefore, my beloved brethren, keep working hard and don't give up, because your labor in Christ is not useless.

- **The collection for the saints (16:1-4).**
  - **Lay aside your portion upon the first day of the week (16:1-2).**
  - **One you choose will take your gift, or accompany me (16:3-4).**

- **Information concerning the collection for the saints (16:1-4):**

Now concerning the collection for the saints, you need to do just as I have instructed the churches of Galatia: on the first day of the week, let each one put aside as God has given him so that it will not have to be gathered when I come. When I come, whomever you choose will be sent to carry your contribution to Jerusalem, and if it seem wise for me to go also, he will accompany me.

Notice that neither the book of Acts, nor the epistle of 1 Corinthians tell many details about this gift to the saints in Jerusalem. There will be more information given in 2 Corinthians and Romans, but it is obvious that personal messengers such as Timothy, Erastus, and others, gave most of the details about the plans. From 2 Corinthians

8:10, we learn that the Corinthians had known about the gift and had been making preparation for some months before this letter was written. Paul tells them how they are to collect the money, and what their own attitudes should be about giving, but very few other details are needed.

- **Close of the epistle (16:5-24).**
  - **Paul's plans (16:5-9):**
    - **Remain in Ephesus until Pentecost,**
    - **Pass through Macedonia,**
    - **Spend the winter in Corinth,**
    - **Go from there to Jerusalem.**
  - **Warnings and greetings (16:10-24).**
- ***See Paul's planned route on your map. His plans will have to change a little, but we will soon learn why in the book of Acts.***

- **Close of the epistle (16:5-24):**

I will come to you after I pass through Macedonia. I hope to spend the winter with you and then to set out on my journey from you. I do not want to stop by only briefly; I hope to stay with you for a while. I plan to remain at Ephesus until Pentecost because a great door of opportunity has been opened for me, but there are many adversaries.

If Timothy comes, see that he dwells among you without fear. He does the work of the Lord as I do, so let no man despise him but help him on his way so that he may come to me. I asked Apollos to come, but he felt it was out of the question. He will come to you when he can.

Be watchful; be steadfast in faith; behave like men; be strong. Let everything you do be done in love.

You know how the household of Stephanas has set themselves to serve the saints. Assist them in their endeavors as well as everyone who helps in the work. I rejoiced at the coming of Stephanas and Fortunatus and Achaicus, because they supplied what was lacking on your part. They refreshed my spirit and yours.

The churches of Asia greet you. Aquila and Prisca *(a short form of Priscilla)* send you greetings, with the church that is in their house. All the brethren greet you.

This is the salutation that I sign with my own hand. If any man does not love the Lord, let him be accursed. O Lord, come. The grace of our Lord Jesus Christ be with you. My love be with you all in Christ Jesus. Amen.

A summary concept:
- **<u>Love, the better way to avoid church problems.</u>**

Thumbnail sketch of 1 Corinthians:

Most of the problems at Corinth were "people problems," rather than false doctrine. The only false doctrine discussed was concerning the resurrection. People were choosing sides after various preachers, the church was harboring a notorious evil-doer, people were determined to get their way, to have their rights, regardless of what happened to the weak who got in the way. They were not conducting themselves in worship as they should, and they were competing over who had the most sensational spiritual gift. Paul shows them that these problems could be not only be solved, but largely avoided, if only they all truly loved God and truly loved one another.

This letter teaches that church problems can be, and must be, solved by love, but the love required is one which is not selfish, a love which will rebuke the evil, one which will not boast itself — a love that relies upon the message of the cross of Christ. Whether the problem is division over personal preferences, immorality, the selfish pursuing of one's own interests without regard to anyone else, or competing with one another over who has the greatest gift — there is a better way: love. Let us learn the lesson of the book in every congregation across our land!

Demetrius and the silversmiths (Acts 19:23-41):

Trouble arises from Gentiles:
- **It is a local affair.**
- **The Roman government is still not involved.**

On more than one occasion in the book of Acts, the "way of Christ" is shortened to "the Way" (see 24:22).

About this time a great stir arose in Ephesus concerning the Way. A certain silversmith named Demetrius made silver shrines of their goddess Diana and he received much income from his craft. He called for a meeting of all his fellow craftsmen.

The items made by Demetrius and his co-workers were mostly small replicas of the temple of Diana in which the goddess was situated. Some statues of the goddess herself have been found. Some of the figures were small enough to be worn as amulets (charms to protect one from danger) on a journey. No figures of silver have been found, but shrines of terra-cotta and marble abound in the area around Ephesus. Silver ones were melted down as they were found for their intrinsic value. The craftsmen included the men who worked to make these shrines in various substances.

Though Diana was called "Artemis" among the Greeks, she was not the same as the Greek goddess Artemis who was "queen and huntress, chaste and fair." This Diana was the local manifestation of the "great mother of gods and men" who had been worshiped in Asia Minor from ancient times.

One can almost hear the rising volume of Demetrius' voice as he stirs up the crowd. The early temple of Diana was burned down in 356 B.C. by a young man named Herostratus who did it "so that his name would go down in history." It was rebuilt on an even grander scale. People all over the Roman empire worshiped her.

Though Demetrius expresses concern for the welfare of their goddess, the main concern of the craftsmen was that their business was suffering.

> Demetrius spoke to the craftsmen, saying:
>
> Gentlemen, you know that it is by this business of ours that we have our wealth. You are also aware that not just at Ephesus, but practically throughout Asia, this Paul has persuaded many people to turn away from Diana by saying that there are no gods made with hands. Therefore not only is there danger that our trade may come to nought, but also that the temple of the great goddess Diana should be made of no account, and that she should be brought down from her magnificence — the one whom all Asia and the world worships!

"Great is Diana of the Ephesians!"

We are meeting new companions of Paul:

- **Erastus has gone with Timothy into Macedonia;**
- **Gaius and Aristarchus are captured here because they were Paul's companions;**
- **Sosthenes joined with Paul in the salutation of 1 Corinthians.**
- **No information is given about when these men joined him, or exactly what role they have played in the work.**

When the craftsmen heard these things, they were filled with rage and began to shout, "Great Diana of the Ephesians!"

As the shouting continued, the city was filled with confusion. Soon a full-scale riot was in progress. People in the streets rushed together into the theater with Gaius and Aristarchus, Macedonians who had been Paul's traveling companions. These two men were in great danger. Paul thought he needed to go into the theater to speak to the people, but the disciples would not let him. Certain of the Asiarchs, who were Paul's friends, sent word to him, begging him not to risk his life in the theater.

This theater was perhaps the largest in the world at that time. It had a diameter of 495 feet and held 24,500 people. A letter from ancient times has been found that condemns the Ephesians for submitting important matters to the decisions of mobs in the theater (Pseudo-Heraclitus, Letter vii, 47).

These Asiarchs were prominent and wealthy men of the provinces who formed a council of Asia which pre-dated Roman rule. From them were chosen the high priests in the cult of Rome and Caesar. In addition to their other duties, they were called upon to provide athletic games, partly, if not wholly, at their own expense, and to preside over them. That they were so immediately accessible on this occasion indicates they were together (normally they lived in different cities) to prepare for some upcoming games.

Two very different examples of the word commonly translated "church," ***ekklesia*****:**

- **It is the word "assembly" in verse 32, which was a mob come together;**
- **It is the word "assembly" in verse 39, which refers to the legislative assembly.**

Pandemonium ruled as one cried out one thing in the mob and others something else. Most in the crowd did not even know what the riot was about. The Jews tried to get the mob to listen to Alexander, a spokesman of theirs. He lifted his hand to get their attention, but when the mob perceived he was a Jew, they all shouted together for about two hours, "Great Diana of the Ephesians!"

Finally the town clerk came out to speak to the crowd. When he had quieted them, he said:

> You men of Ephesus, what man does not know that the city of Ephesus is temple-custodian of the great Diana, and of that which is fallen from Jupiter? Since these things cannot be denied, you ought to be quiet, and to do nothing rash. You have brought these men here who are not temple looters, nor blasphemers of our goddess.
>
> If, therefore, Demetrius and his people have a legitimate complaint against any man, the courts are open, and there are proconsuls; let them accuse one another. If you have other matters, they will be dealt with in the regular assembly. We are in danger of being accused concerning this day's riot, since there is no cause for it, and we will not be able to explain it.

The town clerk quieted the mob and sent them home.

Having said these things, he dismissed the crowd.

The town clerk was the most important man in the city. Decrees which were considered by the public assembly were drafted by him and other planners, and money left for the city was in his charge. As the importance of the assembly declined under Roman rule, his office became more and more important. This town clerk exhibited great intelligence and skill in handling the mob on this occasion.

Paul has spent three years at Ephesus, preaching the whole counsel of God in spite of severe trials.

Paul is still on his third preaching journey.

Label your map:

- **As he leaves Ephesus,**
- **Goes to Troas,**
- **Then across the Aegean Sea to Macedonia.**

By now Paul has spent three very successful years in Ephesus (see Acts 20:31). Acts 19 tells of trouble that arose early in his stay from unbelieving Jews —and now a riot has broken out. Though the riot was quieted on this day, the trouble must not have ended there because Paul begins the second letter to Corinth by describing the hardships in Asia. He even despaired for his life (2 Cor. 1:8-11). As we combine the information given in Acts 19, in 2 Corinthians, and in Acts 20 when Paul talks to the Ephesian elders, it is evident there were persecutions and trials during the whole three years. He says he served the Lord and preached what was needed in tears, and in spite of the severe trials brought about by the plots of the Jews (20:19).

Paul leaves Ephesus and travels to Macedonia (Acts 20:1):

After the uproar ceased, Paul called the disciples to him and exhorted them. Having done this, he set out for Macedonia.

The Summary of 2 Corinthians

"Thanks be to God for His indescribable gift!" (9:15):

- **The God who expects no more of us than we can give;**
- **The God who strengthens us to do more than we think possible;**
- **The God who could take a blasphemer and transform him into one of His most faithful servants.**
- **He is the God who, with trials, also gives blessings and comfort.**

Second Corinthians is a window into the feelings — both of anxiety and of comfort — that the apostle Paul endured during the year touched on so briefly by Luke in Acts 19:21-20:3. It is very rare to have an opportunity to know intimately the heart of a historical character — and certainly rare to see into the heart of a man as great as Paul. Second Corinthians gives us this gift of insight into the great heart of Paul.

It is reassuring to us to know that Paul felt the need for comfort. How did he bear all his trials, the trials that he enumerates in this very book (chapter 11)? The truth is he could hardly bear them at times. One of the greatest lessons of the book is that the furtherance of the kingdom of God is the greatest of causes. The reason why Paul could "keep on keeping on" was that the ministry of the gospel was so great it was worth any cost. Nothing could be permitted to thwart it — but even Paul needed comfort, and he praises the God of all comfort who gives it: the great God who expects no more of us than we can give, the God who strengthens us to do more than we think possible.

Paul's plans have changed:

- **The "door of opportunity" had closed in Ephesus.**
- **It seems he left Ephesus earlier than expected.**

Paul closed the book of 1 Corinthians saying that a "great door of opportunity" was open for him in Ephesus (1 Cor. 16:9). For that reason, and other considerations, we placed the writing of that first book after the burning of the books of magic that is told about in Acts 19:19-20. At that time, Paul was planning to remain in Ephesus until Pentecost, which would be late spring (1 Cor. 16:8). He planned to travel through Macedonia (16:5) on his way to Corinth, where he hoped to spend the winter (16:6) before going on to Jerusalem (16:3) to take the proposed gift for the poor saints there.

When we combine the facts that trouble arose in Ephesus, that Paul had thought he might meet Titus in Troas, and that he has caught up with Timothy in Macedonia, we come to the conclusion that Paul left Ephesus earlier than he had first intended (see 1 Cor. 16:8-9). That great door of opportunity that had opened in Ephesus seems to have closed rapidly. The riot led by Demetrius the silversmith broke out, and though it was stopped that same day, persecution against Paul must have continued, because by the time he wrote his second letter to the Corinthians he described the affliction that arose in Asia as so severe he despaired even of life (2 Cor. 1:8-10). He says that it was only through God, and through the Corinthians' help through their prayers, that he managed to escape.

Paul is deeply burdened:

- **The trouble in Ephesus,**
- **The first letter to Corinth,**
  - **Titus has not reached him with information about how the Corinthians received the letter.**
- **There were persecutions in Macedonia also.**

The book of Acts tells that when Paul left Ephesus on this third preaching trip, he went to Macedonia (20:1), but it is 2 Corinthians that tells that he went northwest from Ephesus to Troas, then across the sea to Macedonia (2:12-13). As he was going through "those parts" of Macedonia (Acts 20:2), he wrote his second letter to the Corinthians.

Paul describes himself as a heavily burdened man as he made the trip. Note how often he mentions his "afflictions" or "suffering" in the first two chapters. The trauma of the riot in Ephesus and the terrible conflict he had endured had taken a severe toll (2 Cor. 1:8-9). He was also deeply troubled over the letter he had written to the Corinthian brethren, because he had been forced to rebuke them sharply. With these burdens, Paul had gone to Troas, hoping to meet Titus with word from Corinth. Though the first letter does not tell who carried it to Corinth, this second letter indicates it was taken by Titus.

When he reached Troas, and Titus was not there, though Paul had an opportunity to preach the gospel, he was too discouraged to make use of it (2 Cor. 2:12-13), so he did not tarry. With an anxious heart he traveled on to Macedonia. But "even when we reached Macedonia our flesh found no relief, but we were afflicted on every side; without were struggles, within were fears" (7:5). This indicates there was persecution in Macedonia also, but no more information is given about what may have caused the trouble. The congregation at Thessalonica had suffered persecution from its beginning, so there may well have been continuing trouble there (see Acts 17:5-9; 1 Thess. 1:6; 3:4; 2 Thess. 1:4-6).

Titus brings good news:
- **Most received the first letter well,**
- **But some are opposing Paul and his message.**

But just then there was good news: Titus came bringing a good report from Corinth (2 Cor. 2:12-13; 7:5-8). The brethren at Corinth had received the letter as they should, and they had corrected some of the problems that had been among them, but it is evident from the second book that some at Corinth were rejecting Paul's message and were trying to deny Paul's apostleship. In answer, Paul wrote this second letter and made one of the strongest defenses of his apostleship to be found in the New Testament. It was very important for that generation (and for all generations since) to understand that Paul's message was reliable. Paul was fully inspired, with full rights from God to instruct saints in the correct ways of God.

2 Corinthians:
- **Written from Macedonia,**
- **Only a few weeks after 1 Corinthians was written from Ephesus.**
- **The year was still A.D. 57.**

Considering that Paul was already in Macedonia when he heard from Corinth (2 Cor. 7:5-6), and that he informs the Corinthians he is coming to see them soon, and he warns them that some from Macedonia might accompany him (9:4), there can be no doubt that this second letter was written from this province. It was only a few months after he had written the first letter.

Paul has caught up with Timothy in Macedonia.

According to Acts 19:22, Paul had sent Timothy and Erastus on ahead of him into Macedonia before the riot broke out in Ephesus. He hoped that Timothy would reach Corinth before Paul himself did, but he was uncertain because he did not know what delays Timothy might find along the way (1 Cor. 16:10). By 2 Corinthians, Paul is joined by Timothy in his salutation (2 Cor. 1:1). Therefore Paul caught up with Timothy in Macedonia.

Since 2 Corinthians is a long book, study this brief outline to get an overall picture in mind.

Summary Outline of 2 Corinthians:
- The God of all comfort provides this comfort in several ways (1:1-7:16).
    - He provides it in our mutual comfort of one another (1:1-2:17).
    - He provides it in giving us the work of preaching the gospel, a ministry so glorious it is worth any cost (3:1-4:18).
    - He provides it in giving a ministry that sustains through divine grace and hope (5:1-7:16).
- Information concerning the gift for the saints of Judea (8:1-9:15).
- Defense of Paul's apostleship (10:1-13:14).
    - Defense of his approach to preaching (10:1-18).
    - Reluctant comparison of himself with his attackers (11:1-33).
    - His great visions, and proof of his apostleship among the Corinthians (12:1-21).
    - Warning (13:1-14).

The letter says:
Greeting (1:1-2):
- **God comforts us in many ways (1:1-7:16).**
- **Praise the God of all comfort (1:3-11):**

The letter says:

Paul and Timothy our brother to the church of God at Corinth:
- **The God of all comfort provides that comfort in several ways (1:1-7:16).**
- Praise God who comforts us in every affliction (1:3-11):

- **God comforts us so that we may comfort others.**
- **As sufferings multiply, so does the comfort.**
- **May you partake of His comfort.**
- **Your prayers helped.**

Praise God who comforts us in all our afflictions, so that we are able to comfort others. As the sufferings we have in Christ multiply, so does the comfort, and our hope for you is that as you partake of the sufferings of Christ, so will you partake of the glory.

I want you brethren to know how near we were to death in Asia. We were very low and sometimes despaired of life, but God delivered us, and He will deliver us. You helped through your prayers, and as prayers were uttered by many, now thanks may be given by many on our behalf.

- ***The theme of the comfort God gives to those who serve Him ties together all the first seven chapters.***

The word "comfort" is used ten times in 1:3-7, while words such as "affliction, suffer, suffering" are found seven times in the same verses. Paul had been in serious trouble, but he knew that all true comfort comes from God, and he was deeply grateful. As he proceeds through the book, he describes different ways God comforted him:

- *The love and encouragement of brethren (1:11-14; 7:13-16);*
- *The knowledge of how great is the challenging work of preaching the gospel (2:14-4:15);*
- *The knowledge of the greatness of the reward (4:16-5:10);*
- *Titus brings good news from Corinth to Paul (7:6);*
- *The thread that it is God who comforts us runs through this entire section.*
  - *One end of the thread is firmly knotted in 1:3-7, and the other end is firmly tied to 7:13-16.*

- ***God has stood by Paul and comforted him, but he needs comfort from his brethren also.***

Paul wants the Corinthians to know how severe his affliction had been in Ephesus, so they will understand why he needs their comfort. If he had not had such a sore period of trial in Ephesus, he might not have minded making a direct trip to Corinth to reprove them and to deal with the evil doers. But he needed comfort himself. That the Corinthians cared enough about Paul to pray for him lets him know that there is love among the Corinthians for him. He and they appreciate each other, and can therefore comfort each other.

- **Paul's change of plans, and why (1:12-2:4):**
  - **By knowing the conduct of each, we each take pride (1:12-14).**
  - **My first plan was to come to you before going to Macedonia (1:15-16).**
  - **Was I "fickle" when I changed my plans? (1:17-22)**

- Paul's change of plans, and why (1:12-2:4):

  In this state, knowing how we delighted in our relationship with you, I planned to come to you and have my spirits lifted by association with you. So my first plan was to come to you from Ephesus so that you could enjoy our company again, to pass by you into Macedonia, and then return to you, and from you to be sent on my journey to Judea.

  When I planned such a course, do you think I was being fickle? Have I been that kind of a person? You know, as does God, that I have not preached a yes/no gospel among you. Is this the way that I and Silas and Timothy have operated among you? No. We have been positive and straightforward in everything.

- **Reasons for changing his plans (1:23-2:4).**
    - **To spare them;**
    - **So they could solve problems before he arrives.**
    - **To make mutual comfort possible.**

I call God for witness that it was to spare you that I decided to change my plans. I knew that if I came with rebuke I would make you sorry, and if I made you sorry, then who would cheer me? So I wrote you, having confidence in you that you could solve the problems. I did not write to make you sorry, but that you might know how much I loved you.

See your map:

- ***See how Paul could have crossed by sea directly from Ephesus to Corinth.***
- ***Contrast that route with the one he took.***

When we first learned of Paul's plans (Acts 19:21-22; 1 Cor. 16:5-9), he was planning to go through Macedonia first, and then proceed to Corinth. But here we learn that earlier he had planned to go straight across from Ephesus to Corinth. Some in Corinth are making the charge that Paul was fickle, that he was afraid to come to Corinth.

In 1:15-22, Paul does not explain why he changed his plans. Instead he shames the Corinthians for even thinking that this change indicated anything vacillating or indecisive about Paul. No, Paul was operating from a principle of the gospel when he made that decision, as he explains in 1:23-2:4. The reasons for Paul's lack of vacillation are rooted in God Himself: "God is faithful," "the Son of God is not yes and no, but yes," "In Him is the yes, wherefore also through Him is the Amen."

- **Forgive and comfort the transgressor (2:5-11):**
    - **Do not let him be consumed in grief,**
    - **Lest it give Satan an advantage.**

- The measures taken against the wrongdoer have worked; it is time to forgive him (2:5-11):

  If anyone has made you sorry, he has caused sorrow, not to me, but to you. What you did about the man guilty of fornication was effective; it did the job. Now it is time to forgive the wrongdoer, lest he be consumed in his grief. Whom you have forgiven, I have forgiven, so that Satan will not succeed in what he is trying to do. We are not ignorant of his tactics.

- **Paul did not find Titus at Troas (2:12-13):**
    - **Paul was too worried to stay and preach.**

- Paul did not find Titus at Troas (2:12-13):

  Furthermore, when I came to Troas to preach the gospel and was given a great opportunity, I found no relief from my worries, because I did not find Titus my brother. So I left Troas and went on into Macedonia.

- ***Paul interrupts himself... Watch to see when he comes back to the report of Titus coming from Corinth.***

Suddenly Paul breaks into a paean of thanks to God and a description of His ministers. We are not told the reason for the abrupt change in his feelings here, but we learn from 7:5-7 that Titus did indeed come and he brought Paul the news he wanted. As in other places in Paul's writings, his interruption of his primary thought is a beautiful point in itself, with this heartfelt description of the work of the preacher of the gospel that is set forth in this section.

- **Thanks be to God who leads us in triumph! (2:14-17)**
    - **We, His ministers, are the aroma of Christ .**
        - **To some: the odor of salvation;**
        - **To others: the smell of death.**

- God comforts by making His ministers sufficient for their task (2:14-17):

    But thanks be to God who always leads us in triumph with Christ, and makes known the aroma of His knowledge in every place. We are the odor of Christ unto God, in them that are saved and in them that perish: to the one a fragrance of life; to the other a fragrance of death. Weigh those who preach in the balance. They are an aroma pleasing to God. Who is sufficient for such a task? Not those who preach from greed and deception, but those who speak as God would have them to, in sincerity.

- ***Paul introduces the topic of chapters 3-7 in 2:14-17, where he describes the servants of God who preach the gospel.***
- ***Paul views us as being led by God in triumph:***
    - ***Presenting the aroma of Christ to the public.***
- ***The work of preaching the gospel is trying and uncertain,***
    - ***But God makes us sufficient.***

The figure of speech in verse 14 is of a Roman Triumph, in which the conquering general was given a parade in Rome where he brought his captives and his trophies to exhibit to the public. Incense was burned in braziers in the streets. Paul views us as being led by God in triumph, making the aroma of the knowledge of Him obvious in all those who preach the gospel This aroma is one that is very pleasing to God, but men regard it in different ways. To those who are saved, it is a fragrance of salvation; but to those who are lost, it is a smell of condemnation. "Who is sufficient for this role?" Paul asks. "But we are not as the many, making merchandise of the word of God, but we speak sincerely in Christ."

When Paul arrived in Macedonia he did not know how things had turned out with the Corinthians. There is much uncertainty in such work, but the work itself is worthy. There is fruit that comes from such work, and even when the work collapses, we know that God wants it done. Sometimes we win, but even when we do not, we know that God is still with us, making us sufficient.

- **You are our "letter of recommendation" (3:1-3):**
    - **Written on your hearts.**
- ***God* makes us adequate as ministers of the new covenant (3:4-6):**
    - **A new covenant that gives life,**
    - **Not of the old one that kills.**

- You are our letter of recommendation (3:1-6):

    Do we need to present our credentials all over again? You are our letter of recommendation, because you are a letter of Christ which we wrote, not with pen and ink, but with the Spirit of God; not on tables of stone, but on tables that are your hearts.

    It is on this basis that we are made sufficient to do the job we have been given. Not that we claim anything for ourselves, but God has made us ministers of a new covenant which gives men life, not of the old one which kills.

- ***Paul says, "Our sufficiency is from God."***
    - ***See 2:16 and 3:5.***

The entire third chapter is a unit describing the great ministry (the work, the task, the charge he had been given) of the gospel in which Paul and his coworkers labored. He says you (the ones who had heard and responded to the message) are our epistle, written upon hearts of flesh. He denies that he and his companions deserve the credit. No, "Our sufficiency is from God," who made them ministers of a new covenant. Paul then contrasts the two covenants. One is the ministra-

tion of death, the ministration of condemnation, whose glory was temporary, even as the glory upon Moses' face was temporary.

- **Glory of the new covenant is far greater than that of the old (3:7-11).**
  - **First covenant was temporary;**
  - **Second is permanent.**

- The glory of the new covenant is far greater than that of the old (3:7-11):

  The glory of the old covenant was temporary. If the ministry of condemnation had glory, it is only fitting that the ministry which brings righteousness should have far greater glory. And if that which was temporary had glory, much more shall that which is permanent have glory.

- **The glory of the new covenant is to be shared (3:12-18):**
  - **We reflect the glory of Christ.**
  - **With faces uncovered, we behold the glory of the Lord,**
    - **We are transformed by it.**

- The glory of the new covenant is to be seen and shared (3:12-18):

  Having such a hope, we speak with boldness. We have no veil before our face such as Moses had (Exod. 34:29-35). Even today, when Moses is read, a veil lies before the hearts of the listeners. But all of us, with faces uncovered, behold as in a mirror, the glory of the Lord, and that glory is transferred to us as we are transformed into the image of Christ.

"Having therefore such a hope...." The hope referred to is of enduring spiritual glory and spiritual life. We have these things because of the glorious new covenant of which we are a part. It is more glorious in that:

- *It is of the spirit, not the letter (3:6),*
- *It is the ministration of the spirit (3:8),*
- *It is the ministration of righteousness (3:9),*
- *It endures; it does not fade away (3:11).*

- **Our hope is of enduring spiritual glory and of spiritual life (3:1-18).**
  - **Moses veiled his face to keep Israel from seeing the glory fade away.**
  - **The glory of the new covenant does not fade away.**

We see a strong and very interesting contrast in this paragraph. Paul says, "We use great boldness of speech regarding the glory of this covenant. This is a glory that remains. We want you to see this glory. We ourselves want to be transformed by this glory."

In the story alluded to, Moses did not veil his face to keep people from seeing the glory that was upon his face from having been in God's presence —he veiled his face to keep them from seeing that glory fade. The old covenant was one in which the glory was inferior, fading, not destined to be permanent. In the new covenant, the veil is removed, and the glory remains. (See Exodus 34:29-35.)

- **Ministers of new covenant speak boldly (4:1-6).**
  - **If anyone cannot perceive our gospel,**
    - **Satan has blinded him.**

- Accordingly, ministers of the new covenant speak boldly (4:1-6):

  Since we have this kind of ministry, we do not despair and give up. We have renounced the hidden things of shame, such as craftiness and deceit *(he has renounced any action that would bring shame upon this treasure)*. If any cannot perceive our gospel, it is because Satan has blinded their eyes so that the light of the gospel of the glory of Christ, who is the image of God, should not dawn upon them.

- **Bodily weaknesses do not affect the value of this great treasure (4:7-15).**
  - **We face death so that you may have life.**
  - **We *must* speak because we believe.**
  - **God will raise us...**

- Weaknesses of the vessels do not detract *(do not bring shame)* from the treasure they contain (4:7-15):

  But we have this great treasure *(the glorious gospel)* in earthen vessels so that the exceeding greatness of the power may clearly be shown to be of God, and not of ourselves. We are constantly being pushed almost beyond endurance, always manifesting the willingness to die for our cause as Christ died. So death works in us, but life in you. But we have no alternative but to speak, for our attitude is the same as that which is written, "We believed, and so we have spoken" (Ps.116:10). We know that the One who raised Jesus from the dead will also raise us, and will present us with you in His presence.

- **We are sustained by this glorious hope (4:16-5:10).**
  - **Our light, temporary affliction works for us an eternal weight of glory (4:16-18).**
  - **Our desire is to be clothed with our eternal body (5:1-5).**
  - **To be with Christ is preferable (5:6-10):**
  - **Whether in the body or with Christ,**
    - **We live to please Him.**

- We are sustained by this glorious hope *(it is worth any cost)* (4:16-5:10):

  Therefore we do not give up, because, though our outward man is decaying, yet our inward man is being renewed every day. For our light affliction, which is only for the moment, works for us more and more exceedingly an eternal weight of glory. Meanwhile, we do not look at the visible, but at the invisible, because the visible will pass away, but the things which are invisible are eternal.

  We long to be clothed in our eternal body, for we know that if this tent in which we live is taken down, we have a building from God, a house not made with hands, eternal, in the heavens. To be with Christ is to be preferred. Facing our dangers, we are of good courage, because we know that while we are in the body we are away from the Lord, and we had rather be with Him. So whether we are at home with the Lord or away from Him, we plan to please Him, because we must all appear before the judgment-seat of Christ to give an account of what we have done in the body.

- **We are moved by the fear of God (5:11-13).**
  - ***The fear of the Lord relates to the judgment described in 5:10.***

- We are moved by the fear of God (5:11-13):

  Since we possess the fear of the Lord, we persuade men. We are not trying to recommend ourselves to you again, but to give you opportunity to be glad of what we have done among you, so that you can answer those who go by mere appearance rather than by what is in the heart.

- **We are compelled to preach by the love of Christ (5:14-15).**

- We are constrained by the love of Christ to conduct our ministry *(complete the task given us)* (5:14-15):

  The love of Christ also compels us to preach the gospel, because we have arrived at the judgment that One indeed died for all. He died for all, so that they could live for Him.

- **In Christ everyone is made new (5:16-19).**

- In Christ everyone is made new (5:16-19):

  Therefore we do not look at people in a fleshly way anymore. Anyone who is in Christ is a new creature. The old things are gone; everything is new. But all these things are brought about by God who gave us this work of reconciling men unto Himself through Christ.

- **As Christ's ambassadors, we beseech men to be reconciled to God (5:20-6:10).**
  - **Today is the day of salvation (5:20-6:2).**
    - **Do not receive the grace of God in vain.**
  - **We give no cause for stumbling (6:3-10).**
    - **We recommend ourselves by our conduct.**

- Through His ambassadors God seeks to reconcile men (5:20-6:10):

  We are ambassadors *(His spokesmen, His representatives)* on behalf of Christ. It is as though God Himself entreats men by us. We beseech you, therefore, be reconciled to God. God made that One who experienced no sin to be as one who sinned on our behalf. Working in cooperation with God, we beg you not to receive the grace of God in vain. As it was said of old, "This is the day of salvation that God has chosen" (Is. 49:8).

  In this work to save men's souls, we conduct ourselves so that we cause no one to stumble. Rather, we recommend ourselves by the way we accept the various hardships that come to us in our work, by kindness, by the Holy Spirit, by genuine love, by the armor of righteousness, by being true even when branded as liars; by being unknown and yet well known, sorrowful yet rejoicing, poor yet making many rich, having nothing, and yet possessing all things.

- ***Paul, what keeps you going when the persecution is so severe?***

Notice how often through this section Paul says, "Therefore... we use great boldness..." (3:12); "we do not lose heart" (4:1, 16); "we are not crushed... not despairing... not forsaken... not destroyed" (4:7-9); "being always of good courage..." (5:6). Paul, how did you keep going when the persecutions were so great? He has given several reasons:

- *The glory of the new covenant (3:1-18).*
  - *It is worth any cost. The afflictions are mere trifles in comparison (4:17-18).*
- *The hope of eternal life is so great (4:14-5:10).*
- *Paul knew he would stand in judgment before God, therefore he feared God (5:10-11).*
- *The love of Christ compels us (5:14-16).*
- *We have been made new in Christ (transformed) (5:17).*
- *God gave us this task of telling the world about the reconciliation that is in Christ (5:17-19).*
  - *Therefore, we are ambassadors for Christ.*

- **We still have affection for you (6:11-13):**
  - **Please have the same for us.**

- We still have affection for you — please have the same for us (6:11-13):

  We still feel open and receptive to you Corinthians. We have no restrictions on our feelings for you. Why don't you respond in kind and open your hearts to accept us.

- **Avoid compromising relationships with evil (6:14-7:1).**
    - **Come out the world and be separate from evil things that defile.**
    - **Let's cleanse ourselves as we develop holiness.**

- Do not enter into compromising relationships with evil (6:14-7:1):

Do not put yourselves into situations which compromise your commitment to God, because we are a temple of the living God. It is as He said, "I will dwell among them and walk among them, and I will be their God, and they will be my people. Therefore come out from the things of the world and be separated from the evil things that defile, and I will be your Father, and you will be my sons and daughters." Having such promises, my beloved friends, let us cleanse ourselves of all contaminations of the flesh and of the spirit as we develop holiness to its perfection.

- ***Note the wording of this basic relationship that God wants with men.***

This is another very beautiful expression of the basic relationship God has always wanted to have with mankind: "If you will obey me, I will be your God, and you will be my people." The passages could be multiplied (Exod. 19:5-6; Lev. 26:12; Jer. 32:38; Ezek. 37:27; Rev. 21:3, and many others).

- **Open your hearts to us; we have not wronged you (7:2-4).**

- Open your hearts to us; we have not wronged you (7:2-4):

Why not open your hearts to us? We have not wronged anyone. You are very precious to me, whether we die together or live together. I feel that I can speak very plainly to you. I am proud of you; I am filled with comfort; I am overjoyed.

- ***At this point Paul returns to his theme of comfort.***

Notice that at this point Paul returns to the theme of 2:12-13; his interruption is complete. He returns to the thought of how the God of all comfort has comforted him in his affliction: Titus has come with a good report from Corinth. Notice that in 7:5, he picks up the thought as if it were the next sentence after 2:13. He hurried on to Macedonia because he was too discouraged to stay in Troas — but the trouble continued in Macedonia. But then Titus came!

- **I rejoice that my reproof has been well received (7:5-16).**
    - **Your sorrow led to your repentance.**

- I rejoice that my reproof has been well received (7:5-16):

When, however, we arrived in Macedonia, we had no comfort. But when Titus came and told me about all you had done to correct matters, I was filled with joy. I do not regret that I made you sorry, because your sorrow was the godly kind, and it moved you to repentance. You did exactly what was right about the one who had misbehaved. So I am comforted. I was especially pleased that Titus found that the things I said about you were true.

- **The collection being made for the poor saints in Jerusalem (8:1-9:15):**
- **The Macedonian churches have been liberal beyond their means (8:1-5).**

- **Concerning the collection being made for the poor saints in Jerusalem (8:1-9:15):**
- The Macedonian churches have been liberal beyond their means (8:1-5):

I want to tell you about the way these Macedonians have contributed of their possessions to the poor saints in Jerusalem.

Though they were poor, they were rich in their liberality. They gave even more than they were really able to give, because they gave themselves first to the Lord..

- **Purpose for the collection (8:6-15).**
  - **To share your abundance with the saints in Jerusalem.**

- Purpose for the collection (8:6-15):

This is why I told Titus to encourage you to finish getting your contribution ready. You were the first to begin a year ago, and now it is time to finish what you began. We are not trying to take what you have and make the poor in Jerusalem rich, leaving you with nothing. We just want you to share your abundance with them.

- **Precautions being taken (8:16-24).**
  - **Approved messengers will take the money.**

- Precautions being taken (8:16-24):

We are conducting this business in such a way as to be open and above board, so that there will be no room for accusations. There will be messengers with us who are approved by the various churches.

- **Be sure your collection is ready (9:1-5).**
  - **This is my reason for writing about this matter.**

- Be sure your collection is ready (9:1-5):

I know that you already know about this collection for the saints, and I know your willingness to help. Indeed, I have been telling others about your willingness in order to spur them to contribute. But now I am writing to be sure you have your offering ready, so that you will not be embarrassed (to say nothing of my embarrassment) by my arriving before you have it collected.

- **God blesses the cheerful, liberal giver (9:6-15).**
  - **He who sows sparingly shall reap sparingly.**

- God blesses the cheerful, liberal giver (9:6-15):

Remember that he who plants lightly will have a light harvest, and he who plants heavily will have a great harvest. The One who supplies seed for the farmer and bread for food, will multiply your seed for planting and will increase the fruits of your righteousness. Through your liberality, many will glorify God and will give thanks to God because of the greatness of God's grace in you. Thanks be to God for His indescribable gift!

The gift Paul is praising in 9:15 is not the specific gift of money from the Gentiles to the Jews, but the gift of grace from God. In this verse, he summarizes all he has said about the greatness of the blessing every saint has in his sharing of this great gift.

- **Paul defends his own apostolic ministry and authority (10:1-13:14):**

- **Defense of his apostolic ministry and authority (10:1-13:14):**

Paul uses touches of sarcasm all through this section, in order to make his points strong — but do not lose sight of what he is saying.

- **His approach to preaching (10:1-18):**

- Paul's defense for his approach to preaching (10:1-18):

Now I, Paul, want to talk to you. You know — the one who is said to be very meek and quiet when among you, and then becomes brave when he is away! It is true that we do not use weapons and

- **Our weapons are not those of the flesh (10:1-6):**
- **But they are mighty before God.**

techniques of the flesh, but our weapons are nevertheless mighty before God to the casting down of fortresses, and able to subdue every thought so as to bring it into obedience to Christ. We are ready to punish all disobedience.

- **I might appear weak, but my authority is real and divinely given (10:7-11).**
  - **The way I am in my letters is the way I plan to be among you.**

You are looking only at what is immediately before you. If anybody trusts that he belongs to Christ — well, so do we. And if I boast abundantly about our authority (which the Lord gave for building you up, not for tearing you down), I will not be made ashamed. I have not meant to try to frighten you in my letters. Some say that I am brave and strong only in my letters, that you should not be frightened and take seriously what I write, because my bodily presence and my word when I am present amount to nothing. Just to silence such talk, let such a one take note of this — the way I am in my letters is also the way I will be when I am among you.

- **Let the one who glories glory in the Lord (10:12-18).**
  - **We sought not to intrude on other men's work,**
  - **We boast within the sphere God has give us.**

Of course, we are not bold enough to compare ourselves with others — but when they measure themselves by themselves, they are without understanding. We were the first to come among you. We sought not to intrude on other men's work, but to preach the gospel in areas even beyond you. Anyone who glories *(boasts)* should do so in the Lord. The one who is truly approved is not the one who recommends himself, but the one whom the Lord recommends.

- **Please indulge me while I state my credentials as an apostle (11:1-4):**
  - **I am worried lest your minds will be led away from Christ.**

- Please indulge me while I state my credentials as an apostle, as a faithful servant of God (11:1-4):

I hope you will bear with me in a little foolishness. I am jealous of you, because I betrothed you to one husband, even Jesus. I am deeply worried that, as Satan deceived Eve, so your minds will be led away from the simplicity and the purity that is toward Christ. It appears that if someone else comes preaching another Jesus, or presenting another disposition, or preaching a different gospel which you did not accept before, that is okay.

- **Paul was not inferior to his adversaries (11:5-6).**

- Paul was not in the least inferior to his adversaries (11:5-6):

I know that I am not one bit behind the foremost of the apostles, because although I am not an "accomplished speaker," I am accomplished in knowledge. But you should already know that!

- **How did I wrong you? (11:7-11):**
  - **By preaching to you free of charge?**
  - **The brethren from Macedonia supplied my every need.**

- Did I do you wrong by not taking anything from you to preach the gospel? (11:7-11).

How did I wrong you? Was it sin that I lowered myself to exalt you by preaching the gospel to you for nothing? I robbed other churches, taking wages of them so that I could serve you. The brethren from Macedonia supplied my every need. I was not a burden to anyone, and I will not let anyone rob me of this glory in Achaia. Why? Is it because I do not love you?! God knows.

- **I am trying to prevent false teachers from deceiving you (11:12-15).**

- I am trying to head off those who would deceive you (11:12-15):

  I am trying to head off those who are false apostles, deceitful operators who pass themselves off as apostles. It should come as no big surprise that there are deceivers, since the devil himself fashions himself into an angel of light.

- **Paul's labors and trials (11:16-33):**
  - **External trials (11:16-27):**
    - **Labored more.**
    - **In prison more.**
    - **Beaten more.**
      - **Five times by the Jews.**
      - **Three times with rods.**
    - **Stoned once.**
    - **Shipwrecked three times.**
      - **A night and a day in the ocean.**
  - **Internal trials (11:28-33):**
    - **Anxiety for the churches.**
  - **Even in Damascus... *(soon after conversion).***

- Paul's labors and trials (11:16-33):

  Do not let anyone think me foolish — but even if someone does, please listen to what I have to say. Seeing that others glory *(boast)*, I will glory also. You apparently have no trouble bearing foolish people. You will put up with a man if he eats you alive, if he takes you prisoner, if he slaps your face. So since others boast of what they have done, I will also. Are they bold, so am I (this is foolishness!). Are they Hebrews? So am I. Are they the seed of Abraham? So am I. Are they assistants of Christ? So am I (I am speaking like a crazy person!). I have labored more than they, been in prison more, been beaten more. Five times the Jews beat me with thirty-nine stripes each time. Three times I was beaten with rods. One time I was stoned; I was shipwrecked three times. *(Remember that the ship wreck recorded in Acts 27 had not happened yet.)* Once I spent a night and a day in the ocean. I have endured far more dangers and sufferings than they.

  Besides all these external things, there are the matters that press upon me daily: anxiety for the churches. Who is weak, and I am not weak? Who stumbles and I do not burn? If I must boast, I will boast of my weaknesses. The God and Father of the Lord Jesus, He knows that I lie not.

  Even in Damascus, the governor under Aretas the king guarded the city in order to take me captive, and through a window I was lowered in a basket by the wall and escaped his hands.

- **Visions and revelations (12:1-10):**
  - **Because of the tremendous visions I saw, I was given a thorn in the flesh.**
  - **I asked the Lord three times to take away it away.**
    - **He said, "My strength is enough."**

- The greatness of his visions and revelations is illustrated by one vision from fourteen years before (12:1-10).

  I am forced to boast, even though I do not wish to do so. If they want to compare revelations, I know a man in Christ who, fourteen years ago, was caught up to the presence of God where he heard unspeakable words which it is not lawful to tell. I do not know whether this man went to heaven in the body or out of it. But because of these tremendous revelations, I was given a thorn in the flesh, so that I would not be exalted too much. I asked the Lord three times to let it depart, but He said, "No, my strength is sufficient for you." I would much rather be weak and have the Lord's strength, than to be strong and not have the Lord's help.

- ***When one realizes he is weak, he reaches to power outside himself.***

Why on earth would one glory in his weaknesses? Paul recognized that his own strength indeed was small. If he relied upon himself, he had nothing, yet men tend to do that when they are strong. When he felt his weakness, however, then he reached out to the strength that was beyond and outside himself, and then he was truly strong. On this basis he would accept and even be glad of his weakness and affliction.

- **The Corinthians saw the signs of an apostle among them (12:11-13).**

- The Corinthians themselves should have testified these things of Paul (12:11-21).

  As I said, I am not one bit less than the foremost apostle. Truly the signs of an apostle were done among you. So in what way do you think you were deprived of anything — unless it was that I did not charge you for my preaching? Forgive me this wrong! My willingness to spend and be spent for you should be sufficient proof of my love for you. This is the third time I am coming to you, and I will not be a burden to you. I will most gladly spend and be spent in your behalf. If I love you more, do you love me less?

  But be that as it may, I did not make myself a burden to you. Since I am so crafty, I took you by deceit! — Did I take advantage of you by anyone I sent to you? I gave Titus instructions and sent a brother with him. Did Titus take advantage of you? Do we not have the same attitude and have we not conducted ourselves the same way?

  Do not think that I have said these things to defend myself. I have said them to edify you, to spare me and you what I must do if I come and find you not as I would have you to be.

- **My willingness to spend myself in your behalf should have shown that my love for you is sincere (12:14-15).**
- **Have I or my associates ever taken advantage of you? (12:16-18).**
- **My "boasting" is not to defend myself, but to help you (12:19-21).**

- **When I arrive, everything will be sorted out, and the power of Christ will be demonstrated (13:1-10).**
  - **I will not spare you.**
  - **Examine yourselves.**

- At Paul's coming everything will be handled, and the power of Christ will be demonstrated (13:1-10):

  When I arrive, at the mouth of two or three witnesses, we will establish everything that has been said. I say again, to those who have sinned, when I come, I will not spare you. You will receive a demonstration of the power of Christ who speaks in me. Examine yourselves to see if you are in the faith. I hope that you can straighten out these matters before I come, so that I will not have to rebuke sharply.

- **Final exhortations and blessing (13:11-14).**

- Final exhortations and benediction (13:11-14):

  Finally, brethren, farewell. Be perfected; be comforted; be of the same mind; live in peace, and the God of love and peace shall be with you.

  May the grace of the Lord Jesus Christ, and the love of God, and the fellowship of the Holy Spirit, be with you all.

Summary concept:

- **It is God who gives us the strength to do our work.**
- **No matter what it takes, it is worth all the effort.**

Thumbnail Sketch of 2 Corinthians:

This second letter to the Corinthians falls into three clearly defined sections:

- *Chapters 1-7: God furnishes comfort to His servants by giving them a glorious ministry.*

- *Chapters 8-9: Be ready with the collection being taken up for the poor saints in Jerusalem.*
- *Chapters 10-13: Paul defends his own apostolic ministry and authority.*

Paul remains in Greece for three months (Acts 20:2-3a):

Paul spends the winter in Corinth, as he had planned.

After passing through the various cities of Macedonia where there were churches, Paul arrived in Greece, where he stayed for three months.

Although the particular city in Greece where he stayed is not specified in Acts, it was no doubt Corinth, because he had written two letters to the brethren there saying he was coming, and he had told them he hoped to spend the winter with them (1 Cor. 16:6). While he was there, he wrote a letter to the church at Rome.

Summary of the book of Romans

Church at Rome:
- **Paul did not start the church at Rome.**
- **He hopes to visit them for the first time,**
  - **After he delivers the gift to the saints in Jerusalem.**

Book of Romans:
- **Written during the winter of A.D. 57,**
- **From the city of Corinth.**

Phoebe:
- **From the church at Cenchrea,**
- **May have taken the letter to Rome.**

Priscilla and Aquila are back in Rome.

Paul started many churches, but he did not start the one at Rome. Most of the saints at Rome were Gentiles (Rom. 11:13), and since Jesus had given Paul the task to work mostly with Gentiles, he wanted very much to visit there. He had tried to go in times past, but so far, problems had arisen so that he had been unable to do so (1:10-13).

Paul wrote the book during the winter he spent at Corinth in Greece on his third missionary journey (Acts 20:2-3). In Romans 15:23-33, he tells of his plans for the next few months. He plans to leave Corinth soon to take the collection from the Gentile Christians to the Jewish Christians in Jerusalem. Then he hopes to make a trip to Spain, and to visit Rome on his way.

Cenchrea was one of the seaports for the city of Corinth, and the church in Cenchrea is mentioned in 16:1, lending further proof that the book of Romans was written from Corinth. Since Paul recommended Phoebe to the brethren at Rome in that same passage, she may have taken the book to them. Nothing else is told about her.

Notice that Priscilla and Aquila are back in Rome. We first met them at Corinth on Paul's first visit to that city, but they had only recently moved there from Italy (Rome) (Acts 18:1-2). Then they accompanied Paul from Corinth to Ephesus (18:18), and were still living there when Paul wrote the first letter to the Corinthians (1 Cor. 16:19). Now, only a few months later, they are back in Rome to be greeted by Paul as he writes this letter (Rom. 16:3-5).

Paul's plans did not work out the way he had hoped. In this letter, after telling the Romans his plans, he asks for their prayers that he might be protected in Jerusalem so that he could safely complete his mission (15:30-32). Instead of his traveling to Rome as a free citizen

Paul will go to Rome:
- **But as a prisoner,**
- **Not as he had planned.**

of the empire, however, he was arrested in Jerusalem by wicked men and was kept in custody in Caesarea for two years, before he was finally transferred to Rome as a prisoner. He was in prison there for two more years before his case was heard. (See Acts 21-28.) Though he was a prisoner in Rome, he was able to preach to all who came to him, and his preaching was effective (Phil. 1:12-13).

The book sets forth God's plan whereby men may be counted righteous.

The book of Romans sets forth the plan God devised for man to be counted righteous. The book is not describing God's own personal righteousness, but rather His plan which provides man forgiveness of his sins so that he may stand righteous before God. The gospel tells that plan. The first 17 verses set forth the core of the message of the whole book.

Keep this short outline before you in order to follow Paul's line of reasoning.

Short outline:
- The theme of the book: The gospel is the power of God unto salvation, **for the just shall live by faith** (1:1-17).
- God's plan for righteousness:
  - Is revealed in the gospel (1:1-17).
  - Is needed by all (1:18-3:20).
  - Is given through faith (3:21-5:11).
  - Solves the problem of sin (5:12-6:23).
  - Overcomes the curse of the law (7:1-25).
  - Provides for all man's spiritual needs (8:1-39).
  - Fulfills the hope of true Israel (9:1-11:36).
  - Demands righteous lives (12:1-15:13).
- Paul's plans for the near future (15:14-33).
- Greetings and closing remarks (16:1-24).

Learn to analyze Paul's style of writing:
- **All study of his books will be easier.**

Paul's style of writing is distinctive. He starts a sentence, picks up one particular word and develops the next thought from that word. Thus his thoughts are tied together as tightly as a puzzle. If one learns to follow his thoughts in this way, all of his writings will be easier to understand. We analyze the first seven verses of Romans in order to illustrate his style. It would be possible to do the whole book this way. Observe how he develops thoughts from the underlined words:

God's plan for righteousness is revealed in the gospel (1:1-17):
- **Greeting (1:1-7)**

Paul's style of writing: Illustrated by Romans 1:1-7:
- **Broken down to its bare core, he says:**
  - **Paul,**
  - **To the Romans saints.**

- **God's plan for righteousness is revealed in the gospel (1:1-17):**
- Greeting and introduction (1:1-7):

Paul:
- A servant of Jesus Christ
- Called to be an apostle
- Separated unto the gospel of God, which was:
  - Promised by prophets in the scriptures
  - Concerning His Son Jesus Christ, who was:
    - Seed of David in the flesh
    - Declared to be the Son of God by the resurrection.
    - Through whom we received:

- **May God's grace and peace be with you.**

But look at how many rich thoughts he has expressed in each step of his greeting.

- Grace
- <u>Apostleship</u> *(a charge)*
  - To <u>call</u> people from all nations to obedience that comes from faith.
    - And <u>you at Rome</u> are some of the called.

To <u>all in Rome</u>:
- Beloved of God
- <u>Called</u> to be saints.

Grace and peace from God... and Christ...

- **I want to preach to you: because the gospel is for all (1:8-17).**
  - **I want to visit you:**
    - **To establish you...**
    - **To be mutually encouraged.**
    - **To have fruit...**
  - **For I am debtor to all.**
  - **For in the gospel, God has revealed His plan to save men.**

- I want to preach to you: because the gospel is for all (1:8-17):

  I give thanks for your faith, and I long to visit you so that I may impart some spiritual gift to you in order to establish you in the faith, and so that we can be mutually encouraged. I also want to have some fruit among you, because, as an apostle, I am a debtor to all — including those of you in Rome. For I am not ashamed of the gospel of Christ, because it is the way God has chosen to offer salvation from sin to everyone who believes, whether he is a Jew or a Gentile. For therein is revealed God's plan of righteousness which comes by faith, just as Habbakuk predicted, "The just shall live by faith" (Hab. 2:4).

God's plan for righteousness is needed by all (1:18-3:20):

- **The Gentiles ignored God and sinned to the extreme (1:18-32).**
  - **They could have known God,**
  - **They chose to ignore Him,**
  - **Therefore God gave them up to their fate.**

- **God's plan for righteousness: needed by all (1:18-3:20):**
- God's wrath against the Gentiles (1:18-32):

  Paul shows a contrast: Mankind *needs* the righteousness that is revealed in God's word, because His wrath *(His judicial anger)* has been revealed from heaven against all ungodliness *(the irreligious; irreverence)*, against all unrighteousness *(immorality)*, and against all those who suppress the truth *(will not hear; seek to keep others from hearing)*. There is no excuse for wickedness because God revealed Himself through the creation, but the Gentiles ignored the evidence and did not glorify Him as God. They could have known God, but they *chose* to reject Him. Therefore, God gave them up to go to their extremes in wickedness (see 1:24, 26, 28). He abandoned them to the fate they chose for themselves.

In our day, the group that would correspond to the Gentiles of Paul's day are the grossly wicked, those who choose to be irreligious, immoral, rejecting all evidence God has left of Himself. They have no excuse. God is angry with them. Their only hope is the gospel.

- **The Jews broke their law also (2:1-29).**
  - **They have no room to boast.**

- God's wrath against the Jews (2:1-29):

  But the Jews are no more righteous before God. They were blessed by God by being given the law of Moses, but they failed to keep their law and stand condemned before God. They have no room to boast over the Gentiles.

- **All have sinned (3:1-20).**
    - **No one has lived without sin. No one!**

Whatever law they lived under, men have not done what they were supposed to do. All stand condemned before God, because all have sinned. And, as long as men have to do every single thing God says in order to be righteous, no one will be righteous — because no one keeps all the law perfectly, with no mistakes. No one!

Individuals who died while still innocent babes, or were mentally retarded to the degree they could not be responsible before God, are not even considered in the book of Romans. Paul is dealing with normal mankind — and all men who have become responsible before God have also sinned and have incurred His anger, and therefore need His forgiveness.

How fortunate it would be if men would avoid theological disputes and merely accept the points being made in texts like this. Paul is not even considering the issue of whether Gentiles could be saved by keeping their own laws. His point is that even the Gentiles' laws incorporated to some degree the principles God would have all men to live by, and that the Gentiles had not kept even those laws perfectly. The result of their interaction with their law was sin.

In our day, the ones who correspond to the Jews of Paul's day are those who profess to be religious, who profess to be God's children, but do not keep God's laws accurately. They are therefore disobedient, and God is angry with them also. Their only hope is the gospel.

God's plan for righteousness: given through faith (3:21-4:25):

- **God has devised a plan for forgiveness (3:21-31):**
    - **Based upon faith in Christ...**
    - **Man can be forgiven.**

- **God has devised a plan for forgiveness: based upon faith in Christ (3:21-4:25):**
- God has devised a plan for forgiveness (3:21-31):

    But God has a new way to save men. It is a plan for forgiveness based upon faith in Christ, rather than upon perfect obedience. It is the gospel *(the good news about what Christ has done)*, and everyone who believes in Christ can be saved, even though he has not kept *all* the commandments God has given *perfectly*. God's new plan allows men to be *forgiven* for the sins they commit.

- **Even Abraham and David were justified by faith, not by perfect lives (4:1-25).**
    - **Abraham *believed* God and it was counted to him as righteousness (Gen. 15:6).**
    - **David learned the blessing of *forgiveness* (Ps. 32:2).**

- The experience of even such men as Abraham and David reflect the futility of seeking one's salvation by one's own merit, and the blessing of justification through faith (4:1-25):

    Even Abraham was not justified by perfect obedience. David learned that it is the *forgiven* man who is blessed. Abraham was justified by faith *before* he was circumcised. It was also before the law was given, because it was God's plan to justify those who follow Abraham's example of faith, not those who seek to be justified by the law.

The first verse of the following section makes it clear that the first four chapters constitute a distinct section in the development of Paul's theme of salvation through faith. Paul states, "Being therefore justified by faith..." So the point of the first four chapters is that by their own efforts to be justified men have known only sin — and therefore God's anger. Therefore God has devised a plan for justification, not based upon sinless obedience, but upon faith in God and in the sacrifice that He has provided.

God's plan for righteousness: solves the problem of sin (5:1-6:23):
- **We can rejoice in our hope (5:1-11).**
  - **We have confidence.**
- **Christ's death more than compensates for the curse caused by Adam's sin (5:12-21).**

- **God's plan for forgiveness solves the problem of sin (5:1-6:23):**
- In Christ we more than gain what was lost in Adam (5:1-21):

Since we are justified by faith we have peace with God and hope for our souls. We can rejoice in our hope, and we can be confident God will not disappoint us. For if God loved us when we were sinners, since we are now justified, will He not love us even more?

All that was lost when Adam sinned, we have more than regained in Christ. Therefore, where sin abounded, the grace of God abounded even more.

Let us now anticipate the next very natural development in the apostle's argument. If salvation is to be based upon faith and forgiveness, and if it is God's grace that deals with our sins, can we just ignore the problem of sin? The concept that this mistaken idea could be based upon is expressed in 5:20: "But where sin abounded, grace did abound more exceedingly." From this thought arises very naturally the question: "Shall we continue in sin that grace may abound?" (6:1). The next section begins with this question.

- **But God's grace demands responsibility on our part (6:1-18):**
  - **We are *committed* to live as servants of Christ.**
  - **Our old man *died*, we arose to live a new life as servants of Christ.**
- **The reward is worth the effort (6:19-23):**
  - **The wages of sin is death;**
  - **The free gift of God is eternal life.**

- Freedom to live a life devoted to sin is absolutely excluded by the commitment we make to God when we become His servants (6:1-23):

But if we can be saved from our sins, if we can be forgiven, should we just not worry any more about sin? May we sin all we want? NO! NO! NO! When we were buried with Him in baptism, we promised to give up sin and to serve God. Our old man of sin *died*, and we arose from baptism as new people, as ones who were committed to be servants of Christ, instead of servants of Satan.

The rewards of the new commitment are worth everything. What benefit did you derive from the service of sin? Only death! But the benefit you derive as servants of God is holiness and eternal life.

One of the greatest questions facing a Jew who contemplated becoming a Christian was what to do with the law of Moses. There would have been a tremendous emotional barrier at the thought of abandoning it. Chapter seven helps to deal with this problem by showing that the situation is parallel with a marriage. Death dissolves the relationship of marriage. Even so, in Christ the Jew died to the law, and was therefore free to be married to another, namely, to Christ.

God's plan for righteousness: overcomes the curse of the law (7:1-25):

- **We have been delivered from the law (7:1-6).**
- **The law identified sinful behavior (7:7-13),**
  - **But as men disobeyed its laws,**
    - **They were trapped in God's wrath.**
- **Even the good man, by himself, struggles with the pressures of sin (7:14-24).**
  - **Defeat is inevitable .**
- **But, man is not alone! He can rely upon Jesus Christ (7:25).**

- **God's new plan for righteousness overcomes the curse of the law (7:1-25):**

  Christ made it possible for us to have an alternative to the law of Moses. For example, when two are married, if one partner dies, the other is free to marry again. So we can now be married to Christ. We have been set free from the law.

  The law was good. It guided us to know what was sin; it identified sinful behavior. Without the law, I could not have known God did not want me to covet. But, though it taught me what sin was, it trapped me in disobedience. Each time I broke one of its commandments, it convicted me of sin.

  Once I knew about sin, though I wanted to do right, I found myself doing wrong; when I knew things I should do, I did not do them. Then I was trapped in sin. Who can save me from such a dreadful situation? Wretched man that I am! I thank God, it has been done through Jesus Christ our Lord.

There has been a good bit of disagreement about the situation of the individual Paul describes in 7:7-25:

- *Is it the Christian who continues to feel the temptation of sin?*
- *Or is it the conscientious sinner who realizes that, in the law itself, there is no relief for his frustrating weakness and sin?*
  - *Even though the verses do describe the feelings Christians have on occasion, the passage is not really dealing with the Christian.*
    - *In terms of this whole letter, the Christian can not be described as one who is dead (vs. 9), slain by sin (vs. 11), sold under sin (vs. 14), in whom sin dwells (vss. 17, 20), in captivity under the law of sin (vs. 23).*
  - *It is the conscientious Jew who would have been most concerned about this problem.*
    - *The curse of the law would be felt most by the conscientious sinner, not by the Christian who had been delivered from it.*
    - *Chapter seven would have a powerful impact upon the spiritually minded Jew who read it.*

God's plan for righteousness: provides for man's spiritual needs (8:1-39):

- **In Christ, instead of condemnation, I have life (8:1-17).**

- **God's plan for righteousness provides for man's spiritual needs (8:1-39):**

  In Christ, you will not be condemned. Your body becomes the place where God's Spirit lives, and the Spirit helps you to live like Jesus. Indeed, that was what God planned — that everyone should be made into a copy of Jesus. I am no longer trapped in the desires

- **Present sufferings cannot compare to the glory that awaits us (8:18-27).**
- **We are secure — nothing can separate us from God (8:28-39).**

of the flesh, because the Spirit teaches me how to live. I can be a child of God!

Therefore our present sufferings are nothing. The glory that awaits us is beyond compare. The Spirit will help us in our weaknesses, and He will intercede on our behalf. Therefore, we can be very secure because nothing can separate us from God — nothing at all!

Chapter 8 is the climax of the book of Romans. Paul has proven that God has devised a plan whereby man can be counted righteous, even though he has sinned. That is, through faith in the sacrifice of Christ, I may be forgiven when I sin — and stand in good favor before God once more. Therefore I have hope! I do not have to stand in fear of condemnation, for I have help from God, from Christ, and from the Spirit — the very ones I angered when I sinned!

But the book continues. The connection between chapters 1-8 and chapters 9-11 is exceedingly powerful. The connection is dependent first upon the ringing declaration at the close of chapter eight that nothing can separate us from the love of God (8:39). This powerful thought raises a question that must be satisfactorily answered or it will entirely destroy the hope that Paul has labored so to give us in the first eight chapters. The question is this: If nothing can separate us from the love of God, then how could He reject His people, the Jews? If God could reject Israel, then how can we hope that nothing will separate us from His love?

God's plan for righteousness: fulfills the hope of Israel (9:1-11:36):

- **But what about the Jews? (9:1-5)**
  - **They had so many blessings,**
  - **But they were separated from the love of God.**
- **God's word did not fail.**
  - **Being a physical descendant of Abraham did not assure God's favor (9:6-18).**
- **God's choices were above the Jews' criticism (9:19-29).**
- **The Gentiles gained righteousness through faith,**
  - **While the Jews lost it by lack of faith (9:30-33).**

- **God's plan for righteousness fulfills the hope of Israel (9:1-11:36)**:
- The plan of God has not failed: it has been His sovereign choice to save those who believe, whether Jew or Gentile (9:1-33):

Oh, you say, "But what about the Jews? When they crucified Jesus, and would not believe on Him, did not God tell them they could not be His special people anymore? So, something separated *them* from God." Yes, they were cut off in spite of their many blessings, and I feel deeply grieved that it is true.

But God's word did not fail. Just because one is a physical descendant of Abraham does not mean he is approved of God. God made some choices even among the physical descendants of Abraham, and those choices were His right to make.

The Jews never objected to God's other choices. Therefore God also has the right to show His mercy to those who had never been offered it before — that is, the Gentiles.

Our conclusion, then, must be that the Gentiles, who did not pursue righteousness, have reached it through faith. The Jews, in pursuing a law of righteousness, did not attain righteousness because they sought for it, not by faith, but by works. They failed to believe in God's Son.

Before analyzing the chapter, look at the primary point of chapter ten. The goal of the law was righteousness for mankind, but that goal was not accomplished through the law itself. It was only possible through faith. Thus Christ is the "end of the law as far as righteousness is concerned to everyone that believes" (10:4). The chapter makes an emphasis upon "everyone." Quoting from the Old Testament, Paul makes the point that it was God's plan to reveal a way of justification that would not be impossible to achieve ("Say not in thy heart, 'Who shall ascend into heaven? or Who shall ascend into the abyss."). This way of salvation would be possible and accessible unto all ("The word is near you, in your mouth, and in your heart), and this way, this message of salvation is the gospel (10:8). Paul explains that it is the man who believes in his heart and confesses with his mouth that Jesus is Lord who will be saved. Notice carefully that we have two broad actions set forth here for men to do: believing and confessing. Notice how the apostle shows how these are the actions all men must render to God, and how the Old Testament itself taught that this privilege would belong to all men. The scripture said, "Whosoever believes on him shall not be put to shame" (Isa. 28:16). "Whosoever" includes everyone, Jew or Gentile. Second, the scriptures say, "Whosoever calls on the name of the Lord shall be saved" (Joel 2:32). That God planned for all men to believe and to call upon the name of the Lord meant that He intended for the gospel to be preached unto them. But Israel did not listen to what God said. Their failure to hear explains their misunderstanding about God's granting the Gentiles repentance unto salvation. They both had opportunity to hear and to know, but in their stubbornness and disobedience, the Jews rejected what God had to say.

- **The Jews tried to establish their own system of righteousness by works,**
    - **And failed because they did not accept God's plan (10:1-4).**
- **Righteousness by faith is based upon faith in the gospel which is preached to all (10:5-15).**
- **Faith comes when men will both hear and believe the message of Christ (10:16-17).**

- God told the Jews beforehand that He intended to justify both Jew and Gentile by faith, but they would not listen (10:1-21):

Brethren, I earnestly pray for Israel that they may be saved, because they are zealous for God, but not in the right way. Being ignorant of God's plan for righteousness, and trying to establish their own way, they did not submit to God's plan.

The righteousness of the law required the *perfect doing* of the law. The righteousness which is by faith is not impossible — it is based upon faith in the word which is preached. This righteousness is for the Jews and Greeks: *whosoever* believes on Him shall not be put to shame, and *whosoever* shall call upon the Lord's name shall be saved. For men to call on the Lord, they had to believe in Him, but before they could believe, they had to hear, and before they could hear, the gospel had to be preached — so God intended of old for the gospel to be preached to all.

But all did not listen to the good news. Isaiah, for example, said, "Lord, who has believed our report?" So faith comes by hearing, and hearing by the word of God. Since they rejected what God said, they could not believe it.

- **The Jews were informed about God's plan to save Gentiles (10:18-21) ,**
  - **But most refused to hear.**

Did the Jews fail to know that God would offer His salvation to the Gentiles because they did not hear? No! God's message was freely preached. Did they have the opportunity to know? Yes! Moses and Isaiah told them, but Israel did not get the message because they were a disobedient, quarrelsome people.

- **God has not rejected His people (11:1-6):**
  - **He saves those who believe on Him and love Him:**
    - **Whether Jew or Gentile.**
- **Most of Israel hardened their hearts (11:7-10):**
  - **Those who believed were chosen.**

- God's choice to save those who believe still stands (11:1-36):

Has God rejected His people? No, because God never planned to save a Jew just because he was a Jew, or refuse to save a Gentile just because he was a Gentile. God always planned to save those who love Him and believe on Him. He did not throw away even one single Jew who believed on Him. As in the days of Elijah, when there was a remnant that had not followed after Baal, so also now there is a remnant in keeping with God's grace.

What Israel as a whole sought for, the chosen ones obtained. The rest were hardened in their minds so that they would not believe.

- **Israel's disobedience furnished the occasion for the Gentiles' salvation (11:11-12).**
- **Paul rejoices in his work among the Gentiles (11:13-16):**
  - **Hoping to provoke his own people to seek salvation.**

Did Israel fall so as to be irretrievably lost? No. Their transgression has furnished an occasion for the Gentiles to have salvation also, so as to provoke Israel to jealousy. If their transgression means such blessings for the world, how much greater blessings, if they were to be saved also!

I am speaking to Gentiles as the apostle to the Gentiles. I rejoice in the work I do in the hope that by helping you to be saved, I may move my people to envy your spiritual blessings, and may save some of them. If their rejection provided the occasion for God's blessings to be offered to the world, what would their acceptance be except life from the dead?

- **Gentiles are not to think that they have been saved because of how righteous they are (11:17-21):**
  - **They stand by their faith.**

If some branches of the olive tree *(the Jews)* have been broken off, and you, a branch from a wild olive *(the Gentiles)* have been grafted in, do not boast. Remember, you do not support the root of the tree; the root supports you. If you say, "Well, branches were broken off so that I might be grafted in," then you need to realize this: the Jews were broken off because they did not believe, and the Gentiles were invited to be in God's kingdom because they did believe. The Gentiles can stay in the kingdom only as long as they are faithful. But if they begin to disbelieve the way the Jews disbelieved, they will be rejected, too. If God were willing to break off the natural branches, then He will not spare you either.

- **Behold the goodness and the severity of God (11:22-24).**

Consider, then, the goodness and the severity of God. He was stern with those who fell, but He is kind to you, if you continue in His grace. Otherwise you will be cut off. The Jews, if they are willing to believe, can be grafted in again. It will be no trouble to God to receive Jews again, because if He could graft wild olive branches into the stock of the tree, then how much more easily the natural branches.

- **Knowledge of God's plan will prevent arrogance on the part of the Gentile Christians (11:25-27).**

I do not want you to be ignorant of God's plan, so you will not be arrogant. Israel has experienced a hardening on the part of some of them so that all who will be saved among the Gentiles may come to God. In this way all Israel *(the spiritual Israel of God)* will be saved.

- **God does not hate the Jews (11:28-32):**
  - **He is perfectly willing for them to be saved from their sins also.**

With regard to the gospel, the Jews have become enemies of God so that the Gentiles might be benefitted, but as far as God's willingness to accept them is concerned, they are beloved because of the fathers. God's gifts and His calling are not subject to change. Just as you were disobedient but now have received the mercy of God, so they too have been judged disobedient in order that they also may receive mercy from God. God has concluded all men disobedient so that He may offer mercy to them all.

- **Doxology (11:33-36):**

Oh the depth of the riches of the wisdom and knowledge of God!

God's plan for righteousness: demands righteous lives (12:1-15:13):

- **In view of God's mercy, let your lives be transformed (12:1-21).**

- **God's plan for righteousness demands a life devoted totally to Him and a transformed mind (12:1-15:13):**
- Our conduct (12:1-21):

Therefore, in view of God's mercy, remember you are to live good lives, presenting your bodies as living sacrifices to God. You are to be transformed, that is, to live your life the way God wants you to live, not some way you might choose.

Let everyone use whatever abilities he has in order to do God's will. Be sincere in your love one toward another. Be kind and sympathetic toward others, willing to help when they are in need. Do not be filled with pride. Never leave even the impression that you are dishonest, and live at peace with all men. Do not seek vengeance for yourselves and do good to your enemies.

- **Fulfill your obligations to others (13:1-14).**

- Our obligations (13:1-14):

Obey the laws of your government because God commands it. Do not carry unfulfilled obligations, except the one to love your brethren; you will never finish discharging that debt. Remember that the day of our destiny is near. Let us live as people of the light, behaving honestly, not in unrestrained immorality.

- **Let your behavior show your concern for the spiritual welfare of your brethren (14:1-23).**
  - **Do not deal harshly with a weak brother on matters of judgment (14:1-12).**

- Treatment of one another (14:1-15:13):

Do not embroil one who is weak in all sorts of arguments on difficult issues. There are things which you may disagree about, things which are not right or wrong in themselves, but matters of judgment. Some will eat meat; others will eat only herbs. Some observe special days; others will observe every day alike. The important thing is to let each one make sure that whatever he does, he does it unto God. You should not go about condemning each other over such things.

- **Do not put a stumbling-block in his path by your actions (14:13-23).**

On the other hand you should be careful not to make another brother stumble by something you do. The kingdom of God is not meat and drink — but righteousness, and peace, and joy in the Holy Spirit. When you do a thing, be confident that it is right. If you are doubtful about it, then do not do it.

- **Reflect the example of Christ, who gave Himself as a sacrifice for others (15:1-13).**

Instead of condemning your weak brother, or putting a stumbling block in his path, let the strong help the weak. Even Jesus did not seek to please Himself, but gave Himself as a sacrifice for others, as it is written: "The reproaches of them that reproached you fell upon me." Now these things that were written before these days were written so that through our patience and comfort we might have hope. May the God of all patience and comfort grant you to be of the same mind toward one another, as Christ would have you to be. Therefore, accept one another (*Jew and Gentile*), just as Christ accepted you for the glory of God, because Christ has been made a servant of the circumcision so that He might bring to pass the promises made to the fathers, and that the Gentiles might glorify God for His mercy, as the scriptures say.

- **May you abound in joy, peace, and hope.**

Now may the God of hope fill you with all joy and peace in believing, that you may abound in hope, in the power of the Holy Spirit.

The implication seems clear that the distinction between strong brethren and weak brethren reflected a distinction also between Jews and Gentiles. Certainly this is the point in 15:1-13. Paul argues:

- *That the strong ought to bear the infirmities of the weak,*
- *That this is what Jesus did,*
- *That the disciples should be of the same mind with one another,*
- *That they should receive one another as Christ had received them.*

He underscores these points by arguing that Jesus became a minister of the Jews in order to fulfil the promises made to the fathers <u>and</u> to enable the Gentiles to glorify God. Four references are cited from the Old Testament to bear witness to this fact. As usual, Paul takes the rather ordinary and uses it to make a point that is sublime.

- **Paul's plans (15:14-33):**

- **Paul's plans for the near future (15:14-33):**

  - **He had preached the gospel from Jerusalem all the way around to Illyricum (15:14-21).**

Since I am the assistant of Jesus Christ unto the Gentiles, I have written more boldly to you. (*This point is made in view of the idea expressed in 15:7-12. Since Paul has a particular connection with the work of Christ among the Gentiles, he writes more pointedly to the Romans. Remember, that though there were certainly Jews among the Roman Christians, Paul states in several passages that he is dealing predominantly with Gentiles: "But I speak to you that are Gentiles" (11:13). In chapter 11 it is especially clear that the apostles is talking to Gentiles. See also 1:13.*) Let me tell you something of which I am proud — I will not boast of anything except what Christ has done through me to

- **Now he hopes to go to Spain (15:22-33):**
    - **To visit Rome on his way,**
    - **After he takes the gift to Jerusalem.**
    - **Pray for me:**
        - **That I may be delivered from unbelievers...**
        - **That the saints will accept the gift.**

produce obedience among the Gentiles by word and deed, through powerful signs, by the power of the Spirit, so that from Jerusalem all the way round to Illyricum *(the territory to the east of the Adriatic Sea)* I have fully preached the gospel of Christ. It has been my policy to go into areas where others have not gone before, so that I would not build upon another man's foundation.

But having completed my mission, and having no other place to go in these parts, and having a great desire to see you, it is my plan to go to Spain, and I hope to see you on my way there and visit a while. But for now, I am heading to Jerusalem to carry an offering for the poor saints in the church there. When I have completed this task, then I plan to come. Pray for me that I may be delivered from those in Judea who do not believe, and that my service will be accepted by the saints there.

- **Greetings and closing remarks (16:1-24).**

- **Greetings and closing remarks (16:1-24):**

  I recommend Phoebe our sister who is a servant of the church in Cenchrea. I would also like to greet Priscilla and Aquila, my helpers in Christ Jesus. Please greet the church in their house, and my many other friends and acquaintances in Rome.

  Those with me greet you also.

- **Doxology (16:25-27).**

- **Doxology (16:25-27):**

  To the only wise God, through Jesus Christ, let the glory be forever.

Thumbnail Sketch of Romans:

There are three main section to the book of Romans. These sections take us through 15:13. The first eight chapters show that justification is through faith in Christ, not through the law. Therefore, we are secure in Christ.

Summary concept:

- **<u>Justification is by faith in Jesus, not through complete obedience of the works of the law.</u>**

In chapters nine through eleven, it is as if Paul anticipated a question: how can we feel secure when God rejected His own people, the Jews? He explains that God did not reject the Jews as such —He rejected unbelievers. Those Jews who did not believe in Jesus were rejected; Gentiles who believed were accepted. Those who remain believers are secure —whether Jews or Gentiles. Paul defends God's right to choose whom He will, and the choice God made was to save those who believe and to reject those who do not believe.

In chapters 12:1 through 15:13, the apostle discusses principles of Christian conduct whereby one dedicates his life to the service of God.

Beginning in 15:14, Paul tells about his own activities, the work he had done until that date, and then his plans for the months ahead. Chapter 16 is filled with greetings to friends Paul had in Rome, and from those who were with him to the saints in Rome.

Paul is still on his third missionary journey.

- **A few months pass between the first and second clauses of Acts 20:3.**

Look on your map:

- **Paul had planned to sail from Corinth, straight for Syria on his way to Jerusalem,**
- **But the Jews plotted to kill him,**
- **So Paul went back through Macedonia.**

These men named were messengers from the various congregations who were involved in collecting the contribution for the saints (see 1 Cor.16:3; 2 Cor. 8:16-21).

Paul's companions to Jerusalem:

- **Sopater**
- **Aristarchus**
- **Secundus**
- **Gaius**
- **Timothy**
- **Tychicus**
- **Trophimus**
- **Luke**

We know Luke is one of the company also, because he uses the pronoun "we" again.

It is very early spring, at the time of the Passover.

Paul Sails to Troas (Acts 20:3b-6):

After three months in Corinth, Paul was ready to leave for Jerusalem. But when he learned of a plot the Jews had made against him *(presumably by setting a trap for him at the docks)*, he was forced to change his travel plans once more. Instead of sailing from Corinth for Jerusalem, he decided to go back through Macedonia.

Accompanying him were Sopater from Berea, Aristarchus and Secundus from Thessalonica, Gaius of Derbe, Timothy *(who was from Lystra)*, and Tychicus and Trophimus from the province of Asia. All these, however, had gone ahead of Paul and Luke, and were waiting for them at Troas. Luke and Paul sailed away from Philippi after the days of unleavened bread *(Passover)*, and joined the others at Troas in five days. In Troas they all waited another seven days.

Some of the men named play an important role in the life of Paul:

- *Aristarchus is mentioned in Acts 19 as one of the men seized by the mob at Ephesus, along with Gaius, who are both identified there as Paul's traveling companions from Macedonia (19:29). Since this Gaius is said to be from Derbe, there is no way to know whether he is the same one who was seized in Ephesus. Gaius was a common name of the day. Aristarchus is later mentioned as Paul's fellow-prisoner (Col. 4:10).*
- *Timothy, who one might describe as Paul's right hand man, was with the group.*
- *Tychicus is closely connected with the church at Ephesus; and later he was the bearer of three of Paul's letters: Ephesians, Colossians, and Philemon (Eph. 6:21-22; Col. 4:7-9; 2 Tim. 4:12).*
- *Trophimus is specifically said to be an Ephesian (Acts 21:29). He has the dubious distinction of being the object of a rumor that Paul had brought a Gentile into the temple. He was seen in Jerusalem with Paul, so the Jews were quick to jump to a false conclusion (21:28-29). Later, when Paul writes his last letter, he tells Timothy that he left Trophimus at Miletus sick (2 Tim. 4:20).*
- *Luke also rejoins the party at Philippi where he has apparently remained from the time of the second missionary journey (Acts 16). Thus we begin another "we" section of the book of Acts (20:5-21:18).*

When Paul, Silas, Timothy, and Luke made the trip across the sea from Troas to Neapolis on the second journey, the trip took only two days (Acts 16:11). This time, traveling in the opposite direction from Neapolis to Troas, it takes five days. The time of year was the first part of April, because that was when the feast of unleavened bread (Passover) took place.

Paul preaches at Troas; Eutychus falls from the window (Acts 20:7-12):

On the first day of the week:
- **The brethren met to break bread.**
- **Paul heals the young man Eutychus.**
- **Paul and the brethren at Troas continued to visit until dawn.**

In Troas, on the first day of the week, when the disciples were gathered together to break bread, Paul preached to them. He planned to leave the following day, so he prolonged his speech until midnight. There were many lamps in the upper story room where they were meeting, and a young man named Eutychus sat in a window. As Paul continued to speak, Eutychus fell asleep. To the horror of everyone, he fell out of the third story window and was taken up dead. But Paul went down and embraced him, saying, "Don't be upset, he is alive."

Afterwards Paul went back upstairs and ate and talked with the brethren a long time, even till dawn broke. Then he departed. Everyone was very much comforted about Eutychus, because he was alive and well.

Teachers need to be prepared to emphasize some points about the Lord's Supper. Do not underestimate the importance of this passage. There are many in the church who do not view this passage as forming any kind of pattern for the time of observing the Lord's Supper. Some wish to dismiss it altogether, saying that it had nothing to do with the Lord's Supper. So let's examine some points about it:

From the context, this first "breaking of bread" must have been the Lord's Supper.
- **If this were the Lord's Supper,**
  - **We have a clear indication from the Bible that God was pleased with their taking it upon the first day of the week.**
- **If someone wants to take the Lord's Supper at some other time,**
  - **He must find some indication from God that the time would be pleasing.**
- **Do I choose to walk in the light of God's revelation,**
  - **Or to walk where God has given no light?**

- *Paul was in a hurry to reach Jerusalem by Pentecost (20:16).*
  - *He was prepared to take quite extraordinary measures to try to make it.*
    - *For example, he decided to sail past Ephesus and meet only with the elders from that church (20:17).*
  - *Yet in Troas, after taking five days to get there from Philippi, he waits seven days (20:6).*
    - *Why did he wait seven days? The only discernible reason is so that he might meet with the brethren and preach to them.*
    - *Now if the breaking of bread mentioned here is a common meal, why did they wait seven days to eat a common meal together? Did the brethren usually meet together for their common meals? If they did, then Paul could have met with them promptly after he arrived and would not have had to tarry seven days.*
- *Though the term "breaking bread" often means eating a regular meal, it was also the term for observing the Lord's Supper.*
  - *The brethren did not meet specifically to hear Paul;*
    - *They met to break bread, and Paul preached to them.*
  - *The context supports the idea that this "breaking bread" was the Lord's Supper.*
- *Though many will agree that this is the Lord's Supper, they argue that one cannot prove from this one example that the Lord's Supper can only be taken on the first day of the week.*

- *But the primary point is this: to know what God wants, we must have a divine indicator of God's will.*
  - *We know that it pleased God for the disciples to meet on the first day of the week to partake of the Lord's Supper because of the record in Acts 20:7.*
  - *If someone wishes to partake of it at some other time, where is the divine indicator that it is God's will for him to do so?*
  - *It becomes a question of whether one wants to walk in the light of God's revelation, or to walk in paths where God has not lighted the way.*
- *Usually those who argue that this was just a common meal are also those who want to prove that the Lord's Supper can be taken at any time, or at no time at all.*

The second mention of "breaking bread" may well have been a common meal.

- *It was a special treat to these early saints for an apostle to be in their midst. Therefore, it is not surprising that Paul spoke to them until midnight, then after the experience with Eutychus, the group went back upstairs, ate together, and continued talking the rest of the night. Think what a privilege it would be if we could have the apostle Paul stop by our home congregation some day! Could you think of any better way to spend some hours?*
  - *Since the group had been together all evening and all night, this second mention of eating was likely a common meal.*
  - *In other words, the disciples met at some hour on the first day of the week (no hour is given) to "break bread," seemingly, as we have shown, to observe the Lord's Supper. Paul was there and preached to them. But then, after midnight and the raising of Eutychus, the brethren went back upstairs, ate together (seemingly a common meal), and continued to visit until daybreak.*

Map assignment:

- **Be sure your map shows Paul's route from Corinth where he spent the winter,**
- **Back through Macedonia, to Troas,**
- **And now by land and sea as he makes his way along the coastline of Asia Minor to Miletus.**
- **Luke is very precise in his details as he tells of this journey.**
  - **Your blank map may not show every island, but you can show the approximate route.**

Paul wants to reach Jerusalem in time for Pentecost, (late spring).

From Troas to Miletus (Acts 20:13-16):

Paul's companions set sail for Assos where they were to meet Paul, because he had decided to walk overland and meet them there. When Paul rejoined them at Assos, they sailed on to Mitylene *(on the island of Lesbos)*. The next day they sailed by Chios *(an island)*, and the third day they touched at Samos *(another island)*. The next day they came to Miletus *(a seaport a few miles south of Ephesus)*. Paul had chosen not to stop at Ephesus itself because he was hurrying, to try, if possible, to make it to Jerusalem by Pentecost.

To get to Assos from Troas, the ship had to sail south around a jutting point of land and then due east to Assos. Because of the round-about journey, Paul could walk across land and join the group without delaying the progress of the ship. The text gives no indication why he chose to do this.

Paul's speech to the elders of Ephesus (Acts 20:17-35):

From Miletus Paul called for the elders of the church at Ephesus so that he could give them a final charge:

He told the Ephesian elders:

- **You know how I conducted myself among you (20:17-21):**
  - **I did not hesitate to preach the things you needed,**
  - **In spite of hardships.**
- **The Spirit warns there will be trouble in Jerusalem (20:22-24):**
  - **But I want to complete the task before me.**
- **You will not see me again (20:25-27):**
  - **I am innocent from the blood of all men,**
  - **Because I have not hesitated to preach the entire will of God.**
- **Therefore guard yourselves and the flock which is among you (20:28-31):**
  - **For false teachers will arise.**
- **I commit you to God's care and to the word of His grace (20:32).**
- **I have left you an example so that you will support the weak (20:33-35).**

> You know how I behaved among you from the first day I arrived in Asia. In all sorts of circumstances I served the Lord in humility and with tears, although I was under many trials because of plots from the Jews. You know I did not hold back anything that you needed to hear, but taught you publicly and from house to house. I have testified to both Jews and Greeks that they must turn to God in repentance and have faith in Jesus Christ.
>
> Now I am compelled by the Spirit to go to Jerusalem, not knowing what will happen to me there, except that the Holy Spirit warns me in every city that fetters and hardships await me. None of these things, however, influence me, nor do I consider my life dear to me as long as I can complete the task the Lord has given me: that of testifying to the gospel of God's grace.
>
> I know that none of you, among whom I have traveled preaching the gospel, will see me again. So I say before you, as you will agree, I am innocent of the blood of all men, because I have not hesitated to proclaim the entire will of God.
>
> Therefore, watch yourselves and guard the flock in which the Holy Spirit has made you overseers, being sure to feed the church of the Lord which He purchased with His own blood. I give you this warning because I know that after I leave, savage wolves will enter in among you and will not spare the flock. Even from among yourselves men will arise, distorting the truth in order to draw away disciples after themselves. Therefore be on your guard! Remember that for three years I ceased not to warn every one night and day with tears.
>
> Now I commit you to God's care, and to the word of His grace which is able to build you up and to give you an inheritance among those who are set apart. I have not coveted any man's silver, or gold, or apparel. You yourselves know that I labored with my own hands to supply my needs and the needs of those who were with me. I have shown you these things so that, as you work, you will support the weak. Remember the words of the Lord Jesus, how He said, "It is more blessed to give than to receive."

Paul and the brethren wept and prayed together.

When Paul had said these things, he knelt down with all of the elders and prayed. They all cried as they embraced him and kissed him. The thing that upset them most was his statement that they would see him no more. Then they accompanied him to the ship.

When Paul wrote Romans:
- **He expected to deliver the gift in Jerusalem,**
- **Then start on his trip to Rome and Spain.**
- **Now he knows trouble awaits him.**
  - **He does not expect to come this way again;**
  - **Though from later epistles, it seems that he did pass back through the area after his imprisonment in Rome (see 1 Tim. 1:3; 2 Tim. 4:12).**

This is the first mention that there will be trouble awaiting Paul in Jerusalem. Only a few weeks earlier, when Paul wrote to the Romans, he was planning to make the trip to Jerusalem to deliver the gift from the Gentile Christians, and then he planned to visit Rome on his way to Spain. He asked that the Romans pray that the gift would be well received and that he would be delivered from the unbelievers in Judea, but at that point he thought he would soon be on his way elsewhere after reaching Jerusalem. (See Romans 15:23-32.) But by the time he talks to these elders from Ephesus, the Spirit has warned him of trouble ahead.

According to I Timothy 1:3, Paul apparently did see the Ephesians again, including at least some of the elders. This situation, therefore, is similar to the one in Acts 27:9-10 in which Paul stated his view based upon his situation and upon certain conclusions he had drawn, but which had not been specifically revealed to him from God. The Spirit had told Paul he was facing bonds and afflictions —and at this point he does not know how severe they may be. Therefore he has expressed a farewell, thinking it may be his final one to them.

Paul and his company sail to Tyre (Acts 21:1-6):

Continue to mark the route:
- **They made connection with a ship to Phoenicia (in the province of Syria),**
  - **On the seacoast just north of Caesarea.**
- **Then sailed south of the island of Cyprus.**
- **On to Syria (to Tyre in Phoenicia).**

After Paul and his companions parted from the elders of Ephesus, they put out to sea and set a course straight to Cos *(an island)*. The next day they went to Rhodes *(a city on the island by the same name. At about this point they left what was considered the Aegean Sea and moved into the waters off the southern coast of Asia Minor)*. From Rhodes they sailed to Patara *(a city in Lycia)* where they found a ship sailing to Phoenicia.

Travelers in that day had to make connections between ships that traveled regular routes in the same manner we have to make connections with various flights, or bus, or train routes.

Disciples at Tyre warn again of trouble in Jerusalem.

From Patara they sailed until they saw Cyprus, and then sailed south of it to Syria. They landed at Tyre where the ship was to unload its cargo. Finding disciples there, they stayed with them for seven days. These disciples warned Paul through the Spirit that he should not go to Jerusalem, but Paul did not hesitate in his plans. When the visiting time was over, he and his companions left to go on their way. All the disciples and their wives and children went out of the city and accompanied them to the beach, where they knelt and prayed together. After saying good-by to one another, Paul and his company boarded the ship and the disciples from Tyre went back home.

The disciples at Tyre warned Paul through the Spirit not to go to Jerusalem. This fact causes a problem if we take it that the Spirit was telling Paul: "Do not go up to Jerusalem," and yet Paul had told the

Paul felt compelled to continue on his way to Jerusalem, in spite of the warnings of persecution, because of the importance of the task before him.

- **The Spirit is telling Paul there will be trouble,**
- **But it is the people who are begging him not to go.**

Ephesian elders he was "bound in the Spirit," or compelled by the Spirit, to make the trip (20:22). Paul was a man who would certainly have done whatever the Spirit said. The explanation is that the Spirit was warning what would happen, but the urging not to go was coming from the people themselves, as they felt deep grief at the idea of his facing such trials. Paul knew that he was headed for trouble, but he felt bound to go, because he had an important task to perform (20:22; 21:13).

The men arrive in Caesarea (Acts 21:7-15):

This is the same Philip who preached to the people of Samaria and to the Ethiopian eunuch in Acts 8.

From Tyre they sailed to Ptolemais where they greeted the brethren and stayed with them for a day. The next day they came to the great seaport of Caesarea and entered into the house of Philip the evangelist who had been one of the seven men chosen to help the apostles back in chapter 6 of Acts. Philip had four daughters who had the gift of prophecy.

We last saw Philip in Acts 8, where the text says he was found at Azotus, and went on his way preaching through the cities until he came to Caesarea (8:40). Apparently he has lived in Caesarea all the time since, a period of over twenty-five years. The year now was A.D. 58.

Paul is warned again — this time by Agabus the prophet.

- **We met this same Agabus back in chapter 11 when he warned of a famine that would come over the land in the days of Claudius.**
- **As a result of his warning at that time:**
    - **Paul and Barnabas took a gift from Antioch to the brethren of Judea (11:27-30; 12:25).**

After they had been there many days, a prophet by the name of Agabus came down from Jerusalem. He went to Paul, took his belt, tied his own hands, and said, "The Holy Spirit says, 'In this manner the Jews in Jerusalem will bind the man who owns this belt, and will turn him over to the Gentiles.'"

Having heard this news, both Paul's traveling companions and the brethren who lived in Caesarea, begged Paul not to go to Jerusalem. But Paul answered them: "What do you think you are doing, weeping and breaking my heart? I am ready not only to be bound, but also to die in Jerusalem for the name of the Lord Jesus."

When he could not be persuaded to change his plans, they gave up and said, "The Lord's will be done."

Afterwards, Paul and the men with him arose and went to Jerusalem. Some of the brethren from Caesarea went with them and brought them to the house of Mnason where they were to stay. Mnason was from Cyprus and was an early disciple.

Paul's companions weep and urge him not to go to Jerusalem:

- **But then accept his decision when he could not be persuaded.**

When Paul arrived in Caesarea he stayed for "many days." It appears from this fact that he did not arrive in Jerusalem in time for the Pentecost feast. We can account for about thirty-five days from the time Paul left Philippi to the time he arrives in Caesarea. In addition we find a considerable leg of his journey for which no time is given (viz., from Patara to Tyre). Finally, we have to add the "many days" at Caesarea. Figuring fifty days (which was the length of time from Passover to Pentecost, see Lev. 23:16) from about April 1, he might still have had time to make it, but the Bible does not say whether he did or did not arrive in time for the feast.

The brethren in Jerusalem received Paul and his company warmly.

Paul arrives in Jerusalem (Acts 21:17):

When they arrived in Jerusalem, the brethren received them warmly.

Review the third journey:

- **Be sure your map is complete.**
- **Know what happened at each place.**

The route:

- **Antioch of Syria**
- **Galatia and Phrygia**
- **Ephesus:**
  - **Book of Galatians**
  - **Book of 1 Corinthians**
- **Troas**
- **Macedonia:**
  - **Book of 2 Corinthians**
- **Corinth:**
  - **Book of Romans**
- **Back through Macedonia**
- **Troas**
- **Miletus**
- **Tyre**
- **Ptolemais**
- **Caesarea**
- **Jerusalem**

The third journey:

After leaving Antioch in Syria, Paul passed through Galatia and Phrygia.

Then, in fulfillment of the promise he had made at the end of the second journey, he returned to Ephesus, where he stayed and preached for three years. While he was there he probably wrote the book of Galatians early in his stay, and definitely wrote 1 Corinthians toward the end of the three years. By the time he wrote that book, he had already made plans to collect a gift from the predominately Gentile congregations to take to the poor saints in Jerusalem.

From Ephesus, he traveled north to Troas, but did not tarry to preach. He continued on to Macedonia, visiting the various congregations as he passed through the province. As he was making his way through Macedonia, he wrote the second letter to the Corinthians.

When he reached Corinth, he spent the winter, and wrote the book of Romans.

In early spring, he started on his way to Jerusalem with the gift that had been collected. But instead of sailing straight from Corinth, he was forced to turn back and travel by land through Macedonia because the Jews had made a plot to kill him.

After passing through Macedonia, he sailed to Troas where he met with the brethren and preached and visited all night long.

He continued his way by land and ship until he reached Miletus, where he called for the elders from Ephesus. By now he had been warned by the Spirit that he will face hardship in Jerusalem. He thinks this is his last chance to encourage these brethren who were dear to him.

He and his companions continue their journey, stopping to visit with brethren at Tyre, Ptolemais, and Caesarea. Warnings continue to come of persecution ahead, but he does not waver in his determination to complete the task of delivering the gift to the Jewish Christians.

He arrives in Jerusalem and finds a warm welcome from the brethren.

Trouble Arises in Jerusalem

(Acts 21:17-28:31)

Paul reported:
- **Told all that God had accomplished among the Gentiles.**
- **James and the elders glorified God.**

Paul arrives in Jerusalem (Acts 21:17-26):

When Paul and his companions arrived in Jerusalem with the gift from the Gentile congregations, the brethren received them warmly. The next day they went in to see James, and all the elders were present. Paul greeted them and told in detail what God had done among the Gentiles through his ministry.

Having heard his report, they glorified God. Then they said to Paul:

The elders to Paul:
- **Many Jewish Christians:**
  - ***<u>All</u> Jews did not reject the gospel.***
  - ***<u>Many</u> believed.***
- **Even the believing Jews thought Paul taught the Jews who lived among the Gentiles to forsake their customs.**
- **The elders advised Paul to pay expenses for a vow,**
  - **To clarify his position on the customs of the Jews.**
- **The elders still firmly believed that the Gentiles did not have to keep the law of Moses.**

> You see, brother, how *many thousands* of the Jews have believed, and all of them are diligent in keeping the law. They have been told that you teach the Jews who live among the Gentiles to stop following after Moses, that you tell them not to circumcise their children, or to live according to the customs of the law. What can be done about this? They are certainly going to hear that you have come.
>
> Therefore, accept this suggestion of ours: there are four men among us who have made a vow. Take these men and purify yourself with them, and pay the expenses they incur in their purification, so that they can have their heads shaved. In that way, everyone will know that there is no truth to these rumors about you, but that you yourself are living in obedience to the law.
>
> As for the Gentile believers, we have written and concluded that they need observe no such thing, except that they should keep themselves from things sacrificed to idols, from blood, from animals that have been strangled, and from fornication.

Paul took their advice.

Accepting their advice, Paul took the men, and the next day, purifying himself along with them, entered into the temple to give notice of the date when the days of purification would end and the offering would be made for each of them.

See Numbers 6 for information about the Nazirite vow.

The vow of the four men was almost certainly a Nazirite vow. At the close of the vow, the hair, which was allowed to grow for the duration of the vow, was shaved and burned in the fire which was under the sacrifice of the peace offering (Num. 6:18). The sacrifices which were to be offered are enumerated in Numbers 6:14-17. The Nazirite was to shave his head in the "day of his cleansing" (Num. 6:9). That "cleansing" was the purification rites these four men were to undergo. Paul would pay for the sacrifices they were to offer and for any other expense incurred. In this way he would show that he had no objection to Jewish Christians following the traditions of their fathers as long as they did not seek to bind them as law. This action was totally consistent with Paul's course of action elsewhere (cf. 1 Cor. 9:20-21).

The vow of these men was different to the one mentioned in Acts 18:18 because it seems that the shaving of the hair in that case was done at the beginning of the vow, not at its end. That vow may have been one not provided for in the law, but one which is mentioned by Josephus as being common among the Jews.

Paul's convictions:
- **The Gentiles were not subject to the law of Moses in any way.**
- **The Jewish Christians could observe the customs of their fathers,**
  - **So long as they did not bind them as law.**

Paul's participation in this vow did not compromise his position toward the law of Moses. One of the hardest battles he fought was over the question of whether the law of Moses was still binding as law upon anyone —whether Jew or Gentile. He particularly fought hard against the Judaizing teachers who tried to force the Gentiles to become subject to the law — and demonstrate that subjection by being circumcised —before they could be saved. But he did not object to the Jewish Christians continuing to follow the customs of their fathers. They could not continue to rely upon the sacrifices of the old law for their forgiveness from sin, but those things such as circumcision of their sons, or vows, could be continued without compromising their allegiance to Christ.

Apostolic example is an important way to establish authority for actions,
- **Unless God demonstrated His disapproval.**

It is important to understand that the only way we can know whether an action of an apostle is one that should be copied or rejected is how it was regarded by God. In this instance, the suggestion came from James (an inspired man) and the elders at Jerusalem. It was accepted and acted upon by Paul (another inspired man). No word of condemnation came from God, so we must assume they acted in accord with His will. God did not leave it in our hands to criticize their actions unless He expressed criticism. For example, we know without doubt that Peter took inappropriate action toward Gentiles at Antioch because he was publicly rebuked by Paul (Gal. 2:11-14). There is no such rebuke from God or from any inspired man on the scene on this occasion, so it is left as an approved, inspired example.

The Jews start a riot (Acts 21:27-36):

Jews from Asia charged:
- **Paul teaches against the people, the law, and the temple.**
- **Now he has brought a Greek into the temple.**

The seven days of purification were almost over when Jews from Asia saw Paul in the temple. They began to stir up the crowd by shouting, "Men of Israel, help! This is the man who teaches everyone against the people, the law, and this place. To add to his guilt, he has brought Greeks into the temple and has defiled this holy place."

These Jews from Asia had seen Trophimus with Paul in the city. Trophimus was an Ephesian who had come in the group of men bringing the gift (20:4). They assumed that Paul had brought him into the temple — but they certainly had not seen him do so.

This trouble:
- **Originated with unbelieving Jews from Asia,**
- **The mob was composed of Jews from Jerusalem.**
- **The Romans rescued Paul.**

The riot grew like a fire. The mob seized Paul and dragged him out of the temple, whereupon the doors of the temple were shut as if they were preventing further defilement. As the Jews were attempting to kill Paul, news came to the tribune of the cohort that all Jerusalem was in an uproar.

Immediately the chief captain *(the tribune)* took soldiers and centurions and ran down *(from the tower of Antonia, the "castle" of 21:34)* into the mob. When the Jews saw the chief captain and his soldiers, they stopped beating Paul. The tribune approached and took Paul into custody, commanding that he be bound with two chains. Then he asked the people who Paul was and what he had done.

The chief captain:
- **Rescued Paul by arresting him.**
- **Inquired who he was and what he had done.**
- **The mob was so aroused, he could learn nothing.**

This question aroused the crowd again. Some shouted one thing and some another so that, because of the uproar, the tribune could not learn anything. He commanded that Paul be taken into the castle *(the tower of Antonia)*. Paul had to be carried by the soldiers to protect him from the violence of the crowd, because the people were furious and kept shouting, "Do away with him."

Gentiles and the temple

The charge that Paul had brought a Gentile into the temple area was a serious one in the eyes of the Jews. There were three courts that surrounded the temple of New Testament days. Anyone might enter the outermost court, which was called the Court of the Gentiles; but it was forbidden, on threat of death, for a Gentile to go into the inner courts. Notices were posted in both Latin and Greek, saying, "No foreigner may enter within this barricade which surrounds the temple and enclosure (its two inner courts). Anyone caught doing so will have himself to blame for his ensuing death" (The Complete Biblical Library, Acts, pp. 519-520).

The Tower of Antonia

The tower of Antonia was a fortress castle adjacent to the northwest wall of the temple court. It had been rebuilt and fortified by Herod the Great. The Romans always kept a cohort of soldiers, usually from 600 to 1,000 men, stationed there to help keep peace among the Jews. Two flights of stairs led down from the tower directly into the Court of the Gentiles. Since the Jews gathered at the temple three times a year for their pilgrimage feasts, the Romans considered the fortress a strategic place to observe the crowds and to keep peace among a subject people who were not loyal in their allegiance to Rome. This chief captain (chiliarch, or tribune) was the man in charge of the cohort of soldiers. The text soon tells us that his name was Claudius Lysias (23:26).

Paul had asked the Romans to pray:
- **That the saints would accept the gift...**
- **That he be delivered from unbelieving Jews...**

Do you remember that Paul asked the saints at Rome to pray for him as he was about to start the trip to Jerusalem? He asked that they pray that he be delivered from the unbelieving in Judea and that the saints would accept the gift he was taking (Rom. 15:30-31). The saints have received him warmly and have glorified God (Acts 21:17, 20), but the unbelieving Jews have now brought trouble, just as Paul had feared, and as the Spirit had foretold.

Paul requests permission to speak (Acts 21:37-40):

The chief captain had bound Paul in chains because he thought he was a terrorist.

Paul asked to speak to the mob:
- **The chief captain granted the request.**

As Paul was about to be brought into the fortress, he spoke to the chief captain: "May I say something to you?"

"Do you speak Greek?" the captain replied. "Are you not the Egyptian who, some time ago, stirred up a rebellion and led the four thousand men of the Assassins into the wilderness?"

Paul replied, "I am a Jew from Tarsus in Cilicia, a citizen of a prominent city, and I would like permission to speak to the people."

The chief captain gave his permission and Paul, standing on the stairs leading into the fortress, motioned with his hand to get everyone's attention. When a great silence came over the crowd, Paul began to speak to them in the Aramaic language.

The Assassins were called Sicarii, because of the dagger, the Sikarios, they used to kill their victims. We would call them terrorists.

The Aramaic language had been the language of the common man in Israel since the days of the captivity. Their original language had been Hebrew, and by this time, most could also speak Greek, but Aramaic was the day-by-day language spoken in the land.

Paul's defense before the mob (Acts 22:1-21):

"Brothers and fathers, listen to my defense which I now make before you." The crowd, hearing that Paul spoke in their own dialect, grew even quieter. Paul continued:

Paul said:
- **I, too, once persecuted this Way.**
- **But the Lord whom I had been persecuting,**
  - **Appeared to me.**
- **The Lord said I would be told what He had planned for me to do.**

> I am a Jew, born in Tarsus of Cilicia, but brought up in this city at the feet of Gamaliel — where I was zealous for God, just as all of you are today, and I persecuted this Way even to death. The high priest and the Sanhedrin can bear witness to these facts. From them I received letters of authority to go to Damascus to find Christians there and to bring them bound to Jerusalem to be punished.
>
> But as I was approaching Damascus, it was about noon when suddenly a bright light shone down from heaven all around me. I fell to the ground and heard a voice saying, "Saul, Saul, why are you persecuting me?" So I said, "Who are you, Lord?" He answered, "I am Jesus of Nazareth, whom you are persecuting."
>
> Now those who were with me saw the light, but they did not understand the words that were spoken to me. I asked, "What do you want me to do, Lord?" and He said, "Get up and go into Damascus, and there you will be told what I have

planned for you to do." Afterward I could not see, because of the magnificence of the light. Those who were with me took me by the hand and guided me into Damascus.

- **Ananias came:**
  - **God wanted me to know His will,**
  - **Because I was to tell all men the things I had seen and heard.**

A very good man named Ananias lived there and enjoyed a good reputation among the Jews. He came to me and said, "Brother Saul, receive your sight," and immediately I could see him. He told me, "The God of our ancestors has planned that you are to know His will, and to see Christ, and to hear a message from His lips — because you are going to act as a witness for Him, telling all men the things you have seen and heard. Now, why keep waiting? Get up and be baptized, calling on the Lord's name."

- **Jesus appeared again and told me to leave Jerusalem quickly.**
  - **I protested...**
  - **But He said, "I am sending you to the Gentiles."**

Some time later, I returned to Jerusalem, and as I was praying in the temple, I fell into a trance. Jesus appeared to me, saying, "Hurry and get out of Jerusalem because they will not accept your testimony about me."

But I said, "Lord, they themselves know that I imprisoned and beat those in every synagogue who believed in you. They know that when your witness Stephen was killed I was there consenting to their actions. I even watched the coats of those who killed him."

But He answered, "Leave here, because I am sending you far away to the Gentiles."

Paul is a Roman citizen (Acts 22:22-29):

The mob was enraged again.
- **The chief captain had to rescue Paul.**
- **He commanded that Paul be scourged to force him to tell his story.**

The crowd listened until Paul said the Lord was sending him to the Gentiles. Then they began shouting and screaming again: "Do away with such a fellow! He is not fit to live!" As they shrieked, they threw off their garments and threw dust into the air.

So the chief captain gave up his effort to learn any more by this means. He commanded that Paul be taken into the castle to be examined by scourging.

In cases like this, Roman procedure was to administer a scourging to persuade the criminal that his best course was to tell everything.

Paul was a Roman citizen:
- **Paul's citizenship was of a higher order than the chief captain's.**
- **It would have been a grave offense if the chief captain had scourged Paul after learning of his citizenship.**

The chief captain left, and as the soldiers were binding Paul for his scourging, he asked the centurion in charge, "Is it legal for you to scourge an uncondemned Roman citizen?"

When the centurion heard this, he hurried to the chief captain and said, "What are you about to do? This man is a Roman!"

Promptly, the tribune came and asked Paul, "Tell me, are you a Roman?"

Paul answered, "Yes."

The chief captain replied, "I had to pay a big price for my citizenship."

Paul said, "But I was born a Roman."

Those who had been about to scourge Paul left the room. The chief captain was afraid now that he knew his prisoner was a Roman citizen and that he had ordered him bound before a condemnation.

Though the chief captain was by now afraid to treat Paul cruelly, he did not release him because he still did not know what charges the Jews had against him. Even if Paul told his side of the story, the chief captain could not be sure it was true until he had heard from the Jews. It was a protection to Paul to be kept away from the Jewish mobs.

Scourging varied in severity according to the purpose of the Romans. For a condemned man, it was part of the death process in which all the cruelty possible was heaped upon the victim. A scourging such as Paul had been about to endure would have been severe, but would probably not have been life-threatening.

Roman law protected citizens from ignoble treatment such as being bound in chains when not yet condemned, and from cruel punishment such as scourging and crucifixion. Though Paul suffered more than most Christians, his citizenship prevented some suffering. Even when he died, it was his Roman citizenship that caused him to be beheaded rather than crucified as Peter was.

Paul's defense before the Jewish Council (Acts 22:30-23:10):

The chief captain tries again to learn the charges against Paul:

- **By taking him before the Jewish Sanhedrin.**

The next day, the chief captain, wishing to learn more about Paul's case, took him before the Sanhedrin and chief priests whom he had commanded to assemble.

Paul began:

- **"I have always tried to do what I thought was right before God."**

Boldly Paul looked at the council and said, "Brethren, I have lived before God in all good conscience until this very day."

No one knows what course Paul's speech would have taken if he had not been interrupted. Probably he planned to say that though he had always done what he thought God wanted him to do, he had been honestly mistaken about God's will when he was persecuting the church.

Paul was interrupted by a slap, at the command of the High Priest.

The high priest, Ananias, commanded those who were close by to slap Paul on the mouth.

This Ananias was not the Annas of Jesus' day. This man came to the position of high priest in A.D. 48 and served until A.D. 59, when he was assassinated by the Sicarii, or assassins. It was now about A.D. 58, so he did not have long to live.

Even under these circumstance, Paul did not consider it appropriate for him to speak against a ruler of his people.

Paul responded quickly, saying, "God will smite you, you whitewashed wall! Do you claim to be sitting to judge me according to the law, and yet you order me to be struck contrary to the law?"

Those who were standing by said, "Do you speak against God's high priest?"

Paul replied, "Brethren, I did not know he was high priest. It is written, 'Do not speak evil of a ruler of the people.'"

What Paul said to Ananias was true, and if his statement that God would smite him referred in a prophetic manner to his death at the hands of assassins a year or so later, then clearly Paul was inspired in his response. Jesus had said that the Holy Spirit would guide the saints in what to say when they were put on trial (Mark 13:9-11). It was, therefore, by the Spirit that Paul spoke. Yet if Paul had known that Ananias was the high priest, he would not have said the words lest he be in violation of Exodus 22:28.

Paul declared he had been called in question over the hope of the resurrection.

- **Sadducees:**
  - **Did not believe in the resurrection, in angels, or spirits.**
- **Pharisees:**
  - **Believed in all three.**

Paul could see he would get no fair hearing in this assembly, so, realizing that the council was divided between Sadducees and Pharisees, he cried out: "Brethren, I am a Pharisee, the son of Pharisees. It is concerning the hope and resurrection of the dead that I am being questioned."

Immediately the council fell to arguing among themselves — the Pharisees against the Sadducees. The Sadducees said that there is no resurrection, neither angels, nor spirits, but the Pharisees believed in all three. The meeting was soon in an uproar. Some of the scribes who were Pharisees stood up and said, "We find no evil in this man, and what if a spirit or an angel has spoken to him?"

Once more, the chief captain rescued Paul from the crowd.

The situation was soon so out of control the chief captain was afraid Paul would be torn in pieces. So he commanded the soldiers to go down and forcibly remove him from the crowd and bring him into the fortress of Antonia.

The Lord comforts Paul (Acts 23:11):

Paul will bear witness to the cause of Christ in Rome itself.

That night the Lord appeared to Paul and said, "Cheer up: as you have testified of me in Jerusalem, so you must bear witness of me at Rome also."

A plot against Paul's life (Acts 23:12-30):

Jews plot to kill Paul.

The next day more than forty Jews banded together under a curse, saying that they would neither eat nor drink until they killed Paul. They told the chief priests and elders about their vow: "We have placed ourselves under a great curse to taste nothing until we kill Paul. This is how you can help us: persuade the council to ask the chief captain to bring Paul down again as if you wanted to find out more details about the case, and before he gets there, we are ready to kill him."

Paul's nephew tells of the plot.

Paul's sister's son heard of the ambush and went into the castle to tell Paul about the plot. Paul called one of the centurions and said, "Take this young man to the chief captain because he has some news for him."

The centurion conducted Paul's nephew to the tribune and said, "Paul the prisoner called me to him and asked me to bring this young man to you because he has something to tell you."

The chief captain took the young man by the hand and led him aside privately and said, "What is it that you have to tell me?"

"The Jews have agreed to ask you to bring Paul down to the Sanhedrin tomorrow, as if they were going to question him more. But do not agree to do so, because more than forty men wait in ambush for him. They have bound themselves under a curse, swearing that they will not eat or drink until they have killed Paul. They are ready, and wait for you to consent to their request."

Then the chief captain sent the young man away, warning him: "Do not tell anyone that you have told me these things."

The chief captain protected Paul again:

- **By sending him to Caesarea under the escort of 470 soldiers.**

As soon as the lad was gone, the chief captain called two centurions and said, "Prepare two hundred soldiers to go to Caesarea. We will also need seventy cavalrymen and two hundred spear men. Tell them to be ready to leave at nine o'clock tonight. Be sure to have an animal ready for Paul to ride also."

While waiting for these preparations to be made, the chief captain wrote a letter to Felix the governor. The letter said:

The letter said:

- **I rescued this man because I had learned he was a Roman.**
- **He is accused of matters concerning the Jews' law.**
- **Not worthy of death.**
- **I learned of a plot against him, so I sent him to you.**
- **His accusers will come to you.**

> Claudius Lysias unto the most excellent governor Felix. Greetings.
>
> This man was seized by the Jews and was about to be killed by them when I came upon them with soldiers and rescued him, since I had learned he was a Roman.
>
> Wishing to know what the Jews had against him, I brought him down into their council. But I found him to be accused of matters having to do with their law. There was no complaint against him worthy of death.
>
> Then when I learned of a plot against his life, I immediately sent him to you, with the plan that his accusers should come and present their case against him before you.
>
> Farewell.

Paul is escorted to Caesarea (Acts 23:31-35):

Caesarea was the official headquarters of the Roman governor of Judea.

- **On the seacoast,**
- **About 70 miles northwest of Jerusalem.**

The soldiers took Paul as commanded and escorted him as far as Antipatris that night. The next day the cavalry went on with Paul, while the soldiers returned to Jerusalem.

The road taken by Paul's guards went northwest to Lydda, on north to Antipatris, and then north to Caesarea — a total distance of seventy miles. Some have criticized this tribune for turning out a small army of 470 men to escort Paul, but the tribune wanted to be certain that no surprise attack would be successful against Paul.

The spear men were probably slingers. The word translated "spearmen" is a word which has been found only three times anywhere: once here, once in the seventh century, and once in the tenth century. The word literally means "those who take something in their right hands." (Lenski, The Interpretation of Acts, p. 949.)

Paul is now a prisoner in Caesarea:

- **Awaiting the Jewish accusers.**

When the escort arrived in Caesarea, they delivered the letter from Claudius Lysias and presented Paul to Felix. When Felix read the letter, he asked Paul what province he was from. When he understood that it was Cilicia, he said, "I will give you a full hearing when your accusers have come." Then Felix gave orders that Paul should be kept in custody at the palace of Herod the Great which now served as the official residence of the governor.

The question about which province Paul was from was in order to determine what jurisdiction he came under. Cilicia was under the governor of Syria. Paul had been arrested in Jerusalem, thus under the jurisdiction of Felix, but being a native of Cilicia, his case, if it involved insurrection, might have to be heard before the governor of Syria. Such an eventuality did not come to pass, but, at this point, Felix had to consider the possibilities.

Felix was procurator of Judea from A.D. 52 until A.D. 60.

- **It is now A.D. 58.**

Felix had been a slave, along with his brother Pallas. The two became freedmen in the house of the mother of Emperor Claudius. Pallas became a favorite of the emperor and was made one of his ministers. He secured the post of procurator of Judea for his brother Felix in A.D. 52.

The Roman historian Tacitus was very critical of Felix, saying, "With all cruelty and lust he exercised the power of a king with the spirit of a slave." Feeling that his brother Pallas could protect him, Felix thought he was at liberty to be as cruel and unprincipled as he wished. (See Tacitus, Annals, Penquin Classics, p. 276.)

Suetonius, another Roman historian, reports that Felix had three wives: Drusilla, princess of Mauritania; Drusilla, the daughter of Herod Agrippa I; and a third wife who is not named. (See Suetonius, Claudius, 28.) Felix ruled until his recall by Nero in A.D. 60. He lost his position as a noteworthy person with the execution of his brother Pallas in A.D. 63.

Paul's defense before Felix (Acts 24:1-23):

The Jews arrive to press charges against Paul.

Five days after Paul left Jerusalem, Ananias the high priest arrived in Caesarea, with some of the elders and an orator named Tertullus who was to present their claims against Paul to the governor.

Tertullus was hired because of his eloquence. It was not that the Jews could not understand Latin or Greek, or that they were unfamiliar with Roman law. The speech was made in Greek, but the Jews could handle either Greek or Latin. Tertullus would insure that the Jews' charges would receive as favorable a hearing as possible. He was their attorney.

When Paul had been called in, Tertullus began to accuse him, saying:

Tertullus said:
- **Felix, you have done great things for our nation.**
- **Please hear this matter.**
- **This fellow is a pest:**
    - **An insurrectionist among Jews...**
    - **A ring-leader in the sect of the Nazarenes.**
    - **He profaned our temple and we arrested him.**
- **We wanted to handle the case ourselves,**
    - **Lysias sent him to you.**

Since you have brought us much peace, and since through your far-sighted policies many problems have been solved for our nation, we gratefully accept every expression of your grace in all places, most excellent Felix.

But, lest I tire you further with these matters, I beg of you to be kind enough to hear a few words. We have found this man a pest and a leader of insurrections throughout the world. He is a ring-leader of the sect of the Nazarenes. Moreover, he dared to profane the temple, so we seized him. We wanted to handle the case ourselves and judge him by our law, but Lysias, with great violence, took him out of our hands and sent him to you.

You will, no doubt, be able to verify these facts by questioning him.

The Jews joined in the accusation with Tertullus, affirming that these charges were true.

The governor made no comment, but nodded to Paul that he could speak. Paul began:

Paul replied:
- **I arrived in Jerusalem only 12 days ago.**
- **I did not arouse the people**
    - **I am not a trouble-maker.**
- **I serve the God of our fathers...**
    - **I hope for a resurrection of the dead as they do.**
    - **I seek a clear conscience...**
- **I came to bring a gift to my people.**

Because I know that you have been a judge of this people for many years *(about five or six years)*, I cheerfully present my case. You can easily verify that it is no more than twelve days since I went up to worship at Jerusalem *(possibly referring to his attending the feast of Pentecost)*. My accusers did not find me debating with anyone in the temple, or stirring up a crowd in the synagogues or anywhere in the city. Neither can they prove their charges against me.

There is this one thing that I confess: I serve the God of our fathers in the Way which they call a sect. In this I do nothing more than believe all the things that are written in the law and in the prophets. My hope is directed to God, a hope that is shared by these men, that there will be a resurrection of both the just and the unjust. Therefore I strive always to keep my conscience clear before God and man.

After some years away, I came to bring a gift for my nation. In the midst of that business, they found me in the

- **I went to the temple to worship.**
  - **No crowd or tumult.**
- **Jews from Asia should make their charge.**
  - **Or, these men should tell you what they found against me in the Sanhedrin.**

temple. I was purified, there was no crowd with me, nor any tumult. But there are certain Jews from Asia who ought to be here to accuse me if they have any case against me. Otherwise, let these men say what crime I have done or what charge they brought against me in their council — unless it was this one statement I made in their midst: "It is concerning the resurrection of the dead that I am questioned before you this day."

Felix kept Paul a prisoner,
- **Waiting for Lysias.**
- **Paul was treated leniently,**
  - **His friends could visit.**

Felix was acquainted with Christianity, so after hearing Paul's defense, he postponed any further discussion by saying: "When Lysias the chief captain comes down, I will decide your case."

Then he told the centurion that Paul was to be kept in custody, but that he was to be given every courtesy, and that his friends were to be allowed free access to the apostle.

Paul speaks to Felix and Drusilla (Acts 24:24-27):

Felix trembled at Paul's message, but did nothing about his life.

After some time, Felix came with Drusilla his wife who was a Jewess. She was the daughter of Herod Agrippa I (Acts 12) and the sister of Bernice and Herod Agrippa II (Acts 26). They sent for Paul to come and speak to them concerning faith in Jesus Christ.

Felix hoped for a bribe to set Paul free.

As Paul reasoned about righteousness, self-control, and the judgment to come, Felix was terrified. He said, "Go away for now. When I have a convenient time, I will call for you."

Two years pass — A.D. 58-60.

When he was succeeded as governor, Felix left Paul in prison in order to please the Jews.

Though Felix was impressed by what Paul taught, he was mainly hoping that he would be offered a bribe to release him. For this reason, he sent for Paul often and conversed with him. Nevertheless, he kept Paul in prison for the two years he remained the governor. Then, when he was succeeded by Porcius Festus, he left Paul a prisoner with the hope it would gain him favor with the Jews. It was now A.D. 60.

Verse 22 states that Felix had some knowledge of this Way of Christ. He and Drusilla wanted more information about what Paul taught — but they did not want to accept the change of life necessary in accepting the message.

The Gospel of Luke:

The book of Luke was probably written while Paul was a prisoner in Caesarea.

There is not enough evidence for us to know exactly when the gospel accounts were written. John did his writing late in the first century, but the other accounts were almost certainly written before the destruction of Jerusalem in A.D. 70. Since the historical account does not follow the history of either Matthew or Mark, we cannot pinpoint a year when the writing of their books would fit. Enough information is given about Luke, however, to give us some insight into when he may have done his writing.

According to Luke 1:1-4, Luke did careful research among the eyewitnesses of Jesus before he wrote his account of the life of Christ.

Luke was in Israel:
- **He came to Jerusalem with Paul.**
- **He will go with Paul to Rome.**
- **He was in Troas and Philippi earlier.**

Therefore, in addition to the inspiration of the Holy Spirit, Luke had first-hand accounts of what Jesus said and did. That means he had to be in the land of Israel in order to have such experience.

As we have already learned, Luke accompanied Paul on this last trip to Jerusalem, and as we will see in Acts 27, he also accompanies Paul as they make their way to the emperor in Rome. Before that, Luke was first in Troas and then in Philippi, from the time Paul arrived in Troas on his second missionary journey until he joined Paul's group for this trip to Jerusalem that we have just described. Now it seems that Luke stayed in the area near Paul during these two years Paul is in prison in Caesarea, so it is the logical time for him to do his investigating and writing about the life and work of Christ. Therefore, the estimated date for the writing of the book of Luke is A.D. 58-60.

Festus learns about Paul (Acts 25:1-5):

Festus — 60-62 A.D.

Festus was of a prominent Roman family. He did not serve very long as a procurator of Judea. By A.D. 62 he was dead, and the wicked Albinus was his successor.

The Jews to Festus:
- **Bring Paul to Jerusalem,**
- **They planned to ambush him on the way.**

Three days after arriving to take over his province, Festus went up to Jerusalem. The chief priests and Jews met with him and pressed their charges against Paul. They asked Festus to bring Paul to Jerusalem for trial, intending to ambush him on the way.

Festus said he would hear the charges in Caesarea.

Festus, however, replied that Paul was in custody in Caesarea and that he was about to go there shortly. He said: "Let those who have power among you go with me, and if there is anything against Paul, let them accuse him."

Paul appeals unto Caesar (Acts 25:6-12):

When the Jews came, Festus asked Paul if he were willing to go to Jerusalem for trial.

After eight or ten days in Jerusalem, Festus returned to Caesarea and the next day sat on the judgment seat of Caesar to hear the case against Paul. When Paul was brought in, the Jews who had come from Jerusalem made many serious charges against him which they could not prove.

Paul replied:
- **I am in Caesar's court.**
- **I have done nothing wrong.**
- **I appeal unto Caesar.**

Paul answered, "I have not done a single thing wrong against the law of the Jews, against the temple, or against Caesar."

Festus, trying to please the Jews, said: "Will you go up to Jerusalem and stand trial before me concerning these matters?"

Paul then gave a stinging reply: "I am standing before Caesar's judgment seat where I am supposed to be judged. I have done nothing wrong to the Jews, and you know it! If I have committed crimes worthy of death, then I will make no effort to evade it. But if none of these things they accuse me of is true, no man has the right to turn me over to them. I appeal unto Caesar."

Festus agreed to send Paul to Caesar.

After conferring with his counselors, Festus said, "You have appealed unto Caesar, to Caesar you will go."

The appeal unto Caesar was a privilege of Roman citizens. It was meant for just such occasions as this. To be fair, Festus did not know of the Jews' plot to kill Paul, but Paul knew of past plots and he had no intention of being placed in their hands. He saw the same desire in Festus to please the Jews that Felix had. After these two years of imprisonment, Paul was convinced there would be no justice for him in Caesarea or Jerusalem.

Festus should have released Paul as an innocent man:
- **But that would have angered his new subjects, the Jews.**

Now Festus was faced with several options. Since Paul was obviously innocent, Festus could and should have set him free; but that would have aroused the wrath of the Jews. He could deny his appeal and continue the trial; but to deny the appeal of a Roman citizen and to try him would involve serious consequences unless Festus had an excellent reason for denying his appeal. Therefore, he took the third alternative, and that was to accept Paul's appeal and send him to Rome. Even that alternative put him in serious difficulties as we shall see.

King Agrippa arrives in Caesarea (Acts 25:13-22):

King Agrippa II:
- **Son of Agrippa I,**
- **Great-grandson of Herod the Great.**

Agrippa II was seventeen when his father died in A.D. 44 (Acts 12), and was considered too young to take over his father's kingdom. He remained in Rome six more years. In A.D. 50 he was made king of Chalcis and was gradually given more and more territory to rule. He was given control of the temple in Jerusalem, and with it the right to choose Jewish high priests. Agrippa made a determined effort to avert the Jewish rebellion that brought about the downfall of Jerusalem, but when he failed, he then threw his support wholeheartedly to the Romans and distanced himself from the Jews. He died in A.D. 101.

Bernice:
- **Sister to Agrippa II**
- **And to Drusilla the wife of Felix.**

Bernice had a rather checkered career. She was the sister of Drusilla and Agrippa II. At an early age she married her uncle Herod, king of Chalcis. When he died, she lived with her brother Agrippa in a state of incest. She married Polemo, the king of Cilicia, to dispel rumors about her relationship with her brother. He married her for her riches. Soon, however, she was back with her brother. She could have stayed with her brother because he lived to an old age, but despite having had several children and being somewhat advanced in age, she became the mistress of Vespasian and then of his son Titus, both of whom served as emperor of Rome.

The visit of Agrippa II to Festus was a formal courtesy call to greet the new procurator.

After some days had passed, Agrippa II came with his sister Bernice to salute the procurator Festus. As they continued to visit for a long time, Festus decided to talk to the king about Paul. He said:

Festus described Paul's case:
- **Left in prison by Felix.**
- **The Jews wanted me to sentence him...**

> There is a certain man who was left in prison by Felix. When I was in Jerusalem, the Jewish leaders made charges against him, wanting me to sentence him for punishment. Of

- **The accused must stand before his accusers...**
- **So, I heard their charges:**
    - **They told of no crime.**
    - **It was some question about a man whom the Jews say is dead and Paul says is alive.**
- **I was confused,**
    - **I asked Paul to go to Jerusalem,**
    - **He refused and appealed to Caesar.**

course I told them that we Romans do not conduct things that way, that we do not make any decision before the accused is able to face the accusers and have an opportunity to make a defense.

So when they arrived here in Caesarea, I promptly had the man brought out. When the accusations were made, however, they had nothing to do with any crime, but simply some controversy concerning their religion. It seems to be about some man named Jesus, who they say is dead, but Paul affirms to be alive.

I was in a quandary about the situation, so I asked Paul if he would be willing to go to Jerusalem and be judged there. But he appealed to Caesar, so I commanded him to be kept until I can send him.

Agrippa asked to hear Paul.
- **The whole Herod family professed to be Jews in religion,**
- **Though they were of Edomite (Idumean) descent.**

Agrippa replied, "I would be very interested in hearing the man myself."

"Tomorrow you shall hear him," answered Festus.

Festus was new to the area so he did not know anything about Jesus, nor about His cause. Felix had been in the area long enough to know a great deal about this Way. Agrippa professed to be a Jew in religion, as did all the Herod family, so he also knew much more about Christianity than Festus did.

Agrippa and Bernice gather with other leaders to hear Paul's defense (Acts 25:23-27):

The next day Agrippa and Bernice arrived in the judgment hall with great ceremony. Chief captains, nobles, and Festus the governor were also there. When everyone was settled, Festus called for Paul to be brought. Before Paul spoke, Festus addressed the assembly to give them a little background in the case. He said:

Festus has a dilemma:
- **He has a prisoner to send to the emperor,**
- **But no charges!**
- **What will the emperor think of a governor who cannot decide a case with no charges?**

King Agrippa, and all of you who are here today, you see this man whom all the Jews made accusation against both in Jerusalem and here. They declare that he ought to die, but I found that he had done nothing worthy of death, and, as he has appealed to Caesar, I have determined to send him. The problem is that I have nothing to write about him to Caesar. This is why I have brought him before you, and especially before you, King Agrippa, so that after you hear his case, perhaps I will have something to write. It seems unreasonable to me to send a prisoner and not send a list of the charges against him.

Paul's defense before Agrippa (Acts 26:1-32):

Agrippa, as the guest of honor, said to Paul, "You may now speak for yourself."

Paul stretched forth his hand and began his defense:

Paul said:
- **King Agrippa, you will understand.**

I am well pleased, King Agrippa, to make my defense before you today regarding the things of which I have been accused, especially because you are intimately acquainted with all the affairs of the Jews. Therefore, I ask you to hear me patiently.

- **The Jews know my life.**

The Jews know about my early life because I grew up and was educated in Jerusalem. If they were willing, they could tell you that in the manner of the strictest segment of our religion I lived a Pharisee. *(Paul knew that Agrippa was aware what the Pharisees believed.)* And now I stand to be judged because of the hope of the fulfillment of the promise which God made to our ancestors. This is the promise all twelve of our tribes are hoping to see fulfilled as they strive to serve God day and night. It is concerning this hope that I am accused by the Jews, O King.

- **I am being judged for the hope all my people have:**
  - **The promises God made to our ancestors.**

Why is it considered incredible to you that God raises the dead?

- **Why think it strange that God can raise the dead?**

In my youth I too thought that I should oppose the name of Jesus of Nazareth. So I persecuted men and women in Jerusalem and even in foreign cities. I was insanely angry at them. I put many saints in prison and cast my vote against them when they were put to death.

- **I, too, opposed Jesus and His followers.**

I was even on my way to Damascus for this very purpose when at midday, O King, I saw a light from heaven, brighter than the noonday sun. We all fell to the ground, and then I heard a voice speaking to me in the Aramaic language: "Saul, Saul, why do you persecute me? It is hard for you to kick against the ox-goad." I said, "Who are you, Lord?" and the Lord said, "I am Jesus of Nazareth whom you are persecuting. But get up and stand on your feet because I have appeared to you so that you can be a servant and a witness both of the things you have seen of me and of the things that I will show you. I will deliver you from the people *(the Jews)* and from the Gentiles to whom I am sending you. You are to open their eyes so they can turn from darkness to light and from the power of Satan unto God, so they can receive remission of sins and an inheritance among those whom I make special through their faith in me."

  - **But Jesus appeared to me from heaven so that:**
    - **I could be a servant and a witness..**
  - **He gave me a task to perform.**

Therefore, O King Agrippa, I did not disobey that heavenly vision. First to those in Damascus, then in Jerusalem, and throughout all the country of Judea, and also to the Gentiles,

  - **I have spent my life obeying that charge:**
    - **Preaching to Jews**
    - **And to Gentiles.**

- **That is why the Jews arrested me and tried to kill me.**

- **I have taught only what Moses and the prophets foretold.**

I preached that they should repent and turn to God and prove their repentance by their works.

It is for this reason that the Jews seized me in the temple and tried to kill me. With the help of God I stand to this day, witnessing to the small and the great. I have said nothing but what the prophets and Moses foretold would happen: namely, that the Christ must suffer death and how He, through His resurrection, should proclaim light both to the people *(Israelites)* and to the Gentiles.

Festus did not understand: "Paul, you are insane!"

As Paul thus made his defense, at this point Festus interrupted, crying in a loud voice, "Paul, your much learning is driving you insane."

But Paul replied:

Paul replied:
- **I am not insane.**
- **The King understands.**
- **He knows and believes what the prophets have said.**

I am not crazy, most excellent Festus. No, I speak words of truth and reason. The king here, to whom I have spoken without restraint, knows all about these things. I am certain that not one of these things is concealed from him, because this matter did not occur in some hidden corner.

King Agrippa, do you believe the prophets? I know you believe.

Agrippa said: "Almost thou persuadest me to be a Christian."

King Agrippa responded, "In short order you would make me a Christian."

And Paul answered, "I wish to God that both in short order and in great measure, not you alone, but also everyone who is here today, might become what I am, except for these bonds."

This man is not worthy of death or imprisonment.

But Paul got no farther. The king stood up, along with Festus and Bernice, and then everyone else. When they had withdrawn to private quarters, they discussed the case and agreed: "This man has done nothing to deserve death or imprisonment."

Then, not knowing of the plot against Paul if he had been taken to Jerusalem for trial, Agrippa told Festus, "He could have been set free if he had not appealed to Caesar."

By denying the resurrection of Christ:
- **The Pharisees showed their lack of faith in one of their primary doctrines.**
- **Paul is still pursuing the same faith he had as a young Pharisee.**

As with all the speeches in Acts, Paul made particular points that were appropriate for his audience. Paul tells that in his younger days he was a devoted Pharisee. One of the chief points of the Pharisees' belief was the resurrection —yet when it came time to express their faith in the resurrection, they denied it. The Gentiles also had difficulty believing in a resurrection (Acts 17:32), so Paul asks, "Why do you consider it incredible that God would raise the dead?" Paul affirmed that his present work was in pursuit of the same faith and hope in God and in the resurrection that he had when he was a young Pharisee.

Paul's argument based upon the details of his conversion was a convincing one, and one that he used on different occasions in his preaching and writing. Paul's complete change in the pattern of his life still defies explanation unless one accepts that Christ did appear to him on the road to Damascus. It was fitting here to show that he, too, had misunderstood Jesus of Nazareth, just as the Jews who were accusing him, until he saw Jesus alive in heaven.

The complete change in Paul's life defies explanation if the Lord did not appear to him.

Paul says, "Wherefore I was not disobedient to the heavenly vision." His obedience meant that he devoted his life to the preaching of Christ. Yet it was the same hope foretold by the prophets and by Moses that he and the other Jews had believed all of their lives.

Except for this chain of events, such people as Felix, Festus, Agrippa, and the others present would never have heard the gospel proclaimed. Even a quiet reading of the speech impresses one with the fervor and intensity of the speaker. Paul's audience was wrapped up completely in his presentation. This speech was a rare one for the people of this audience to hear. They were used to hearing beautiful speeches with art and device of rhetoric, but they did not often hear a speech which made its appeal to truth. Nor did they often hear a speech by one so sincere and so passionate about what he believed.

The Lord foretold that Paul would bear witness to His name before kings and rulers (Acts 9:15).

By Festus' outburst that Paul was raving, he indicated both how much he was caught up in the address and his complete bewilderment because of his ignorance of the situation among the Jews. Paul's response to Festus breathes a spirit of calmness and rationality. No one there could possibly have believed this man was really insane.

Paul made his strongest appeal to Agrippa: "Do you believe the prophets?" If he really did, then as Paul had clearly shown, that faith inevitably leads to Christ. If he did not, then he denied his commitment to Judaism and to the temple over which he had charge.

Agrippa responded. But how did he respond? Did he mean, "You have me nearly ready to become a Christian," or did he mean, "In such short order you would make me a Christian?"? Was Agrippa sincere? We cannot read his heart, but everything else we know about Agrippa's life would indicate: No. Therefore it is likely he meant, "Merely on the basis of my faith in the prophets, you would have me become a Christian?" It was likely a response to show his peers that he was not carried away — but it is also likely that he was deeply impressed. He shows that he knew something about "Christians" because he is the only one who used that term on this occasion. Paul's answer to Agrippa involves not a whether this or that, but a both this and that: "both in short order and in great measure" is the best interpretation of the phrase.

Was Agrippa sincerely saying he was almost persuaded to be a Christian?

Notice that Agrippa uses the name "Christian."

Acts 26 takes its place in Acts with the other great speeches: Peter's speech on Pentecost (chapter 2); Stephen's speech to the Sanhedrin (chapter 7); Paul's speech in Antioch (chapter 13); his speech on Mars Hill (chapter 17); and his speech to the Jewish mob (chapter 22).

Paul's Journey to Rome
(Acts 27:1-28:16)

As we have shown, though Luke does not mention himself by name in the book of Acts, he was likely in the area of Palestine the whole two years Paul was in prison in Jerusalem and Caesarea. Now the historical account specifically includes him again. The last "we-section" in Acts is 27:1-28:16, as Luke accompanies Paul on his trip to Rome. The time is the fall of A.D. 60.

It is early fall of A.D. 60.

It seems strange that Festus waited so late in the year to send Paul away, because weather played a very important part in traveling in that day. Sea travel was impossible during the months of November, December, and January. Some authorities are exact, saying that after November 11 all sea travel ceased until March 10. It could be that Festus himself did not arrive in Judea until late summer. It could be that there was a delay until a ship capable of taking a group of prisoners came to Caesarea.

Sea-travel halted during the winter because of dangerous weather conditions.
- **Yet this trip began in the fall.**

The right currents and wind were essentials in navigation because their ships were sailing vessels rather than the power driven ships of our day. For example, the authorities could not simply say, "Sail down to Egypt and find a ship going to Rome." Currents off Palestine flow north; therefore it was easy for a vessel to sail north, and that is what this ship did. From the account, it is clear that Julius, the centurion in charge, was given the authority to use his discretion in making connections.

Paul and other prisoners were in the custody of a centurion named Julius.
- **Luke and Aristarchus accompany Paul.**

The vessel taken was a coaster based in Adramyttium, a port located at the head of a deep bay northeast of the island of Lesbos in the Aegean Sea. The ship was headed for home, planning to stop at places along the coast of Asia.

In 2 Corinthians 11:23-29, Paul tells of the various afflictions he had suffered. Included in the list are these expressions: "Thrice I suffered shipwreck, a night and a day I have been in the deep...in perils of waters...in perils in the sea..." But remember, that book was written before the shipwreck described here in Acts 27.

This shipwreck is not included in the list of afflictions in 2 Corinthians.

Label your blank map at the end of the chapter to show this journey to Rome. Luke is very specific as he describes the route. You will understand the story better if you take time to look where they are and why they chose the route they did.

Label your map.

Shipwreck (Acts 27:1-44):

When it was time for Paul to sail, the Roman authorities gave him and other prisoners into the custody of a centurion by the name of

The trip:
- **Sidon:**
  - **Friends gave Paul the things he needed.**
- **Cyprus:**
  - **They sailed between Cyprus and the mainland of Asia Minor,**
  - **Seeking the best winds for their needs.**
- **Myra:**
  - **Julius transferred his passengers to a grain ship from Alexandria on its way to Rome.**
- **Cnidus:**
  - **They lost the shelter of the coast,**
  - **Put out to open sea.**
- **Crete:**
  - **The ship turned south to the southern side of Crete,**
  - **Trying to find land to protect them from the contrary winds.**
- **Fair Havens:**
  - **Paul said winter here.**
  - **It was in the last half of October, or later.**
- **Phoenix:**
  - **The captain wanted to reach Phoenix,**
  - **A better harbor in which to winter.**

Julius, who was stationed with the Augustan cohort. The soldiers and their prisoners boarded a ship from Adramyttium, along with Luke and Aristarchus who were accompanying Paul. They set sail heading north.

One day *(and 67 miles)* later, they stopped briefly at Sidon where the centurion allowed Paul to go to his friends in the city and receive the things he needed. From Sidon they continued their journey north.

The prevailing winds in that area blow to the east. By sailing close to the island of Cyprus, keeping it on their left, they avoided these winds as they sailed west. A current flows to the west between the southern shore of Asia Minor and Cyprus, so by leaving their sails down, they could sail west even when the winds were against them. In addition, because of certain land formations or other factors, there are winds which normally blow to the west for a distance. This trip was proving difficult, however, because the winds were contrary.

Having sailed through the waters off Cilicia and Pamphylia, they came to Myra on the coast of Lycia. There the centurion found a grain ship based in Alexandria, Egypt, which was headed for Rome. It was a large ship, able to hold a cargo of grain and to carry 276 people (see verse 37).

Setting sail, they spent many days hugging the coast and seeking to go west. Their way was slow and difficult because the winds continued in the wrong direction. At Cnidus they reached the western end of Asia Minor and had to put out to open sea, so they turned southwest and sailed to the south side of Crete. They crept along with difficulty until they finally arrived at a place called Fair Havens near the city of Lasea.

By this time, the difficulty of their travel had delayed their progress toward Rome so much that it was getting late in the season to continue sailing. The Fast of the Atonement *(the day when the Israelites were commanded to "afflict" their souls (Lev. 16:29)*, was already past, so it was the middle of October or later. Paul warned those in charge saying, "Sirs, I am of the opinion that to go on will bring us injury and loss, not only of the cargo and the ship, but also of our lives." Nevertheless, the centurion agreed with the sailing master and the captain instead of Paul. It was natural that he thought they knew better than Paul.

The captain and sailing master had no idea at all of striking out for Rome. That option was out. Their present location, however, was not a good one. If they could make it just a few more miles west, they would have a much better harbor in which to anchor for the winter. And it was still early enough in the season for them to think they could make that short distance with no problem.

So when a breeze blew gently from the south, they thought they could use the wind and sail the few miles to Phoenix. Instead, no sooner had they set out, than a gale called Euraquilo came sweeping down from the north over the mountains of Crete. The ship was caught,

A fierce storm arose:
- **The ship was blown off course,**
- **Driven before the wind.**

and not being able to face the wind, was forced to turn about and run with the wind.

The "tempestuous" wind was literally a "tuphon." The word sounds similar to typhoon — and it was a similar kind of storm — but "typhoon" comes from the Chinese word "Tai-Fung." Euraquilo, or Euroclydon, was merely the name given this kind of fierce storm. Its etymology is not relevant in this case.

- **Island of Cauda:**
  - **They secured the life-boat,**
  - **Wrapped the ship with cables,**
  - **Lowered the sails,**
  - **Let the ship be driven by the storm.**

Very quickly they came to the small island of Cauda. In its shelter they were able to get the boat secured *(a lifeboat, probably of considerable size)*. That job done, they wrapped the sailing ship with cables which would help to keep it from coming apart in the waves. They were very afraid that the storm would drive them into the waters off north Africa, the Syrtis, lying between Carthage and Cyrene, where they would be shipwrecked on a shoal or sandbar. Therefore with fear, they lowered the sails, and were driven by the storm.

- **Grave danger that they might be driven into the shoals and sandbars off the coast of Africa.**

Authorities on sailing tell how, in circumstances such as these, a small sail was usually left on the bow to let the wind pull the ship along. If they steered to the right as near the wind as possible, calculations have shown that they would reach Melita in about 13 days —just as Luke describes.

Seasoned sailors describe the rigors of such a storm: the bucking forward and backward from wave crest to trough, the ship cavorting like a wild horse; the constant screaming of the wind in the rigging until the ears were numb; the blowing spray which stung like needles; the rain soaking everything exposed; the constant fear of death at any moment; and all of this for two solid weeks!

- **Two weeks seeing neither sun nor stars, being violently storm-tossed:**
  - **First day after Cauda:**
    - **Threw cargo overboard.**
  - **Next day (3rd day of the storm):**
    - **Threw off the ship's tackle.**
  - **Many days:**
    - **All hope gone.**
  - **Paul reassured them:**
    - **Take food;**
    - **Ship will be lost,**
    - **But no lives will be lost.**

The storm reached such proportions they began to cast items overboard *(probably heavy items of freight lashed to the deck)*. On the third day they began dumping the furniture of the ship. As the days went by without sight of the sun in the day, or stars at night, in the grip of such a storm, all on board began to give up hope of surviving the tempest.

During the violent and dreary days of the storm, little food, if any, had been eaten. Paul stood in their midst and said, "You men should have listened to me when I warned you not to sail from Crete. Then we would have escaped all this misfortune and loss. But cheer up, because there will not be loss of life. The ship will be lost, but no one will die. I know this because this very night my God, to whom I belong and whom I serve, sent an angel to tell me, 'Do not be afraid, Paul. It is necessary for you to appear before Caesar, and God has graciously granted you the lives of all these who sail with you.' Therefore, cheer up, sirs, because I believe that it will be just as God has said. However, we will be shipwrecked on some island."

- **Fourteenth night:**
  - **Sailors discovered they were approaching land.**
  - **They cast anchor,**
    - **And longed for daylight!**

- **The sailors tried to leave the ship in the lifeboat,**
  - **Paul warned that they must stay with the ship,**
  - **Or all lives would be forfeited.**

- **Paul ate food,**
  - **Urged the others to do the same,**
  - **Assuring them that no life would be lost.**

- **Threw the wheat overboard.**

- **Daybreak:**
  - **They drove the ship in toward the beach,**
  - **It hit a reef and stuck tight.**
    - **It began to break apart.**

- **All reached shore by swimming or floating.**
-
- **Julius saved all the prisoners in order to save Paul.**

About the middle of the fourteenth night, as the vessel was borne along through the sea, the sailors *(the crew)* began to suspect that they were approaching land, but they had no idea where they were. When they checked the depth, they found it to be 120 feet deep. Soon they sounded again *(checked the depth by lowering a weight on a line into the water)*, and found it only ninety feet. Fearing that they would crash upon breakers, they cast out four anchors from the stern *(the rear end of the ship)* and prayed earnestly for daylight to come.

The sailors were unwilling to wait and see how Paul's prophecy would turn out. He had said the ship would be lost and they wanted to escape it, so they lowered the lifeboat into the sea as if they were going to set anchors from the bow. In other words, the anchors would be laid from the bow as far out to the sides and rear as possible.

Paul, however, was not deceived. He knew this maneuver was a pretext: what the sailors were really about to do was to take the lifeboat and attempt to reach shore in it. Ordinarily their chances of reaching the shore would have been better that way. Paul told the centurion and the soldiers: "Unless these remain in the ship, you yourselves cannot be saved." Promptly the soldiers went forward, slashed the ropes which held the boat and let her fall off. *(If the sailors left on the lifeboat, there would be no crew to bring the ship closer into land, and it was too far out to sea for the others to find safety.)*

As daylight approached, Paul pleaded with everyone to eat, saying: "For two weeks now you have been continually without food. I beg you to eat something to insure your safety, because not even one hair of anyone's head will perish." When he had said these words, he gave thanks to God in the presence of all of them and broke off a chunk of bread and began to eat. Then the others, being cheered, began to eat. The total number of people on board was 276.

After eating, they lightened the ship by throwing the wheat into the sea. This measure would make the ship ride high in the water as it moved toward the shore so that it could go in as close as possible.

At daybreak they could see land, but they could not recognize where they were. They found a sort of bay with a beach into which they decided to drive the ship, if they could. Casting off the anchors, they loosed the rudders so they could steer the ship. Then hoisting the foresail, they made for the beach. As the ship moved forward, it struck the bottom and grounded itself. Now that the ship was stuck, it could no longer flex with the waves, so the pounding of the water began to break the ship apart.

The soldiers wanted to kill the prisoners lest one escape. But the centurion, intent on saving Paul, refused to let them take the action and ordered those who could swim to go overboard and get to land first. The rest could make their way by floating on boards or whatever floating object they could find from the ship. In such a manner, everyone reached shore safely.

A winter spent on Malta (Acts 28:1-10):

- **Island of Melita:**
  - **They found non-Greek speaking people.**

After reaching the shore, they learned that the name of the island was Melita *(Malta)*. The people of the island, who were barbarians *(not Greek speaking people)*, showed unusual kindness. They kindled a fire and took in all the shipwrecked victims because of the continuing rain and the cold.

- **Paul:**
  - **Bitten by a poisonous snake,**
    - **But is unharmed.**
    - **The people decided he was a god.**

Paul busied himself helping with the fire. He gathered an armful of firewood and placed it on the fire. Roused by the heat, a viper from the wood bit Paul on the hand. When the people of the island saw the creature hanging from his hand they said, "Surely this man is a murderer. Though he has escaped the sea, justice has not allowed him to live."

The apostle, however, shook the snake off into the fire and suffered no harm whatever. The natives continued to watch Paul, expecting him to swell or to fall down dead. After a long time, when nothing bad happened to him, they changed their minds and said he was a god.

- **He healed the father of leading man of the island,**
  - **Then all others who were brought to him.**
- **The people showed great kindness to Paul and his companions.**

Not far away was the villa of the First of the island, a man named Publius. He received the ship's party and gave them a place to stay for three days. *(The First was the Roman representative who ruled the island under the oversight of the governor of Sicily.)* The father of Publius was sick in bed with fever and dysentery. When Paul learned of the situation, he went in and after praying, healed him by laying his hands upon him.

When word of this miracle spread, the rest of the people who had diseases came to be healed. The people of the island had been unusually kind from the first, but when Paul healed their sick, they could not do enough for him and the other shipwreck victims.

Think of the impact Paul's life and miracles had on Julius the centurion and others of the ship's party who had occasion to be close to the apostle. The evidence shows that Paul was much esteemed by the centurion and probably by the entire ship's company. Now, by this shipwreck, the people of the island have a chance to hear the story of Christ.

A barbarian:
- **A foreigner, one who did not speak Greek,**
- **Therefore one outside the normal culture of the day.**

Luke calls the people on the island "barbarians." That word gives an incorrect connotation to us. Our dictionary describes a barbarian as "one whose culture is between savagery and civilization; a member of an uncivilized tribe or race." The meaning of the Greek word in the first century meant a "foreigner, one who did not speak Greek." Since most of the people of the Mediterranean world spoke Greek, gradually the term barbarian took on the negative connotation we give it because it described one outside the typical civilization of the day. By this one word, Luke tells us that the natives on this small island were non-Greek speaking. Since Paul was an apostle he had the full gift of speaking in tongues (see 1 Cor. 14:18), so he could communicate with them immediately in their own language.

The Book of Acts:

Luke probably began writing the book of Acts while he and Paul were still in the area of Judea and Galilee, shortly after he finished writing the book of Luke. That would fit, because the first twelve chapters of Acts tell of events that took place in Jerusalem and the surrounding area. But it is evident it was not finished until he and Paul made the trip to Rome together since he describes that trip and its wreck so vividly.

The book of Acts was written about this time.

The last half of the book, telling the stories of Paul's work, may well have been written during this winter on the island of Melita. It was finished, however, before Paul's first trial before Nero in A.D. 62/63 because Luke does not tell of the outcome of that trial, nor of any of the events that occurred after that. Therefore we place the writing of the book between A.D. 60 and 64, almost certainly narrowing the date to A.D. 60-61, except for the last note that states that Paul was in Rome a full two years before his trial.

Paul reaches Rome (Acts 28:11-16):

When spring arrived:

- **The ship's company set sail toward Rome on a ship from Alexandria that had wintered on the island.**
- **Syracuse in Sicily**
- **Rhegium**
- **Puteoli:**
    - **They disembarked to make the rest of the trip by land.**
    - **Stayed for one week.**

Traveling overland:

- **Brethren from Rome came to meet Paul,**
- **He was greatly encouraged.**

Rome:

- **Though still a prisoner, Paul was treated leniently.**
- **Stayed in a hired house with a guard.**

After spending the three months of winter on the island, the ship's company set sail aboard a ship of Alexandria which had wintered there. The ship's name was the Two Brothers. *(Castor and Pollux, two sons of Zeus by Leda according to Greek mythology, were the tutelary gods of sailors.)*

From Malta they sailed eighty miles to Syracuse on the eastern shore of Sicily. After three days there, they sailed seventy miles, tacking the ship *(that is, taking a zig-zag course in order to use the winds available)*, to Rhegium located on the southern tip of the toe of the boot of Italy. For one day they waited for the south wind to blow. Then aided by this good wind, they traveled the 180 miles or so to Puteoli, arriving the very next day. Here Paul disembarked and began the overland journey to Rome. The brethren at Puteoli urged Paul and his companions to stay with them for a week.

With very heavy traffic constantly going to and from Rome, it is not surprising that the brethren in Rome heard of Paul's arrival. One delegation from the church came and met Paul and his company at Appii Forum, about forty miles from Rome. A second group met them at Three Taverns, about ten miles farther along the way. The brethren in Rome had heard all about Paul's situation, and thus showed their love and concern. When Paul saw them, he thanked God and was greatly encouraged.

When Paul arrived in Rome, the government continued to treat him very leniently. They allowed him to stay in private quarters with only one Roman soldier as guard.

Paul would have been able to see the volcanic mountain of Vesuvius which was located very near Puteoli. The year was A.D. 61.

It was only eighteen years until that volcano erupted, killing thousands and burying the city of Pompeii. In that eruption, Drusilla the wife of Felix and their son were killed.

The main road through Italy to Rome was the Appian Way, which was begun by and named after the Roman censor Appius Claudius Caecus about 312 B.C. It was more than 365 miles long, running from Rome to Brundisium. It did not pass through Puteoli, but Paul and his companions probably joined the famous highway at Capua.

We must marvel at how co-operative Julius the centurion was in all these things. How impressed he and the other Roman soldiers had to be by the behavior of these Christians!

Remember that Paul had written a letter to the Romans saints back in the winter of A.D. 57. Paul's fame as an apostle had spread far and wide. Also the word carried from Puteoli to Rome would have included the news that Paul was being brought for trial. It is unlikely the brethren had heard any other way because no message could have beaten Paul to Rome, because all ships would have been delayed by the same fierce weather conditions Paul's companions found.

Paul to the Jewish leaders:

- **I have done no wrong,**
  - **I was delivered a prisoner from the Jews into the hands of the Romans.**
- **The Romans wanted to set me free,**
  - **Jews objected.**
  - **I appealed to Caesar.**
- **I make no complaint against my nation to the emperor.**
- **I wear these chains for the sake of the hope of Israel.**

Paul reasons with the Jews of Rome (Acts 28:17-28):

When Paul had been in Rome three days, he called the Jewish leaders to him and said:

> Brethren, though I had done nothing against our people or the customs of our fathers, I was delivered a prisoner to the Romans while I was in Jerusalem. When the Roman officials examined my case, they desired to set me free since I had committed no crime. But when the Jews opposed it, I was forced to appeal to Caesar. I have no intention of accusing my nation. Therefore, I called you together, because it is for the hope of Israel that I am bound with this chain *(referring to the soldier guarding him).*

The Jews had received no word from Judea about Paul:

- **They wanted to hear him speak to learn more about "this sect."**

The Jews answered: "We have received no letters from Judea about you, nor has any of the brethren come to us and to tell us any critical thing about you. But we do want to hear what you think, because we know that this sect of which you are a part is criticized by everyone."

Paul's day of preaching:

- **He told them about Jesus and the kingdom of God.**
- **Presenting evidence from Moses and the prophets.**

A certain day was agreed upon, and at that time a large number of Jews gathered in Paul's house. He reasoned with them, testifying about the kingdom of God, and persuading them about Jesus. He spent the whole day bringing forth his evidence from the law of Moses and the prophets.

Finally Paul quoted a warning Isaiah had given to the ancestors of the Jews (Isa. 6:9-10). Isaiah had been charged to go and tell the people what God wanted them to do. The prophet was to preach to them until

Some believed, others did not:
- **Isaiah's warning fit the occasion.**
- **The Gentiles listened to the message better than the Jews.**

they stopped their ears and closed their eyes. The warning concerned a people who were already rejecting God. God hardens such a generation by continuing to tell them what they need to know. Paul said, "Be careful that this warning does not come to apply to you. You must know that God has commanded that these things be preached to the Gentiles, and they will listen."

When these words had been spoken, the Jews left, disagreeing among themselves and discussing the things which they had heard.

What a mighty discourse this must have been! Think about that Roman soldier sitting or standing nearby hearing all of this.

Luke used a carefully balanced expression to say some believed the things spoken, and some disbelieved —perhaps meaning that the Jews were divided about half and half. Usually if the division were lop-sided, Luke used words such as few in contrast with many.

Two more years pass:
- **Paul still a prisoner,**
- **Awaiting his trial before the Emperor Nero.**
- **He preached freely to all who came to him.**

Paul remains a prisoner in Rome for two years (Acts 28:30-31):

For two years Paul lived in his rented house in Rome, and during this time received all those who came to him. He preached the kingdom of God and the facts about Jesus. No one sought to hinder him from this work.

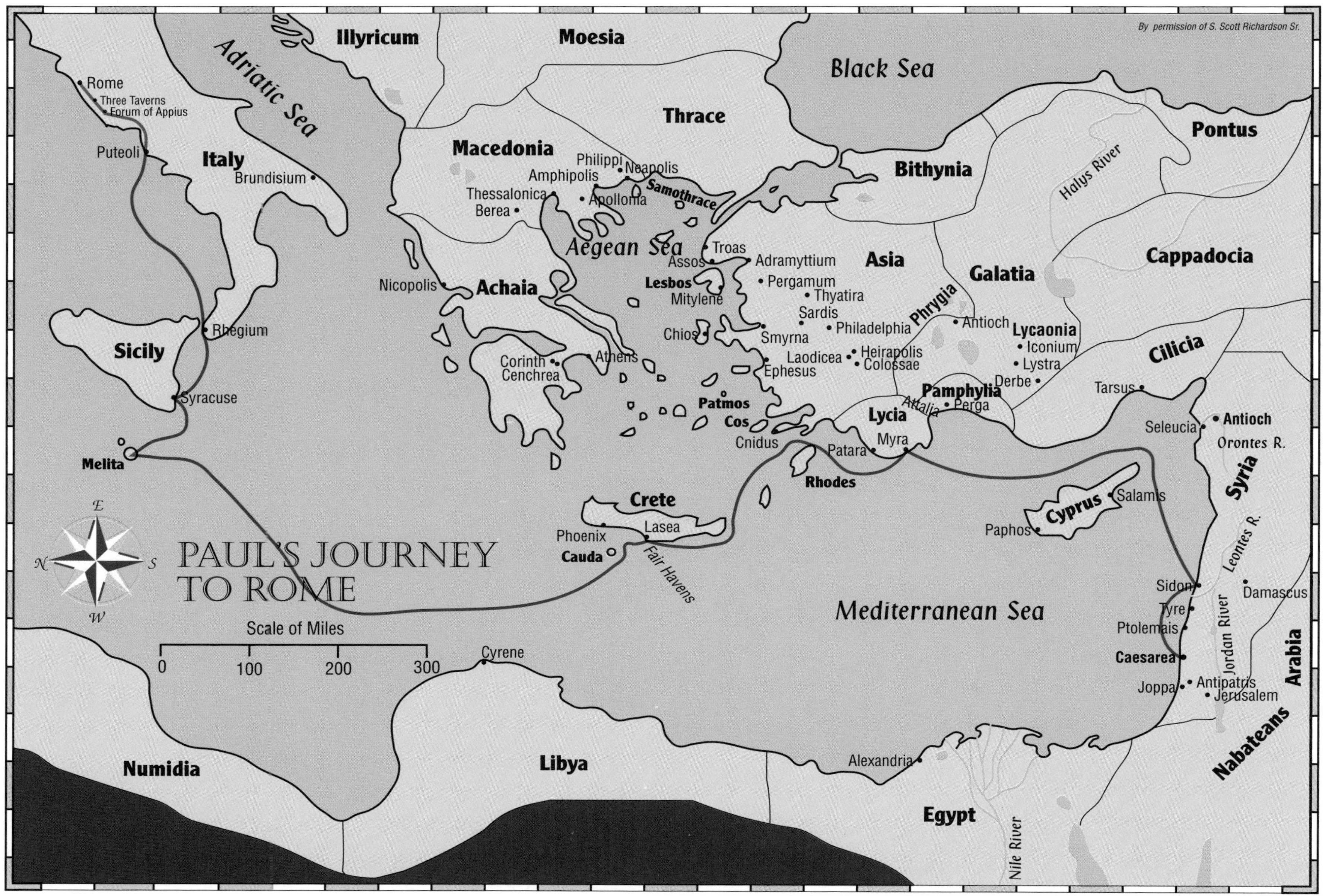
PAUL'S JOURNEY TO ROME
By permission of S. Scott Richardson Sr.
Scale of Miles
0
100
200
300
E
N
S
W
Illyricum
Moesia
Black Sea
Adriatic Sea
Thrace
Pontus
Rome
Three Taverns
Forum of Appius
Puteoli
Italy
Brundisium
Macedonia
Philippi
Neapolis
Amphipolis
Samothrace
Thessalonica
Apollonia
Berea
Bithynia
Halys River
Aegean Sea
Troas
Assos
Adramyttium
Asia
Galatia
Cappadocia
Nicopolis
Achaia
Lesbos
Mitylene
Pergamum
Thyatira
Sardis
Philadelphia
Phrygia
Antioch
Lycaonia
Iconium
Lystra
Derbe
Sicily
Rhegium
Chios
Smyrna
Laodicea
Heirapolis
Colossae
Ephesus
Corinth
Cenchrea
Athens
Cilicia
Tarsus
Syracuse
Patmos
Cos
Cnidus
Pamphylia
Attalia
Perga
Lycia
Myra
Patara
Rhodes
Seleucia
Antioch
Orontes R.
Syria
Melita
Crete
Lasea
Phoenix
Cauda
Fair Havens
Cyprus
Salamis
Paphos
Leontes R.
Sidon
Damascus
Tyre
Ptolemais
Caesarea
Jordan River
Arabia
Joppa
Antipatris
Jerusalem
Mediterranean Sea
Cyrene
Alexandria
Nabateans
Numidia
Libya
Egypt
Nile River

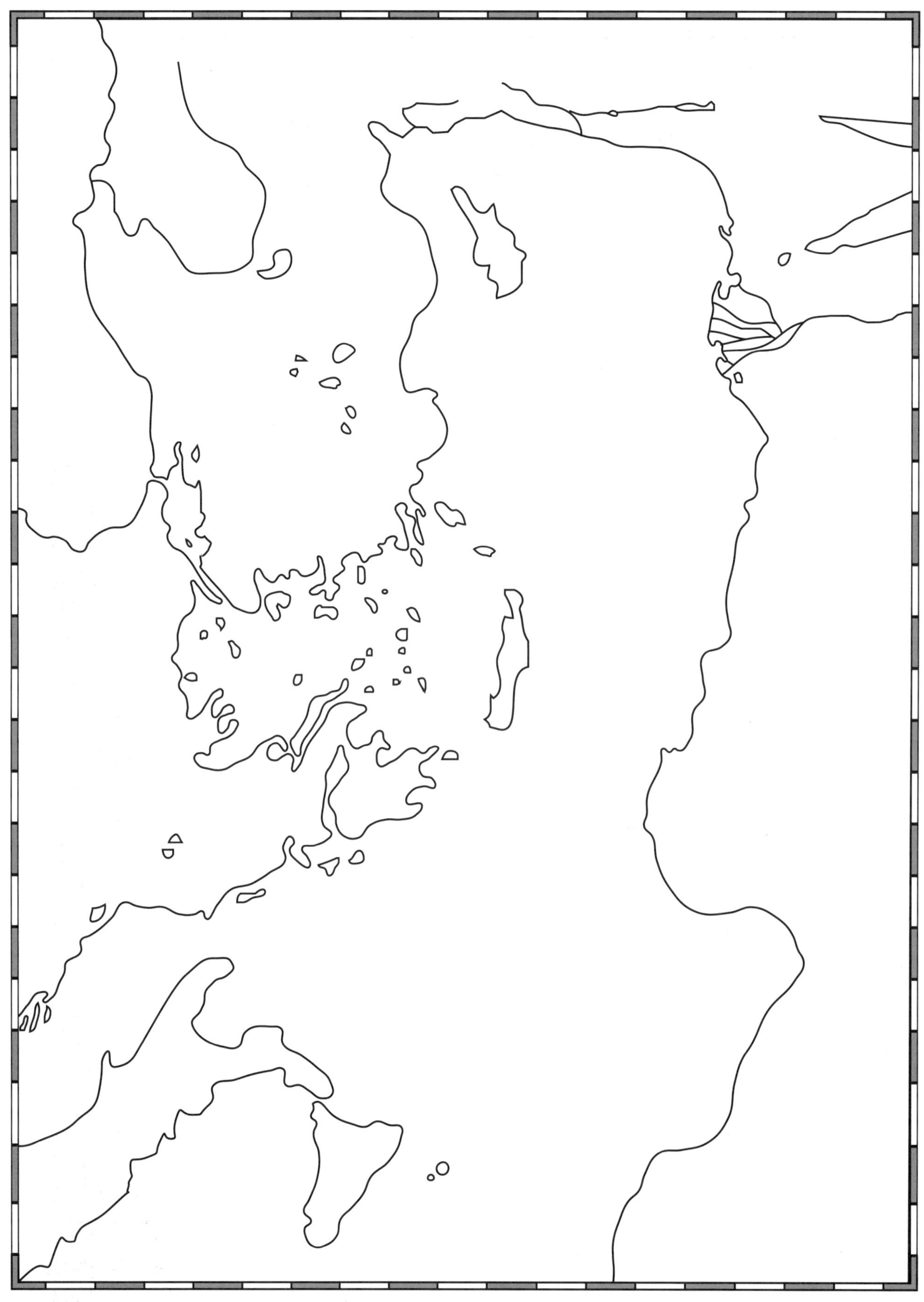

Paul's Life After the Book of Acts
(Ephesians. Philippians. Colossians. Philemon. 1 Timothy. 2 Timothy. and Titus)

After the book of Acts, there is no inspired history of Paul's work, yet his life and work continued. The only inspired information we can glean is from the seven epistles he wrote after he arrived in Rome. We will put together the details we can learn from his writings, plus some details from secular sources, and piece together the rest of his story to the best of our ability.

Paul in prison at Rome:

Paul in prison:
- **2 years in Caesarea**
- **2 years in Rome**
  - **Awaiting his trial.**
  - **A.D. 61-63.**

At the close of Acts the apostle Paul was a prisoner in Rome for two full years (Acts 28:30-31), after spending the preceding two years as a prisoner in Caesarea (Acts 24:27). Festus began his term as governor of Judea in A.D. 60. He sent Paul to Rome that fall; the ship was wrecked, and Paul and the others spent the winter on the island of Melita. They reached Rome in the spring of 61, where he remained until sometime during A.D. 63.

Nero: emperor A.D. 54 to 68.

Nero was emperor of Rome from A.D. 54 to 68. Thus, it was Nero who heard Paul's case (although probably Nero did not hear the case personally because emperors usually had a representative to deal with such matters). Until this time, the Roman government had not discovered Christianity was a new, separate religion from Judaism. If they had heard of it at all, they would have assumed it was just another Jewish sect.

During the years at Rome:
- **Paul in his own hired house with a guard.**
- **Preached to all who came.**
- **Saints came and went.**
- **Wrote Ephesians, Philippians, Colossians, and Philemon.**

The two years Paul spent in Rome were busy ones from the beginning. The hired house in which he resided was apparently spacious enough because it accommodated the large number of Jews who met with Paul almost immediately after he arrived in Rome (Acts 28:23). Likely, Luke and Aristarchus stayed with him in this house (Acts 27:2; 28:16). Other saints came and went during the time he was in the city. The rent was paid through gifts of money sent to Paul from brethren such as the Philippians (see Phil. 4:10, 18). From this house, Paul will write Ephesians, Philippians, Colossians, and Philemon.

Even though Paul was a prisoner, he welcomed all who came to him, and he preached boldly and without hindrance (Acts 28:30-31). The book of Philippians adds the information that he was able to preach to some even in important positions in the household of Caesar (Phil. 1:13; 4:22).

Why would God let Paul remain a prisoner for four years? Why did He not release Paul as He had on other occasions? No one knows all the answers, but some can be surmised by the circumstances. Paul was not on the sidelines even in prison. He has preached to kings and rulers, to centurions, to people on an island, now to Jews and saints in Rome, and to Roman guards. He will write four letters while he is here in Rome. But during all of these four years he was protected from his enemies. The same guard that kept Paul a prisoner kept his enemies away from him. Perhaps God was giving His bruised and battered servant a time to rest in a safe place (See Galatians 6:17 and 2 Corinthians 11:16-33.)

Paul's prison letters:

By prison letters, we refer to Ephesians, Philippians, Colossians, and Philemon. The evidence makes it almost certain that these letters were written fairly close together by Paul from Rome during this first imprisonment there. Look at the evidence:

Evidence that Paul wrote these letters from Rome:

- **Paul was a prisoner, near the Praetorian guard.**

- *Look how the books can be linked together:*
  - *In Ephesians Paul refers to himself as a prisoner (3:1; 4:1; 6:20).*
  - *In Philippians he refers to his bonds (1:7, 13, 17), to the Praetorian guard (1:13), and to Caesar's household (4:22). These references show Paul was in bonds in Rome.*
  - *In Colossians, he refers to himself as a prisoner (4:3, 10, a fellow-<u>prisoner</u> to Aristarchus).*
  - *In Philemon he mentions his bonds (verses 9-10), and that Epaphras was another fellow-<u>prisoner</u> (verse 23).*
  - *So all four of these books mention Paul's imprisonment.*
    - *There were only two prolonged imprisonments that Paul suffered during the story of Acts:*
      - *The one in Caesarea for two years (Acts 24:27),*
      - *And the one in Rome for two years (Acts 28:30).*
        - *The Praetorian guard and Caesar's household were in Rome, not Caesarea.*

- **The books of Ephesians, Colossians, and Philemon were carried by Tychicus and Onesimus.**

- *Tychicus and Onesimus carried three of the letters.*
  - *The letter to Ephesus was carried by Tychicus (Eph. 6:21-22).*
    - *Tychicus was from the province of Asia, and may have been from Ephesus itself (Acts 20:4).*
  - *The letter to Colossae was carried by Tychicus (Col. 4:7-9).*
    - *Onesimus is associated with Tychicus on this trip.*
  - *Tychicus and Onesimus also took a letter to a man named Philemon.*
    - *This letter was written in behalf of Onesimus whom Paul met and converted in Rome.*

- **Look on your map:**
  - **Find Ephesus and Colossae in Asia.**
  - **Find Philippi in Macedonia.**

- *Paul sent a message to Archippus in the letter to the Colossians and then greets him as he begins his letter to Philemon (Col.4:17; Philemon 2).*
  - *Therefore, we conclude that both Philemon and Archippus were members of the church at Colossae.*
- *The letters to Ephesus, to Colossae, and to Philemon could easily be carried by the same person because the places and persons were all in the province of Asia.*

- **Philippians was carried by Epaphroditus.**

- *The letter to the Philippians, however, though written at approximately the same time, was likely carried by Epaphroditus (Phil. 2:25-30).*

- **Paul expected to be released soon.**

- *Paul expected to be released shortly when he wrote these epistles.*
  - *He told the Philippians that he "trusted in the Lord that he himself would come to them shortly" (Phil. 2:23-24).*
  - *He told Philemon to prepare him a lodging because he hoped that through his prayers he would be granted unto him (verse 22).*
  - *He was released after the emperor heard his case this time, but he was killed at the end of his second imprisonment at Rome.*

- **Ephesians and Colossians are companion books.**

- *Another point that helps prove that Ephesians was not written at Caesarea, but at Rome about the same time as Colossians, is the similarity between the two books.*
  - *It is much more logical to assume that they were written about the same time than that they were written three or four years apart and were as nearly alike as they are.*

The books were sent in the early spring of 63.

All four of these letters were written toward the end of Paul's two years in Rome, since he hoped to be released soon. Therefore, they were written in the fall or winter of 62 or in the early spring of 63. They must have been ready for the men to take with them as soon as travel could begin in the spring of 63. We will study the letters in two groups: the three letters sent to the province of Asia, and then the letter sent to Philippi. We will study them in this order: Ephesians, Colossians, Philemon, and then Philippians.

Summary of Ephesians

Almost no personal notes.

There are very few personal notes in the book of Ephesians. No one joins Paul in the greeting, and he greets no one by name, which is surprising because he worked three years in Ephesus on his third missionary journey. Tychicus is obviously with Paul at this time, because he is sending him to tell the Ephesians about his own personal situation.

Even though it is a relatively short book, Ephesians has one of the richest themes to be found in the whole New Testament. It is a description of the blessings God has provided for all saints through Christ and then a reminder that with these blessings come responsibilities. Because of the richness of its message, let us analyze it carefully.

The book can be easily outlined. It falls into two major divisions: God has given us every spiritual blessing in Christ (chapters 1-3). Therefore, live accordingly (chapters 4-6).

Ephesians 1:3-14 is the opening movement in the book, and there are few passages in the Bible that are richer or filled with loftier thoughts. Verse three is an example. In it the distinctive thought of the book is summarized: "Blessed be the God and Father of our Lord Jesus Christ, who has blessed us with every spiritual blessing in the heavenly places in Christ." Look at the mighty thoughts in this one verse:

- *"Blessed be God..." is an expression of deep praise of Jehovah who has chosen to bless us.*
- *"with every spiritual blessing..." God has given us <u>every</u> spiritual blessing that could be imagined.*
- *"...in Christ." God's whole scheme for man, His whole plan is provided through Christ. Everything is summed up in Him.*

Listen now to the music of Paul's great symphony. The letter says:

Paul to the saints at Ephesus:

- God has given us all spiritual blessings in Christ (1:1-3:21):
- Look what God has done for us (1:3-14):

Let God be praised because He has blessed us with every spiritual blessing there is in Christ. (*Now look as the apostle piles up these blessings.)* He **chose** us in Christ before the foundation of the world, so that we should be holy and blameless before Him (1:4). He **planned our adoption** as sons through Jesus, according to the good pleasure of His will *(by His kind intention)* (1:5), according to the glory of **His grace which He bestowed on us** in the Beloved (1:6). In whom *(the Beloved)* **we have redemption** through His blood by the forgiveness of our trespasses, according to the riches of **His grace (1:7) which He lavished upon us** in all wisdom and insight (1:8). He has **made known to us the mystery of His will** (1:9), so that, in the fulness of the times, He might sum up all things in Christ — in heaven and on earth (1:10).

In Him **we have obtained an inheritance**, having been predestined according to the purpose of the One who works all things after the counsel of His will (1:11). All this was to the end that we who first trusted in Christ should be to the praise of His glory. In Christ, whom you trusted and believed, **you were sealed with the Holy Spirit** as a pledge *(a down payment)* of our inheritance until the redemption of God's possessions, to the praise of His glory.

Short Outline:

- **God has given us every spiritual blessing in Christ (1:1-3:21).**
- **Therefore live accordingly (4:1-6:24).**

The letter says:

God has given us all spiritual blessings in Christ (1:1-3:21).

- **Look what He has done for us (1:3-14):**
  - **Chose us (1:4)**
  - **Adopted us (1:5)**
  - **Bestowed His grace upon us (1:6, 7, 8)**
  - **Redeemed us by forgiving our sins (1:7)**
  - **Made us know His mystery (1:9)**
  - **Gave us an inheritance (1:11)**
  - **Gave us a down payment until time for God to receive His possession (1:13-14).**
- **He did it all through Christ:**
  - **Expressions such as "In Christ," "in Him," "through Jesus Christ," "in the Beloved" occur ten times in 1:3-14 (1:3, 4, 5, 6, 7, 9, 10, 13).**
- **By His eternal purpose:**
  - **Before the foundation of the world (1:4),**
  - **According to:**
    - **The kind intention of His will (1:5)**
    - **The riches of His grace (1:7-8)**
    - **His purpose who works all things after the counsel of His will (1:11).**

- **So that *(for a purpose)*:**
  - **We should be holy and blameless (1:4)**
  - **To the praise of His glory (1:6, 12, 14)**
  - **With a view to summing up all things in Christ (1:10).**

Paul is not teaching an individual, Calvinistic kind of predestination that does not permit the operation of man's free will No, he is saying that God determined how He would save men before He made the worlds. He determined that Christ would be the sacrifice, He would be the One through whom all redemption would come, and He determined that all those who accepted His grace could be adopted as sons of God. What blessings! But God did all of this for a purpose. Even here in this first main paragraph, Paul says that God made His plans and carried them out in Christ in order to make it possible for us to be the kind of people He wants, to the praise of His glory.

- **For this reason, I pray (1:15-23):**
  - **That God may:**
    - **Give you a spirit of wisdom...**
    - **Enlighten your heart...**
  - **So that you may know:**
    - **The hope of His calling,**
    - **The riches of His inheritance,**
    - **The surpassing greatness of His power toward us who believe.**
  - **According to:**
    - **The working of His power...**
    - **Which He used when He raised Jesus from the dead and exalted Him.**

- For this reason *(in view of all the blessings God gives through Christ),* I pray (1:15-23):

  I have heard of your faith in Christ and your love for all the saints, so I include you in my prayers. I give thanks for you, but more importantly I pray that God may give you a spirit of wisdom in the knowledge of Him, that He may enlighten the eyes of your heart, so that you may know the hope of His calling, the riches of His inheritance, and the surpassing greatness of His power toward us who believe.

  The way to grasp these blessings is through the working of His mighty power — the same power that He brought about in Christ when He raised Him from the dead and seated Him at His own right hand. He made Him far above all rule, above every name. He put everything in subjection to Him and gave Him to be head over all things to the church which is His body, the fulness of Him who fills all in all.

Having reminded the Ephesians of God's sublime blessings, his prayer for the Ephesians (and for all saints since) is that they may fully appropriate the richness of these blessings, which are their inheritance. Through God's plan they (and we) have access to the same power that raised Jesus Christ from the dead. Paul is saying, "Grasp that power. Reach the potential these blessings give you."

Having taken us soaring in celestial realms, Paul brings us to earth by pointing out that when God gave these blessings, we were dead. The contrast between our deadness and the greatness of God's blessings magnifies the blessings.

- **And you, DEAD... (2:1-10)**
  - **In sins**
  - **Walking like the world**
  - **In lusts of the flesh**

  - **God showed His mercy**
    - **Made us alive**

- God granted all these wonderful blessings at a time when we were dead (2:1-10): *(Compare this passage to Romans 5:1-11.)*

  In contrast to all the blessings God has given, you were *dead!* You were still in your trespasses and sins; you still *walked* according to the course of this world, still living in the lusts of your flesh. But God was rich in His mercy, because He loved us. Even when we were dead in our sins, He made us alive with Christ and raised

- **So that we might see the riches of His grace...**
  - **A grace He gave us so that we could be His being *(His craft)*,**
  - **Designed for and functioning in good works He prepared.**

us up to sit with Him in heavenly places — so that He might show the surpassing riches of His grace in Christ Jesus.

Realize that it is through grace *(undeserved favor)* that you have been saved through your faith. You did not earn it — it is a gift of God. It is not because of your great works, lest you should boast. No, you are *His* workmanship *(His craft)* which He created in Christ. He designed you for good works which He has prepared for us to *walk* in.

The first words of 2:1 are jolting. Literally, the wording is, "And you — dead!" The New American Standard has it: "And you were dead in your trespasses and sins." Now look at the whole thought: "God gave you these incomparable blessings, and you were dead!!" The reason for these blessings is found within God and His mercy, not in anything we did to deserve them.

It is interesting to note, beginning with 2:10, how often Paul uses the word "walk" during the course of this epistle (2:10; 4:1, 17; 5:2, 8, 15). With this verse, Paul is introducing the second key thought of the book: As a result of God's blessings, He has made us something we were not before. We are the result of His craftsmanship, made to walk in His ways and to do His works.

- **You Gentiles were farther from God than were the Jews (2:11-22):**
  - **Separate from Christ...**
  - **Having no hope...**
  - **But now brought near by the blood of Christ...**

- You Gentiles were even farther away from God than were the Jews (2:11-22):

  You were separate from Christ, excluded from the commonwealth of Israel, strangers to the covenants of promise, having no hope, without God in the world. But now you have been brought near by the blood of Christ. He is our peace; He made both groups one by breaking down the dividing wall that was the Law of Moses, thus establishing peace. He reconciled both Jew and Gentile in one body, putting to death the hatred between them. He preached to those far and near, so that we both have access to the Father.

It is obvious that the thrust of Paul's comments is to Gentiles. In bold tones he sets forth the absolutely desolate condition the Gentiles were in. BUT....

- **No longer aliens...**
- **Access to the Father,**
- **Fellow citizens,**
- **Part of God's family,**
- **Part of His temple.**

You are no longer strangers and aliens. You are fellow citizens with the saints. You are part of God's household that is built upon the foundation of the apostles and prophets with Jesus as the corner stone. In Jesus the whole building fits together and grows into a holy temple in the Lord as a dwelling for God in the Spirit.

What incredible blessings Paul is describing! Actually to become a part of the dwelling place of God! Do not take these blessings for granted. Do not forget gratitude.

- **For this reason... I have a prayer for you Gentiles (3:1, 14-19):**

He interrupts himself, but we will come back to the interruption in a moment.

- For this reason... I bow my knees before God (3:1, 14-19):

Paul identifies himself as "the prisoner of Christ Jesus for the sake of you Gentiles." He is about to express a prayer he makes, but when he refers to himself as a prisoner of Christ in behalf of the Gentiles, the thought leads him to speak of the great grace God gave to him in his ministry to the Gentiles. I think we often miss what Paul prays for, so let's leave this interruption for a moment in order to see what his prayer is for the Gentiles. Then we will look at the interruption.

- **May God grant that:**
  - **You be strengthened with power... so that:**
    - **Christ may dwell in your hearts...**
    - **You may grasp the depths of God's riches...**
    - **You may know the love of Christ...**
    - **You may be filled with the fulness of God.**

For this reason *(in view of all that God has done for us, in view of how helpless we were without God's grace, and in view of Paul's special ministry in behalf of the Gentiles)*, I bow my knees before the Father on your behalf. I pray that God will grant that you will be strengthened with power in the inner man, and that Christ may dwell in your hearts through faith. I want this for you so that you may be able **to comprehend** *(grasp, catch hold of, hold tight)* the breadth, the length, the height, and the depth, and **to know** the **love of Christ** that surpasses knowledge, so that you may be filled up to all the fulness of God.

The object of "comprehend" and of "know" is the love of Christ. Paul's prayer is that the Ephesians will take full advantage of all that God offers. It is as if God has a great treasure room. He bids us go in and gather all we can carry. It is sad that many Christians are satisfied with only a bauble or two and never take the fulness of the blessings God so freely offers.

- **Doxology (3:20-21).**

- Doxology (3:20-21):

Now to Him who is able to do exceeding abundantly above all that we ask or think, according to the power that works within us, to Him be the glory in the church and in Christ Jesus to all generations forever and ever. Amen.

Each saint receives his measure of the blessings provided, to the degree that he puts to work the power that God has put at his disposal. That power is Christ dwelling in our hearts by faith (see Col. 1:27). Now that God has done His work, it is up to me.

Back to Paul's interruption.

- **For the sake of the Gentiles... (3:1-13)**
  - **God gave me a charge to the Gentiles.**
  - **He revealed his mystery,**
  - **I wrote it, so you can read and understand it.**
  - **The mystery is that the Gentiles may share in God's blessings.**

- *Back to Paul's interruption:* I am a prisoner... for the sake of you Gentiles (3:1-13):

You do know about the stewardship I was given from God, do you not? God revealed His mystery to me, and I wrote it down so that when you read it you can understand what I know about the mystery of God. This is the mystery that was hidden in ages past, but has now been made known to the apostles and prophets. This great mystery is that the **Gentiles** are fellow heirs, fellow members of the body, fellow partakers of the promise through the gospel.

- **I was granted the privilege of telling it...**
- **Revealing God's wisdom:**
    - **Planned from eternity,**
    - **Accomplished through Christ.**

And God granted *me* this great privilege of telling the Gentiles the unfathomable riches of Christ, to bring to light the mystery that was hidden so long — so that the many sided wisdom of God might be made known through the church *(through the whole plan that brought about the church)*. All of this wisdom was in accordance with His eternal purpose, and was accomplished through Christ Jesus, in whom we have boldness and access to God. Therefore do not lose heart at my trials, because they are for your glory.

Walk in a manner worthy of your calling (4:1-6:24):

- **God has given us everything we need to reach full spiritual maturity (4:1-16).**
    - **Walk in humility...**
    - **Keep the unity of the Spirit...**
    - **Use the gifts Christ gave:**
        - **To build up the body of Christ,**
        - **Until all attain full spiritual maturity.**
    - **No longer children...**
    - **Grow as each joint does its part.**

- Therefore *(in view of the great blessings you have been given)* I, Paul, the prisoner for your sake, beg you to walk in a manner worthy of your calling (4:1-6:24):
- The greatness of the blessings increases the greatness of the responsibilities (4:1-16):

Walk as your great calling requires you: in humility, gentleness, patience, forbearing one another in love. Keep the unity of the Spirit: one body, one Spirit, one hope, one Lord, one faith, one baptism, one God. Christ gave gifts unto men when He returned to heaven: everything we need in order to do all He requires. He gave us apostles, evangelists, pastors and teachers in order to achieve the building up of the body of Christ until we all attain to the unity of the faith, and until we reach full spiritual maturity.

As a result of the growth made possible by Christ's gifts we are no longer children, tossed by every wave of false doctrine. But, speaking the truth in love, we are to grow up in all ways in Christ, from whom the whole body receives its nourishment as each joint does its part to enable the body to grow.

- **Do not walk like the Gentiles (4:17-5:21):**
    - **Put off the old man... and put on the new man (4:17-24).**
    - **Put away the practice of sin (4:25-32).**
    - **Walk in love (5:1-2).**
    - **Walk as children of light (5:3-14).**

- Do not walk like the Gentiles (4:17-5:21):

You no longer *walk* as the Gentiles do with their aimless lives and with their minds wilfully ignorant of God. You have put away the old man which becomes more corrupt by the lusts of deceit, and you have put on the new character God has made possible for you to have.

Your lives must reflect this new character: do not lie; but rather, speak the truth. Do not be given to wrath. Do not steal; instead, make an honest living so that you can help others. Do not let filthy speech come out of your mouth, but that which is wholesome. Do not disappoint the Spirit of God. Put away bitterness, wrath, anger, clamor, ranting, and all malice. In their place, be kind, tenderhearted, forgiving, just as God in Christ has forgiven you.

You are the beloved children of God. Imitate your Father as children are supposed to do, and *walk* in love in the same way Christ loved you.

Do not even discuss such things as fornication, impurity, or greed. Let there be no filthy talking or coarse jesting among you; instead use your tongues for giving thanks. Do not let anyone deceive you, because you know that no one who does these things has any inheritance in the kingdom of God. You used to be children of darkness, but now you are light in the Lord; so *walk* as children of light. Do not participate in the deeds of darkness, but rather expose them to the light.

- **Walk carefully, being filled with the Spirit (5:15-21).**

Walk carefully, looking about you lest you fall into temptation. Use your time wisely because the days are evil. Understand the will of the Lord. Do not be drunk with wine, but be filled with the Spirit. Speak to one another in psalms and hymns and spiritual songs in order to give thanks to God and to encourage one another.

- **Be wise in your various relationships (5:22-6:9):**
  - **Husbands and wives (5:22-33).**
  - **Children and parents (6:1-4).**
  - **Servants and masters (6:5-9).**

- Be subject one to another; wise in your various relationships (5:22-6:9):

In all your relationships, see that you are subject to one another as the situation requires. Wives, be in subjection to your husbands as the church is subject to Christ. Husbands, love your wives as Christ loved the church and gave Himself up for it.

Children, obey your parents and honor them, for this is what God wants you to do. And fathers, be sure to rear your children in the discipline and instruction of the Lord.

Servants, be obedient to those who are your masters in this life. Work whether they are watching you or not. Work for them as if you were working for Christ. And you masters, treat your slaves fairly because you too have a Master who is in heaven.

- **Put on the whole armor to be ready to meet the foe (6:10-20).**

- Put on the whole armor in order to be ready to meet the forces of evil (6:10-20):

Finally, be strong in the Lord and in the strength of His might. Stand firm. Know your enemy. Put on the whole armor of God so that you can stand against the wiles of the devil. Remember that you are wrestling against spirit beings, so take the full armor so that you will be armed and ready. Pray always. Be on the alert. And when you pray, pray for me also that I will have the courage to keep on preaching the gospel, for which I am an ambassador in chains.

If the great apostle Paul needed the prayers of others that he might have boldness to preach —even when the going was hard —all the rest of us need the same prayers from and for each other.

- **Tychicus will tell you about my situation (6:21-22).**

- Tychicus will tell you about my situation (6:21-22):

Tychicus will tell you everything about my personal situation. It is for this purpose that I have sent him.

- **Benediction (6:23-24).**

- Benediction (6:23-24):

Peace and love be to the brethren, along with faith from the Father and the Lord Jesus Christ. Grace be with all those who love our Lord with a love that is incorruptible.

Thumbnail sketch of Ephesians:

The book of Ephesians extols the richness of God's blessings. Christians have been given every spiritual blessing that exists —and all of them are given through Christ. God has called us to be His children. It is as if God has a treasure room of blessings that are available to the Ephesians (and to all saints), and Paul wants them to take full advantage of everything God has provided (chapters 1-3).

Concept of Ephesians: God's rich blessings bring great responsibilities.

But then, of equal importance, if the saint wants God's blessings, he must meet the responsibilities that accompany them. God's blessings have always been conditional. Since we have been offered such privileges, let us live as becomes children of God. Let our walk be in Christ; let it be a life that glorifies God in every way (chapters 4-6).

Summary of Colossians

Almost certainly Epaphras established the church at Colossae, not Paul (Col. 1:7; 4:13). It is at least implied that Paul had never personally preached in the city of Colossae, because he seems to include the saints there among those who had never seen his face (2:1).

Epaphras:

- **From Colossae,**
- **Visited Paul in Rome.**
- **Is called Paul's fellow-prisoner in Philemon.**

At some point, Epaphras visited Paul in Rome and told him about the progress of the saints in Colossae (1:7). In response, Paul wrote them a letter and sent it by the hands of Tychicus and Onesimus (4:7-9). In addition, they also carried the letter to the church at Ephesus (Eph. 6:21-22). It seems logical that since Epaphras had come from Colossae, and a letter was being sent there, he would have taken it as he returned home, but Epaphras is called Paul's fellow-prisoner in the book of Philemon (verse 23). No details are given about the circumstances that kept Epaphras from carrying the letter.

Paul's companions:
Timothy
Epaphras
Tychicus
Onesimus
Aristarchus
Luke
Mark
Jesus (Justus)
Demas

Tychicus and Onesimus are leaving to carry the letters.

Though Paul was a prisoner a long way from the area where he had done most of his work, notice his companions at this time. Timothy joins in the salutation to the church at Colossae (1:1) and to Philemon (verse 1). Epaphras was still in Rome (Col. 4:12-13). Tychicus and Onesimus have been with Paul, but he is sending them to Colossae with the letters (4:7-9).

Aristarchus, who accompanied Paul on the trip to Rome (Acts 27:2), is with him and is called a fellow-prisoner (Col. 4:10). No information is given about what happened to cause him to be imprisoned. Some have thought Paul may have used a figure of speech, and that Aristarchus and Epaphras were both "prisoners" in that they had voluntarily chosen to stay in Rome with Paul. But that does not necessarily fit, because Paul does not use that expression about his other associates, including Luke, who also accompanied him on the trip to Rome and is with him at this time (Col. 4:14). This may be an indication that the persecution against the saints was intensifying, though the Roman government had not yet gotten directly involved.

Mark is the same one who started out with Paul and Barnabas on their first preaching journey, and then turned back. Now he is with Paul, and Paul recommends him to the Colossians (4:10). Jesus (Justus) and Demas are also there (4:11, 14). Nothing else is known about this Jesus. Demas will forsake Paul when he is imprisoned the second time in Rome (2 Tim. 4:10). This is the passage where Luke is called a physician (4:14) and where Mark is called Barnabas' relative (4:10).

A letter to Laodicea?

A statement in Colossians 4:16 has raised questions in the minds of readers for generations — and no one knows the answers. It says: "When this letter is read among you, have it read to the church at Laodicea, and you read my letter to them also." What letter? There is no letter in the New Testament called the Laodicean letter! Obviously, we do not have every word the apostle wrote in his lifetime, and this letter seems to be one of those things. Some have wondered if the letter we call Ephesians could be this letter to Laodicea, and that the name of the congregation to whom it was addressed got lost at some point. There are two reasons for wondering if it could be. First, the letters Ephesians and Colossians are companion letters and make points that are understood best when studied together; and, second, it seems unusual that Paul sends no personal greetings to Ephesus where he had spent three years in very diligent work. Perhaps there is merit in that answer to the question, but know that no one can give a certain answer. Be assured, however, that we have the full information that the Holy Spirit determined was necessary for us to have the full counsel of God.

Short outline:

- **Christ is everything you need (1:1-29).**
- **Do not let anyone spoil what you have (2:1-23).**
- **A picture of the true child of God (3:1-4:18).**

The theme of Colossians has been stated as Christ the fulness of God — and that is a very important part of the letter. But let's be a little more specific and practical in our approach to the theme and state it this way: Christ is all you need. In Him you have all the blessings of God. Therefore you do not need anything or anyone else. This theme is argued throughout the book, but it is especially stated in 2:3: "Christ, in whom are all the treasures of wisdom and knowledge hidden," and in 2:8-12: "Take heed lest there shall be any one that maketh spoil of you through his philosophy and vain deceit, after the tradition of men, after the rudiments of the world, and not after Christ: for in Him dwelleth all the fulness of the Godhead bodily, and in Him ye are made full, who is the head of all principality and power ..."

The Colossian letter says:

Paul says:

Salutation (1:1-2).

- **We are thankful (1:3-8):**
  - **For your faith,**
  - **For your love toward all the saints:**

Paul and Timothy to the brethren at Colossae:

- We give thanks for your conversion (1:3-8):

  We thank God the Father every time we pray, because of your faith in Christ and because of your love toward all the saints. This love is based upon the common hope of life in heaven which you heard about in the gospel, which has come to you, even as it is

- **Based upon the common hope of heaven.**
- **The gospel is bearing fruit in your life.**

bearing fruit in all the world. The gospel has been producing fruit in you since you first heard it from Epaphras.

Keep in mind the parallels between Colossians and Ephesians. The preceding paragraph (1:3-8) is comparable to Ephesians 1:15-16. In this first paragraph, Paul says, "We are glad to hear that you have become faithful Christians." In the next paragraph (1:9-14), he prays for their full growth and development. Compare to Ephesians 1:17-19.

- **We pray for your further growth in Christ, that you may (1:9-14):**
  - **Be filled with all knowledge,**
  - **Have all spiritual wisdom and insight;**
  - **Walk in a manner worthy of the Lord,**
    - **So that you may please Him...**
  - **Be strengthened with His power...**
    - **The One who rescued us... forgave us...**

- We pray for your further growth in Christ (1:9-14):

Since we first heard of your faith, we have not ceased to pray that you may be filled with all knowledge of His will, so as to have all spiritual wisdom and insight. We pray that you walk in a manner worthy of the Lord, so that you may please Him by bearing fruit in every good work and by growing in the knowledge of God.

We also pray that you may be strengthened with His power, so that you may be steadfast, giving thanks to the Father who fitted us for our lot as saints of light. He rescued us out of the tyranny of darkness and brought us into the kingdom of the Son He loved. It is in Him we have our redemption, the forgiveness of our sins.

Next comes an eloquent description of the majesty of Christ, but there is a very practical reason for this portrayal at this point. Paul is wanting them to see that their spiritual blessings exist because of ***who Christ is****. Compare this section to Ephesians 1:20-23. This portrayal of Jesus is a very clear affirmation of His Deity.*

- **The glories of Christ and of His position (1:15-20):**
  - **He is:**
    - **The image of God (1:15).**
    - **Ranked first in all creation (1:16).**
    - **The Creator and Sustainer of all things (1:16-17).**
    - **Head of the church (1:18).**
    - **Fullness of the Father (1:19).**
    - **The One who reconciles (1:20).**

- The glory of Christ and of His position (1:15-20):

Christ is the true image of the invisible God, the first-ranked of all creation *(every creature)*. In Him were created all things: things in the heavens and things upon the earth, things visible and invisible. In Him all the beings of power were created. He is before all things, and in Him all things hold together.

Not only is He the firstborn of all creation, He is also the head of the body, the church. He is the one who began all things, the firstborn from the dead, so that among all things He might have the preeminence, the first rank.

He has this rank because it was exactly what the Father wanted, so that the full character and nature of Deity dwell in Him. It was also the pleasure of God to reconcile all things to Himself through the blood of His cross, whether things upon earth, or things in the heavens.

"Firstborn" does not mean that Jesus was first created and then everything else began through Him. Rather, the term has to do with rank. Among all things created Jesus holds first rank. He entered into the realm of created things by becoming a man, but He was God before

creation, and through Him everything created was made. Compare this statement that "all things were created by Him..." to John 1:1-3. Jesus was and is Deity, with God in the very beginning, and everything came into being through Him.

- **Though once enemies of God, you were reconciled (1:21-23):**
  - **So that:**
    - **He may present you holy, without blemish;**
  - **If you remain steadfast...**

- You were enemies of God, until you were reconciled (1:21-23):
  Compare this paragraph with Ephesians 2:11-22.

  Though in former times you were alienated from God, and enemies because of your evil works, yet now you have been reconciled through Christ so that you may be presented holy and without blemish before Him. For this goal to be accomplished, however, you must remain grounded and steadfast, and not moved away from the hope of the gospel which you heard, which has been preached in all creation, and of which I have been made a servant.

- **I rejoice that I could tell the mystery of Christ (1:24-29):**
  - **I rejoice in my suffering...**
  - **God bestowed this ministry on your behalf, that I might:**
    - **Tell the mystery to Gentiles, which is:**
      - **Christ in you, the hope of glory.**
    - **Present everyone perfect in Christ.**
  - **To this end I work hard.**

- I rejoice in my part in making known the mystery of Christ (1:24-29):

After describing the power and majesty of Christ, and relating His power and majesty to the blessings of the Colossians, Paul does the same thing with regard to the ministry he has been given among the Gentiles. See Ephesians 3:1-13.

I am very happy to be able to do my share of Christ's suffering for His body's sake, that is, the church. I was made a servant of that church in keeping with the responsibility which I was given. You see, in ages past, the plan of God was not revealed, but now it has been put into the light for His saints. To them He has made known the riches of the glory of this mystery among the Gentiles, which is Christ in you, the hope of glory. Therefore we proclaim Christ, teaching every man so that we can present everyone perfect in Christ. To this end I toil diligently.

Some outline chapter two as a warning against Judaizing teachers, and it certainly is that, but the first few verses (1-5) are closely related to the ideas of 1:15-29. Often as Paul is making a transition, he blends together the themes he has been discussing, and introduces the topic of the next phase of his reasoning. Reminding them therefore of Christ, who is the source of all blessings, he also warns them against those who would deceive them (2:4).Compare 2:2 with the much-expanded version of the thought in Ephesians 4:1-16.

- **I work so that (2:1-5):**
  - **You may be comforted by your unity,**
    - **Sharing in the riches...**

- I work hard so that you may be comforted by unity and so that you may know the mystery of Christ (2:1-5):

  I want you to know how greatly I work for you, for those at Laodicea, and for all those who have not seen my face. My efforts are so that your hearts may be comforted, being knit together in love, and joined together, sharing in all the riches of the fullness of

- **You may know the mystery of Christ...**
  - **Where all treasures are hidden.**

understanding. I work that all may know the mystery of God which is Christ, in whom all the treasures of wisdom and knowledge are hidden. I am saying these things to warn you not to be deceived by smooth-talking false teachers.

- **Walk in Christ as you were taught (2:6-7).**

- Walk in Christ as you were taught (2:6-7):

  As you first received Christ the Lord, continue to walk in Him and be established in Him.

- **Beware of philosophical Judaism (2:8-15):**
  - **Do not let anyone take away what you have.**
  - **The fullness of Deity dwells in Him (2:9).**
  - **In Him you are made full (2:10).**
  - **In Him the body of flesh is put away (2:11).**
  - **You were buried with Him in baptism (2:12).**
  - **Made alive in Him (2:13).**
  - **Delivered from the law of Moses by Him (2:14).**
  - **He has won the victory (2:15).**

- Beware of philosophical Judaism (2:8-15):
  (Remember that 2:8-12 captures the theme of Colossians.)

  Be careful, therefore, lest anyone take advantage of you through his philosophy and vain deceit, emphasizing the rudimentary things of the world instead of Christ.

  All the fullness of Deity dwells in Him, and in Him you are made full. In Him you were circumcised, but not with the circumcision of Moses. In *your* circumcision, you put off *the whole body of flesh.* You were buried with Him through baptism, from which you were raised with Him through faith in the operation of God who raised Him from the dead.

  Even though you were dead through your trespasses, God made you alive with Christ (*compare with Eph. 2:1*). He forgave us all of our trespasses, and blotted out the bond which was written in decrees against us *(the law of Moses)*. He took it out of the way, nailing it to the cross. Having defeated His enemies, He displayed to all His triumph over them.

Among the things accomplished in Jesus Christ, Paul mentions the spiritual blessings of putting off the body of the flesh, being made alive, being forgiven, but one of the great blessings in Christ is what He has done with regard to the law of Moses. He has delivered us from the law, a law of commandments contained in ordinances.

- **So do not submit to restrictions that men would place upon you (2:16-23):**
  - **Do not let anyone condemn you in regard to food, drink, or special days (2:16-17).**
  - **Do not be enticed by those who devise their own worship to impress people with their piety (2:18-19).**

- So do not submit to the restrictions that men would place upon you (2:16-23):

  So do not let anyone condemn you regarding food, or drink, or in reference to a feast day, or a new moon, or a sabbath day *(rules from the old law)*. Those were but shadows of things to come; the substance belongs to Christ.

  Do not let any man rob you of your prize by his showy, pretended humility and by his recommending, for example, the worship of angels. He is talking about things he has not seen, and is puffed up. He does not hold fast to the Head, from whom the body, which is supplied and knit together through the various parts, grows and prospers.

  If you died with Christ to the things regulated by the law, do not subject yourselves to rules: "Do not handle this," "Do not taste that,"

- **Do not subject yourselves to commandments men make up to impress others with their holiness (2:20-23).**

"Do not touch so-and-so," all of which things are destined to perish. Oh, these things have a *show* of wisdom in self-devised worship, and in making a display of humility and severity with the body, but they are of no value against giving in to the flesh.

The peculiar doctrines mentioned above indicate that these particular Judaizing teachers may have been some kind of local cult of Judaizers. At least they were making demands that are not mentioned in other passages, but nothing is known for sure about them.

- **Picture of the true child of God (3:1-4:6):**
  - **Concentrate on heavenly things (3:1-4).**
  - **Put away sinful attitudes (3:5-11).**
  - **Put on positive characteristics (3:12-17).**
  - **Human responsibilities (3:18-4:1):**
    - **Wives and husbands (3:18-19).**
    - **Children and parents (3:20-21).**
    - **Servants and masters (3:22-4:1).**
  - **Continue steadfastly in prayer (4:2-4).**
  - **Walk wisely among those who are not Christians (4:5-6).**

- Picture of the true Christian life without the philosophies of Judaism (3:1-4:6): *(Compare with Ephesians 4-6.)*

If then you were raised with Christ, seek the things which are above, where Christ is, seated at God's right hand. Concentrate on the things that are above, not on the things upon the earth.

Put to death, therefore, the evil practices and the wicked disposition which are of this world. You have put off the old man with his activities, and have put on the new man which is constantly being remodeled to be like Christ.

Cultivate, as God's chosen ones, a heart of compassion, kindness, lowliness, and meekness, forbearing one another, and forgiving one another just as the Lord forgave you. Let the word of Christ dwell in you richly in all wisdom, teaching and warning one another in psalms, hymns, and spiritual songs. And whatever you say or do, let it be in the name of the Lord.

Wives, be in subjection to your husbands as the Lord desires. Husbands, love your wives, and do not look down on them.

Children, obey your parents in all things, because this is well-pleasing in the Lord. Fathers, provoke not your children, so that they will not be discouraged.

Servants, obey your masters according to the flesh. Serve them sincerely, work energetically for them, as unto the Lord, because it is from the *Lord* you will receive your inheritance. Masters, be sure to treat your slaves fairly, knowing that you also have a master who is in heaven.

Keep on praying, no matter what comes. And pray for us also, so that God may open to us a door for the word, to speak the mystery of Christ for which I am in bonds.

Remember to walk wisely toward those who are outsiders. Let your speech always be appropriate and apt, so you will know just how to answer each one.

- **Tychicus will tell you about my affairs (4:7-9).**

- Tychicus and Onesimus will tell you about my situation (4:7-9): *(See Ephesians 6:21-22.)*

Tychicus will tell you all the news about me. He and Onesimus will comfort your hearts and will let you know everything that is happening here.

- **Greetings (4:10-18).**
  - **Read the letter to Laodicea.**

- Greetings and close (4:10-18):
  Those with me send their greetings to you. Give my greetings to the brethren in Laodicea and to those with you. Also, when you have read this letter, exchange letters with the Laodiceans. Remind Archippus to fulfill the stewardship he was given in the Lord.

Thumbnail sketch of Colossians:

We have seen that Colossians and Ephesians are very similar, yet the emphasis is different. In Colossians Paul is dealing with an error which is threatening, namely, some "off-brand" Judaism, stressing rules, angel worship, etc. He, therefore, presents Christ as the fullness of God, the One in whom we are complete. Paul tells the church at Colossae: Do not let anyone come in and tell you that you need his rituals and his commandments and his wisdom. In Christ you have the gospel, you have salvation, you have life, you have everything you need. It is in chapters one and two where we see this point stressed the most. The emphasis continues in chapters three and four, but it is not as pronounced as it is in the first two chapters.

Concept:
Christ is all you need.
Do not let anyone spoil what you have.

Summary of Philemon

Philemon is a personal letter from Paul to his friend Philemon, who seems to have been a member of the church at Colossae (Col. 4:9). Apparently Paul had converted him, because Paul says Philemon owed him his life (Philemon 19). A slave of Philemon's, by the name of Onesimus, ran away. In Rome, Onesimus met Paul and was converted by him. Paul sent Onesimus back to Philemon in the company of Tychicus who was taking letters to Ephesus and Colossae. Paul asks Philemon to receive Onesimus again as a servant, and as a brother in Christ as well (Philemon 10-16).

Paul wrote:

Onesimus:
- **A runaway slave,**
  - **Belonging to Philemon,**
- **Converted by Paul.**
- **Returning to Philemon.**

The personal letter from Paul to Philemon says:
- **Salutation (verses 1-3).**

Paul and Timothy to Philemon, and to Apphia our sister, to Archippus, and to the church in your house:

Archippus is mentioned also in the letter to the Colossians (Col. 4:17). This fact is one of the reasons why we believe Philemon was a member of the church at Colossae.

- **I give thanks for your faith and love (verses 4-7).**

Every time I pray, I thank God because of your faith in Christ and for your love for the saints. I pray that the sharing of your faith may bring about good results in all areas of life. I have had much joy and comfort through your love, knowing that many saints have been encouraged through you, my brother.

- **I am sending Onesimus back to you, as a beloved child of mine (verses 8-14).**

Therefore, though I would not hesitate to command those things that are necessary, yet for love's sake I had rather make a request of you in behalf of Onesimus, my child whom I have begotten while in my bonds. Once he was unprofitable to you, but now he is profitable to you and to me. So I have sent him back to you, a part of my own heart. I would have preferred to keep him with me, but without your consent, I would do no such thing lest your goodness in letting me keep him as my helper be a matter of necessity and not free will.

- **Receive him as a brother (verses 15-17).**

Think about it like this: perhaps he was separated from you for a while so that you would have him for ever. He is no longer just a servant, but also a brother who is loved, especially by me, but how much more to you, both in the flesh and in the Lord.

- **I will pay anything he owes you (verses 18-20).**

If he owes you anything, put it to my account. I, Paul, write this with my own hand: I will repay it. I do not need to remind you that you owe me your own self besides. Yes, my brother, I would like to make a profit from you in this matter; cheer my heart by doing as I ask.

- **Please prepare a place for me to stay... I hope to come soon (verses 21-22).**

I write you, confident that you will do even more than I have asked. In addition, prepare me a place to stay, because I hope that through your prayers, I will be able to come to you.

- **Greetings and benediction (verses 23-25).**

Epaphras, Mark, Aristarchus, Demas, and Luke, my fellow-workers, greet you. May Christ be with you.

Thumbnail sketch of Philemon:

This letter was written to ask Philemon to receive his slave back as a beloved brother. It does not breathe fear that Philemon might receive Onesimus harshly. Paul has every confidence that Philemon will accept his slave without any punishment.

Concept:
<u>Please receive your slave Onesimus back as a brother</u>.

It is interesting to remember that both Ephesians and Colossians contain instructions for the conduct of both slaves and masters. It is easy to see why the need for such instructions would be upon Paul's mind. His conversations with Onesimus, and his knowledge of the situation of slaves and masters in general, would have encouraged him to deal with the subject —with the approval and guidance of the Holy Spirit.

<u>Summary of Philippians</u>

Epaphroditus brought a gift from the church at Philippi.

Early in A.D. 63, a man named Epaphroditus brought Paul a gift from the church at Philippi (Phil. 2:25). Paul sent a return letter expressing his appreciation for the gift and for all the people there. It was almost time for his trial before Nero. He hoped to be released soon and he hoped to visit Philippi again (2:23-24). Remember that, though the three letters —Ephesians, Colossians, and Philemon —could be carried by the same messengers, this fourth prison epistle could not, because Philippi was located up in Macedonia, while the others were located in the province of Asia.

The church at Philippi was begun on Paul's second journey.

Philippi seems to have been a special church to Paul. They remained in close contact with him even from the first day he left them (4:15-16). Now it is close to ten years since the church started with the conversion of Lydia, the Philippian jailer and others (Acts 16). Remember also that Luke stayed behind when Paul and Silas left the city on the second journey, and he remained there until the close of Paul's third journey (Acts 16:40 — "they left"; 20:5-6 — "we sailed"). His influence must have been a great help to the congregation.

Main points:

- **Gratitude**
- **Exhortations:**
  - **Remain faithful.**
  - **Beware of false teachers.**

Paul hopes to be released after his hearing before Nero, but he does not know for sure what lies before him. So this letter to the Philippians is not only an expression of gratitude for their concern for him, but it is also an exhortation that Paul thinks may be his last one to them: "Be faithful no matter what comes."

The Philippian letter says:

- **Salutation (1:1-2).**
- **Paul's gratitude and prayer (1:3-11):**
  - **I give thanks for your help in furthering the gospel.**
  - **We have shared in trials and labor.**
  - **I long to see you.**
  - **I pray that your love may abound...**
  - **That you will be able to discern good and evil.**
- **Paul's joy in the spread of the gospel (1:12-26):**
  - **My experiences have helped spread the gospel (1:12-13).**
  - **Brethren are bolder to speak the word of the Lord (1:14-18).**
    - **Others speak from jealousy...**
  - **To be with Christ is much better for me,**
    - **But for your sake, it is better that I remain (1:19-26).**

Paul said:

Paul and Timothy, to all the saints at Philippi:

- Paul's gratitude and prayer for the Philippians (1:3-11):

  I thank God every time I think of you, praying with joy in my heart, because of your help in the furtherance of the gospel to this very day. I have every confidence that He who began a good work among you will perfect it until the day of Christ. It is only right for me to feel this way toward you since you have me in your heart, because we have shared God's grace in all my trials and labors. God knows how I long to see you, holding the same tender feelings toward you that were characteristic of Jesus. I pray also that your love will abound more and more in all knowledge and discernment. Then you will be able to distinguish between good and evil, so that you may be pure and without offense at the judgment.

- Paul's joy in the spread of the gospel (1:12-26):

  Brethren, my experiences have turned out to be a help to the spread of the gospel rather than a hindrance. The fact that I am in bonds because of my devotion to Christ has become known throughout the whole praetorian guard.

  Moreover, since the brethren here have seen how my situation is going, they are bolder to speak the word of the Lord. There are some, of course, who preach Christ from the motive of jealousy and competition. This does not bother me. I simply rejoice that the gospel is preached.

  I proceed on the assumption that through your prayers and the supply of the Spirit of Christ, I may magnify Christ in my body whether I live or die. I do not know what I would like best. One side of me would strongly prefer to go and be with Christ, because that would be far better. On the other hand, I feel that I am still needed here for your sake. On this basis, I have confidence that I will remain.

Some authorities say that imprisonment in Rome was of a military character, and that the barracks of various troops in the city were used as prisons. It is thought that when a prisoner was allowed, as Paul was, to live in his own rented dwelling, when his trial came up, he was transferred to the prison where those who were on trial were kept in custody. If this were the situation, it is easy to see how the true reason for Paul's imprisonment could become known throughout a whole troop more easily than if he were guarded by only one man right up to his trial. Most likely the praetorian guard refers to the praefecti praetorio into whose custody those who came on appeal from the provinces were placed.

The affliction that some thought to raise for Paul "in his bonds" was that they thought that by their actions in making converts, they might make Paul chagrined that he was in prison and could not do what they were doing; or they might have thought they would make Paul's lot worse by spreading the gospel more. No details are given.

- **Three admonitions:**
  - **Stand fast (1:27-30):**
    - **In unity...**
    - **Not afraid:**
      - **Evidence of your salvation.**

- Three admonitions follow (1:27-2:18):
- The first admonition: Whether I come or not, please remain faithful (1:27-30):

But whether I come and see you or remain absent, let your lives be worthy of the gospel. Stand fast, in perfect unity, working together for the faith of the gospel. Do not be frightened by your affliction which, to your adversaries, is a sign of wickedness. To you, however, it is evidence of your salvation, because not only have you come to believe in Christ, but to suffer for Him as well.

- **Have the mind of Christ (2:1-11):**
  - **Deal with each other in humility (2:1-4).**
    - **Be considerate.**
  - **Have the attitude of Christ (2:5-11):**
    - **Humility and obedience.**
    - **Even to the point of death on the cross.**

- The second admonition: Have the disposition of Christ as you deal with each other (2:1-11).

If those in Christ should encourage one another and have tender feelings toward one another, make my joy full by having that kind of disposition toward each other. Do not do anything through feuding and pride. Instead, in lowliness of mind, let each of you consider the other better than himself. And do not be preoccupied with your own affairs; but rather consider the affairs of others as well.

You need to have the attitude of Christ. He existed in the form of God, yet He did not consider His equality with God as something He could not let go. Rather, He emptied Himself of His divine prerogatives and became a servant, subject unto God. And having taken the position of a man, He humbled Himself, becoming obedient even unto death, yes, even to death on the cross.

- **In return, God exalted Him above all.**

Therefore God exalted Him to the point that He is above all things. In His name every knee must bow and every tongue confess that He is Lord, to the glory of God.

- **Be light-bearers (2:12-18):**
  - **Continue to obey... blameless... lights in this dark world.**

- The third admonition: Hold forth the word of light (2:12-18).

So, as I was saying, continue to obey the word, and do those things which will bring about your final salvation. Live so as to be blameless and harmless, children of God without flaw in the midst of a crooked and perverse generation. In the midst of such moral and spiritual darkness you are seen as lights in the world, holding out the word of life.

- **Timothy and Epaphroditus (2:19-30):**
  - **As soon as I learn how things will go with me, I will send Timothy (2:19-24).**
  - **Till then, I am sending Epaphroditus (2:25-30).**

- Paul explains his actions regarding Timothy and Epaphroditus (2:19-30):

I hope to send Timothy to you soon so that I can be encouraged about your condition. I do not have anyone like him, who will genuinely care about your situation. As soon as I see how things are going to go with me, I plan to send him to you, and I trust in the Lord that I will also come to you shortly.

Till then I felt it necessary to send Epaphroditus, my brother and fellow worker, and your messenger and servant for my needs, back to you. He has been homesick for you and has been especially concerned, knowing that you had heard he was sick. The fact is he *was* sick; he nearly died, but God had mercy on him, and on me, so that I did not have to bear sorrow stacked upon sorrow. So I have sent him back so that you may rejoice. Therefore receive him with joy, and honor him because he came close to death, doing for me what you wished.

- **Warning against Judaizers (3:1-4:1):**
  - **Beware of those who turn circumcision into a mere mutilation of the flesh (3:1-3).**
  - **I could brag about the flesh also — if it were of any value (3:4-6).**
  - **I count all such things worthless for the excellency of Christ (3:7-16).**

- Warning against Judaizing teachers (3:1-4:1):

Finally, my brethren, rejoice in the Lord. To keep on warning you about things you need to know is not bothersome to me, but it is safe for you. Look out for the dogs, look out for those who work evil, and for those who turn the rite of circumcision into merely a mutilation of the flesh. *We* are the circumcision: we who worship according to the Spirit of God, and glory in Christ, and do not put our confidence in the flesh.

If one thinks he has reason to boast about fleshly attainments, I have more. I could brag that I was circumcised on the eighth day, that I come from the stock of Israel, of the tribe of Benjamin, a Hebrew of Hebrews. Regarding the law I was a Pharisee. Zeal? Why, I persecuted the church! And with regard to the righteousness of the law, I was blameless.

But these things mean nothing to me. I have cast these and all other things behind me and consider them to be loss for the most important thing of all, which is the splendor of the knowledge of Christ. Yes, I have cast these things away that I may put forth every effort to reach the goal line so that I can receive the prize of the high calling of God in Christ. Let all of us who are full-grown have a similar attitude.

- **A contrast (3:17-4:1):**
    - **False teachers whose god is their belly,**
    - **And Christians whose citizenship is in heaven.**

Brethren, imitate me, and note those who walk after our example. For there are many who walk in a manner unworthy of Christ. Their destiny is destruction, their god is their belly, and they glory in the things they should be ashamed of.

On the other hand, *our* citizenship is in heaven, from which we look for Jesus our Savior to come. He will transform the body of our humiliation so that it will be like the body of His glory. Wherefore, my brethren, whom I love and long for, my joy and my crown, stand fast in the Lord.

- **Euodia and Syntyche (4:2-3):**
    - **Work together...**

- Exhortation to Euodia and Syntyche (4:2-3):

I want to encourage Euodia and Syntyche to have the same attitude and to work together. Yes, and I beseech you also, true companion, to help these women, because they labored with me in the gospel, along with Clement, and the rest of my co-workers, whose names are in the book of life.

- **Exhortations to all (4:4-9):**
    - **Rejoice in the Lord.**
    - **Be not anxious...**
        - **Pray...**
        - **The peace of God will guard your hearts.**
    - **Think on things honorable.**

- Exhortations to all (4:4-9):

Rejoice in the Lord, and I repeat, rejoice! Let your gentleness be displayed toward all men. The Lord is at hand; do not be anxious about anything, but in everything that concerns you, in prayer and requests, with thanksgiving, make your requests known to God, and the peace of God which passes understanding will guard your hearts and your thoughts in Christ.

Finally, brethren, think only on the best, the most wholesome of things. You do as you saw and heard me do, and the God of peace will be with you.

The next paragraph is a remarkable demonstration of the spirituality of the apostle Paul. He basically says, I am so glad that you sent your gift, not because I needed it and did not know what I was going to do, but because of what it tells me about you spiritually. You see, I have learned to do without or to enjoy having.

- **Paul's gratitude to the Philippians (4:10-20):**
    - **I have learned to be content (4:10-13).**
    -
    - **But I seek the spiritual profit that will come to you as a result of your generosity (4:14-20).**

- Paul's gratitude to the Philippians (4:10-20):

I rejoice greatly in the Lord that you remembered me again. It was not that you had forgotten, but that you did not have opportunity to help.

I am not speaking to you now about what I lacked, because I have learned to be content in whatever state I am. I know how to be filled and how to be hungry. I can do all things through Christ who strengthens me. But you did well to help me in my affliction. You Philippians know that when I left you and went on to Thessalonica you sent to my need once and again. It is not that I seek for the gift, but I seek for the fruit that thus is credited to your account.

But now I have everything I need and am filled, because Epaphroditus brought the things from you, a very pleasing sacrifice in the sight of God. And my God will supply your every need also. To Him be the glory for ever and ever.

- **Greetings and benediction (4:21-23).**

- Greetings and benediction (4:21-23):

  Greet every saint in Christ. The brethren with me send greetings. All the saints greet you, especially those of Caesar's household.

  May the grace of Christ be with your spirit.

Concept:
<u>Joy in the Lord.</u>

Thumbnail sketch of Philippians:

The epistle to the Philippians contains much that is personal and much that is spiritual. Paul had a special relationship with the Philippians. He expresses his affection for them and gives them an account of the things that had happened to him. It is a very profound "thank you" letter. Remember that this letter filled with joy and gratitude was written by a man in prison —unjustly imprisoned because of his faith in Christ.

Paul's concern for the spiritual welfare of the Philippians moves him to encourage them to behave as Christians and to beware of false teachers. He expresses his gratitude for their gift and is glad for the spiritual benefits they will derive from their generosity.

Paul's trial

Information is sketchy:
- **Some from 1 Timothy, Titus, 2 Timothy,**
- **And a few notes from the writings of the early Christians (the "church fathers").**

The Bible does not tell us anything about Paul's trial before the emperor. From evidence found in some of his epistles, and in some of the statements of the church fathers, it seems evident that Paul was released for a time. We have very few details about his work during the short time he was free. What we have comes from the epistles of 1 Timothy and Titus which were written at this time. Since there is no inspired history of this period, we need to look carefully at the scant evidence we do have.

Paul expected to be released:
- **He planned to visit:**
  - **Philemon at Colossae,**
  - **And the brethren in Philippi.**

- *In two of the epistles written during the two year stay in Rome, Paul shows that he expected to be released:*
  - *He told the Philippians that he hoped to come to them shortly (Phil. 2:24).*
  - *He told his friend Philemon to prepare a lodging for him because he hoped to visit him soon (Philemon 22).*

From the evidence, we can be reasonably certain that, upon his release from prison, Paul headed for the region of the Aegean Sea: Greece, Macedonia, and Asia.

He left Timothy in Ephesus as he went into Macedonia.
- **This does not fit into the stories of Acts.**

- *In his first letter to Timothy, he said, "As I exhorted thee to tarry in Ephesus when I was going into Macedonia..." (1 Tim. 1:3).*
  - *This situation did not occur during any of the three missionary journeys recorded in Acts.*
  - *Paul passed through Ephesus twice in Acts: once at the close of his second journey (Acts 18:18-21), and once, for a three year stay, on his third journey (Acts 19:1; 20:31).*
  - *The first time, he left Ephesus headed for Jerusalem, not Macedonia.*
  - *The second time he left Ephesus headed for Macedonia (Acts 20:1), but he did not <u>leave</u> Timothy in Ephesus; rather, he <u>sent</u> Timothy ahead into Macedonia (Acts 19:22).*
  - *Therefore the time referred to in 1 Timothy 1:3 must have occurred after Paul's first prison term.*

He left Titus in Crete:
- **But Paul did not preach in Crete during the time of Acts.**

- *The apostle left Titus in Crete (Tit. 1:5).*
  - *We know of no time Paul went by Crete in the book of Acts except during his journey to Rome.*
    - *There is no evidence that Titus was with him at that time,*
    - *Nor is there evidence that Paul made more than the briefest of visits to what must have been an insignificant harbor (Fair Havens) (Acts 27:8).*
  - *Therefore the trip to Crete referred to in the letter to Titus must have taken place in the period following Paul's release from prison in Rome.*

He plans to winter in Nicopolis:
- **But he did not go there during his three preaching journeys.**

- *Paul plans to spend the winter in Nicopolis (Tit. 3:12).*
  - *Nicopolis was a city on the shore of the Adriatic Sea in the province of Achaia, several miles northwest of the city of Corinth.*
  - *There is no mention in Acts of his going to Nicopolis, much less spending a winter there.*
  - *So this is further evidence that Paul was released from prison and that he was busy visiting various congregations and preaching at every opportunity during this period.*

At the time of his second letter to Timothy:
- **He expected to be executed soon.**
- **He had left Trophimus sick in Miletus.**

- *Paul wrote Timothy a second letter:*
  - *By then he was back in prison and he expected to be executed (2 Tim. 4:7).*
  - *But in this letter, he referred to a time not long before when he left Trophimus in Miletus sick (2 Tim. 4:20).*
    - *This situation does not fit anything in Acts.*

- *Therefore it, too, must belong to the period between his imprisonments.*

• He had left a cloak and books at Troas.

- *He had also left a cloak and some books at Troas and asked that Timothy bring them with him when he joined Paul (2 Tim. 4:13).*

By 2 Timothy:
• Only Luke is with him as his immediate companion,
• Though other brethren are in the city.

- *There were several friends with Paul in Rome when he wrote Colossians and Philemon (Col 4:7-17; Philemon 23-24).*
  - *By the time he writes 2 Timothy, only Luke is with him (2 Tim. 4:9-12, 19-21).*
  - *Others had been there, but were no longer with him.*
  - *Though there is some repetition of the men mentioned in 2 Timothy and in the earlier books, it is not the same group of men.*

Eusebius' records:
• Paul was released after the first imprisonment,
• Continued his work for a time.

- *These facts cited are the most valuable and specific scriptural evidence that Paul was released from prison the first time and that he traveled extensively, continuing his work in the gospel.*
  - *To these Biblical facts, we add the witness of the early church historian Eusebius who says of Paul:*
    - *"After pleading his cause, he is said to have been sent again upon the ministry of preaching, and after a second visit to the city [Rome] that he finished his life with martyrdom" (Eusebius' Ecclesiastical History, Book II, Chapter 22).*

If our timing is correct:
• The trial in Rome was early in A.D. 63.

Paul's possible itinerary after his release:

His possible itinerary:
• From Rome to Crete,
** • He left Titus to finish "setting in order" the things lacking.**
• To Ephesus,
• To Colossae to visit Philemon,
• And back to Ephesus, where he left Timothy.
• On to Macedonia, and probably to Greece.
** • He wrote letters to Timothy and Titus.**
** • It was not yet winter,**
**   • He asks Titus to join him in Nicopolis.**

Though estimates vary, we feel the evidence is strongest that Paul was released no later than the summer of A.D. 63, more likely in the spring of that year. Upon his release, it seems he headed for the province of Asia. There are different views about the most likely route. Some have Paul traveling from Rome to Brundisium, across the Adriatic Sea, and into Macedonia through the back door. This explanation, however, does not account for the facts very well. More likely Paul's journey took him from Rome to Crete (look at your map). After a brief time there, the apostle left Titus on the island to set in order the things that were lacking and to appoint elders in every city (Tit. 1:5). He probably went next to Ephesus (1 Tim. 1:3). While there he could have conveniently made the planned visit with Philemon at Colossae (Philemon 22).

After his stay in Ephesus (leaving Timothy there, 1 Tim. 1:3), he traveled to Macedonia (1 Tim. 1:3) and visited Philippi, which he had also planned to do (Phil. 2:24). Sometime after leaving Ephesus, Paul wrote to Timothy, perhaps while in Macedonia or in Greece. At about the same time, he wrote to Titus, asking him to meet him in Nicopolis because he planned to spend the winter there (Tit. 3:12). This itinerary may not be the exact one Paul followed, but it avoids needless back-tracking and seems to be a logical arrangement.

No evidence of raging persecution:
- **Therefore, almost certainly, it was still A.D. 63.**

Note that in neither 1 Timothy nor Titus is there any evidence of raging persecution. Therefore these books were almost certainly written in the fall of 63, since it is clear that it was not yet winter when he wrote to Titus (Tit. 3:12). If this were the fall of 64, the situation would be totally different because Nero's persecutions would already have begun. We will discuss those persecutions, and why they arose, after we survey the letters of 1 Timothy and Titus.

Summary of 1 Timothy

Timothy has been Paul's most faithful companion since the early part of the second missionary journey.
- **"No man like minded."**

Timothy has been Paul's most faithful companion since he chose to accept Paul's invitation to go with him from Lystra on the second missionary journey (Acts 16:1-3). Timothy must have been a very young man at that point. Paul used him over and over as his special messenger (see Acts 18:5; 1 Thessalonians 3:1-6; Acts 19:22; 1 Corinthians 4:17; 16:10-11). He was one of the group of men who made the trip to Jerusalem to take the gift to the saints (Act 20:4). He joins Paul in the greeting in six of his epistles (1 and 2 Thessalonians, 2 Corinthians, Colossians, Philemon, and Philippians). Paul described him as "my beloved and faithful child in the Lord" (1 Cor. 4:17). Truly Paul had no one else who was such a "kindred spirit," serving as a child with his father (see Phil. 2:19-23). These letters that Paul writes to Timothy, as his own life draws near the close, show that Timothy is continuing to be that faithful servant, ready to do whatever needs to be done.

Short outline:
- **Instructions to the household of God (1:3-3:16).**
- **Instructions to Timothy about his ministry (4:1-6:21).**

The book of 1 Timothy is a personal letter from an older preacher to his younger protégé, but it is also a very practical book for every child of God. The first half of the book is filled with instructions for conduct within the family of God (the church). The second half is advice every preacher —young or old —needs as he faces the task of fulfilling his own ministry in proclaiming the gospel.

Paul says:

Paul's first letter to Timothy:

- **Greeting (1:1-2).**
- **Instructions to the house of God (1:3-3:16):**
- **Paul's charge to Timothy (1:3-11):**
  - **Warn men not to teach false doctrine (1:3-4).**

Paul to Timothy, my genuine child in the faith:
- Instructions to the house *(the family)* of God (1:3-3:16):
- Reminder of Paul's charge to Timothy (1:3-11)

When I left Ephesus going into Macedonia, I urged you to remain there so that you could charge certain ones not to teach false doctrine and not to waste time on fiction and fables.

The point of my command was to bring about love from a pure heart and a good conscience and true faith, but some have turned aside from these things and have set themselves up as teachers of

- **Our goal is love from a good conscience and a sincere faith.**
  - **Beware of those who turn aside and misuse the law (1:5-11).**

the law, though they do not understand what they are talking about. The law is a good thing, but it is made for the lawless and rebellious, for the ungodly and sinners, for the unholy and profane, for murderers of fathers and murderers of mothers, for manslayers and for all others whose behavior is contrary to the gospel which was entrusted to me.

The responsibility Paul gave Timothy as he was leaving Ephesus was to combat the false teaching of Judaism. The same charge would fit in any generation, as Paul would urge a preacher to oppose false teaching in whatever form it appears. Having reminded Timothy of this work, he points out that the ultimate purpose of his work is to help the church to grow, to help saints develop. Paul particularly addresses this expanded purpose in the letter, for this is the task that both Paul and Timothy had. It is typical of Paul to mention an idea — that the gospel was entrusted to him — and then to write a beautiful essay on the mercy and grace of the Lord who saved him and gave him such a wonderful work to do.

- **I am grateful the Lord appointed me to His service (1:12-16).**
  - **I was a sinner:**
    - **An ignorant one;**
    - **I am a prime example of God's mercy.**
  - **Doxology (1:17).**

- I am grateful the Lord appointed me to His service (1:12-16):

  I am deeply grateful that Christ Jesus counted me faithful and appointed me to His service, though I was a persecutor and a blasphemer. But I found mercy because I did it ignorantly in unbelief. I serve as a prime example of how long-suffering Christ can be, so that others can be encouraged to believe unto eternal life.

  Now unto the King eternal, immortal, invisible, the only God, be honor and glory for ever and ever. Amen.

- **I renew my charge to you, Timothy (1:18-20):**
  - **Conduct the good warfare... maintain the faith...**

- I renew my charge to you, Timothy (1:18-20):

  I am giving you this responsibility, my son Timothy, according to the prophecies which preceded you, that by them you may conduct the good warfare, maintaining the faith and a good conscience which some have rejected.

These "prophecies" were most likely prophecies made concerning Timothy himself. 1 Timothy 4:14 mentions "the gift that is in thee, which was given thee by prophecy, with the laying on of the hands of the presbytery." The presbytery would have been the elders or presbyters of the church at Lystra. These prophecies, given by someone such as Paul, Silas, or some other prophet, were likely spoken as Timothy was being appointed to the work of preaching the gospel. No further details are given. The laying on of hands served as a way of commending someone to a work (see Acts 13:3); the laying on of the hands of an apostle could impart the Holy Spirit to someone, but it was only an apostle who could transfer such a gift (see Acts 8:17-21 and the notes we included with that passage).

Paul begins now to give Timothy some specific instructions for the behavior of the saints, the members of the house or family of God.

- **Pray for all (2:1-15):**
  - **Pray for rulers (2:1-7):**
    - **So that we may live in peace... in godly behavior.**
    - **So that men may come to salvation.**
  - **Let men pray in every place.**
  - **Let women be in quietness (2:8-15):**
    - **In their clothing (2:9).**
    - **In their conduct (2:10, 15).**
    - **In their learning and teaching (2:11-14).**

- Let prayers be made for all (2:1-15):

First of all, I urge that prayers be made for all men: for kings and for all those who are in authority, so that we can live peaceful lives in all godliness and sober behavior. This is acceptable to God who would have all men to be saved. There is one God, and one mediator between God and men — that is the one man, Christ Jesus. He gave Himself a ransom for everyone, and I was appointed a preacher and an apostle to tell men of His sacrifice.

I desire therefore that men pray in every place, lifting up hands that are holy in conduct. Likewise, I would that women dress themselves in a meek and sober way, not with flashy clothes and jewelry, but, which is only fitting in women professing reverence for God, with good works.

Let a woman learn in a quiet manner. I do not permit a woman to teach nor to have dominion over a man, because Adam was first made, then Eve. Also Adam was not beguiled, but the woman was beguiled and thereby fell into transgression. Nevertheless, she will be saved in connection with her child-rearing, if she continue in faith and love and sanctification with a serious approach to life.

There is a sharp contrast between the commanded behavior of men and women. Men are to pray in every place; women are not to teach or to have dominion over a man. She is to learn in quietness. Notice that the reasons Paul gives for this distinction have nothing to do with tradition or the rules of society. The reasons are rooted in the creation itself, and in the first sin. She was created second; and the role of submission was one of the consequences placed upon Eve when she allowed herself to be deceived by the serpent. A godly woman has completed the task God has given her when she has quietly fulfilled her role as wife and mother, serving the Lord in faith and love.

- **Qualifications for workers (3:1-13):**
  - **For elders (3:1-7):**
    - **Above reproach,**
    - **Husband of one wife,**
    - **Temperate,**
    - **Sober minded,**
    - **Respectable,**
    - **Hospitable,**
    - **Able to teach,**
    - **Not given to wine,**
    - **Not violent,**
    - **Not covetous,**
    - **Children under control,**
    - **Not a novice,**

- Qualifications for workers (3:1-13):

True and reliable is the statement: If a man desires the office of a bishop, he desires a good work. Therefore a bishop must have no charge of wrong-doing which can be lodged against him *(above reproach; blameless)*. He must be the husband of one wife, one who manages his family well, with his children under control with all dignity: for if he does not know how to rule well his own household, how will he take care of the church of God? He must be temperate *(vigilant)*, prudent *(sober-minded)*, of good behavior *(respectable)*, hospitable, able to teach, gentle *(patient)*. He must not be addicted to wine, not violent *(pugnacious; no brawler)*, not greedy for money *(free from the love of money)*, not quarrelsome, not covetous. He must be a mature man, a seasoned Christian, lest

- **Good reputation.**
- **For deacons (3:8-13):**
  - **Reverent,**
  - **Not double-tongued,**
  - **Not given to wine,**
  - **Not greedy,**
  - **Holding the mystery of God with a pure conscience,**
  - **Blameless.**
  - **Husband of one wife,**
  - **Ruling his household well.**
- **Women (3:11):**
  - **Reverent,**
  - **Not slanderers,**
  - **Temperate,**
  - **Faithful in all things.**

he be lifted up with pride. He must have a good reputation with those who are outside the church so that he will not fall into reproach and snare of the devil.

Deacons, likewise, must be good men of proven character: reverent *(men of dignity)*; not double-tongued, or addicted to wine; not fond of sordid gain; holding the mystery of the faith with a clear conscience. He must be the husband of one wife and he must be able to manage his children and household well. Let them be tested first, and then let them serve as deacons if they are beyond reproach. For those who serve well as deacons obtain for themselves a high standing and great confidence in the faith that is in Christ Jesus.

Women *(their wives)* also must be serious *(dignified)*, not slanderers *(malicious gossips)*, temperate and faithful in all things.

These qualifications were not "suggestions" on Paul's part. Notice that he says a bishop or a deacon "must be," he "must have" these various character traits. In order to give the clearest interpretation of the meanings Paul included in the qualifications, we have included synonyms that are found in different translations of this text. It is God's will that there be experienced men who serve as His appointed overseers of the flock. See Titus 1:5-9 and 1 Peter 5:1-4 for further information on the subject.

- **Purpose for these instructions (3:14-16):**
  - **So you may know how to behave in the family of God (3:14-15);**
  - **For the story of Christ is great (3:16).**

- Purpose for these instructions (3:14-16):

I write these things to you, hoping to come to you shortly, but if I tarry a long time, so that you will know how men should behave themselves in the household of God, which is the church of the living God.

Without question the mystery of godliness is great. It tells of One who was presented in the flesh, justified in the spirit, seen of angels, preached among the nations, believed on in the world, and received up into glory.

- **Instructions for Timothy's work (4:1-6:21):**
- **Take heed to yourself (4:1-16):**
  - **Because apostasy <u>will</u> come (4:1-5).**
  - **Take careful heed to your own life (4:6-16):**
    - **Warn brethren (4:6).**
    - **Avoid fables (4:7).**
  - **Practice godliness:**

- Instructions for Timothy's work (4:1-6:21):
- Take heed to yourself (4:1-16):

We must know how men should behave, because the Spirit says plainly that some will depart from the faith, listening to false doctrines which originate with the demons. They will speak lies in hypocrisy, having their own conscience seared as with a hot iron. They will forbid to marry and command that people abstain from meats that God gave to be received with thanksgiving.

If you inform the brethren of these things, you will be a good servant of Christ, nourished by the good doctrine you have followed till now. But refuse all profane and silly stories. Instead, spend your time practicing godliness. Bodily exercise is profitable for a little, but godliness is profitable for all things, since it has the

- **That is of true value (4:7-10).**
- **Continue teaching, reading, exhorting (4:11, 13).**
- **Be an example in every facet of life (4:12).**
- **Do not neglect the gift you were given (4:14).**
- **Guard yourself and your teaching (4:15-16).**

promise of the life which is now and of the life to come. It is because we hope in God that we make all these efforts.

Command and teach these things. Give no one even the slightest reason to discount you because of your youth. Be an example to those who believe, in speech, in behavior, in love, in faith, and in purity. Till I come, pay attention to public reading, to encouraging, to instructing. Do not neglect the gift given you by means of prophecy with the laying on of the hands of the elders. Be diligent in these things; concentrate completely upon them so that the progress you have made may be obvious to everyone. Pay careful attention to yourself and to your teaching. In this way you will save both yourself and those who hear you.

- **Be careful how you deal with people (5:1-6:2):**
  - **People of different ages (5:1-2).**
  - **Older widows (5:3-10, 16):**
    - **Teach families to care for their own (5:4, 8, 16).**
    - **Help only those with no means for support (5:3-10).**
    - **Do not burden the church (5:16).**
  - **Younger widows (5:11-16).**
  - **Elders (5:17-25):**
    - **Reward an elder's service (5:17-18).**
    - **Rebuke an elder who sins (5:19-21).**
    - **Do not to be hasty in choosing men (5:22).**

- Be careful how you deal with various people in the church (5:1-6:2):

Do not deal roughly with an older man, but exhort him as you would a father. Treat the younger men as brothers, the older women as mothers, and the younger women as sisters, in all purity.

Honor those who are widows indeed *(truly alone)*, without any means of support. Teach families to provide for their own relatives *(widows)*, in order to show piety at home and to recompense parents. If any will not provide for his own, especially those of his own household, he has denied the faith and is worse than an infidel. If a woman has dependent widows, let her assist them so that the church will not be burdened. Let none be enrolled as a widow to be helped by the church, who is under sixty years old. She must have been the wife of one man; having a good reputation; one who has shown hospitality, and has devoted herself to good works.

Do not enroll the younger widows, lest they become idle and busybodies, talking of things they should not. They need to marry, bear children, and see after their families.

Let elders that rule well be counted worthy of double honor, especially those who labor in the word and in instruction. The scriptures say, "You shall not muzzle the ox when he treads out the grain," and "The laborer is worthy of his hire."

Do not receive an accusation against an elder unless there are two or more witnesses to back up the charge. Those who *have* sinned, rebuke publicly that the rest may be afraid of doing wrong.

Be sure you do these things without partiality. Do not choose men hastily. Be careful not to involve yourself in other men's sin.

- **Timothy, look after your health (5:23).**

- Timothy, take care of your health (5:23):

Do not keep on drinking water; use a little wine for your stomach's sake and your frequent infirmities.

- **Discern the works of men — good or bad (5:24-25).**

- Discern the works of a man (5:24-25):

  Some men's sins are quite obvious even before investigation; with some men the sins are not so obvious, but may be learned with observation. Likewise, a man's good works may not be immediately obvious, but the slightest investigation will bring them to light.

- **Servants and masters (6:1-2).**

- Servants and masters (6:1-2):

  Let those who are servants honor their masters so that the gospel will not be blasphemed. Those who have believing masters, let them not set them at nought because they are brethren. Let them instead serve them even more diligently, knowing that those who benefit from their labors are both believing and beloved.

- **Beware of false teachers motivated by greed (6:3-10).**
  - **A false teacher may teach from a hope of gain (6:3-5).**
  - **Godliness is great gain:**
    - **True contentment (6:6-10).**

- Beware of false teachers who are motivated by greed (6:3-10):

  If any one teaches a different doctrine than the words of Christ, he is puffed up, quarrelsome, and does not know what truth is. He thinks of godliness as a way of gain.

  Godliness *is* a way of gain when it is combined with contentment, because we brought nothing into the world; neither shall we carry anything out of it. So if we have food and clothes we will be content.

  Those who set their hearts on being rich fall into many foolish and harmful lusts such as drown men in destruction. This is because the love of money is the root of all kinds of evil.

- **Fight the good fight of faith (6:11-14):**
  - **Pursue the right things.**

- Fight the good fight of faith (6:11-14):

  But you, O man of God, flee such things and pursue righteousness, godliness, faith, love, and steadfastness. Fight the good fight of faith. I charge you in the sight of God and of Christ Jesus that you keep the commandment without spot or reproach until Christ comes again.

- **Doxology (6:15-16).**

- Doxology (6:15-16):

  At the right time He will show Him who is the blessed and only Potentate, the King of kings and Lord of lords, who only has immortality, dwelling in light unapproachable, whom no man has seen or can see. To Him be honor and power eternal. Amen.

- **Warn the rich (6:17-19):**
  - **Not high-minded.**
  - **Full of good works.**

- Warn the rich not to be high-minded, but to be full of good works (6:17-19):

  Charge those who are rich in this world's goods to be not high-minded nor to have their hopes set on the uncertainty of riches, but on God. Tell them to do good and to be rich in good deeds, laying up treasures for the life to come.

- **Final charge to Timothy (6:20-21).**

- Final charge to Timothy (6:20-21):

  O Timothy, guard what has been placed in your care. Be careful to avoid the profane babblings and opposition of knowledge, which is not knowledge at all.

  Grace be with you.

Concept:
<u>Timothy's responsibilities as an evangelist</u>.

Thumbnail sketch of 1 Timothy:

Paul was placing great responsibilities into Timothy's hands as a servant of the gospel. Three times Paul specifically gives a "charge" to Timothy (1:5, 18; 6:13). Such a charge is given numerous times in the epistle using different terms, such as, "I exhort" (2:8; 3:14-15; 4:6, 11 and others). From such references we conclude that the theme of this letter is the work which Paul entrusts to Timothy and his instructions about how to do this work.

His love for and confidence in Timothy is everywhere evident. The genuine care an evangelist is to have for people, his careful study and teaching, are also very much the message of 1 Timothy. The letter is practical and profound. Paul touches on both congregational affairs (public prayers, elders, widows, e.g.), and individual affairs (exhortation to servants and to the rich). He shows his concern for Timothy's own welfare. It is the message of an older preacher to a younger preacher who will be fulfilling the charge for the years ahead.

<u>Summary of Titus</u>

Titus:

- **Probably written in the fall of A.D. 63,**
- **From either Macedonia or Greece.**

This epistle was written about the same time as 1 Timothy. The book does not tell where Paul was, nor whether the letter to Titus was written shortly before or after 1 Timothy. Paul mentions Tychicus who was from Asia (Acts 20:4), and who carried the letters from Paul to the Ephesians, to the Colossians, and to Philemon (Eph. 6:21-22; Col. 4:7-9). Paul may, therefore, have still been in Asia. His plan, however, was to spend the winter in Nicopolis which was a long way from Asia, indicating Paul was more likely in either Macedonia or Greece on his way to Nicopolis., Since it, too, is a letter from the older apostle to a younger preacher, the book of Titus is very similar to the book of 1 Timothy.

- **He was another of Paul's faithful co-workers:**
  - **Since the conference in Jerusalem at the end of the first missionary journey.**

Titus was selected to go with Paul and Barnabas when they went to Jerusalem to consult with the apostles and elders about the question of whether the Gentiles were required to be circumcised before they could be saved (Acts 15). Titus was a Gentile convert, and Paul chose to take him as a test case. After the discussion, Titus was not required to be circumcised or to keep the law of Moses in any way (Gal. 2:1-3). Later, during the third journey, Paul wrote to the Corinthians from the city of Ephesus, and he sent it by the hands of Titus. Then Titus joined Paul in Macedonia, giving a report from Corinth, and Paul sent him back with a second letter (see 2 Cor. 2:12-13; 7:5-7; 8:16-24). Now he has been left in Crete to do a needed work (Tit. 1:5).

Paul said:

Paul's letter to Titus says:
- **Greeting (1:1-4).**
  - **A full, rich greeting.**
- **I left you in Crete to appoint elders in every city (1:5-16):**
  - **Qualifications (1:5-9):**
    - **Blameless,**
    - **Husband of one wife,**
    - **Believing children,**
      - **Not rebellious.**
    - **Above reproach,**
    - **Not self-willed,**
    - **No hot temper,**
    - **Not given to wine,**
    - **No striker,**
    - **No love for sordid gain,**
    - **Hospitable,**
    - **Lover of good,**
    - **Sober, just, holy,**
    - **Temperate,**
  - **Holding fast the sound doctrine (1:10-16):**
    - **So that they:**
      - **Can exhort,**
      - **Rebuke the false teachers.**

Paul to Titus, my true child according to our common faith.

- I left you in Crete to appoint elders in every city (1:5-16):
  (Compare with 1 Timothy 3:1-7.)

  This is the reason I left you in Crete: to set in order the things that need to be corrected and to appoint elders in every city. Choose men who are blameless, the husband of one wife; a man whose children believe, and are not accused of riot *(dissipation)* or rebellion. The bishop must be of sterling character *(above reproach)* as God's steward; not self-willed or quick-tempered; not addicted to wine, no striker, not fond of sordid gain *(filthy lucre)*. He is to be a hospitable man; loving good men *(loving what is good)*, sober *(sensible)*, just, devout *(holy)*, temperate *(self-controlled)*. He must be well informed in the truth so that he can exhort in sound doctrine and refute false teachers.

  These false teachers are very destructive and they *must be* silenced before they destroy whole houses. One of their own prophets wrote, "Cretans are always liars, evil beasts, idle gluttons." This statement is true. Therefore rebuke them sharply. Exhort them to be sound in the faith, not paying attention to Jewish fables.

Notice that the reason Paul emphasizes here why elders must be well informed is so that the false teachers can be stopped — and he says the teachers are so destructive they must be stopped, before they destroy whole families. Elders have a grave responsibility. They are to "watch for the souls" of the flock and they will give an account for how well they carry out their responsibilities (Heb. 13:17).

- **Teaching various classes of individuals (2:1-15):**
  - **Speak sound doctrine to (2:1):**
    - **Aged men (2:2),**
    - **Aged women (2:3),**
    - **Younger women (2:4-5),**
    - **Younger men (2:6).**
    - **You be an example (2:7-8).**
  - **Servants (2:9-10).**

- Teaching various classes of individuals (2:1-15):
  (Compare to 1 Timothy 5:1-6:2.)

  In contrast to the false teachers, you speak the things which are characteristic of sound doctrine. Tell the older men to have self-control, to be serious, understanding what life is all about. Tell aged women to be reverent in their attitude, not vicious gossips, nor enslaved to much wine, teaching what is good. Let the older women encourage the younger women to love their husbands, to love their children, to be serious, pure, workers at home, kind, and to be in subjection to their own husbands. Teach the young men to be serious in their approach to life. Make yourself an example in everything you do and teach. Live so that the enemy may be put to shame, having nothing bad to say about us.

  Tell servants to be in subjection to their own masters, to be well-pleasing to them, not depriving them of the gain they should

- **The grace of God teaches us to live seriously and righteously (2:11-14).**
- **Teach all these things (2:15).**

have from their work. In this way, they will beautifully decorate the doctrine of God.

For the grace of God has appeared, bringing salvation, and teaching us to deny irreverence and worldly lusts, so that we may live seriously, and righteously, and godly in this present age while we look for the coming of the Lord.

Speak and teach these things and reprove with all authority. Let no man set you at naught.

- **Various commands (3:1-11):**
  - **Saints must conduct themselves properly (3:1-2).**
  - **Once we lived at the call of our lusts and pleasures (3:3).**
    - **But God saved us (3:4-7).**
  - **Continue teaching these things (3:8-9).**
  - **After warnings:**
    - **Reject the trouble-maker (3:10-11).**

- Various commands (3:1-11):

Help the saints to be in subjection to rulers, to be ready to do every good deed. Remind them to speak evil of no one, not to be contentious, to be gentle, showing consideration for others.

Once we were all foolish, disobedient, deceived, and living our lives in lusts and pleasures. We were unconcerned with God's ways, and were filled with envy, and malice, and we hated one another.

But when God bestowed His kindness upon us in His Son, we were saved through His mercy, not by works which we did to earn us righteousness, but through the washing of rebirth and by the renovation of the Holy Spirit. Thus He has made it possible for us to be heirs according as we hope for eternal life.

I want you to go on affirming these things so that those who believe may be careful to keep up their good work. These things are good and profitable, but shun foolish questions and speculations, and fusses, because they are unprofitable.

After warning a man intent on being a trouble-maker, reject him. Realize that he is on the wrong course. He is sinning and has condemned himself.

- **Personal remarks and benediction (3:12-15):**
  - **Try to join me for the winter in Nicopolis (3:12).**

- Personal remarks and benediction (3:12-15):

When I send Artemas to you, or Tychicus, try hard to meet me in Nicopolis, for that is where I plan to spend the winter. Make every effort to send Zenas and Apollos on their journey, so that they will have what they need.

All that are with me greet you. Grace be with you all.

Concept:
<u>Titus's responsibilities as an evangelist.</u>

Thumbnail sketch of Titus:

Though the letter to Titus is very similar in content to 1 Timothy, it is not as personal a letter, because it seems Paul and Titus had not worked together as closely as Paul had with Timothy. The message of the book concerns the responsibilities Titus had been given. Therefore, he also is given guidelines on selecting men to be elders. He is told about things he needs to emphasize about the personal conduct of the Christians on Crete, and he is told to be an example in his own life.

Any preacher of the gospel, whether young or old, would do well to read the books of 1 Timothy and Titus frequently.

Paul's Activities After Writing 1 Timothy and Titus

Did Paul go to Spain?
- **Difficult years have passed since that first plan was made.**
- **If he did, it was after he visited Asia and Macedonia.**

At one time it was Paul's intention to go to Spain, and to visit Rome on his way. But that statement was made before Paul took the gift to the saints in Jerusalem at the end of his third missionary journey (Rom. 15:22-29). By the time he wrote to the Philippians (Phil. 2:24), and to Philemon (verse 22) about his intention to come to them, it had been more than four years since he wrote that letter to the Romans. Many things had happened in the intervening years — including four years of imprisonment, two of which had been in Rome itself. If he did go to Spain after his release, it was surely after he visited the places where he had already planted the gospel.

Did Paul go to Spain? There are those who argue that he went even farther, as far as Britain. It is an intriguing thought, because Britain is in "our world." To say that Paul went to either Spain or Great Britain is to have him visit "our world."

- **No Biblical evidence that he did so.**
- **But Clement said:**
  - **Paul "...and come to extreme limit of the west..."**

There is no Biblical evidence that he did so, though there is a little historical basis for the speculation. Clement of Rome was a contemporary of Paul, and may have been the Clement mentioned in Philippians 4:3. He wrote a letter to the Corinthians during the persecutions that raged under Domitian, toward the close of the first century. In the letter he said of Paul: "Having taught righteousness to the whole world, and come to the extreme limit of the west, and suffered martyrdom under the prefects..." (The First Epistle of Clement to the Corinthians, Chap. 5). It is this note about which the controversy swirls.

- **No one knows the answer.**

Even though the Bible does not mention such a trip, it would do no violence to the scriptures that are given to say that he went there. We are given so few details about his travels after his release from prison, it is impossible to be specific about his work.

Up until this point, we can be fairly certain we have Paul's epistles placed at about the right points in the history. And until after his imprisonment, we know the routes he traveled because the book of Acts gives enough information for us to follow his trail. Even after the first imprisonment, we can piece together a fairly accurate picture of his work for the next few weeks or months, though possibly not in the exact order described because there are too few details to know for sure. The biggest questions arise about this period after he wrote the first letter to Timothy and the one to Titus. Did he go to Spain? How long was it before he was captured again and executed? No one knows. Perhaps Clement's reference was to Spain, since Paul had earlier expressed his hope to go there, but time was very limited before trouble broke out again, so almost certainly he did not go farther than Spain, even if he went that far.

Outbreak of Persecution Under Nero

Time was limited before trouble broke out again:
- **Fire broke out in Rome on July 19, A.D. 64.**
- **Nero blamed the Christians.**
- **Therefore a terrible persecution broke out:**
  - **The first one instigated by the Roman government.**

On July 19, A.D. 64, a terrible fire broke out in the city of Rome. Ten out of fourteen districts of the city burned down. Tacitus reports that many thought the fire might have been instigated by Nero. He also states that in order to divert attention from himself, Nero "fabricated scapegoats — and punished with every refinement the notoriously depraved Christians." The historian goes on to describe the horrible persecutions inflicted upon the Christians:

> *First, Nero had self-acknowledged Christians arrested. Then, on their information, large numbers of others were condemned —not so much for incendiarism [arson, referring to their supposed guilt for the burning of Rome] as for their anti-social tendencies [a translator's footnote adds, "But this phrase (odio humani generis) may instead mean 'because the human race detested them' "]. Their deaths were made farcical. Dressed in wild animals' skins, they were torn to pieces by dogs, or crucified, or made into torches to be ignited after dark as substitutes for daylight. Nero provided his Gardens for the spectacle, and exhibited displays in the Circus, at which he mingled with the crowd — or stood in a chariot, dressed as a charioteer. Despite their guilt as Christians, and the ruthless punishment it deserved, the victims were pitied. For it was felt that they were being sacrificed to one man's brutality rather than to the national interest. (Tacitus, Annals, Penguin Classics edition, pp. 365, 366.)*

Tacitus describes the horrors of Nero's persecutions:
- **Later persecutions by Rome were worse,**
- **But this one was shocking because it was the first.**

Another footnote adds this comment:

> *Tacitus seems to hesitate (as often) between two versions. Were the Christians persecuted as incendiaries or as Christians? Our other sources know nothing of the former charge. Probably they were persecuted as an illegal association potentially guilty of violence or subversiveness (i.e., treason), but although the attack created a sinister precedent, its main purpose at the time was merely to distract attention from rumors against Nero by finding a suitable scapegoat. Christian beliefs are unlikely to have been attacked as such. It has often been disputed whether Nero's government regarded the Christians as a sect of the Jews (who had received unfavorable treatment from Tiberius and Claudius, but may now have obtained protection through the influence of Poppaea). (p. 366.)*

Nero was seeking scape-goats, and he sacrificed Christians to his own brutality.
- **Christian beliefs likely played no part in causing the persecutions.**

Peter is slain; Paul is imprisoned the second time:

Clement tells of the martyrdom of both Peter and Paul (Clement's First Epistle to the Corinthians). Eusebius, the historian, informs us that Peter and Paul were both slain in Rome by Nero, that Paul was beheaded, and Peter was crucified (Eusebius, Ecclesiastical History, Book II, Chap. 25).

Eusebius quotes from Dionysius, bishop of Corinth, who said Peter and Paul died about the same time (Eusebius, p. 80). Some authorities, however, think that Peter was killed in 64, while Paul was away from Rome, and that Paul was killed in 66 after he came back from Spain. A plausible case can be made, but it is almost altogether guesswork.

Peter was crucified
- **In about A.D. 64 or 65.**

Paul was imprisoned again:
- **And then beheaded.**
- **Probably in about A.D. 66.**

Therefore, probably sometime in A.D. 64 or 65, Peter was crucified in Rome. With Peter's death, the prophecy of Jesus, which He Himself made to Peter, was fulfilled (John 21:18-19). Peter had grown to be a very different person from what he was when he first met Jesus.

Persecution from Jews:
- **If they rejected the Christ,**
  - **No wonder they rejected His followers.**
- **The Judaizing teachers were problems,**
  - **But they were dealing with a difficult question regarding the Gentiles and the old law.**

Persecution from Romans:
- **Romans had no regard for human life.**
- **The decree is from the emperor,**
  - **So there would be protection from a government official.**

This time of persecution at the order of Nero must have been very frightening to the early Christians. They had suffered persecution since the beginning of the church, but it had been from the Jews who rejected Jesus as the Christ, or from Jewish converts who were trying to bind the old law on the Gentiles. If Gentiles had gotten involved in a persecution, it was a local dispute. But now the government itself, at the order of the emperor, is fighting the Christians!

Though the Jews would fly into a fit of rage and stone Stephen (Acts 7), or imprison saints (Acts 8), or try to beat Paul (Acts 21:26-36), they were at least a more understood source of trouble. The Judaizing teachers were a major problem to the early Christians, but it was understandable that the question of the relationship of the Gentiles to the old law would be a difficult one to the Jews. But the Romans had no regard for human life; they tortured their victims for pleasure. For a decree from the emperor to go out denouncing the Christians was a terrible thing to happen. Conditions only get worse in the years ahead.

It is uncertain how far out into the provinces Nero's persecution reached, but many saints were killed in Rome. The first Epistle of Peter, dealing with persecution, was addressed to brethren in the various provinces of Asia Minor, so it reached out into the provinces at least to some degree. Well known men such as Peter and now Paul are being killed or imprisoned. No one knows how many others died.

No details are known about Paul's being taken into custody, but tradition is unanimous that he came to Rome — whether as a prisoner or voluntarily, we do not know — and there he died. Before his death, he wrote his last letter, a very poignant letter to Timothy, his child in the faith.

Summary of 2 Timothy

Paul's last letter says:

- **Salutation (1:1-2).**
- **Please remain faithful (1:3-2:13):**
  - **I thank God:**
    - **For your affection for me (1:3-4);**
    - **And for your genuine faith (1:5).**
  - **Stir up the gift within you (1:6).**
- **We have shared the great work of preaching the gospel (1:7-14):**
  - **God did not give us a spirit of fear (1:7).**
  - **Therefore share in suffering (1:8-11):**
    - **Not ashamed of:**
      - **The testimony of our Lord,**
      - **Or of me, His prisoner.**
  - **I am not ashamed:**
    - **Because I know Him whom I have believed (1:12).**
  - **Protect and defend the gospel which has been placed in your care (1:13-14).**

Paul wrote:

Paul to Timothy, my beloved child.

- Please remain faithful (1:3-2:13):
- I thank God for you, and I wish I could see you (1:1-6):

I thank God for you, Timothy. O how often I think of you when I pray to God, day and night. I remember your tears, and I know how much you care for me. How I wish I could have you with me to comfort me!

As I have thought about you, I have been reminded of the genuine faith you have — faith which was in your grandmother Lois, and in your mother Eunice, and is now in you. Therefore I want to remind you to stir up *(kindle afresh)* the gift which is in you, which was given you through the laying on of my hands.

Timothy would have received the gift of the Holy Spirit through the laying on of Paul's hands, though no details are given. Timothy would certainly need the guidance of the Spirit as he faced the difficult future ahead of him. Paul is reminding him of the blessing in his hands. Sometimes we forget our greatest blessings at the very moments we need them most.

- We have shared the great work of preaching the gospel (1:7-14):

Remember that God has not put in us a feeling of fear, but of power and discipline. Therefore do not be ashamed of the testimony of our Lord, nor of me his prisoner. Be willing to suffer hardship.

You and I, Timothy, have been given a part in the greatest work there is: the preaching of the purpose and grace of God which has been shown in the coming of Jesus Christ. He abolished death and has brought to the light life and immortality through the gospel. It is for this great cause that I suffer these things. Yet I am not ashamed, for I know Him whom I have believed, and am persuaded that He is able to keep safely that which I have committed unto Him in view of that coming day.

Hold to the pattern of sound words which you heard from me. And guard, through the Holy Spirit who dwells in us, the treasure which was placed in your charge.

Even strong men such as Timothy needed to be encouraged to stand fast in the face of hard times. Many were turning away in fear, as is evident from the very next paragraph.

- **Those of Asia abandoned me (1:15-18):**
  - **But Onesiphorus has been a true friend**

- Those of Asia abandoned me; but Onesiphorus has been a true friend (1:15-18):

  You know how all that were in Asia turned away from me, of whom are Phygellus and Hermogenes. But may the Lord grant mercy to the house of Onesiphorus because he has often come to my aid. He was not ashamed of my chain, for when he was in Rome, he kept searching until he found me. And you know very well in how many things he served at Ephesus.

- **Remain faithful as a good soldier (2:1-7):**
  - **Teach others (2:1-2).**
  - **Suffer hardship (2:3).**
  - **Do not become entangled in affairs of this life (2:4-7).**

- Remain faithful as a good soldier of Christ Jesus (2:1-7):

  Therefore, my child, be strong in the grace which is in Jesus. And the things you have heard from me among many witnesses, entrust them to faithful men, who will in turn be able to teach them to others also.

  Suffer hardship with me, as a good soldier of Christ. Remember that no soldier on campaign entangles himself in the affairs of life, so that he can please the one who enlisted him. Also remember that no one can win in the games unless he follows the rules. Consider what I have said, because the Lord will give you understanding.

- **I endure all things for the sake of the chosen (2:8-13):**
  - **So that they can receive salvation.**

- I endure all things for the sake of those who have been chosen (2:8-13):

  Remember Jesus Christ for whose sake I suffer bonds as if I were a criminal. But it is for the sake of those who are chosen that I endure all these things, so that they can receive salvation with the ultimate glory Christ plans for them. The saying is good, that if we die with Him, we shall also live with Him. But if we deny Him, He will also deny us.

- **Prepare for the Master's use (2:14-26):**
  - **Ignore things of no consequence, or that lead to destruction (2:14, 16-19).**
  - **Know how to handle God's word (2:15).**
  - **Be a vessel of honor (2:20-21).**
  - **Run from youthful lusts (2:22a).**
  - **Cultivate characteristics the Lord's servant should have (2:22-26).**

- Let each one prepare himself for the Master's use (2:14-26):

  Remind the brethren not to strive about things of no consequence. Work hard to present yourself approved unto God, a workman who knows how to handle the word of God. Avoid those things which will detract from your usefulness to the Lord, and will even lead to your downfall. In every house there are all kinds of containers, some for honorable uses, some for very dirty uses. If a man will purge himself from dishonorable things, then he will be a vessel of honor unto the Lord.

  Run from youthful lusts and pursue righteousness. Avoid foolish and ignorant questions, because they just cause strife. The Lord's servant must not be one who quarrels with others, but one who is gentle to all, apt to teach, forbearing, in meekness correcting those who oppose the truth. Perhaps God will give them the opportunity to repent and to recover themselves from the snare of the devil.

- **Grievous times are coming (3:1-17):**
  - **Menace of false teachers (3:1-13):**
    - **They *will* come.**
    - **They will lead people astray.**
  - **Timothy, be a contrast to the unfaithful (3:14-17):**
    - **Persecutions will come,**
      - **But God will deliver.**
    - **Rely upon the scriptures:**
      - **The man of God has everything he needs.**

- For grievous times are coming (3:1-17):

Be aware that grievous times will come. Men will be selfish, lovers of money, boastful, ranting and raving, without natural affection, and you will not be able to reason with them. They will put on a front of being godly, but will have kept from themselves the power thereof. Turn away from these people. Such people will always be troublemakers, leading people astray.

But you follow my teaching, conduct, purpose, faith, long-suffering, love and steadfastness. You know very well what kind of sufferings I endured at Antioch, at Iconium, at Lystra — but the Lord delivered me from everyone of them. The fact is that everyone who lives godly in Christ Jesus will suffer persecution.

Remain in the things which you have learned and have been assured of, realizing from whom you learned them. From the merest infant you have known the sacred writings which are able to make you wise unto salvation. All scripture is given by the inspiration of God and is profitable for teaching, for reproof, for correction, for instruction in righteousness so that the man of God may have everything he needs to do God's will.

Notice that as Paul is warning Timothy of the grievous times to come, it is not the severe persecutions ahead that Paul is concerned about. It is the false teachers who will come; it is the destructive work of those who profess godliness while at the same time living self-centered, wicked lives. They will destroy the saints much more surely than any threats from the governmental persecutions. Let us heed the warnings about our greatest enemies.

Here in Paul's last letter he makes one of the most inclusive, strongest affirmations of the inspiration of the scriptures to be found in the whole Bible. <u>All</u> scripture is inspired. Timothy, you have everything you need in order to be equipped to every good work. Paul would no longer be available to advise Timothy, but he had all the wisdom of God within his grasp. We, too, have that same word of God in our hands — with the same blessings it provided for Timothy. Let us remember to use it wisely.

- **Paul's final charge to Timothy (4:1-8):**
  - **You stand in the presence of God (4:1).**
  - **Preach the word (4:2-4):**
    - **No matter what happens —**
    - **People will not want to hear.**
  - **Fulfill your task (4:5).**

- Paul's final charge to Timothy (4:1-8):

I charge you before God and before Christ Jesus, who will judge the living and the dead both by His appearing and by His kingdom: preach the word. Stand ready in good times and in bad; convict, rebuke, admonish with all long-suffering and doctrine. The time will come when the people will not endure sound doctrine. Rather, having itching ears, they will seek teachers of their own choosing to preach what they wish to hear. But you remain firm and do the work of an evangelist.

I am already being poured out as a drink offering, and it is time for me to go. I have fought the good fight; I have finished the

- **I am being offered as a sacrifice to God (4:6-8):**
  - **A crown awaits me.**

course; I have kept the faith. From now on there is a crown of righteousness laid up for me which the Lord, the righteous judge, will give to me in that day; and not to me only, but also to all those who look forward to His coming.

- **Paul's situation (4:9-18):**
  - **Please come (4:9).**
  - **Only Luke is with me;**
  - **Some deserted me;**
  - **Others I have sent where there was need.**
  - **Beware of Alexander the coppersmith (4:14-15).**
  - **All forsook me during my trial (4:16-18):**
    - **The Lord stood by me,**
    - **And He will not forsake me.**

- Paul's situation regarding friends and supporters (4:9-18):

Make every effort to come to me, because Demas has abandoned me, having loved this present world. Crescens has gone to Galatia, Titus to Dalmatia. Only Luke is with me. Bring Mark with you because he is useful to me as an assistant. But Tychicus I am sending to Ephesus. The cloak that I left in Troas with Carpus, please bring with you. Also bring the scrolls, especially the parchments *(vellum scrolls)*.

Alexander the coppersmith did me much evil. The Lord will pay him as he deserves. But beware of him because he greatly withstood our words.

At my first hearing no one was at my side. Everyone forsook me; may it not be held to their account. The Lord stood by me, though, and will continue to stand by me. He will deliver me from every evil work, and will save me unto His heavenly kingdom. To Him be the glory for ever and ever.

- **Greetings and benediction (4:19-22).**
  - **Try hard to come before winter (4:21).**

- Greetings and benediction (4:19-22):

Greet Prisca and Aquila, and the house of Onesiphorus. Erastus remained at Corinth, but Trophimus I left sick at Miletus.

Make every effort to come before winter. Eubulus greets you, and Pudens, and Linus, and Claudia, and all the brethren. The Lord be with your spirit. Grace be with you.

Priscilla and Aquila are no longer in Rome.

From the closing verses of 2 Timothy we see that Paul did more traveling after the writing of 1 Timothy and Titus. Erastus remained at Corinth; he left Trophimus at Miletus, and he had left a cloak at Troas. We do not have enough details to fit this into a framework, however.

Also notice that Prisca (Priscilla) and Aquila are no longer in Rome. It is likely that they, as many other Christians, fled the city, thinking to find greater safety in the provinces.

Paul asks Timothy to try hard to come before winter. Remember that all shipping stopped during the winter months. If Timothy did not make it before winter, it would be spring before he could possibly get there — and Paul's time was short.

Concept:
<u>Timothy, no matter what happens, or if others are unfaithful, please remain faithful</u>.

Thumbnail sketch of 2 Timothy:

The theme of the letter is: "Timothy, remain faithful as a preacher of the word. Please do not give up! Follow my example and finish your work as an evangelist, as I have finished mine as a preacher and an apostle. Cling to faith in Jesus Christ, a faith which was planted in you when you were a baby." Paul holds before Timothy, as an example, both his afflictions and his anticipated reward. How valuable is such a message to us as well!

Paul's work is finished:

It gives us sad pause to realize that, with these words, the writings of Paul are ended. It has now been nearly 2,000 years since he died. For these years he has enjoyed the fruits of his labors —the crown that was awaiting him! Having followed Paul's life through Acts and in the study of his epistles, we feel that we have come to know him as a friend. We can feel the loss with the saints who loved him.

Is it possible to grasp the emotions of Timothy as he read this letter? If Timothy made it to Rome before winter, he probably was there for the execution of his "beloved father in the faith." Yet the tone of the letter is triumphant. There are tones of sorrow when Paul speaks of those who have turned away from him, but it was a sad time for the church, a dreadful time, when many did turn away from the faith. Nevertheless, the apostle could say, "I know Him whom I have believed" and, "I have fought the good fight."

It was likely about 65/66 A.D. when Paul was killed.

Death of Paul:

Most likely, about A.D. 65/66 the great apostle to the Gentiles was beheaded. Once more his Roman citizenship proved a blessing, because, though to be beheaded would be dreadful, it did not bring the prolonged suffering that crucifixion or other cruel forms of death brought.

He is the primary character of the story in 17 chapters of Acts.

Thirteen of his letters are included in our Bible.

With the death of Paul we say goodby to the man who, next to Christ, did more to build and strengthen the church than anyone else. The books he left behind have been a source of information and strength to all Christians who have lived in the generations since. Obviously the Holy Spirit thought his example was one we needed to know, because seventeen chapters of the book of Acts follow his work as the primary character, and thirteen letters he wrote (87 chapters) are included in our Bible.

His death was a day of grief to the saints:

- **But a day of release for Paul.**

His incredible life, full of suffering and fruitful labor, was over. It was a day of grief for the saints, but a day of victory for him —a day of release from suffering. At last he could depart and be with Christ, which was "very far better" (Phil. 1:23).